Transactions of the Royal Historical Society

SIXTH SERIES

XXVIII

CAMBRIDGE
UNIVERSITY PRESS

Published by the Press Syndicate of the University of Cambridge
University Printing House, Shaftesbury Road, Cambridge CB2 8BS,
United Kingdom
One Liberty Plaza, Floor 20, New York, NY 10006, USA
477 Williamstown Road, Port Melbourne, VIC 3207, Australia
C/Orense, 4, Planta 13, 28020 Madrid, Spain
Lower Ground Floor, Nautica Building, The Water Club,
Beach Road, Granger Bay, 8005 Cape Town, South Africa

First published 2018

A catalogue record for this book is available from the British Library

ISBN 9781108484664 hardback

SUBSCRIPTIONS. The serial publications of the Royal Historical Society, *Royal Historical Society Transactions* (ISSN 0080-4401) and Camden Fifth Series (ISSN 0960-1163) volumes, may be purchased together on annual subscription. The 2018 subscription price, which includes print and electronic access (but not VAT), is £195 (US $325 in the USA, Canada, and Mexico) and includes Camden Fifth Series, volumes 54 and 55 and Transactions Sixth Series, volume 28 (published in December). The electronic-only price available to institutional subscribers is £163 (US $272 in the USA, Canada, and Mexico). Japanese prices are available from Kinokuniya Company Ltd, PO. Box 55, Chitose, Tokyo 156, Japan. EU subscribers (outside the UK) who are not registered for VAT should add VAT at their country's rate. VAT registered subscribers should provide their VAT registration number. Prices include delivery by air.

Subscription orders, which must be accompanied by payment, may be sent to a bookseller, subscription agent, or direct to the publisher: Cambridge University Press, University Printing House, Shaftesbury Road, Cambridge CB2 8BS, UK; or in the USA, Canada, and Mexico: Cambridge University Press, Journals Fulfillment Department, One Liberty Plaza, Floor 20, New York, NY 10006, USA.

SINGLE VOLUMES AND BACK VOLUMES. A list of Royal Historical Society volumes available from Cambridge University Press may be obtained from the Humanities Marketing Department at the address above.

Printed in the UK by Bell & Bain Ltd, Glasgow

CONTENTS

Transactions of the RHS 28 (2018), pp. 1–3 © Royal Historical Society 2018
doi:10.1017/S0080440118000154

ALIVE – AND STILL KICKING: THE RHS AT 150

By Margot C. Finn

Marking and reflecting on the Royal Historical Society's major anniversaries has not typically been a function of our *Transactions*. In his presidential address of February 1918, C. W. C. Oman unsurprisingly made no mention of the Society's fiftieth anniversary. Noting that he was employed at Whitehall in three different types of war work and had read only one book of history in the past year, Oman identified himself 'as one of the much-cursed tribe of censors' employed by the government to police dissemination of contemporary historical records, and proceeded to use this vantage point to reflect on what we now term 'fake news', that is 'the genesis and development of Rumours, Reports, and Legends of a false or exaggerated sort, during times of military or political crisis'.[1] Like Oman before him, R. A. (Robin) Humphreys, president of the Society at its centenary in 1968, failed to note this milestone in the *Transactions* – indeed, no presidential address from 1968 was published by the Society, with *A Centenary Guide to the Publications of the Royal Historical Society 1868–1968* instead appearing to mark this anniversary.[2]

Ian Archer's '150 Years of Royal Historical Society Publishing' in this volume thus represents an innovation – one that merits being read alongside both the articles here (drawn from our past year of public lectures and symposia), and also our new anniversary blog, *Historical Transactions* (https://blog.royalhistsoc.org/). Archer's survey, informed not only by our archive and publications but also by his many years of sterling service for the Society as a literary director, provides several salutary reminders that the RHS is not now as pioneering as we may wish to think. He observes that women historians were prominent in the Society's publications – winning two-thirds of the RHS Alexander Prizes between 1898 and 1917 and accounting for 40 per cent of published papers in the 1920s, for example – long before the advent of second-wave feminism. Furthermore, earlier incarnations of the RHS (like the Society in 2018)

---

[1] C. W. C. Oman, 'Presidential Address', *Transactions of the Royal Historical Society*, fourth series, 1 (1918), 3.
[2] Alexander Taylor Milne, *A Centenary Guide to the Publications of the Royal Historical Society 1868–1968: And of the Former Camden Society 1838–1897* (1968).

aspired to reflect global rather than only national histories: Robin Humphreys, significantly, was the founding director of the Institute of Latin American Studies during his RHS presidency – alerting us to more diverse organisational and disciplinary histories than we typically acknowledge. The scope of the articles in the 150th anniversary *Transactions* is thus pleasing but perhaps not path-breaking in its wide range. Taking readers from late twelfth-century France and Scotland through the social and cultural histories of the Catholic Reformation and seventeenth-century English gender relations, it considers the material, military and revolutionary histories of India, Japan and Russia before grappling with twentieth- and twenty-first century socio-economic and political discontent, respectively, in Northern Ireland and North America.

This is not to underplay the distance the RHS has travelled since its foundation, or the further distance it needs to travel in the next decades. In his preface to the first volume of the *Transactions*, published in 1872, Charles Rogers described the Society's aims as 'the reproduction and illustration of rare historical tracts, and the recovery, from recondite sources, of materials which might illustrate the less explored paths of national and provincial history'.[3] Just as the geographical and methodological scope of this volume demonstrates that 'national and provincial history' no longer suffices for the RHS, so too the programme of activities that feed into our publications no longer fits this narrow mould. Supporting excellence in historical scholarship remains at the heart of what we do, but we are (I hope) now increasingly aware of the danger of mistaking exclusivity for excellence. The development of public history (and the award of our 2018 Public History Prizes), the proliferation of online resources (including the Society's *Bibliography of British and Irish History*) and the advent of open access publication (soon to become the RHS's key mode of disseminating early career researchers' books) all register our commitment to render the 'recondite' discoverable by an expanding community of historical practitioners. The research the Society's working groups on race, ethnicity and gender equality have been conducting throughout the 150th anniversary year has provided repeated, often painful, reminders of why access and inclusivity both matter in historical practice, and are often so difficult to accomplish in institutions in which historical teaching and research are conducted.

Managed variously by amateur and professional archivists, librarians, museum experts, publishers and historians (almost all unpaid for their labours and wearing multiple hats whilst balancing too many plates), the RHS has soldiered on over a century and a half. Ian Archer

---

[3]   Charles Rogers, 'Preface', *Transactions of the Royal Historical Society*, old series, 1 (1872), 3.

quotes G. R. Elton's complaint of 1973, after assuming the presidency, that the Society's 'Victorian hangover is powerful, manifest and stifling'. Today, that legacy is to be sure still manifest, but arguably it is far less powerful and less stifling, as well as increasingly understood to have been more nuanced, contradictory and dynamic than Elton supposed. The 2018 *Transactions* – like the anniversary blog, public lectures, regional visits and symposia, publication and public history prizes, grants for early career historians and policy interventions – demonstrate forcibly that the RHS is much more than alive and still kicking as it exits its sesquicentennial year.

Transactions of the RHS 28 (2018), pp. 5–32 © Royal Historical Society 2018
doi:10.1017/S0080440118000026

TRANSACTIONS OF THE

ROYAL HISTORICAL SOCIETY

PRESIDENTIAL ADDRESS

By Margot C. Finn

MATERIAL TURNS IN BRITISH HISTORY: I. LOOT*

READ 24 NOVEMBER 2017

ABSTRACT. This address explores the writing of history in Britain during the Georgian and Victorian eras, arguing for the need both to trace British historiographical genealogies along routes that extend from Europe to the Indian subcontinent and to acknowledge the importance of material histories for this evolution. Focusing on military men who served in the East India Company during the Third Anglo-Maratha and Pindari War (1817–18), it examines the entangled histories of material loot, booty and prize on the one hand, and archival and history-writing practices developed by British military officers on the other. Active in these military campaigns and in post-conflict administration of conquered territories, a cadre of Company officers (assisted by 'native' interlocutors trained in Indian historical traditions) elaborated historical practices that we more conventionally associate with the Rankean historiographical innovations of the Victorian era. The Royal Historical Society's own history is shaped by these cross-cultural material encounters.

In the presidential address he delivered in 2009, Colin Jones noted that most of his predecessors at the helm of the Royal Historical Society (RHS) had been English historians, and had chosen to frame their four successive annual lectures around 'the state of a key issue or else to offer a synthesis in regard to some knotty problem or major theme in, usually, English history'. His approach to the anniversary lectures, as a French historian with eclectic tastes, was to range 'more widely and more disparately than is the presidential custom', so as to play to his strengths while following his interests. Like Goldilocks sampling the Bear family's porridge, I have borrowed selectively from these contrasting presidential paradigms. Like most previous incumbents, I too am an English or British historian, but like Colin before me in his 'French Crossings' lectures, I intend to connect Britain's so-called 'island

*I am especially grateful for comments and suggestions from Penelope J. Corfield, Felix Driver, Jagjeet Lally and Sue Stronge.

history' to its wider European and global moorings.[1] To do so, I too will range widely in my four lectures over time and space. However, in keeping with the majority of my presidential forebears, I will retain the predominant convention of articulating a sustained focus. I do so not by offering 'a synthesis' that addresses a continuous narrative or 'knotty problem', but rather by opting to explore, through four different case-studies, the implications for modern British history of the cluster of methodological practices within our discipline known collectively as the 'material turn'.

I use the phrase 'material turn' in two linked senses, one relating to material culture and the other to material or economic life. Since at least the 1980s, historians have increasingly turned to material objects as primary sources that can illuminate aspects of the past which are obscured if we attend to textual evidence alone. Drawing from disciplines that include anthropology, archaeology and sociology, they have found in material culture rich new records of the past and novel ways of explaining human behaviours in historical contexts. Some within this school count objects listed in textual sources such as inventories and wills, and derive from these quantitative data new insights into past social worlds.[2] Others are inspired by theorists who argue that material objects not only shape but actively collude in social processes and historical change. Rather than resting in humans alone, historical agency – these proponents of the material turn argue – resides in a fluid, animating interface that connects material things to persons.[3] Human histories are thus both entangled in and propelled by the force of 'vibrant matter'.[4]

A second type of material turn has ensued from historians' growing disenchantment with the perceived excesses of linguistic and cultural analysis, the twin methodologies that increasingly supplanted social, economic and political history-writing from the 1980s onward.[5] Tempering the claims of the linguistic and cultural turns of these decades, historians

---

[1]   Colin Jones, 'French Crossings: I. Tales of Two Cities', *Transactions of the Royal Historical Society*, 20 (2010), 1–26, at 2.

[2]   Pioneering studies of this kind include Maxine Berg, 'Women's Consumption and the Industrial Classes of Eighteenth-Century England', *Journal of Social History*, 30 (1996), 415–34; and Lorna Wetherill, *Consumer Behaviour and Material Culture in Britain, 1660–1760* (1996). For an overview of more recent iterations of this approach, see *Writing Material Culture History*, ed. Anne Gerritsen and Giorgio Riello (2014), esp. 1–13.

[3]   Bruno Latour, *Reassembling the Social: An Introduction to Actor-Network-Theory* (Oxford, 2005). For an analysis of these trends within British history, see Frank Trentmann, 'Materiality in the Future of History: Things, Practices, and Politics', *Journal of British Studies*, 48 (2009), 283–307.

[4]   Jane Bennett, *Vibrant Matter: A Political Ecology of Things* (Durham, NC, 2010).

[5]   See the vigorous debates between RHS presidents on these themes: Peter Mandler, 'The Problem with Cultural History', *Cultural and Social History*, 1 (2004), 94–117; Colin Jones, 'Peter Mandler's "Problem with Cultural History", or, Is Playtime Over?', *Cultural*

are now reclaiming (and reformulating) traditions of materialist history that developed in the Victorian era and dominated our discipline for much of the twentieth century. 'Fifty years ago, history was anchored in what Geoff Eley and Keith Nield term a "sovereign materialism"', Kenneth Lipartito has recently observed. In contrast, 'Much of the debate in the profession over the past half-century has been about establishing the authority of ideas, values, and identities independent of coarse materiality or narrow economic interests.' Combining cultural and linguistic historians' earlier insights with a renewed conviction that economic and material life profoundly shape the course of history, a rising methodological pulse within present-day historical analysis, he observes, argues that 'Things, nature, technologies…and commodities count, not just as cultural representations or referents in language, but in their own right.'[6]

For scholars of eighteenth- and nineteenth-century Britain – my own field of specialism – the rise of these two versions of the material turn has been closely associated with the decline of a more insular, national narrative of British history, and with the corresponding growth of interest in Britain's imperial landscapes. Whereas foundational interpretations of the economic history of modern Britain focused on domestic coal mining, iron smelting and cotton manufacture, more recent materially minded researchers have turned instead to histories of sugar, tea and chintz.[7] The Caribbean, the Cape and the Indian subcontinent have emerged in this context as vital fonts of British goods, British identities and British power.[8] In this paper, I explore a further frontier of this nexus of imperial and material connections by turning to the practice of history-writing itself. Focusing on material histories of loot that

and Social History, 1 (2004), 209–15; and Peter Mandler, 'Problems in Cultural History: A Reply', Cultural and Social History, 1 (2004), 326–32.

[6] Kenneth Lipartito, 'Reassembling the Economic: New Departures in Historical Materialism', American Historical Review, 121 (2016), 101–39, at 101.

[7] The earlier focus on production and indigenous growth is for example captured in The Economic History of Britain since 1700, I: 1700–1860, ed. Roderick Floud and Donald McCloskey (Cambridge, 1981). Sidney Mintz's Sweetness and Power: The Place of Sugar in Modern History (New York, 1985) marked an early turning point. Exemplary of British historians' attention to consumers and material goods are, for example, Maxine Berg, Luxury and Pleasure in Eighteenth-Century Britain (Oxford, 2005); Beverly Lemire, Fashion's Favourite: The Cotton Trade and the Consumer in Britain, 1660–1800 (Oxford, 1991); and Erika Rappaport, A Thirst for Empire: How Tea Shaped the Modern World (Princeton, 2017).

[8] Examples of this rapidly expanding literature include Catherine Hall, Keith McClelland, Nicholas Draper, Kate Donnington and Rachel Land, Legacies of British Slave-Ownership: Colonial Slavery and the Formation of Victorian Britain (Cambridge, 2014); John McAleer, Britain's Maritime Empire: Southern Africa, the South Atlantic and the Indian Ocean, 1763–1820 (Cambridge, 2017); Sadiah Qureshi, Peoples on Parade: Exhibitions, Empire, and Anthropology in Nineteenth-Century Britain (Chicago, 2011); and Kathleen Wilson, The Island Race: Englishness, Empire, and Gender in the Eighteenth Century (2002).

reach from the seventeenth century through and beyond the Victorian era and which stretch geographically from south India to Scotland, I explore the relationship between plunder, on the one hand, and the writing of history, on the other. In doing so, I seek to bring Georgian-era imperial and material histories home to bear on the discipline of history in Victorian Britain in the first decades of the RHS's operation. Colonial loot and military booty, I argue, played an active role in inciting historical practice in nineteenth-century Britain. On the eve of our sesquicentennial anniversary year, it is fitting to reflect back on that neglected material history.

I

Let me begin by sketching the main accepted narrative of how history as a discipline developed in Britain in the Georgian and Victorian eras. Three successive phases of history-writing dominate received under-standing of the nineteenth-century discipline. From the publication of David Hume's *History of England* in 1754 and of William Robertson's *History of Scotland* in 1759 to the end of the Napoleonic Wars, Scottish Enlightenment thinking held sway within British history. Cosmopolitan in tone, the phenomenally popular histories penned in this period became increasingly 'conjectural' in their methodology. Deduction from assumed universal principles of human behaviour shaped the Enlightenment historical paradigm, which traced a progressive arc from 'rude' and 'barbaric' early societies to modern, commercial 'civili-sations'. Human nature – innately both inquisitive and acquisitive – was in this conjectural model 'the engine bringing both limitless potential energy and dramatic forward motion to…history'.[9] Written in Scotland, England and on the European continent by men employed as librarians, chaplains, private tutors, personal secretaries and university professors, this was at its core a textual and philosophical mode of histor-ical interpretation. This domestic variant of Enlightenment history was typically composed at a distance from the European and imperial wars that raged in these decades, by men (and occasionally women) safely ensconced within the comforts of the urban salon or the domestic home.[10]

The years after 1815 – so the accepted narrative tells us – witnessed a sharp constriction of British historians' vision. This period, stretching roughly to the Franco-Prussian War of 1870–1, saw the Scottish

---

[9] David Allen, 'Scottish Historical Writing of the Enlightenment', in *The Oxford History of Historical Writing*, III: *1400–1800*, ed. José Rabasa, Masayuki Sato, Edoardo Tortarolo, and Daniel Woolf (Oxford, 2012), 497–517, citation 507.

[10] Karen O'Brien, *Narratives of Enlightenment: Cosmopolitan History from Voltaire to Gibbon* (Cambridge, 1997).

Enlightenment paradigm subsumed within so-called Whig history.[11] In John Burrow's formulation of this 'Liberal descent', the late Georgian and early Victorian Whig writers who monopolised history after 1815 discerned 'in English history the continuous presence…of an abiding spirit of liberty', an overweening liberal force-field that lent their writing an inherently celebratory, nationalist tone.[12] This school of historians borrowed liberally from literary sources and took much pride in literary style, but its practitioners' predominant concern was to champion a politics of freedom and progress. Associated with a coterie of white, male, propertied authors that included Thomas Babington Macaulay (1800–59), William Stubbs (1825–1901) and Edward Freeman (1823–92), the Whig tradition, in Michael Bentley's description, 'saw as imperative the task of communicating their work to the widest audiences…to mould its taste…to a tradition of constitutional continuity stemming from Saxon liberties through Magna Carta and the Bill of Rights to the Hanoverian…mixed constitution…that accounted for Britain's, and especially England's, greatness'.[13]

Puncturing this triumphalist liberal narrative of British history from the 1870s onwards was a third historiographical epoch, which saw the growing impact in Britain of assumptions and working methods pioneered in Prussia from the 1820s by Leopold von Ranke.[14] The Rankean school was characterised by an (ostensibly novel) empiricist emphasis on facts and a deep belief in the virtues of immersion in manuscript archives. As Anthony Grafton observes, 'collections of primary sources…acted on Ranke like clover on a pig'.[15] These tenets challenged not only the conjectural methodology of Enlightenment history but also the Whig historians' reliance on literary sources and liberal ideals to narrate the triumphal progress of the English nation.[16] British historians' acceptance of continental European methodologies, to be sure, was patchy. But champions of Ranke nonetheless numbered both among the foremost historians of late Victorian and Edwardian Britain and among the founding fathers of the RHS. British historians who 'studied in Germany and returned

---

[11] Colin Kidd, 'The "Strange Death of Scottish History" Revisited: Constructions of the Past in Scotland, c. 1790–1914', *Scottish Historical Review*, 76 (1997), 86–102.

[12] 'Whig history…is, by definition, a success story: the story of the triumph of constitutional liberty and representative institutions', Burrow observed. J. W. Burrow, *A Liberal Descent: Victorian Historians and the English Past* (Cambridge, 1981), 3.

[13] Michael Bentley, 'Shape and Pattern in British Historical Writing, 1815–1945', in *The Oxford History of Historical Writing*, IV: *1800–1945*, ed. Stuart Macintyre, Juan Maiguashca and Attila Pók (Oxford, 2011), 209.

[14] Georg G. Iggers, 'The Intellectual Foundations of Nineteenth-Century "Scientific" History', in *Oxford History of Historical Writing*, IV, ed. Macintyre, Maiguashca and Pók, 41–58.

[15] Anthony Grafton, *The Footnote: A Curious History* (1997), 35.

[16] Iggers, 'Intellectual Foundations', 47–50; Bentley, 'Shape and Pattern', 212–16.

to England with a passion for research' included distinguished RHS fellows, council members, vice presidents and presidents such as Samuel Gardiner (1829–1902), Sir John Robert Seeley (1834–95), Charles Firth (1857–1936) and Sir George Prothero (1848–1922).[17]

The historical traditions of the world beyond the Occident were progressively effaced as these three phases of history-writing unfolded. Scottish Enlightenment historians, although domiciled in Europe, allowed their imaginations to range freely beyond these familiar Western precincts. Their curiosity about the wider world was matched with a methodological proclivity for cross-cultural comparison, further feeding their global outlook.[18] At Edinburgh, William Robertson (1721–93) followed his 1759 and 1769 works on Scottish and continental European history with a 1777 *History of America* and a 1791 *Historical Disquisition concerning the Knowledge which the Ancients Had of India.*[19] Domestic British engagement with extra-European histories was both mirrored and extended by the labours of Enlightenment-era 'Orientalist' scholars on the Indian subcontinent. Typically employed in the East India Company's civil service, men such as William 'Oriental' Jones (1746–94), John Howell (1711–98) and the Perthshire Orientalist Alexander Dow (1735/6–79) deployed their new knowledge of Asian languages to write Enlightenment histories of the subcontinent.[20] Crucially, these Orientalists' scholarly labours drew upon not only the linguistic expertise but also the manuscripts and methodologies of Indian scribal elites – Hindu and Muslim bureaucrats and scholars schooled in their own vibrant traditions of historical scholarship.[21]

Nineteenth-century British Whig historians were, in contrast, contemptuous of both Asian history and Asian history-writing. The publication of James Mill's militantly utilitarian *History of British India* in 1817 set

[17] William C. Lubenow, *'Only Connect': Learned Societies in Nineteenth-Century Britain* (Woodbridge, 2015), 109.

[18] O'Brien, *Narratives of Enlightenment*; Joanna de Groot, *Empire and History Writing in Britain c. 1750–2012* (Manchester, 2013), chs. 1–2.

[19] For Robertson's Indian and cosmopolitan histories, see O'Brien, *Narratives of Enlightenment.*, esp. chs. 4–5; Stewart Brown, 'William Robertson, Early Orientalism and the *Historical Disquisition* on India in 1791', *Scottish Historical Review*, 88 (2009), 289–312; and *William Robertson and the Expansion of Empire*, ed. S. J. Brown (Cambridge, 1997).

[20] Brown, 'William Robertson', 296–9, notes the prominence of Scots in Orientalist scholarship of this era. See more broadly Jane Rendall, 'Scottish Orientalism: From Robertson to James Mill', *Historical Journal*, 25 (1982), 43–69.

[21] David Ludden, 'Orientalist Empiricism: Transformations of Colonial Knowledge', in *Orientalism and the Postcolonial Predicament: Perspectives on South Asia*, ed. Carol Breckenridge and Peter van der Veer (Philadelphia, 1993), 250–78; Rama Sundari Mantena, *The Origins of Modern Historiography in India: Antiquarianism and Philology, 1780–1880* (New York, 2012); Phillip B. Wagoner, 'Precolonial Intellectuals and the Production of Colonial Knowledge', *Comparative Studies in Society and History*, 45 (2003), 783–814.

the prevailing, derogatory tone, for Mill argued that India lacked a history: dominated by despotism, its culture and polity had failed to manifest progress.[22] In Macaulay's works, this disdain for the subcontinent reached new, morbid heights. As Catherine Hall has argued, his distaste for both India and Indians – born of his bureaucratic labours on the subcontinent in the 1830s – became an integral component of his liberal historical vision.[23] Notoriously, Macaulay in 1835 asserted 'the intrinsic superiority of…Western literature' and (acknowledging that he had 'no knowledge of either Sanscrit or Arabic') claimed 'that a single shelf of a good European library was worth the whole native literature of India and Arabia'.[24] Nor did the Rankean historiographical revolution of the later Victorian years reverse this trend. Georg Iggers has observed that Ranke declined 'to deal with the histories of China and India because he claims that they have no histories in any real sense, but are stagnant and thus at best have "natural histories"'.[25]

Taken together, these three phases of British and European history-writing suggest a lineage for the discipline that uncannily resembles the interior decor of the RHS Council Room (Figure 1). In this materialised representation of our discipline's evolution in Britain, modern historical practice appears to march forward as generations of be-suited, bearded white men give way to generations of be-suited, clean-shaven white men. Surrounded by books and manuscripts culled (in the best Rankean tradition) from British and European archives, their presidential portraits on our walls give no hint of these men's investment in (and our inheritance from) Britain's empire and its history – substantial although these often were. Yet this image of the RHS conceals cross-cultural historical traditions, embedded in the imperial past, which contributed to the making of modern British histories. By turning to the Anglo-Maratha War of 1817–18, I hope to disrupt the seemingly natural British and European progression – to 'provincialise' this historiography, in Dipesh Chakrabarty's resonant phrase[26] – and to begin to recover the vibrant alternatives to the Whig and Rankean Victorian traditions that emerge from our own woodwork, if we take a material turn.

[22] Javed Majeed, *Ungoverned Imaginings: James Mill's 'The History of British India' and Orientalism* (Oxford, 1992), ch. 4, esp. 135–7, 148–9.

[23] Burrow, *Liberal Descent*, 62–4; Catherine Hall, *Macaulay and Son: Architects of Imperial Britain* (2012), ch. 5.

[24] Thomas Macaulay, 'Minute on Education' (2 Feb. 1835), www.columbia.edu/itc/mealac/pritchett/00generallinks/macaulay/txt_minute_education_1835.html.

[25] Iggers, 'Intellectual Foundations', 48.

[26] Dipesh Chakrabarty, *Provincializing Europe: Postcolonial Thought and Historical Difference* (Princeton, 2000).

Figure 1 Royal Historical Society Council Room, November 2017: the walls are decorated with portraits of each of the Society's past presidents. Photograph: James Dawkins.

II

Britain waged three Anglo-Maratha Wars between 1775 and 1818. The focus here, the Third (also known as the Pindari) War began in 1817 and ended in 1818, with mopping-up campaigns extending into the following year.[27] The terms 'Third Anglo-Maratha War' and 'Pindari War' describe two intertwined conflicts fought contemporaneously on overlapping ground by conjoined British armies. Both phrases are misleading, not least because they suggest Manichean oppositions. For these wars did not unilaterally pitch the British against the Marathas – the Hindu claimants to the western lands of the crumbling Islamic Mughal empire. Nor did they set the British unambiguously against the Pindaris – freebooting raiders who exploited the endemic military dislocation in western India after 1800 to sweep down into the fertile Deccan from their strongholds on the banks of the Narbudda. Rather than dualistic combat, these years saw the East India Company's army ally with selected Maratha chiefs even as they battled against others in their campaign to suppress the so-called Pindari hordes. Maratha princes likewise allied selectively with and against each other, the British and the Pindaris. Their armies were fundamentally hybrid: Arab, European and Indian Muslim mercenaries joined Hindu princely armies in their efforts to fight free of British control in the Anglo-Maratha and Pindari Wars.[28]

Loot and plunder were central aspects of these battles, a circumstance that reflects much longer traditions of warfare in Central and South Asia. The wars originated in autumn 1817 with a major British campaign to suppress what the British termed the 'predatory system', the increasingly violent plundering expeditions mounted in the Deccan by Pindari horsemen. The etymology of 'Pindari' is unclear: contemporaries variously ascribed Afghan, Jat and Maratha origins to these mobile warriors. The first credible reference to them, as mercenaries in the Mughal army, dates from 1689.[29] By the later eighteenth century, Pindaris were instead mercenaries in the Maratha armies of the successor states fighting free from the Mughal grip.[30] Shifts of allegiance such as this were characteristic of Pindari strategy. Light horsemen armed with spears and matchlocks and organised into parties of from 1,000 to 3,000 men, they were highly mobile freebooters. On horseback they could cover up to fifty miles in a single day, operating only loosely linked to the armies of their sometime Maratha allies. Charged with

---

[27] Stewart Gordon, *The Marathas 1600–1818* (Cambridge, 1993), 163–77; Reginald George Burton, *The Mahratta and Pindari War. Compiled for General Staff, India* (Simla, 1910).

[28] Randolf G. S. Cooper, *The Anglo-Maratha Campaigns and the Contest for India: The Struggle for Control of the South Asian Military Economy* (Cambridge, 2003); Mesrob Vartavarian, 'Pacification and Patronage in the Maratha Deccan, 1803–1818', *Modern Asian Studies*, 50 (2016), 1749–91.

[29] Philip F. McEldowney, 'Pindari Society and the Establishment of British Paramountcy in India' (MA dissertation, University of Wisconsin, 1966), 5.

[30] *Ibid.*, 6; Mahrendra Prakash Roy, *Origin, Growth, and Suppression of the Pindaris* (New Delhi, 1973), offers the most comprehensive overview.

harassing enemy camps and villages, their function was not to stand and fight but rather to ride and plunder. They swept rapidly into enemy territory, seized any valuable booty, loaded up their hardy steeds, set fire to looted habitations and sped onward to their next victims.[31] One British observer compared the Pindaris to Cossacks on the Russian steppes. They practised 'rapine, accompanied by every enormity of fire and sword, upon the peaceful subjects of the regular governments', he commented. 'The cruelties they perpetuated were beyond belief.'[32]

In the aftermath of the Second Anglo-Maratha War, Pindari depredations escalated sharply. Defeat in the Second War had forced the leaders of the Maratha Confederacy to cede substantial territory to the British. The peace treaties these leaders signed swelled the Pindari ranks by depriving tens of thousands of armed mercenaries of employment. British officials estimated that there were fewer than 3,000 Pindari horsemen in 1800; by 1817, this figure had risen to between 25,000 and 50,000.[33] In the intervening years, the Pindaris turned to increasingly autonomous campaigns of plunder, disrupting trade, despoiling villages and stripping assets from territories farmed for revenue by the Marathas, the English East India Company and Muslim princely states. A handful of successful Pindari leaders acquired great wealth and built military followings that rivalled those of the Maratha chiefs they had earlier served.[34]

As mounting piles of booty enabled the Pindaris to construct new power bases by recruiting men from the Deccan's growing pool of unemployed mercenaries, atrocity stories proliferated in British commercial and military accounts. An East India Company investigation of 1815 reported that 339 villages had been plundered by Pindaris, with 182 persons killed, 505 wounded and 3,603 tortured.[35] By 1816, Pindari raids threatened the Company's territories from Madras to Bombay.[36] Responding to this crisis, in autumn 1817 Francis Rawdon-Hastings (1754–1826), governor general of India, formed two armies to crush the Pindari threat: the so-called Grand Army, under his own command, and the Army of the Deccan, led by Sir Thomas Hislop (1764–1843). Mustering 114,000 men in ten divisions, these two armies – Hastings's Grand Army marching from the north and Hislop's Deccan Army up

[31] Vartavarian, 'Pacification and Patronage', 1756–67.
[32] Henry T. Prinsep, *History of the Political and Military Transactions in India during the Administration of the Marquis of Hastings 1813–1823* (2 vols., 1825), I, 36–7, 38, 39.
[33] McEldowney, 'Pindari Society', 9.
[34] Vartavarian, 'Pacification and Patronage', 1759–61.
[35] Prinsep, *History of the Political*, II, 333–4.
[36] *Bombay Gazette*, 4 Sept. 1816, 1 Jan. 1817.

from the south – sought to force the Pindaris home to the banks of the Narbudda.[37]

This mass deployment of British forces against the Pindaris precipitated the Third Anglo-Maratha War, by affording disaffected Maratha chiefs an opportunity to reassert their claims to western India, while the British were distracted by their campaign to suppress the Pindaris. A loose, often internally divided congeries of princely kingdoms, the Maratha Confederacy or empire traced its origins to the seventeenth-century warrior Shivaji Bhonsale (1630–80). Shivaji had won a decisive battle over the forces of the western Deccan's ruling dynasty in 1659, defeating his opposing general – so legend proclaimed – by eviscerating him with a *baghnaka*, a lethal weapon shaped like a tiger's claw.[38] His success in the next decades in contesting Mughal might rested on a sophisticated system of plunder that converted military loot into government revenue. James Grant Duff (1789–1858) – a captain in the Bombay army and the father of the RHS's fourth president – detailed Shivaiji's system of loot as statecraft in his 1826 history of the Marathas. 'All plunder...was the property of government', he reported. 'It was brought at stated times to Sivajee's...public audience, and individuals formally displayed and delivered their captures.' The phrase '*to plunder the enemy*', he observed, 'is to this day used by the Mahrattas to express a victory, of which it is in their estimation the only real proof'.[39]

Crowned Maratha monarch in 1674, Shivaji founded the dynasty to which Maratha princes still, in the 1800s, owed spiritual allegiance. But by the later eighteenth century, Maratha power was wielded not by the Satara Rajas descended from this founding father, but rather by the *peshwa* or prime minister, based at Poona (present-day Pune). In 1802, on the eve of the Second Anglo-Maratha War, the British had deposed the sitting *peshwa* and installed in his place (as a puppet ruler) Baji Rao II (1775–1851). Shackled to the British by an extortionately costly alliance, Baji Rao fumed, schemed and – in November 1817 – waged open war against his oppressive allies.[40] While the British began to move against the Pindaris, Baji Rao's army looted and burned to the ground Poona Residency, the East India Company's regional seat and the official home of its chief diplomat, Mountstuart Elphinstone (1779–1859). Elphinstone – later to become a noted historian – escaped

---

[37] R. G. Burton, 'A Hundred Years Ago: The Mahratta and Pindari War', *Royal United Services Institution Journal*, 62 (1917), 800–11.

[38] For the *baghnaka*, and the context of its use, see Anna Jackson and Amir Jaffer with Deepika Ahlaway, *Maharaja: The Splendour of India's Royal Courts* (2009), 16–17. For Shivaji, see James Laine, *Shivaji: Hindu King in Islamic India* (Oxford, 2003).

[39] James Grant Duff, *A History of the Mahrattas* (3 vols., 1826), I, 229.

[40] Suman G. Vaida, *Peshwa Bajirao II and the Downfall of the Maratha Power* (Nagpur, 1976).

the Residency with his retainers, but his library of rare Persian, Sanskrit, Hindi and Marathi books and manuscripts was destroyed in the flames.[41]

Baji Rao's treachery was swiftly compounded by the defection to his cause of other Maratha chiefs. These events compelled the two British armies formed to suppress the Pindaris to fight simultaneously on multiple fronts. In the next months, these armies gradually forced the Pindaris toward the hills and jungles of the Narbudda by a pincer-like movement between Hastings's Grand Army, and Hislop's Deccan divisions. As they retreated, Baji Rao and his Maratha allies – assisted on occasion by fleeing Pindaris – evaded capture by the Deccan Army's infantry and cavalry. Rumoured to be simultaneously in multiple, far-flung corners of the Deccan and moving with little resistance through the territories of Britain's supposed allies, Baji Rao was to evade capture until June 1818. In the meantime, epidemic cholera struck the British forces, exacerbating the heavy toll of their military losses. As British casualties mounted, the senior officers orchestrating pursuit of the *peshwa* across the Deccan struggled to maintain authority over their own forces. Plunder and looting – the very practices the Pindari War had been waged to suppress – now emerged as a shared *modus operandi* of Pindari, Maratha and British alike.[42]

Since the reign of Shivaji in the seventeenth century, loot had been the vital cog around which Maratha military strategy turned, just as plunder later became the prime goal and military function of the Pindaris. These extractive modes of warfare extended far beyond the Maratha territories and were entrenched in India long before Europeans established a substantial territorial presence. It was plunder that provided much of the capital that allowed Afghan, Sikh, Jat and Maratha freebooters, active from Central Asia down to the Deccan, to attract and deploy the mercenary horsemen who secured the new regional states that displaced Mughal imperial rule. In this turbulent political era, Jos Gomans observes, 'there was no clear-cut distinction between war and peace and between plundering and revenue collection…In fact, looting was considered as an irregular form of tax collection by the enemy.' Hoards of accumulated plunder functioned for Indian princely aspirants as private banks which 'could be used…to attract new adventurers or converted into ready cash by sale'.[43] Loot, moreover, provided the essential glue that made both Indian and British multi-ethnic armies coalesce and function: 'the best way of keeping an army…together was…the prospect of…plunder'.[44]

[41] Grant Duff, *History*, III, 427–8; Prinsep, *History of the Political*, II, 57.

[42] Vartavarian, 'Pacification and Patronage', 1769–72.

[43] Jos. J. L. Gomans, *The Rise of the Indo-Afghan Empire, c. 1710–1780* (Leiden, 1995), 136–7, 138–9.

[44] *Ibid.*, 142.

The British presence added to these Central and South Asian traditions of extractive statecraft one novel component predicated on European conventions of war. This new factor was the prize system. Legal structures for adjudicating the allocation of ships and cargoes seized in war had developed in the sixteenth century in maritime Europe, and from the seventeenth century Admiralty courts oversaw the distribution of so-called prize, the spoils of British naval combat.[45] Military prize as it developed in seventeenth-century Britain was, in sharp contrast, ramshackle, partisan, Byzantine and tortuously slow. Whereas legal courts adjudicated maritime prize, only the sovereign had the ultimate authority to determine which officers and men should enjoy proceeds from the sale of booty captured in territorial campaigns. In theory, the prospect of military prize granted by the king bolstered soldiers' valour in the battlefield whilst diminishing their incentive to engage in indiscriminate plunder at or before the point of victory. Battlefield practice, however, departed radically from this ideal, for prize procedure demanded labyrinthine bureaucracy and delayed gratification, while loot lay readily and immediately at hand. Under prize procedure, in the aftermath of each territorial battle, commanding officers established committees responsible both for collecting, inventorying and disposing of booty seized from the enemy and for compiling detailed lists of who had served under whom in each campaign – thereby seeking to establish combatants' entitlement to prize.[46] These voluminous records were then sent to Whitehall, for the sovereign's consideration. Already onerous in European theatres of war, these cumbersome prize processes were rendered yet more burdensome in the Anglo-Maratha campaigns by the vast distances that booty, documents, and men traversed; by the cacophony of languages spoken by officers and their men; and by the sheer scale of plundered material objects that surfaced in the course of the Deccan Army's protracted pursuit of the *peshwa*.[47]

As they were chased by the Deccan Army from hill forts to princely courts, from princely courts to jungles and from jungles to the plains, Baji Row and his allies mobilised their accumulated hoards of treasure to attract mercenaries, to provision their armies and to purchase the silence of neutral princes through whose territories they fled.

[45] Francis Deák and Philip C. Jessup, 'Early Prize Court Procedure: Part One', *University of Pennsylvania Law Review*, 82 (1934), 677–94, esp. 679–82; Shavana Musa, 'Tides and Tribulations: English Prize Law and the Law of Nations in the Seventeenth Century', *Journal of the History of International Law*, 17 (2015), 47–82.

[46] Harris Prendergast, *The Law relating to Officers in the Army* (1855), ch. 7.

[47] The disputes over the so-called 'Deccan Prize Money' of the Third Anglo-Maratha War are chronicled in British Library (henceforth BL), MSS Eur F88/447. The main Deccan Prize ledgers, extending in many volumes from 1819 to 1850, are found in BL, IOR/L/AG/24/24.

Comprising jewels, textiles, plate, gold and silver coins, religious statues and weaponry, this liquid capital was variously heavy, fragile, cumbersome to pack and difficult to transport or conceal. Its materiality – its heft, its size, its configuration and composition – shaped its appeal, use and value, both in transit and, if captured by the British, once revealed. Packed in bullock carts, loaded onto camels, dispatched on the backs of horses and elephants, vast sums of treasure flowed across the Deccan to fund Maratha warfare.

The siege and capture of Rhygur Fort illustrate the material, cultural and military processes simultaneously at play as Maratha treasure was transmogrified into British booty and set on its rocky road to becoming British prize. Rhygur had played a vital military and ritual role in Shivaji's seventeenth-century empire, but its strategic importance was heightened in 1818 by the fact that it was to this fort and its commandant, Narroba Outia (who also served as Baji Rao's treasurer), that the *peshwa* had dispatched his wife for safety. Women played active roles in Maratha war and politics. Shivaji's mother, Jijabai (1598–1674) figures prominently in the Maratha *powadas* (heroic poems) that chronicled her son's military victories; wives, widows and mothers featured conspicuously among the Maratha rulers who contested Mughal power in the following decades.[48] At least one female leader was beheaded by her clan during the Pindari War, to remove her from power.[49] In warfare, the wives of Maratha and Pindari chieftains were also instrumental in transporting princely treasure. Reporting the movements of the Pindari Chitu in January 1818, the *Bombay Gazette* noted that his party included 'six elephants, two for the conveyance of his Wife, Son, and Mother, and the rest…laden with Treasure'.[50] Where there were insurgent Indian women, British military men rightly suspected, there was also likely to be loot, or prospective prize.[51] When, after eighteen days of bombardment by British artillery, Rhygur at last capitulated, the attention of Lieutenant-Colonel David Prother and his men was fixed equally on its commandant, Narroba, and on the *peshwa*'s wife, Bhai Sahib.

The terms of capitulation agreed at Rhygur stipulated that all of the *peshwa*'s treasure hidden in the fort, as well as two-thirds of Narroba's personal fortune, was to become British booty. Early estimates suggested

---

[48] Prachi Deshpande, *Creative Pasts: Historical Memory and Identity in Western India, 1700–1960* (New York, 2007), 57–60; Gordon, *Marathas*, 160–2. See more broadly V. S. Kadam, 'The Institution of Marriage and Position of Women in Eighteenth-Century Maharashtra', *Indian Economic and Social History Review*, 25 (1988), 341–70.

[49] *Bombay Gazette*, 21 Jan. 1818.

[50] *Ibid.*, 28 Jan. 1818.

[51] Local villagers who fled to the hill forts to escape warfare took their moveable property with them, but these goods were vulnerable to seizure as booty. See for example Grant Duff, *History*, II, 429–31.

that the coin alone of the *peshwa*'s ample hoard comprised 19,000 gold mohurs and 4½ lacs of silver rupees.[52] Booty seized in warfare, this wealth was vibrant matter, animated with the potential to become military prize, through the king's gift in England.[53] As Prother's men dug into the walls of the fort to extract the *peshwa*'s concealed hoard of treasure, rumours of its vast extent proliferated. So too did suspicion that Narroba's men would carry British booty with them as they marched in defeat from the fort. The discovery of thirty-eight empty money bags within Rhygur's walls fuelled already rampant speculation along these lines. As the peace negotiations and search for booty continued, claims that Narroba's servants were sewing gold coins into their turbans, so as to carry illicit property to their master's home in Poona, reached a hysterical pitch.[54]

Already seething, these rumours escalated after Narroba's troops marched out, for the combined impact of the prize committee's inventory of the *peshwa*'s hoard and the departure for Poona of the *peshwa*'s wife brought home to observers both the vast extent of the wealth mobilised by the Marathas in this war and the unlikelihood of ever seizing it in full. Prother's prize committee documented page after page of booty, the proceeds of which might – or, might not – someday be awarded to the Deccan Army, at the king's pleasure. Having itemised sixteen boxes, bags and baskets of jewels and gold ornaments, the prize committee required a further 180 numbered bags to bundle the remaining items for transport. Solid gold bracelets, armlets set with pearls and diamonds, head ornaments, gold rings, garnet pendants, silver bangles and shawls figured in these ledgers, alongside a gold helmet, a gold lion and a gold elephant.[55] The departure of the *peshwa*'s wife inevitably stoked British suspicions that booty was slipping through their hands and returning with her to replenish the *peshwa*'s dispersed and mobile treasuries. Propriety dictated that neither she nor her female servants could be searched, and Maratha dress was well suited to conceal mobile treasure. Prother duly extracted prize from the Bhai Sahib of 29,000 rupees in coin, two horses, nineteen gold or silver figures of gods, jewels, plate and textiles.[56]

Glistening in the sunlight, fascinating the connoisseurial eye, heavy in the hand, the consignment of material booty and prospective prize from

---

[52] Petition of Lt-Colonel David Prother to the privy council (1833), BL, MSS Eur, F88/447, 184.

[53] For 'vibrant matter' and the 'vital materiality' that links persons, things and political agency, see Bennett, *Vibrant Matter*.

[54] Prother Petition, BL, MSS Eur, F88/447, 184–5.

[55] Rhyghur Prize Committee Proceedings, May 1818, BL, MSS Eur F88/447, 416–18.

[56] Prother to Lt-Colonel Leighton, 12 May 1818, BL, MSS Eur F88/447, 417.

Rhygur paled in the imagination when compared to the potential booty that had surely accompanied the Bhai to Poona. The stakes were high. Prize money could eclipse officers' military pay. Arthur Wellesley – who as the duke of Wellington was later to be appointed Deccan Prize Fund's senior trustee in London – had netted £25,000 of prize for his service in the first two Anglo-Maratha Wars.[57] The Rhygur officers' high expectations, however, were dealt a severe blow when the dust of battle settled. Prother was an experienced commanding officer: between December 1817 and April 1818, his forces succeeded in capturing eighteen Maratha hill forts. But neither he nor his officers spoke Marathi, the language in which the Rhygur treaty of capitulation was drawn up. To their fury, once he had reached the safety of Poona and assumed the identity of a mere civilian, they discovered that Narroba's oral agreement to surrender two-thirds of his property as booty was absent from the treaty's written stipulations.[58] Infighting and mutual accusations of blame were soon rife among the British officers serving in the Deccan, entangling a broader constellation of officials in adjudicating claims about loot, booty and prize.

III

The men who were instrumental in these booty disputes were all clients in the patronage network of Mountstuart Elphinstone. Captains John Briggs (1785–1875), James Grant Duff (1789–1858) and Henry Dundas Robertson (1790–1845) were, like Elphinstone himself, Scots or of Scottish descent.[59] They formed a close-knit Celtic administrative network based in Deccan outposts that stretched from Poona and Satara in the north to Khandesh in the south. Feeding vital information to each other and to Elphinstone as they struggled to impose order in the wake of war, they encouraged agriculture, battled epidemic cholera, laboured to suppress looting (by Pindari, Maratha and British troops) and sought to ensure that legitimate booty seized by the army divisions that continued to chase insurgents across their territories was secured either for the East India Company's coffers or for military prize committees. In performing these duties, both perforce and by inclination, Elphinstone's men became enthusiastic historians.

[57] Cooper, *Anglo-Maratha Campaigns*, 377 n. 168.
[58] Prother Petition, BL, MSS Eur F88/447, 184–7.
[59] For the wider Scottish tradition of Orientalist administration, see Joanna Frew, 'Scottish Backgrounds and Indian Experiences in the Late Eighteenth Century', *Journal of Scottish Historical Studies*, 34 (2014), 167–98; Martha McLaren, *British India and British Scotland: Career Building, Empire Building and a Scottish School of Thought on Indian Governance* (Akron, 2001); and Avril Powell, *Scottish Orientalists and India: The Muir Brothers, Religion, Education and Empire* (Woodbridge, 2011).

The fundamental incoherence and the extraordinary inconvenience of military prize processes are under-examined leitmotifs of British imperial warfare, and in India the vagaries of prize assumed an exaggerated form. Basic questions about how Indian booty should be capitalised remained unanswered until after 1857.[60] To whom should the king attribute booty seized from the Marathas – and thus, to whom should he confer prize money? Was payment for booty owed to the Company's directors in London, to its governors in India or to officers and troops? Were only men engaged in actual combat in a given battle entitled to prize, or was the Deccan Army collectively entitled to any and all Maratha booty? Did the Grand Army merit prize alongside the Deccan Army – notwithstanding that its divisions, preoccupied with suppressing the Pindaris, did not participate in the campaigns against the *peshwa*? Lack of secure knowledge that war booty would indeed result in prize payments encouraged British officers and their troops to loot alongside Indian mercenaries and villagers. John Briggs, himself already embroiled in a fierce dispute with fellow-officers over his seizure for the Company of the famed Nassak diamond, condemned 'the enormities committed by the Europeans, & natives', observing that in Khandesh it was under British officers' oversight that 'property...and...household goods were carried off, the temples polluted'.[61] In this febrile military context, producing historical narratives that either justified or discredited claims to prize came to occupy many Company men alongside their efforts to bring the *peshwa*'s territories under control.

The private letters of James Grant Duff, Elphinstone's man in Satara, and John Briggs, his man in Khandesh, demonstrate how key officers were drawn ineluctably into historical research and publication by the demands and opportunities of military employment.[62] As they laboured to restore order in the Deccan, Grant Duff and Briggs wrote regularly for (and with) advice and information both to each other and to their patron, who carefully archived their letters as he rebuilt his library after the sack of Poona Residency. Their voluminous correspondence preserved, chronicled and interpreted the vital dates, key personnel, official documents and confused events of successive battles, establishing an historical

---

[60] Raffi Gregorian, 'Unfit for Service: British Law and Looting in India in the Mid-Nineteenth Century', *South Asia*, 13 (1990), 63–84.

[61] John Briggs to Mountstuart Elphinstone (henceforth ME), 25 Apr. 1818, BL, MSS Eur F88/201, 56. For the disputed Nassak diamond, see Evan Bell, *Memoir of General John Briggs, of the Madras Army; With Comments on Some of his Words and Work* (1885), 61–71.

[62] The broader contours of military service as a medium of colonial knowledge formation are explored in Nicholas Dirks, 'Colonial Histories and Native Informants: Biography of an Archive', in *Orientalism*, ed. Breckenridge and van der Veer, 279–313; and Douglas Peers, 'Colonial Knowledge and the Military in India, 1780–1860', *Journal of Imperial and Commonwealth History*, 33 (2006), 157–80.

matrix from which a stable narrative of the Deccan campaign could be assembled. Like colonial knowledge production more broadly, these historical endeavours relied fundamentally on the expertise of 'native' informants and interlocutors. Exploiting the skills and collections of a dense network of Maratha and Persianate scribes and badgering local princes for access to their genealogical collections, Briggs and Grant Duff immersed themselves in Indian historical manuscripts.[63]

Their private correspondence pullulates with an enthusiasm for archival documents, original research and evidence-based historical analysis that pre-dates publication of the German historian Leopold von Ranke's first book and pre-figures many of the methodologies he would later champion from his base in German universities and European state archives. In these officers' letters, the conjectural methodologies of Scottish Enlightenment history were put into productive dialogue not only with the administrative demands of military pacification but with Maratha and Mughal traditions of historical writing – themselves shaped by pragmatic administrative and military agendas, and likewise in flux in these years.[64] Plunder in the midst of battle and prize claims in the aftermath of war both fuelled and problematized these military men's labours. The correspondence sent by James Grant Duff and John Briggs to Elphinstone was larded with reports of actual looting, suspected booty and putative prize, and with repeated pleas for assistance in distinguishing between these troublesomely labile material categories. 'Treasure-hunting does indeed make men keen – here is Grant [Duff] who set his face against it writing volumes to shew how laudable it is', Henry Dundas Robertson observed to Elphinstone in 1818.[65] Over time, this burgeoning correspondence grew to encompass much wider narratives of state formation and empire-building.

From 1818, constantly consulting Maratha manuscripts in his search for evidence of the location of hidden treasure, Grant Duff began to collect and transcribe his own proprietary Maratha archive. From his research in the primary materials he used to search for booty and to

[63] Deshpande, *Creative Pasts*, 77–8; James Grant Duff (henceforth JGD) to ME, 28 Dec. 1819, BL, MSS Eur F88/205, 70v–74v.
[64] For Maratha historical traditions, see Sumit Guha, 'Speaking Historically: The Changing Voices of Historical Narration in Western India, 1400–1900', *American Historical Review*, 109 (2004), 1084–103; for wider Indian historiographical traditions relevant to these British officers, see Kumkum Chatterjee, *The Culture of History in Early Modern India: Persianization and Mughal Culture in Bengal* (New Delhi, 2009), and Velcheru Rao, David Shulman and Sanjay Subrahmanyam, *Textures of Time: Writing History in South India 1600–1800* (New York, 2003).
[65] Henry Dundas Robertson to ME, 3 Sept. 1818, BL, MSS Eur F88/201, 97. Robertson himself reported having 'dreamt the whole night of large Boxes of gold' carried away by Maratha antagonists. Robertson to ME, [1818], BL, MSS Eur F88/201, 216r–v.

allocate pensions to toppled warlords, it was but a short step to historical scholarship. 'I shall have the whole of them copied', he wrote to Elphinstone of his collected manuscripts in July 1819. 'A long time ago I had a <u>floating idea</u> of throwing some light on Mahratta History, the possession of such materials...enables me to authenticate a great deal of what concerns this country.'[66] With Elphinstone's encouragement, Grant Duff now committed to write the history of 'the <u>modern expansion</u>' of the Deccan states.[67] By 1820, he had begun to write a book, acknowledging ruefully that 'I had no conception of the labour' this would entail.[68] In Khandesh, John Briggs also turned his attention from booty disputes to historical research, and the pair agreed a division of labour, with Briggs focusing on the Mughal empire and Grant Duff on the Marathas.[69] Grant Duff's letters to Elphinstone were now animated not by stories of hidden treasure but by reports of progress on his book manuscript and insistent requests for feedback on his draft chapters.[70]

Availing himself of a vibrant community of British military officer-historians, Grant Duff sent his burgeoning manuscript out from Satara for successive rounds of peer review, developing normative practices of anonymity that will be familiar to present-day professional historians. The reason that he had asked for readers' feedback to be written not on the manuscript itself but on separate slips of paper, he explained to Elphinstone, was 'that I may have the benefit of several opinions without one opinion being influenced by another'.[71] Then as now, subjection to peer review was often painful, but Grant Duff accepted criticism stoically, resorting to military metaphor to signal the virtues of this stringent discipline. 'Kennedy has given my 1st Volume such a castigation! the lash clotted with my blood is still whirling in his hand...and I really think that most of what he has said is very fair', he observed philosophically.[72]

Neither Grant Duff's manuscript, which he completed in Britain and published as a three-volume tome in 1826, nor John Briggs's four-volume 1829 *History of the Rise of the Mahomedan Power in India*, embraced the emerging orthodoxies of Whig history, any more than they relied upon Whig methods of analysis. Grant Duff was dismissive of James Mill's 1817 *History of British India*, a work damning of Indians and Indian history alike but which the Whig historian Thomas Macaulay would later hail

---

[66] JGD to ME, 19 [July 1819], BL, MSS Eur F88/205, 74.
[67] JGD to ME, 2 Aug. 1819, BL, MSS Eur F88/205, 84v.
[68] JGD to ME, 8 Aug. 1820, BL, MSS Eur F88/205, 123.
[69] JGD to ME, 12 Aug. 1820, BL, MSS Eur F88/205, 126.
[70] JGD to ME, 14 Mar. 1822, BL, MSS Eur F88/205, 158.
[71] JGD to ME, 14 Mar. 1822, BL, MSS Eur F88/205, 158.
[72] JGD to ME, 29 Dec. 1822, BL, MSS Eur F88/206, 18.

as 'the greatest historical work which has appeared in our language since Gibbon'.[73] In Grant Duff's contrasting estimation, Mill suffered from 'an inclination to find fault where he does not really understand, a total want of genius and the want of an Indian spirit'.[74] Unlike Mill, both Grant Duff and Briggs recognised that the Marathas had a history and had evolved their own historiographical traditions to interpret it. They openly acknowledged that their weighty tomes rested on original documents and research produced by Indian forebears and Indian co-producers of historical scholarship. Grant Duff's preface duly thanked East India Company men but also praised Brahmin and Maratha friends for the generosity of their scribal assistance, gifts of manuscripts and guidance with historical interpretation.[75] Briggs's acknowledgement of the labours of his Indian *munshi* both named this fellow-historian and imbued him with distinction. 'Fortunately the person who was my first assistant in 1812 remained with me till I left India in 1827, and his whole life has been devoted to the study of Indian history', he informed his readers. This individual, 'to whom I feel myself bound to say I owe so much is Meer Ally Khan…a person of good family in…Agra'.[76]

Both Briggs and Grant Duff, indeed, wrote scathingly in their histories about misguided British interpretations of Indians. Briggs's work was a translation, annotation and elaboration of the Muslim historian Mahomed Kasim Ferishta's (1560–1620) treatise, and offered an explicit defence of both Indian history and Indian historians. 'The perusal of their history cannot be otherwise than instructive if it be merely to show the certain effects of good and bad government among a people whom our ignorance disposes us to consider as devoid of moral energy', he asserted in his preface. 'It is not my intention to dilate on the origin of this misconception of the Indian character…a volume would not suffice to point out all the instances to the contrary with which the work abounds', he concluded.[77] In Grant Duff's *History of the Mahrattas*, even the Pindaris – notwithstanding their propensity to plunder and enacting murderous violence – were accorded some sympathy. For Grant Duff blamed the development of their predatory system on 'the half measures and selfish policy adopted by the British government'.[78]

Rejecting the emerging verities of Whig history, Grant Duff's treatise instead bears the impress of earlier strands of Scottish conjectural history,

---

[73] Cited by Hall, *Macaulay and Son*, 209.
[74] JGD to ME, 21 Feb. 1822, BL, MSS Eur F88/205, 152v.
[75] Grant Duff, *History*, I, viii–x.
[76] John Briggs, *History of the Rise of Mahomedan Power in India, till the Year A.D. 1612…* (4 vols., 1829), I, xiii.
[77] *Ibid.*, xv–xvi.
[78] Grant Duff, *History*, I, 330. See also I, 389.

in which a society's level of civilisation could be gauged by the status of its women – with higher female status betokening higher levels of civilisation.[79] 'The women of the Mahratta country are well treated; they are helpmates, but by no means the slaves of their husbands; nor are they in the degraded state...which some travellers have described', he asserted at the outset of his *History*.[80] Compatible with conjectural methodology, this assessment was also rooted in military praxis. It reflected Grant Duff's repeated contests for authority over the youthful Raja of Satara with the Raja's widowed mother, who was understandingly reluctant to cede power to the British and emphatically capable of exercising independent agency. Reporting one of many standoffs between the Raja and his mother to Elphinstone in 1818, Grant Duff had observed that 'the old lady turned and looked...as if she could have spit in his face or kicked his shins, or tore his little snub nose off, & the poor little fellow was so cowed that I quite pitied him in having such a b_ of a mother'.[81]

Grant Duff's *History* married his conjectural reflections with 'modern' historical methodologies that included not only deep archival research (referenced in footnotes) but also an appreciation of material culture that resonates with the arguments of recent historians who have taken the material turn. Illustrations of Maratha weaponry punctuate the pages of his *History*, in which Grant Duff depicted the weapons themselves as animating agents of Maratha history. Experienced commanding officers in the Deccan typically allowed defeated mercenaries to retain their swords and daggers, which they understood to be not inert objects but rather named heirlooms to which powerful identities and histories were attached. First in the battlefield and then from his base at Satara, Grant Duff had closely observed the function of such material objects as vibrant matter. In his interpretation, the Maratha archive comprised both historical manuscripts and political things-cum-persons. Shivaji's sword, he reported in his *History*, 'which he named after the goddess Bhowanee [Bhavani], is still preserved by the Raja of Satara with the utmost veneration, and has all the honours of an idol paid to it'. In a footnote, Grant Duff added that the sword's 'whole history is recorded by the hereditary historian of the family'.[82] So great was his appreciation of the power of Maratha material culture, indeed, that Grant Duff's archival acquisitions appear to have crossed

---

[79] Karen O'Brien, *Women and Enlightenment in Eighteenth-Century Britain* (Cambridge, 2009), esp. ch. 2; Silvia Sebastiani, '"Race", Women and Progress in the Scottish Enlightenment', in *Women, Gender and Enlightenment*, ed. Sarah Knott and Barbara Taylor (Basingstoke, 2005), 75–96.
[80] Grant Duff, *History*, I, 18.
[81] JGD to ME, [1818], BL, MSS Eur F88/204, 10v.
[82] Grant Duff, *History*, I, 298.

Figure 2 The *baghnaka* or tiger claw, reputedly used by Shivaji, taken to Britain by James Grant Duff and subsequently donated by the family to the Victoria and Albert Museum. © Victoria and Albert Museum, London.

the porous boundaries that divided plunder, loot, booty and prize. Gifted to the Victoria and Albert Museum in 1971, the *baghnaka* or tiger claw (Figure 2) that made its way from Satara to his home in Scotland in the 1820s figures in family legend as the very weapon used by Shivaji to eviscerate his rival and thereby establish the Maratha empire.[83]

IV

Resting on plunder and its suppression, born of booty and its administration, activated by the pursuit and deflection of prize claims, late Georgian history-writing in India suggests an alternative trajectory from the Scottish Enlightenment to disciplinary modernity than the one conventionally traced through liberal Whigs to the Rankean historians of the later Victorian era.[84] Both loot – a term with Sanskrit and Hindi origins that reflect its extended history as a military modality in Central and South Asia – and prize – a practice developed by European nation-states to regulate plunder in first their domestic and

[83] For the family's genealogy of this object, see http://collections.vam.ac.uk/item/O134202/tiger-claws-unknown/.

[84] Grafton, *The Footnote*, challenges the conventional chronology of historiographical 'modernity' in referencing, but confines his argument to a European context.

then their imperial wars – shaped the practice of nineteenth-century British history-writing. Warfare on the Indian subcontinent promoted an evidence-based vein of historiography deeply rooted in British and Indian archives of the imperial state. Through the operation of the prize system, booty was freighted with expectations of material profit that only precise historical narratives supported by documentary evidence could deliver, once battle had ceased and the army's post-conflict systems had lumbered into gear. Entitlement to prize required proof of battle; evidence about where, how and when booty had been seized; and contextual information on its provenance – in short, it demanded historical documents and historical analysis.

Instrumental resort to the archives constructed by Elphinstone and his men can be tracked through their correspondence well beyond the 1820s, as the officers whose booty disputes they had adjudicated in India returned to Britain and appealed to the treasury, the privy council, chancery, parliament and the press for payment of prize from the Pindari War. Company men clamorous for prize appealed to Elphinstone's collection of private letters and government documents, using these manuscripts to substantiate their narratives of the Deccan campaigns and thus to justify their receipt of prize.[85] References to published histories (themselves based on private archives) written in the wake of battle further augmented these efforts.[86] Defeated Marathas likewise appealed to these manuscripts to advance counter-claims against British seizure of the *peshwa*'s treasure.[87] Constantly delayed, repeatedly interrupted and never enough, the successive royal warrants that belatedly released prize awards from sale of the Deccan booty in the 1820s, 1830s and 1840s go far to explain the appeal of loot today over prize tomorrow in the British empire. The Third Anglo-Maratha and Pindari War ended in 1818, but the final payment recorded in the Deccan Prize ledgers dates from 1897, and (at this late date) was inevitably made not to an actual combatant of the campaigns but to a long-deceased officer's adult children.[88]

---

[85] See for example the many letters and draft replies in BL, MSS Eur F88/447.

[86] Examples include BL, MSS Eur F88/447, 334v–338; contemporary histories used to substantiate claims included Prinsep, *History of the Political*, esp. II, 12–13, and Valentine Blacker, *Memoir of the Operations of the British Army in India during the Mahratta War of 1817, 1818, & 1819* (1821).

[87] See esp. Arthur James Lewis, *A Letter to the Right Honourable the Lords Commissioners of His Majesty's Treasury, relative to the Claim of the Representatives of Naroba Govind Ouita on the Deccan Prize Fund* (1833), and Haruki Inagaki, 'Law, Agency and Emergency in British Imperial Politics: Conflict between the Government and the King's Court in Bombay in the 1820s', *East Asian Journal of British History*, 5 (2016), 207–24, esp. 217–22.

[88] The recipients were assistant surgeon Thomas Tomkinson (£17 13s 2d, 1874); Mrs Catherine Carmody (on behalf of Sergeant Patrick Carmody, deceased, 6s 8d, 1896) and

What happened in Britain to the innovative historical methodologies forged in these Indian wars?[89] Can we discern any legacies of James Grant Duff's pioneering archival research, his appreciation of Indian history or his enthusiasm for Maratha material culture in the works of his son, Mountstuart Elphinstone Grant Duff (1829–1906), fourth president of the RHS (Figure 3)? At first glance, the answer to this question appears to be an emphatic negative: James Grant Duff's Indian legacy was ostensibly effaced in Britain by the triumph of the Whigs. Notwithstanding he read German fluently and spent much time on the continent consorting with European intellectuals, the influence of Ranke is absent from M. E. Grant Duff's historical writings. Best known for his talent for 'collecting interesting...historical anecdotes, pithy sayings and literary curiosities', he was a fixture in Victorian gentlemen's clubs.[90] His *Notes from a Diary* begins, unpromisingly but not uncharacteristically, by recording his first sighting of an olive.[91]

Explicit adherence to the Whig interpretation of British freedom coloured M .E. Grant Duff's approach to India. It was he who initiated the RHS's annual presidential addresses, but the pages of the *Transactions* reveal scant evidence of his father's historiographical footprint. Bereft of footnotes, Grant Duff's eight anniversary lectures typically found their inspiration not in archives but in texts by classical authors such as Tacitus, evidence he combined with personal reminiscences of eminent Victorian men among his friends. Only his last lecture, in 1899, engaged substantially with India, and his analysis – decisively shaped by the 'calamity' of the 1857–8 Mutiny and Rebellion – was steeped in the tenets of liberal imperialism.[92] Whereas his father's years in India had produced an historical interpretation that recognised Marathas as effective state-builders with their own historical traditions, M. E. Grant Duff instead drew upon his experience as governor of Madras Presidency (1881–6) to infantilise Indians and Indian politics. 'Demands are made from time to time for even more self-Government but they are altogether in the nature of the cries of children to whom

the children of the late Lt-Colonel Charles Heath (£69 17s 9d, 1897), BL, IOR/L/AG/24/25/8, 414.

[89] On the subcontinent, Grant Duff's *History* became a standard text in the increasingly Anglicised curriculum for men – both Indian and British – serving the Company, and after 1850 its canonical status was such that it spurred fierce Indian nationalist critiques of British imposition of Western education. Deshpande, *Creative Pasts*, 80–5, 94–114.

[90] 'Sir Mountstuart Grant Duff', *Times*, 13 Jan. 1906, 17.

[91] Mountstuart Elphinstone Grant Duff, *Notes from a Diary 1851–1872* (1897), I, 1.

[92] M. E. Grant Duff, 'Presidential Address', *Transactions of the Royal Historical Society*, 13 (1899), 9. Liberal imperialism's infantilisation of Indians is underlined by Uday Mehta, *Liberalism and Empire: A Study in Nineteenth-Century British Liberal Thought* (Chicago, 1999); and Theodore Koditschek, *Liberalism, Imperialism and the Historical Imagination: Nineteenth-Century Visions of Great Britain* (Cambridge, 2011).

Figure 3 The Right Honourable Sir Mountstuart Elphinstone Grant Duff (1829–1906), president of the Royal Historical Society, 1891–99. RHS Archives.

their nurses refuse the enjoyment which they expect to derive from a case of razors', he observed, praising 'the impartial justice' with which the British government had treated 'our Indian fellow subjects'.[93]

93 Grant Duff, 'Presidential Address', 6.

To trace the enduring imprint of the Indian careers of men such as James Grant Duff on British history-writing, we must dig a little deeper, and look in rather different (and more material) directions. Two vantage points are arguably most productive. The first is recognition that the material wealth that allowed M. E. Grant Duff to rise to the RHS presidency and to support other Victorian learned societies – he presided, for example, over the Royal Geographical Society as well – was substantially Indian in origin. Named after his father's East India Company patron, who had naturally stood as his godfather, Grant Duff enjoyed an education and social status derived from Indian capital. His father's net worth at death in 1858 was £43,354 10s 1d (well over £4 million at current values); his military savings, prize payments and Company pension allowed James Grant Duff to leave an Aberdeenshire country estate to this, his eldest son. Together with money inherited from M. E. Grant Duff's mother – the daughter of an eminent Company physician and botanist – this Indian hoard ensured that whereas his father at sixteen had left school in Scotland for military service on the subcontinent, the son would attend the Edinburgh Academy, matriculate at Balliol, be called to the Inner Temple, serve as a Liberal MP and be appointed to the lucrative governorship of Madras.[94]

A second legacy is revealed in M. E. Grant Duff's travel-writing – a genre in which (in contrast to his presidential lectures), he placed the Company colonialism of his father's generation into explicit dialogue with post-Mutiny politics. In this text, material objects emerged both as bearers of meaningful Indian histories that could still speak to Britons and Marathas alike and as emblems of the economic modernity which – he suggested – would one day render India eligible for liberal freedoms. His 1876 *Notes of an Indian Journey* saw Grant Duff use his father's 1826 *History* to reflect on the Marathas' pathway to modernity. Here, extended quotations from his father's book allowed M. E. Grant Duff to construct a 'picturesque' history in which British officers such as James Grant Duff chased Pindaris and the 'unmitigated scoundrels' of the Maratha 'nation' from their hill forts to establish a precarious colonial rule.[95] As a site of political power, Satara (which 'was within an ace of giving trouble in 1857') served in this interpretation as a problematic emblem of the tenacity of Maratha historical consciousness. 'I confess I did not much like the look of things…at Satara', he opined. 'The people seem to cherish the recollections of old times quite as much as is desirable, and while they are peculiarly attentive to the representative

---

[94] H. C. G. Matthew, 'Duff, Sir Mountstuart Elphinstone Grant (1829–1906)', *Oxford Dictionary of National Biography* (Oxford, 2008).

[95] Mountstuart E. Grant Duff, *Notes of an Indian Journey* (1876), 221, 220.

of the Satara family, they rather fail in the respect paid throughout the empire to the local British authority.'⁹⁶

Like his father before him, M. E. Grant Duff braided material histories into his political analyses, recognising the vital force of things as agents of both historical memory and historical change. At Satara, his Maratha hosts brought out Shivaji's iconic sword and *baghnaka* (the pair of which had allegedly accompanied James Grant Duff home to Britain):

> In the course of the day, Bhowanee (Sivajee's sword) came to visit me. She is a fine Genoa blade...I say she, for to this day she is treated in all respects, not as a thing, but as a goddess...With her came other interesting objects, among them two Wagnucks which her illustrious owner used on one critical occasion...one is a facsimile of that in my possession.⁹⁷

Couched in the language of vibrant matter, M. E. Grant Duff's description of Maratha material artefacts echoed his father's recognition of the power of objects to serve as historical archives. From this base, he elaborated a material future for Indian manufacture in which reproduction of traditional 'native' wares – textiles, carpets and enamels, of which he was himself a keen consumer – for British markets would fuel modernisation on the subcontinent.⁹⁸

Still figuring in the footnotes of scholarship on South and Central Asia today, the works of East India Company military historians such as James Grant Duff form part of a much broader Victorian corpus of military history that is also rich in social, cultural, material and political evidence, commentary and analysis.⁹⁹ Many of these works conform very poorly to Whig paradigms and methodologies, a finding that should not surprise us. Military men who – like James Grant Duff – peppered requests in their private correspondence for peer review of their book manuscripts with casual comments about the necessity of quelling plunder by summary hangings or firing insurgents from cannons may well have found the language of liberalism inadequate to the task of empire.¹⁰⁰ Men, moreover, who had privileged access both to original records of overturned states and to rich collections of Indian material culture were unlikely to be impressed by the Whigs' belated discovery of the archive. History-writing was an integral accompaniment and consequence of British military campaigns in India. Already in the 1810s

---

⁹⁶ *Ibid.*, 232, 231.

⁹⁷ *Ibid.*, 231.

⁹⁸ *Ibid.*, 28, 58, 70, 138 149.

⁹⁹ Peers, 'Colonial Knowledge', offers an excellent introductory analysis of the production of scholarly works by military men. Bonnie Smith notes the broader, non-academic context in which much Victorian history was produced (by women as well as men) in her *The Gender of History: Men, Women and Historical Practice* (Cambridge, MA, 1998).

¹⁰⁰ See for example JGD to ME, 6 Feb. 1819, BL, MSS Eur F88/205, 2–4v.

and 1820s, the military officers charged with distributing the spoils of imperial warfare were also experimenting with many of the modes of historical practice now current within the discipline today. They did so in active dialogue with Indian historians, trained in a rich tapestry of 'native' historiographical traditions. By taking the material turn and inserting loot back into our narratives of history-writing, we can thus also take important steps in the wider project of acknowledging our discipline's cross-cultural, global formation.

Transactions of the RHS 28 (2018), pp. 33–64 © Royal Historical Society 2018
doi:10.1017/S0080440118000038

FORMALISING ARISTOCRATIC POWER IN ROYAL *ACTA* IN LATE TWELFTH- AND EARLY THIRTEENTH-CENTURY FRANCE AND SCOTLAND*

By Alice Taylor

Whitfield Prize Winner

ABSTRACT. Our understanding of the development of secular institutional governments in Europe during the central Middle Ages has long been shaped by an implicit or explicit opposition between royal and lay aristocratic power. That is to say, the growth of public, institutional and/or bureaucratic central authorities involved the decline and/or exclusion of noble aristocratic power, which thus necessarily operated in a zero-sum game. While much research has shown that this conflict-driven narrative is problematic, it remains in our understanding as a rather shadowy but still powerful causal force of governmental development during this period. This paper compares the changing conceptualisation of the relationship between royal and aristocratic power in the French and Scottish kingdoms to demonstrate, first, how narratives built at the periphery of Europe have important contributions to make and challenges to make to those formed from the core areas of Europe and, second, that state formation did not involve a decline in aristocratic power. Instead, the evidence from royal *acta* in both kingdoms shows that aristocratic power was formalised at a central level, and then built into the forms of government which were emerging in very different ways in both kingdoms in the late twelfth and early thirteenth centuries. Set in broader perspective, this suggests that governmental development involved an intensification of existing structures of elite power, not a diminution.

To say that the twelfth and thirteenth centuries witnessed the development of secular and ecclesiastical government across Europe is to say nothing new. However, for polities ruled by the authority of single,

*I am grateful to Chris Wickham, Alice Rio, Paul Hyams, Matthew McHaffie, John Sabapathy and Dauvit Broun for reading drafts of this paper, and particularly to Susan Reynolds for her heavy critique. All infelicities are my own responsibility. It has also benefited from the comments of the anonymous peer reviewers as well as from my presentation of early versions at the Sir James Lydon Research Seminar in Medieval History at Trinity College Dublin, the Medieval History Seminar at All Souls College, Oxford, and the colloquium held at Glasgow in April 2017, 'Identifying Governmental Forms in Europe, 1100–1350: Palaeography, Diplomatics and History'. This paper is a research output of the AHRC-funded project, *Models of Authority: Scottish Charters and the Emergence of Government, 1100–1250* (Grant Ref: AH/L008041/1).

secular individuals – kings, dukes and counts – how we understand that process is still an open question.[1] The traditional view has been that centralised governmental institutions in these polities developed out of a structural opposition between royal and aristocratic power. This narrative used to be expressed primarily in two ways. First, it was told as the growth of the 'public' against the 'private': bureaucratic governments with emergent judicial institutions developed across Europe during the twelfth and thirteenth centuries at the expense of private lordship, intruding ever more deeply into the capacity of lords to raise revenue, wage war and hold their own courts.[2] The second way essentially told this narrative in reverse: states developed when the most quintessentially private form of authority – lordship – grew to such an extent that it created a public state which (at least in theory) governed (at least some of) its people through institutions and offered them justice in its courts. The concept of 'feudal monarchy', introduced into historical analysis in the early twentieth century but abandoned in print over the century's last quarter, was at its heart a narrative of state formation, showing how governments developed by institutionalising the demands of lordship at the expense of other lords.[3]

The characterisation of royal and aristocratic is well known to be an inadequate one, not least because some polities were ruled by dukes, counts or councils rather than by kings, nor were political elites in secular states wholly lay.[4] At its heart, however, the characterisation

---

[1] This is not the case for communes, for which see C. Wickham, *Sleepwalking into a New World: The Emergence of Italian City Communes in the Twelfth Century* (Princeton, 2015).

[2] See the survey in S. Reynolds, 'The Historiography of the Medieval State', in *Companion to Historiography*, ed. M. Bentley (1997), 117–38. The most recent and wideranging position on medieval government is T. N. Bisson, *The Crisis of the Twelfth Century: Power, Lordship and the Origins of European Government* (Princeton, 2009), which, although putting forward a different explanation for the emergence of institutional government and being explicitly critical of Weber, nonetheless adopts an implicitly oppositional narrative (particularly 293–304). For the sharp distinction between public and private as underlying the medieval state outside of the historical discipline, see M. Mann, *The Sources of Social Power*, I: *A History of Power from the Beginning to A.D. 1760* (Cambridge, 1986), 390–3.

[3] J. R. Strayer, *On the Medieval Origins of the Modern State*, with forewords by C. Tilly and W. C. Jordan (Princeton, 2005), 3–56; T. N. Bisson, 'The Problem of Feudal Monarchy: Aragon, Catalonia, and France', *Speculum*, 53 (1978), 460–78.

[4] By an aristocrat, I mean a lay (non-urban) elite, defined legally and socio-economically. For difficulties with the word 'aristocratic', see T. Reuter, 'The Medieval Nobility in Twentieth-Century Historiography', in *Companion to Historiography*, ed. Bentley, 177–202; and in a German historiographical context, T. Reuter, 'Forms of Lordship in German Historiography', in *Pour une anthropologie du prélèvement seigneurial dans les campagnes médiévales (XIe – XIVe siècles): réalités et représentations paysannes*, ed. M. Bourin and P. Martínez Sopena (Paris, 2004), 51–61. I have retained it here because I am not making an argument about the phenomenon and/or practice of lordship. Aristocratic, however, remains a problematic adjective, having connotations with cultural behaviour and social ambition as much as formal status, and is certainly problematic in an urban perspective, where lay elites in towns were

speaks to a structural tension between central, ruling authorities and the power and authority of elites who are, in theory, ruled by them. This tension has been explored and in many cases neutralised in recent scholarship, which has shown that the power of rulers and lords cooperated as much as came into conflict.[5] Yet no narrative of practical cooperation during the central Middle Ages has thus far fully explained how this cooperation worked with, through or against governments *as* they institutionalised; cooperation either works outside administrative institutions (as in late thirteenth-century France) or in their absence (as in the German kingdom-empire under Frederick Barbarossa).[6] As a result, the place of a structural opposition between royal and aristocratic power within accounts of medieval state formation remains ambiguous, no longer accepted yet not wholly discarded and not replaced. The aim of this paper is thus to explore the changing relationship between royal and aristocratic power in two polities in Europe rather far north of the Alps – the kingdom of the Franks and the kingdom of the Scots – and in so doing remove that oppositional relationship as a causal force of secular state formation in both polities and question its importance more generally.

Why choose the French and Scottish kingdoms, particularly as they are so profoundly different in size and wealth? The French kingdom is an obvious choice as it has been held up as one of the normative case-studies for a conflict-driven narrative of state formation. In the French kingdom, royal power was long thought to have grown at the expense of aristocratic power in a zero-sum game: kings first exercised their pre-existing feudal rights over lay aristocrats in the *regnum Francorum* and then explicitly hacked at the heart of aristocratic power by issuing proclamations against seigneurial violence and their right to wage war.[7] Less explicit conflict between royal and non-royal lay power was also evident in the

often distinguished from landed aristocrats (although in that sense it is helpful in this paper, which is not examining urban elites). For the increasing focus on bishops as key political actors, see S. T. Ambler, *Bishops in the Political Community of England, 1213–1272* (Oxford, 2017).

[5] For example, J. Firnhaber-Baker, *Violence and the State in Languedoc, 1250–1400* (Cambridge, 2014).

[6] T. Reuter, 'The Medieval German *Sonderweg*? The Empire and its Rulers in the High Middle Ages', in his *Medieval Polities and Modern Mentalities*, ed. J. L. Nelson (Cambridge, 2006), 388–412.

[7] The literature is vast; see, for the traditional position, L. Halphen, 'La place de la royauté dans le système féodal', *Revue historique*, 172 (1933), 249–56; and J. W. Baldwin, *The Government of Philip Augustus: Foundations of French Royal Power in the Middle Ages* (Berkeley, 1986), 259–303. See also J.-P. Poly and É. Bournazel, *La mutation féodale* (3rd edn, Paris, 2004), 204–23. For a new understanding of the transformation of homage over the twelfth century, see K. van Eickels, *Vom inszenierten Konsens zum systematisierten Konflikt. Die englisch-französischen Beziehungen und ihre Wahrnehmung an der Wende vom Hoch-zum Spätmittelalter* (Stuttgart, 2002). For a new outline of the growth of French royal power, which anticipates much of what follows (although it concentrates on reconceptualising

institutions of government themselves and the people who worked within them. Major aristocrats (titled and non-titled) did not often play formal roles within French royal government; indeed, there was an increasing spatial and functional separation between titled aristocrats and court-based governmental servants, moving from, as Dejoux has recently put it, the 'new men' of Philip Augustus, to the *baillis* and clerks of the *parlement* under Louis IX, to the 'knights and clerks of the king of the last Capetians'.[8] The judicial system was similarly structured, developing formal routes of appeal from seigneurial courts to the centre, appeals which underlay the functioning of the thirteenth-century French *parlement*.[9] Crucial to the operation of the royal judicial (and indeed financial) system were inquests, which were used not only to investigate the abuses of royal officials against localities and local jurisdictions but also to recover 'usurped' regalian rights and, although the immediate governmental aims of Louis IX inquests have recently been convincingly challenged, it remains that their very activity served to embed royal authority further into the consciousness of increasingly geographically widespread localities.[10]

If the French kingdom traditionally offers an example of a conflict-driven narrative, then what does the kingdom of the Scots offer? For a start, any example of institutionalisation, in which aristocratic and royal power do not represent competing interests but are instead part of the same governing system, inherently challenges the traditional model of state formation outlined above. This is what we find in late twelfth- and thirteenth-century Scotland, which is rarely compared to any place in Europe other than England (and, less commonly, Ireland and Norway). Although it is common for Scottish royal government to be seen as an England in miniature, owing to its adoption and adaptation of some of the institutions and legal procedures of the southern kingdom, it has to be stressed that the structures of power – and therefore the institutions of rule which were created – were profoundly different in

the eleventh century), see D. Barthélemy, *Nouvelle histoire des Capétiens, 987–1214* (Paris, 2012), particularly 296–9, 321–2.

[8] M. Dejoux, 'Gouverner par l'enquête en France, de Philippe Auguste aux derniers Capétiens', *French Historical Studies*, 37 (2014), 271–302, at 298–9; for governmental personnel, see Baldwin, *Government of Philip Augustus*, 106–36.

[9] J. Hilaire, *La construction de l'état de droit dans les archives judiciaires de la cour de France au XIIIe siècle* (Paris, 2011), particularly 67–92; A. Harding, *Medieval Law and the Foundations of the State* (Oxford, 2002), chs. 5 and 6.

[10] M. Dejoux, *Les enquêtes de saint Louis: gouverner et sauver son âme* (Paris, 2014), 371–9, has demonstrated the inquests' personally reparative aims, stressing their symbolic unifying power, which allowed for local complaints against the king, personalised through its officials, to be heard and pacified through acknowledgement without the explicit aim of reform, but which simultaneously operated as a force of subjection by placing the idea of government and royal authority at the heart of local society.

Scotland compared to those of England. Unlike in England, aristocratic power was well integrated into the central institutional framework of royal power in late twelfth- and thirteenth-century Scotland, the period when administrative units of government developed across the core area of the kingdom north and south of the Firth of Forth.[11] Aristocratic courts were not excluded from the developing royal justice system but were built into royal legislation: unlike in England, where knights of the shire took an oath to preserve the king's peace in local counties, in Scotland, this oath (explicitly modelled on its English counterpart) was taken by the lay and ecclesiastical *magnates* to uphold the peace in their lands.[12] There was no class of 'new men' who staffed the emerging bureaucracy: major lay aristocrats served alongside bishops as the leading figures of the royal financial and judicial administration (so earls served as justiciars, chamberlains and, less often, sheriffs, while bishops and abbots were frequently chancellors). Crucially, this government developed a relatively complex and increasingly standardised set of administrative and judicial procedures, all communicated in writing, and royal brieves (equivalent to English writs, although different in scope) could initiate cases in aristocratic courts as well as bring them into royal courts. In this sense, later twelfth- and thirteenth-century Scotland provides an example of royal government not growing in opposition to aristocratic power but, instead, formalising it as a territorial authority and formally incorporating it into the structures of rulership and government within a single polity.

Scotland could be dismissed as a mere quirk on the periphery of Europe, not politically important nor financially weighty enough to challenge a narrative built at the core of Europe. Indeed, it can and indeed has been seen as a rather extreme example of 'Europeanization' or its insular counterpart, Anglicization, with its government – its sheriffs, justiciars, brieve system, even documentary form – all being based on 'English' counterparts.[13] However, the core/periphery opposition as a way of understanding change in general has been criticised, both as tool for understanding Europe in the central Middle Ages and more

---

[11] A. Taylor, *The Shape of the State in Medieval Scotland, 1124–1290* (Oxford, 2016), with summary of argument at 438–55. The difference would not, however, be so profound at a local level: see K. J. Stringer, 'Law, Governance and Jurisdiction', in *Northern England and Southern Scotland in the Central Middle Ages*, ed. K. J. Stringer and A. J. L. Winchester (Woodbridge, 2017), 87–136, particularly 131–2.

[12] Taylor, *Shape of the State*, 169–72.

[13] The defining approach remains R. Bartlett, *The Making of Europe: Conquest, Colonisation and Cultural Change, 950–1350* (1993), whose power came from its subtle treatment of 'peripheral' areas. For a comparative approach which emphatically does not adopt the framework of core/periphery, see C. Wickham, *Medieval Europe* (New Haven, 2016).

broadly.[14] There are multiple cores and multiple peripheries all working simultaneously and, even when influence and adoption of practices, concepts and institutions found at 'cores' can be identified, they work out very differently in their new hosts. Accordingly, we should not dismiss alternative narratives found on our traditional peripheries: we should instead take them seriously and work out their implications in comparative perspective.

This article is therefore an experiment in comparative history: were the institutional governments which developed in the late twelfth- and early thirteenth-century Scottish and French kingdoms really founded on such opposite manifestations of the relationship between royal and non-royal power? It will be argued that, although the French experience seems superficially more conflict-driven than the Scottish, there are certain structural similarities between the two kingdoms in how the relationship between royal and aristocratic power was conceptualised. The comparison itself will be based on the internal diplomatic of royal written acts drawn up over the period, which offer comparable source bases. Throughout the period defined in this paper, *acta* were drawn up in the names of kings of both kingdoms, yet 'chancery'-produced documents only start to predominate among each surviving corpus towards the end of the twelfth century. In neither did any form of systematic record of all outgoing documentation take place under Philip Augustus, three famous 'registres' – *codices* containing outgoing and incoming *acta* and other administrative royal and non-royal documents – were produced but these *registres* did not keep a copy of all documents issued. In short, for most of the period covered by this paper, royal acts offer a stable corpus of evidence with which to compare the two kingdoms.

In addition, the method of studying those acts – diplomatics – is particularly useful in this context. Diplomatics is one of history's auxiliary sciences and encompasses the technical and diagnostic study of the internal and external features of documents, traditionally those with some juridical value.[15] But while diplomatics has traditionally concentrated on the identification and development of different types of documents and their internal structures and formulae, there has been less attention given in general to what changing patterns of small formulae within twelfth- and thirteenth-century *acta* actually mean. What do the

---

[14] See below pp. 60–1.
[15] For the focus on juridical documents, see T. Kölzer, 'Diplomatics', in *Handbook of Medieval Studies: Terms – Methods – Trends*, ed. A. Classen (Berlin, 2010), 405–23. That being said, diplomatics has expanded its reach to include non-juridical documents, as acknowledged in O. Guyotjeannin and L. Morelle, 'Tradition et réception de l'acte médiéval: jalons pour un bilan des recherches', *Archiv für Diplomatik*, 53 (2007), 367–403.

formulae of royal acts reveal about how the normative relationship between royal and aristocratic power was communicated?[16] For France, this paper will argue that, as in Scotland, the internal formulae of royal *acta* shifted towards the end of the twelfth century to create a formal representation of legitimate aristocratic power which framed, if not created, a new political discourse and a new legal framework for these relationships of power. In both polities, the relationship between royal and aristocratic power did change, but in both, the parties to that relationship were more, not less, secure in their positions, although the consequences of this security were different in each kingdom. Institutional government thus did not mark a structural move against the phenomenon of aristocratic power but rather changed its terms: it gave it form, as part of the process of governmental consolidation itself. This process was achieved through discursive cooperation, rather than practical conflict, and manifested itself differently in different polities.

I Comparison of the source base

Comparative history is founded on knowing what one is comparing, so how do the two source bases size up against one another? This is particularly important when comparing two kingdoms of such different size and scale as France and Scotland. The political composition of both kingdoms was different; the symbolic relationships of French kings with non-royal rulers within their own kingdom was profoundly and more directly competitive (particularly when those dukes and counts were also kings or other rulers elsewhere) than in Scotland, where eleventh- and twelfth-century competition centred on the kingship itself from individuals originating in different branches of a widely defined royal kin.[17]

Despite these differences, it is worth noticing some similarities. In both kingdoms, the number of surviving royal charters increases steadily over the twelfth century, as happened elsewhere in Europe.[18] If one divides the number of surviving documents by the reign length, one is left with

---

[16] The potential of the methods of diplomatics and palaeography to illuminate medieval communication more broadly is examined in, among many, *Ruling the Script in the Middle Ages: Formal Aspects of Written Communication*, ed. S. Barret, D. Stutzmann and G. Vogeler (Turnhout, 2017). For particularly creative ways of thinking about legal norms and charter formulae, see P. R. Hyams, 'The Charter as a Source for the Early Common Law', *Journal of Legal History*, 12 (1991), 173–89; J. Hudson, *Land, Law and Lordship in Anglo-Norman England* (Oxford, 1994); M. W. McHaffie, 'Law and Violence in Eleventh-Century France', *Past and Present*, 238 (2018), 3–41.

[17] R. Oram, *Domination and Lordship: Scotland 1070 to 1230* (Edinburgh, 2007), 64–74, 108–22, 140–5.

[18] M. Clanchy, *From Memory to Written Record: England, 1066–1307* (3rd edn, Oxford, 2013); P. Bertrand, 'À propos de la révolution de l'écrit (X^e – XIIIe siècles): considerations inactuelles', *Médiévales*, 56 (2009), 75–92.

a *per annum* mean of the rates of survival. This of course bears little resemblance to the actual numbers of documents produced and so cannot be indicative of overall change. Nevertheless, the similarity in the overall trajectory of the figures remains striking, particularly as the archival context for preservation is similar. In Scotland, the numbers of surviving charters 1124–1214 *per annum* are: 5.4 surviving acts per year for David I (1124–53), 13.5 per year for Mael Coluim IV (1153–65) and 10.7 for William (1165–1214). The spike in the figures for Mael Coluim IV is interesting but explainable: Mael Coluim's reign was considerably shorter than William's (twelve years as opposed to forty-nine) and, in general across Western Europe in this period, proportionally far more charters were confirmed in the first few years of a king's reign. In addition, 11 out of Mael Coluim's 161 surviving charters were drawn up for Scone Abbey on a single occasion to replace the charters which the abbey claimed to have lost in a recent fire.[19] Furthermore, scribes of the 'king's chapel' (*capella regis*) produced an ever-increasing proportion of surviving original charters during the reign of William the Lion (1165–1214).[20]

Rates of survival of French royal charters are higher but broadly comparable. According to figures calculated by John Baldwin (based in part on notes from Jean Dufour and Michel Nortier), between 1059 and 1203, 5.7 *actes per annum* survive from the reign of Philip I (1059–1108), 14.0 *per annum* under Louis VI (1108–37), 19.1 *per annum* under Louis VII (1137–80) and 28.1 under Philip Augustus (1180–1223), up to 1203.[21] In 1204, the earliest 'cartulary-register', containing transcripts of royal and non-royal *actes* (among other items), Register A, began to be compiled, whereupon the figure leaps to 41.1 *per annum*, which is no longer statistically comparable to either corpus.[22] Yet, in both, the proportion of 'issuer-

[19] *The Charters of David I, 1124–53, and of his Son, Henry, Earl of Northumberland, 1139–52*, ed. G. W. S. Barrow (Woodbridge, 1999); *Regesta Regum Scotorum*, I: *The Acts of Malcolm IV, 1152–65*, ed. G. W. S. Barrow (Edinburgh, 1960) (henceforth *RRS*, I); *Regesta Regum Scotorum*, II: *The Acts of William I, 1165–1214*, ed. G. W. S. Barrow with collaboration of W. W. Scott (Edinburgh, 1971) (henceforth *RRS*, II). These numbers do not include charters classified as spurious or non-contemporary but do include those which are, at present, being classed as non-contemporary either in their diplomatic or their palaeography as part of the research on the database for the AHRC-funded project, *Models of Authority: Scottish Charters and the Emergence of Government, 1100–1250* (Grant Ref: AH/L008041/1, and online at www.modelsofauthority.ac.uk).

[20] For royal scribes, see *RRS*, II, 88–90; discussed by D. Broun, *Scottish Independence and the Idea of Britain from the Picts to Alexander III* (Edinburgh, 2007), 191–206.

[21] J. Baldwin, 'The Kingdom of the Franks from Louis VI to Philip II (a) Crown and Government', in *The New Cambridge Medieval History*, IV: *c. 1024 – c. 1198*, ed. D. Luscombe and J. Riley-Smith (Cambridge, 2004), 510–29, at 510–11, and n. 1.

[22] *Recueil des actes de Philippe Ier, roi de France (1059–1108)*, ed. M. Prou (Paris, 1908); *Recueil des actes de Louis VI, roi de France (1108–1137)*, ed. J. Dufour (4 vols., Paris, 1992–4). The acts of Louis VII have still not been edited but see *Études sur les actes de Louis VII*, ed. A. Luchaire (Paris, 1885). For Philip Augustus, *Recueil des actes de Philippe Auguste roi de*

produced' documents also increased: kings were increasingly having acts written in their own name, produced 'in house', although the numbers of people involved in creating, drafting, authenticating and issuing these documents may well still have been small.[23] Thus, although the numbers are far greater on the French side, the two kingdoms witness the broader trend: across twelfth-century Europe, more documents were being produced by the institution of kingship itself.[24]

Quite apart from scale, there are also some significant differences, of which there is space here to highlight only one. This is that Latin charters (defined here generically as some form of Latin document structured by the threefold division of protocol, text and eschatocol and having some form of legal function) only began to be drawn up and issued in the names of its kings in the twelfth century in the Scottish kingdom, while documents issued in the name of some form of *rex Francorum* survive from the early seventh century onwards.[25] This difference is important. The *novelty* of the Latin act in the twelfth-century kingdom of the Scots has prompted far greater historiographical examination of the capacity of the charter itself to reframe the political, social and economic landscape it claimed to represent than is the case in most work on French royal charters of the same period. For example, a long-standing question posed by Scottish historiography is how far the language of fiefs, inheritance and service both affected and represented changing conceptions of elite power in the twelfth-century kingdom, and particularly the kingdom in the first half of the twelfth century, the period when Latin acts were adopted by Scottish kings. The historiography has also focused on how far this new written lexicon of territorial power – adapted from English example – destroyed, adapted or retained Gaelic words which represented rights

France, ed. H.-F. Delaborde, C. Petit-Dutaillis, J. Monicat and M. Nortier (6 vols., Paris, 1916–2005) (henceforth *Recueil*). For the registers, see *Les registres de Philippe Auguste*, ed. J. Baldwin with F. Gasparri, M. Nortier and E. Lalou (Paris, 1992); J. Baldwin, 'Les premiers registres Capétiens de Philippe Auguste à Louis IX', in *Décrire, inventorier, enregistrer entre Seine et Rhine au moyen âge: formes, fonctions et usages des écrits de gestion*, ed. X. Hermand, J.-F. Nieus and É. Renard (Paris, 2012), 105–22.

[23] J. Dufour, 'Peut-on parler d'une organisation de la chancellerie de Philippe Auguste?', *Archiv für Diplomatik*, 41 (1995), 249–61.

[24] R.-H. Bautier, 'Les actes de la chancellerie royale française sous les règnes de Louis VII (1137–80) et Philippe Auguste (1180–1223)', in *Typologie der Königsurkunden*, ed. J. Bistřický (Olmütz, 1998), 99–113, at 106–7, 110.

[25] For the issue in Scotland, see D. Broun, 'The Adoption of Brieves in Scotland', in *Charters and Charter Scholarship in Britain and Ireland*, ed. M. T. Flanagan and J. A. Green (Basingstoke, 2005), 164–83; M. Hammond, 'The Adoption and Routinization of Scottish Royal Charter Production for Lay Beneficiaries, 1124–95', *Anglo-Norman Studies*, 36 (2014), 91–115; for France, see, among many, H. Reimitz, *History, Frankish Identity and the Framing of Western Ethnicity, 550–850* (Cambridge, 2015), 98–102.

over land.[26] To take an example: *cuit* – a Gaelic word meaning 'portion', which has been taken to mean a tribute render taken from land and rendered to elite title-holders – appears only in the Gaelic property records transcribed into the gospel book of Deer in the early twelfth century (but recording much earlier gifts) but was neither transposed nor transliterated in the Latin charter record. Put simply, the absence of written documents means that what *cuit* meant, where it went and what replaced it has become a much more pressing and open question than it would have been if we could track its lexical and linguistic changes through earlier material.[27]

By contrast, changes in the internal form of French royal acts have either received less attention or are considered as secondary to the broader subject of political change in the second half of the twelfth century. In particular, attention is given to the major territorial expansion of the effective authority of French kingship under Philip Augustus and how preexisting ideas of the relationship between the king and other rulers within the French kingdom were extended to help cement this expansion (famously, the example that kings could receive but not perform homage).[28] Therefore, when small-scale internal diplomatic change is considered in French twelfth-century royal acts, the discussion focuses on how existing representations of the relationship between the king and his aristocrats were applied more ambitiously over a wider territorial area, whereas, for the Scottish kingdom, scholarship has focused on the effect which an obviously new vocabulary of elite power had on earlier power structures. We therefore need to interrogate how far this difference in national historiographical emphasis is borne out by the evidence itself.

II The representation of aristocratic power in Scottish royal charters

What can we see in Scottish royal charters?[29] Some background is required before answering this question. Over the twelfth century,

---

[26] My preliminary attempt to make sense of it is in Taylor, *Shape of the State*, 176–87, and see also the insights in S. Reynolds, 'Fiefs and Vassals in Scotland: A View from Outside', *Scottish Historical Review*, 82 (2003), 176–93.

[27] For an explanation, see D. Broun, 'Statehood and Lordship in "Scotland" before the Mid-Twelfth Century', *Innes Review*, 66 (2015), 1–71, at 20–4.

[28] Baldwin, *Government of Philip Augustus*, 260–6, although see Barthélemy, *Nouvelle histoire*, 289–322. This is despite the vast amount which has been done on 'les modalités de l'intégration'. See, as an example, *La royauté capétienne et le Midi au temps de Guillaume de Nogaret. Actes du colloque de Montpellier et Nîmes (29 et 30 novembre 2013)*, ed. B. Moreau and J. Théry (Nîmes, 2015). For the position on royal homage, see Halphen, 'La place de la royauté'; Baldwin, *Government of Philip Augustus*, 259–303.

[29] What follows summarises the content and argument made in Taylor, *Shape of the State*, 26–83, 102–13, 157–64, 172–87.

there was a significant change to the definitional basis of elite power: many forms of elite authority – to say nothing of official authority – became territorialised. An example of this would be what happened to the rank of *mormaer* (a Gaelic title, Latinised as *comes*, meaning 'great steward' or 'sea steward'). *Mormaír* held the highest ranking secular title under the king north of the Firth of Forth, and exercised extensive authority over a province, being primarily responsible for levying the provincial host. Over the twelfth century, however, the *mormaer* gradually stopped exercising extensive power over his titular province as a whole (the provinces of Fife, Mar, Buchan, Strathearn and Atholl all have attested *mormaír* in the first half of the twelfth century) and began to exercise more exclusive, intensive power over a limited area *within* his province, over a territory known as a *comitatus* ('earldom') from the 1170s at the latest.[30] The *mormaír* stopped raising common army service from their whole province and, instead, by the early thirteenth century had responsibility only for the levy of the common army from their *comitatus*, raising men and provisions from their lands in the same way as bishops, abbots, thanes, and knights did from theirs. *Mormaír* thus changed in two ways. First, they stopped being lords exercising extensive power at a provincial level over multiple, more local, authorities; like other lords, they started exercising intensive power only over their own lands. Second, *mormaír*-land was seen to be held from the king. What happened to *mormaír* represents a major reorientation in the conceptualisation of elite lay power by which, during the second half of the twelfth century, elite lay power was territorialised and defined through *connected* landholding, that is, they were said in charters to hold their land from the king. These two developments coincided in twelfth-century Scotland but their precise form was not set. The most obvious example is from the twelfth-century German kingdom where not only were some major rulers granted extensive privileges in imperial diplomas which defined their *beneficia* or *feoda* as being part of the empire (*imperium*) or *regnum* – rather than held of the person of the king/emperor, as in Scotland – but also whose local and regional power territorialised and intensified particularly from the later twelfth century onwards.[31]

---

[30] For extensive and intensive power, see Mann, *Sources of Social Power*, I, 7–8.

[31] R. Schieffer, 'Das Lehnswesen in den deutschen Königsurkunden von Lothar III. bis Fridrich I', in *Das Lehnswesen im Hochmittelalter: Forschungskonstrukte – Quellenbefunde – Deutungsrelevanz*, ed. J. Dendorfer and R. Deutinger (Ostfildern, 2010), 79–90; B. Arnold, *Princes and Territories in Medieval Germany* (Cambridge, 1991), chs. 1 and 3; *The Origins of German Principalities, 1100–1350: Essays by German Historians*, ed. G. A. Loud and J. Schenk (Oxford, 2017); H. Vollrath, 'Politische Ordnungsvorstellungen und politisches Handeln im Vergleich. Philipp II. August von Frankreich und Friedrich Barbarossa im Konflikt mit ihren mächtigsten Fürsten', in *Political Thought and the Realities of Power in the Middle Ages*, ed. J. Canning and O.-G. Oexle (Göttingen, 1998), 33–52.

A closer study of the internal form of Scottish royal charters only confirms this broader trend.[32] First, authentic royal charters recording land gifts to lay elites under King David I (1124–53) often described these gifts in personal terms. Land was to be held, 'with all those customs which Ranulf Meschin ever had in Carlisle and in his land of Cumberland' or 'as Udard the sheriff held it'. Phrases such as these could denote an extensive and undefined authority over a large tract of territory (as in the first example) but did not have to (as in the second example).[33] On occasion, it was specified that a beneficiary would hold his land from the king but this was in no way a standard requirement; indeed, there is only one authentic example of this from the reign of David I. However, this changed. It became standard by the 1170s for charters to command that land should be held 'from the king and his heirs' and, moreover, *in feudo et hereditate* ('in feu and heritage', to use Scots legal terminology) to specify a perpetual, heritable gift.[34] This too was a change: perennial inheritance was not often specified in charters of David's reign. Sometimes, the heritable capacity of the land was entirely absent, sometimes it was explicitly limited to a single generation and sometimes perennial inheritance was specified.[35] But it is only in the first decade of the reign of William the Lion

---

[32] What follows accepts the arguments presented in Hammond, 'Adoption and Routinization'.

[33] But what precisely that meant was not made explicit, although one can reasonably assume that everyone was *expected* to know (or at least have the capacity to interpret) what customs Ranulf Meschin had and how Udard had held the land. The point, however, was that it was left open. See D. Broun, 'The Property Records in the Book of Deer as a Source for Early Scottish Society', in *Studies on the Book of Deer*, ed. K. Forsyth (Dublin, 2008), 313–60, at 328–9.

[34] The emergence of *in feudo et hereditate* as a standard part of Scottish royal charters is difficult to track precisely, partly because the extent to which early royal charters were later reworked is only just being worked out. In David's reign, there are four single sheet charters surviving, of which three (*Charters of David I*, nos. 16, 54, 210) are products of the nascent Scottish writing office, while a fourth (*Charters of David I*, no. 53) seems to be a later reworking by Durham of no. 54. Of the three, therefore, no. 54 (1136×7) contains the phrase 'In feudo ⁊ In hereditate sibi ⁊ heredibus'; while no. 210 contains the phrase 'in feudo ⁊ hereditate illi ⁊ heredi suo'. There is no standardised form in Mael Coluim's reign either: the (contextually) famous charter of the king to Walter fitz Alan is an early thirteenth-century copy, containing an inflated text (*RRS*, I, no. 183). Yet the charter issued for Ralph Frebern (*RRS*, I, no. 256, issued 1162×4) does contain the phrase 'in feudo ⁊ hereditate'. This only survives as an eighteenth-century facsimile, although it is possible to detect the same hand which also drafted others of Mael Coluim's charters: *Diplomata Scotiæ: Selectus Diplomatum et Numismatum Scotiæ Thesaurus*, ed. J. Anderson (Edinburgh, 1739), plate 25. For this development in England, see Hudson, *Land, Law and Lordship*, 94–7.

[35] Inheritance limited to a single generation might have been used in royal charters of Mael Coluim IV (1153–65). The clearest example, however, survives in antiquary transcript, which has been tampered with (at least in the eschatocol); London, British Library, MS Harley, 4693, fo. 46r (printed *RRS*, I, no. 190).

(1165–1214), that we can be sure that the drafters of royal charters regularly categorised lay land as being given and held *in feudo et hereditate*, which were held *de rege*, and that they understood 'inheritance' as a perennial concept.[36] Finally, during the 1170s and 1180s, scribes in the *capella regis* introduced charter formulae which explicitly related to the rights of lay beneficiaries to jurisdiction over their land.[37] This formula was borrowed from English charter diplomatic but also added the words 'furca et fossa', denoting the right to a gallows and an ordeal pit, that is, rights to punishment and proof in cases concerning life and limb.[38] In addition, reference to a kingdom-wide set of (unnamed) practices started to be made primarily in *non*-royal charters. Land was to be held 'as freely and quit as other lands are held in the kingdom of the Scots/ Scotland'. This formula first appeared in the 1150s but took off in the 1190s, occurring in just over 30 per cent of all surviving non-royal charters known to have been issued during that decade.[39]

What these developments in charter diplomatic show is that elite power had come to be understood in royal charters as based on coherent pieces of inherited land, held with rights of jurisdiction, which was described as being held from the king. It was thus understood in abstracted and generally standardised terms. This is an important point for Scotland, where the historiography has long focused on 'new' methods of landholding among an immigrant 'Anglo-Norman' aristocracy in the twelfth century and the 'old' methods exercised and/or abandoned by the Gaelic-speaking native aristocracy. But this new vocabulary of power emerging in the 1160s and 1170s was applied to everyone, regardless of origin. Elites cooperated with it because it had become the lexical register to understand their own authority. Even the authority to hold a court had become dependent not primarily on status or rank but on holding land, either from the king or from another lord. Being a court-holder, therefore, automatically meant cooperating with a changed political discourse. There was a new lexical register to express territorialised power that simply did not exist in the 1140s, but did by the 1190s, and which constituted a new, written, definition of elite power, used routinely. This does not mean that there was (yet) a distinct category of tenure 'in feu'; that

---

[36] For the earlier chronology in England, see Hudson, *Land, Law and Lordship*, ch. 3.

[37] Discussed by many, but see the essential work of Barrow (ed.), *RRS*, ii, 49–51. The internal diplomatic of the only surviving text of the formula in Mael Coluim IV's reign (*RRS*, i, no. 184) is non-contemporary to the period, and represents, at the very least, an updating of the original charter.

[38] Some charters could be quite specific about the location of pits, see *RRS*, ii, no. 152; on the decline (or abolition) of the ordeal in Scotland, see Taylor, *Shape of the State*, 280–4.

[39] For a full examination of this, see D. Broun, 'Kingdom and Identity: A Scottish Perspective', in *Northern England and Southern Scotland*, ed. Stringer and Winchester, 31–85.

development was a phenomenon of the second half of the thirteenth century, evidenced explicitly by legislation issued as late as 1318 by Robert I.[40] But it did mean that lay aristocratic power was understood as a uniform phenomenon (even if individual cases differed in practice), based on the holding of hereditable land 'from' the king and commanding clear and autonomous jurisdictional privileges.

The change which occurred over the twelfth century was thus twofold. First, aristocratic power itself changed: it became more limited to defined territories but was exercised in a more intensive and exclusive way. Second, the written definition of this power shifted from being understood on personal, individualised terms to being generalised and abstracted. The personalised early twelfth-century royal charters had given way to the abstracted and standardised charters of the 1170s and beyond. But these two changes had not come at the expense of aristocratic power itself: there was no zero-sum game between it and royal power. Elites exercised more autonomous power in their own lands than they had previously, with more individual responsibilities and liabilities. In addition, lords themselves had more opportunities to enhance their own status, power and finances through participating in the changed structures of royal government. As sketched out above, by the 1190s, the ways in which kings of Scots were ruling had transformed. By legislation of 1184, it was expected that new local royal officials, 'sheriffs' (*uicecomites*), would hold their courts every forty days and that a central court, which all major lay and ecclesiastical magnates had to attend, would be held under the authority of another new official, the royal justice. Accounting procedures were also developing through an itinerant audit of sheriff's revenue collections. Scottish government was institutionalising: royal courts had been created and their functioning, in theory, standardised. These changes eventually incorporated this new formal representation of aristocratic power: royal statutes (agreed by magnates) did not just introduce legal reform in royal courts, they expected the same procedures to be followed in aristocratic courts. In this way, aristocratic power was part of royal power and vice-versa, rather than each operating in structural opposition to the other.[41]

III Differences in source type, and the example of Guigues, count of Forez, 1163–7

What does this matter for French royal diplomatic? After all, the situation is entirely different. First, there was already a strong political

---

[40] *The Records of the Parliaments of Scotland to 1707*, gen. ed. K. Brown (St Andrews, 2011), 1318/27 (online at: www.rps.ac.uk/mss/1318/27 accessed 1 Oct. 2017), and *Scottish Formularies*, ed. A. A. M. Duncan, Stair Society 58 (Edinburgh, 2011), A20/21.

[41] See Taylor, *Shape of the State*, chs. 5 and 6.

discourse about non-royal dependence on the king in the *regnum Francorum* which is simply absent in the Scottish kingdom or at most undocumented. Some of this was emanating from Suger and Saint-Denis[42] but, by the 1160s, there are good indications that it was a regular part of political talk and thinking, whether royal or non-royal.[43] Royal diplomas contained references to the extensive authority of the king's *corona*, a concept which was strategically appealed to in documents and letters issued under the names of other lords, non-royal rulers and churchmen.[44] Chroniclers too adopted a language of elite dependence on the king within the French *regnum*. Hugh of Poitiers, for example, in his Vézelay chronicle, recorded Henry the Liberal, count of Champagne, threatening Louis VII with the transfer of his county to Frederick Barbarossa, despite admitting that he held it *de fisco regis* and *de feodo regis* (both expressions are used).[45] Yet royal diplomas for lay elites and non-royal rulers did not, until (roughly) the last two decades of the twelfth century, use this language frequently or routinely, as they did later.

The difference between the presentation of the relationship between royal and aristocratic power in royal diplomas as opposed to other non-juridical, non-royal chronicles and letters will be illustrated by a single case. In early summer 1163, Guigues, count of Forez, had a letter written to Louis VII.[46] In it, the count wondered why the king had not commanded him to do anything concerning the king's recent campaign in the Auvergne – 'since I am yours, since I was raised by you to knighthood, since my father committed me to your care and protection (*sub cura et tutela vestra*), and since my whole land belongs to you'. The count continued: 'for I would have been there with you in your army, had not Count Girard [of Mâcon] and the schismatics of Lyon

---

[42] For Suger's statements in his *de rebus in administratione gestis*, see *Oeuvres complètes de Suger*, ed. A. Lecoy de la Marche (Paris, 1867), 161–2. For the notion that *homagium* distinguished the *comes Normannie* from the *rex Francorum*, see the *Brevis Relatio* on the *c.* 945 agreement (E. M. C. van Houts, 'The *Brevis Relatio de Guillelmo Nobilissimo Comite Normannorum*, Written by a Monk of Battle Abbey, Edited with a Historical Commentary', Camden Fifth Series 10 (1997), 5–48, at 45).

[43] For the performance of homage, see J. Gillingham, 'Doing Homage to the King of France', in *Henry II: New Interpretations*, ed. C. Harper-Bill and N. Vincent (Woodbridge, 2007), 63–84; M. Aurell, 'Philippe Auguste et les Plantagenêt', in *Autour de Philippe Auguste*, ed. M. Aurell and Y. Sassier (Paris, 2017), 27–69.

[44] See, as representative, Y. Sassier, 'La *corona regni*: émergence d'une *persona ficta* dans la France du XIIe siècle', in *La puissance royale: image et pouvoir de l'antiquité au moyen âge*, ed. E. Santinelli and C.-G. Schwentzel (Rennes, 2012), 99–110.

[45] Hugh of Poitiers, *Monumenta Vizeliacensia: textes relatifs à l'histoire de l'abbaye de Vézelay*, ed. R. B. C. Huygens (2 vols., Turnhout, 1976–80), trans. *The Vézelay Chronicle*, trans. J. Scott and J. O. Ward (Binghampton, 1992), 242, 243.

[46] Most recently discussed in *Lyon, entre empire et royaume (843–1601): textes et documents*, ed. A. Charansonnet, J.-L. Gaulin, P. Mounier and S. Rau (Paris, 2015), 223–6, which includes full details on its preservation in the 'Saint-Victor' register.

come into my land with an armed force'. Why had they come? Guigues continued: 'For they had come not only to disinherit me – if they could have – but also, more than that, to transfer my county (*comitatum meum*), which is from your crown (*qui de corona vestra est*), to the empire of the Teutons.'[47] This is particularly striking given that Forez was quite literally on the boundary between the French *regnum* and the Roman *imperium*, and, indeed, it was during the 1140s that the idea emerged that the Rhône (and the Saône) was indeed the frontier between the empire and the French kingdom.[48] It might be thought that the complexity of this region explains Guigues's recourse to such unifying yet necessarily equally divisive ideas. However, the concept of the king's crown – of which individual churches, counties, duchies and mere land could all constitute a part – was used increasingly in letters, diplomas and charters from the Second Crusade onwards.[49] As Sassier has shown, the king's *corona* established '[une] sorte de cercle idéal dont chaque église du royaume serait un joyau ou un *membrum*, dont dépendrait chaque fief ou chaque vassal du roi'.[50] Indeed, the reference to the king's crown could also be used by third parties in order to appeal to the king to persuade him to do things he did not necessarily want to do. It is clear that Stephen, abbot of Cluny, knew this well in 1166, when he petitioned Louis VII for help against the count of Mâcon in Burgundy, exhorting the king to remember that Burgundy was part of Louis's kingdom as well and that no good would come to the 'body' of the kingdom if one of its parts (Burgundy) perished through sickness while the other (France) abounded in health.[51]

It is important, however, to understand these claims not as legally enforceable realities but, instead, as part of a complex political discourse, which was distinct from the relationships constructed, claimed and recorded in charters and diplomas. In the paschal year 1167, Louis VII met Guigues of Forez at Bourges and a surviving diploma records what happened. The diploma takes the form of a chirograph, one of three of this type of record surviving as an original from Louis's reign.

---

[47] *Recueil des historiens des Gaules et de la France*, vol. 16, new ed. L. Delisle (Paris, 1878), no. 161, p. 49.

[48] *Lyon, entre empire et royaume*, ed. Charansonnet, Gaulin, Mounier and Rau, 179–80, 183–7, 230–5.

[49] For Suger's role, see Sassier, 'La *corona regni*', 102–3.

[50] Y. Sassier, *Structures du pouvoir, royauté et res publica: France, IXe – XIIe siècle* (Rouen, 2004), 215.

[51] *Recueil des historiens des Gaules et de la France*, vol. 16, 130–1: 'Quid prodest in eodem corpore sic partis alterius provideri saluti, quod altera morbo depereat? Quasdam plerumque latius videmus serpere lues, et dum minus mala caventur, ex insperato sana putridis vitiari. Non sola Francia de regno vestro est, licet sibi nomen Regis specialius retinuerit. Est et Burgundia vestra. Nihil magis illi quam isti debetis.'

It is a reasonable assumption that, as the surviving copy was kept in the Trésor, the second copy – if not more, for diploma-chirographs could be drawn up in multiple copies – would have been kept by Guigues.[52] The simple diploma states that Guigues, the king's 'friend' (*amicus*), came to 'us and our court' to settle his business. At Bourges, 'he received from us the castles which he had never before had from a lord', that is, Montbrison and Montsupt, and did homage and fealty for them (*de eis*) to the king (*nobis*). The diploma continued: 'rejoicing in the bond he had entered into with us, and eagerly desiring to transfer (*trahere*) himself to us, he also placed in our homage (*in hominium nostrum*) these other castles'. This was not the end of the agreement between the two. The diploma records that the count then asked the king for the *ius* which he had as a result of the royal *dignitas* in six further castles 'to increase his fief', and this, the king said, 'by the counsel of our *fideles*... we have granted to him, and confirm with our seal, with the monogram of our name inscribed below'.

There are two noteworthy points here. First, the (admittedly terse) narrative structure seems, at this point, to be a standard part of the (admittedly few) surviving twelfth-century diplomas recording royal gifts or confirmations of land to lay elites.[53] This is important because, as we shall see, this narrative structure of the text of the diploma eventually gave way to an entirely different way of recording gift-giving and confirmation to lay individuals. But the narrative structure is important here because it renders the agreement between Louis and Guigues both personal and performed, while at the same time invoking some legal norms and concepts which were clear to them but not to us. The diploma presents their relationship as, broadly, a voluntary one, confirmed and constituted by legal norms. After Guigues had performed homage and sworn fealty (which he had never done before) for two castles (Montbrison being the *caput* of his county), he rejoiced in his actions and transferred more of his castles into the king's homage.

The narrative and personal style of this 1167 diploma is important and I will return to it. Of immediate relevance here, however, is the diploma's statement that Guigues, the king's *amicus*, had 'never before' held his two major castles from a lord, as he was now doing from Louis. This new relationship was cemented by the performance of homage and the swearing of fealty. This seems to be directly at odds with the letter written under Guigues's name to Louis VII only three years earlier (at the

[52] Paris, Archives Nationales, K24, no. 14 (paschal year 1167); calendared in *Études*, ed. Luchaire, no. 537, and printed in *Monuments historiques*, ed. J. Tardiff (Paris, 1866), no. 602. On its chirograph form, see F. Gasparri, *L'écriture des actes de Louis VI, Louis VII et Philippe Auguste* (Geneva and Paris, 1973), 116–17.

[53] For an earlier example, see *Recueil Louis VI*, no. 65.

most). This letter proclaimed that Guigues's 'whole land' belonged to the king and, indeed, his whole county was 'of the king's crown'. The distinction here between the political claims of the letter and the legally framed diploma is important. By appealing to the king's *corona*, the letter invoked a formal, territorially connected relationship between king and count which was, in fact, only explicitly created by the 1167 diploma, issued a few years later, which stresses the novelty of the arrangement confirmed between the two parties. The claim in Guigues's letter – that his 'whole land belonged' to the king – seems to be directly contradicted by the diploma's statement that Guigues had never before held two of his chief castles from a lord. Although this is a simple point, it is worth stressing: there was a different and more limited register of the relationship between Louis and Guigues in the diploma than was present in the non-juridical letter. Of course, diplomas themselves did contain extremely ambitious statements about, among other things, the power and authority of the king's majesty and crown.[54] But, when describing the individual relations between king and count, it seems that, as late as 1167, one had to be rather more circumspect.

The flexibility of the conceptual frameworks used to describe the relationship between the king and aristocrats therefore differed between charters and letters and, indeed, charters and chronicles. Letters and chronicles contained highly politicised understandings of power relations but these types of document were not understood as containing legal value. They could thus interpret French royal territorial supremacy liberally and contextually to support or challenge the different aims and ambitions of the parties concerned. This was different in diplomas. Leaving aside the 1167 diploma's representation of Guigues's emotional response to his new relationship with the king as of one of great happiness and joy, we can see that the document provided a quite simple view of Guigues's new status: he had *more* rights in his land and, by holding them 'of' the king, created a new relationship which looked forward, rather than backwards, was cemented by Guigues's performance of

---

[54] See the examples in Sassier, 'La *corona regni*', 103–4; and, most obviously, in the 'golden bull' issued for Aldebert, bishop of Mende in 1161, in which Aldebert acknowledged that his bishopric was held of the kingdom's crown (*de corona regni nostri*) and swore *fidelitas* (*Layettes de Trésor des chartes*, ed. A. Teulet (Paris, 1863) (henceforth *Layettes*), i, no. 168). The powers granted to Aldebert were great, but the personalised construction of the relationship between bishop, bishopric, king and crown is still present in the diploma, and it is of note that the celebratory short chronicle written around 1170 by a clerk of Mende does not mention this but instead 'in perpetuum regiam potestatem plenamque juridictionem super omnes homines'; *Chronicon breve de gestis Aldeberti*, in *Les miracles de Saint Privat, suivis des Opuscules d'Aldebert III, évêque de Mende*, ed. C. Brunel (Paris, 1912), also discussed in Bisson, *Crisis*, 312–14, but with different emphases.

homage and fealty and was not wholly in contradiction of his own local power.

The key point about these precisely constructed narratives is that they seem to have been legally descriptive: they described the relationship which two parties entered and did so in non-standard terms, without making anything like the same claims Guigues had made in his earlier letter. That is, although they used and invoked well-trodden yet broad concepts (such as *homagium*, *fidelitas* and *ius*), they *applied* them to describe a relationship performed and constructed at Louis's court in Bourges. Louis's surviving diplomas for lay people are formulaically very different in narrative and word order, although sometimes the same words appear.[55] There was, in short, no standard lexical framework which could be used to describe the relationship between kings and other aristocrats, lords or non-royal rulers, in abstract and replicable terms. The noteworthy point, however, is not the diversity of internal lexical form in the 1160s, but that this personalised diversity was replaced with standardised and abstracted formulae during the first two decades of the reign of Philip Augustus.

IV Creating forms of legitimate aristocratic power

Perhaps from as early as the mid-1180s, but certainly from the mid-1190s, there is an identifiable explosion in French royal *acta* in the number of formulae used to describe the way in which land, rents and monies were given and what was expected as a result.[56] These formulae appear in royal *acta* regardless of type; thus, they appear in both diplomas and the less solemn *chartes*, a developing type of document which out-numbered diplomas among Philip Augustus's surviving acts from the mid-1190s onwards.[57] Philip's *acta* start regularly recording that land or monies were to be given by the king or were to be held by the beneficiary 'in fief and homage' (*in feodum et hominagium*), 'in fief and liege homage' (*in feodum et hominagium ligium*), 'in liege homage' (*in ligium hominagium*) or in 'liege fief' (*in feodum ligium*), with the beneficiary having done *hominagium*

---

[55] See the examples in *Études*, ed. Luchaire, nos. 353, 537, 636.

[56] The earliest surviving appearance of *in feodum et hominagium ligium* seems to be the diploma partially copied into the *Livre noir* of Saint-Maur-des-Fossés (s.xiii); printed *Recueil*, I, no. 121, issued in the paschal year 1184. The orthography is *homagium ligium*, which may be significant, or may just be the copyist's preference; I have not examined the manuscript. For other early examples, mostly preserved in the registers (particularly A), see *Recueil*, II, nos. 556, 560, 764, 770, 793, 794 (both cancelled), 797, 798, 801. The 1184 example is important, as it predates the loss of the French royal archives at Fréteval in 1194.

[57] For the tendency to over-typologise diplomatic developments under Philip Augustus, see S. Barret and J.-F. Moufflet, 'Forms, Typology and Normalisation: French Royal Charters in the Thirteenth Century', in *Identifying Governmental Forms in Europe, c. 1100 – c. 1300: Palaeography, Diplomatics and History*, ed. A. Taylor, forthcoming.

to the king. In the 1190s, there was much variety in the formulae used; however, to give land *in feodum et hominagium ligium* and *in hominagium ligium* eventually became standard. 'Liege homage' is an interesting phenomenon, denoting the performance of homage to the chief lord. The attractiveness of the concept to rulers, both royal and non-royal, is clear but should not be assumed, as many rulers (including the king of Scots) did not make use of it, nor did those who did use it all the time.[58] This is a simple example of how the formula was used in a royal charter, which survives as an original from 1212, and concerns land in the Auvergne.[59]

> Philip, by God's grace, king of the Franks. All whom these letters reach know that we have given to our beloved and sworn man, Bertrand de la Tour, the castle of Orcet, and Montpeyroux, and Coudes, with their pertinents, to be held from us and our heirs in perpetuity, in fief and liege homage (*in feodum et hominagium ligium*), saving any external right, as Bertrand himself was holding these things on the Wednesday before the feast of St John the Baptist, when I received his homage about this matter.[60]

There are three notable points about *in feodum et hominagium ligium* and other related formulae. First, they are inherently non-personal and thus create a framework into which individuals, monies and lands could fit. In this, they differ from diplomatic practice under Louis VII when narratives were written into diplomas to fit the individual case. Also, unlike the use of homage in Louis VII's diplomas, the appearance of *hominagium* in the formula *in feodum et hominagium ligium* did not in itself denote the performance of homage (the Bertrand de la Tour example is a clear example of this; his performance is added to the end of the standard formula).[61] Second, these formulae describe only lay relations, which is striking in France, given that churchmen and ecclesiastical and monastic institutions are recorded as holding *feoda* (whatever that meant) and receiving homage in their own charters and agreements.[62] Based on

---

[58] See Aurell, 'Philippe Auguste', 55–60, for its use in French high politics.

[59] The appearance of the formula *in feodum et hominagium ligium* and other, similar, formulae has been noticed before, but can be analysed as Norman-inspired phenomena, resulting from Philip's conquest of the duchy in 1202–3, although many survive in Register A, which is very Norman-focused. See S. Reynolds, *Fiefs and Vassals: The Medieval Evidence Reinterpreted* (Oxford, 1994), 276–8, and scholarship cited there. See particularly Bisson, 'The Problem of Feudal Monarchy', 473–7, and revisited in Bisson, *Crisis*, 305–6, which states that the 'management of vassals, fiefs and tenurial obligations could easily be integrated with new techniques of power'. The difference is that I would argue that the 'management of vassals' etc. was *part* of the new techniques of power.

[60] *Recueil*, III, no. 1251. Charter here is used generically.

[61] However, it is of note that some earlier examples did, see *ibid.*, II, nos. 734–5.

[62] See, for example, the famous diploma about the county of Amiens, in *Recueil*, I, no. 139, also no. 445. The relationship between counts and (arch)bishoprics is also interesting. In 1179 (at Lateran III), William, archbishop of Reims, obtained a papal bull from Alexander III stating that Henry, count of Champagne, was 'known to have a fief from

their use, it seems that these formulae were intended to describe relations between lay people.

Third, the formula *in feodum et hominagium ligium* or *in hominagium ligium* was, in its infancy, a consciously *royal* tag or identification. Only later, in the thirteenth century, does it appear in the internal diplomatic of the *acta* of other non-royal rulers and lords. This is obviously a difficult statement to prove quantifiably.[63] That being said, I have not been able to find another pre-1190 non-royal example by searching the *Chartae Galliae* or *Diplomatica Belgica* databases or through preliminary searches through collections of major counts, in particular those of Champagne, whose records are notable for the presence of early inquests into the status of their men, adding the status label 'ligius' where appropriate.[64] The orthography of *hominagium*, with the additional three minims constituting the 'in', is also relatively unusual. There are, found through *Chartae Galliae*, only a few early examples from the cartulary of Saint-Aubin from the 1080s.[65] The suggestion that a formulation of *in feodum et hominagium ligium* and other related formulae was originally consciously a royal one is, on the other hand, shown on the few attested occasions when Philip's writing office reissued documents previously issued under another ruler's authority. In May 1199, Philip confirmed a charter of Arthur, duke of Brittany, granting the sénéchal-ship of Anjou and Maine to Guillaume des Roches.[66] In August 1204, after Philip learned of Arthur's death, the document was issued again, this time solely as Philip's gift. But whereas his earlier confirmation had used the formula *in feodum et hereditatem*, which was probably present in

your church, which he is held to do liege homage (*ligium hominium*) to you, save the king's *fidelitas*'. The precise wording of this bull would have been drafted by Reims; see *Documents relatifs au comté de Champagne et de Brie, 1172–1361*, ed. A. Longnon (Paris, 1901), I, 466 (no. 2).

[63] The obvious point that the concept of liege homage itself was not a primarily French royal formulation still needs to be stated; see the liege homage of Simon, duke of Lotharingia, kinsman of Philip of Flanders, 'against all men save the emperor' in an agreement made in Philip's court in 1179 (*De oorkonden der graven van Vlaanderen (juli 1128–september 1191)*, III: *Regering van Filips van de Elzas*, ed. T. de Hemptinne, A. Verhulst and L. de Mey (Brussels, 2009), no. 536, 29–31; online at www.diplomatica-belgica.be/, ID 8617: accessed 31 Jan. 2018). The earliest datable mention of *ligius* has been suggested by West to come from the region west of the Meuse in 1055; C. West, *Reframing the Feudal Revolution: Political and Social Transformation between Marne and Moselle, c. 800 – c. 1100* (Cambridge, 2013), 210–11, and n. 48.

[64] The earliest is from 1172, and is printed in *Documents*, ed. Longnon, I, 1–53.

[65] *Cartulaire de l'abbaye de Saint-Aubin*, ed. B. de Brousillon and E. Lelong (3 vols., Angers, 1896–1903), I, nos. 73, 127; *Chartae Galliae* also provides examples from the abbey of Saint-Crépin-le-Grand, Soissons: Acte n°212797 in *Chartae Galliae*: www.cn-telma.fr/chartae-galliae/charte212797/ [1146], and the cathedral of Amiens in 1167 (Acte n°201735 in *Chartae Galliae*): www.cn-telma.fr/chartae-galliae/charte201735.

[66] *Recueil*, II, no. 608.

Arthur's original charter (which no longer survives), his later confirmation, issued after having taken Anjou and Maine into his own hands, used *in ligium hominagium* and excised the 'foreign' formula *in feodum et hereditatem*, thus reconfiguring it according to the standards of his own writing office.[67]

Thus, from perhaps as early as the mid-1180s, a new range of small-scale, diplomatic formulae were gradually introduced into French royal charters to denote lay relations between exclusively the French king and aristocrats. These formulae appear first to have been introduced for gifts of land and monies within the old French domaine but, crucially, could be applied to all levels of society and to different geographical regions with very different relations with the French kingship. The point was that the formulae claimed to level all recipients; they all had the same relationship with the king *qua* king, which placed, in theory not practice, the lordship held by Bertrand de la Tour in the Auvergne in the same position vis-à-vis the king as the countess, her son and county of Champagne.[68] The major ideas which lay behind it were that the public, legitimate basis of *all* aristocratic power was territory, hereditability, dependence on the king and, increasingly, kingdom-wide. Unsurprisingly, it was within this new conception of aristocratic power, and in particular the emphasis on homage, that Philip's government began to propagate statements which pertained to inheritance, succession and the conceptual authority of the king's court to judge the complaints of his ruled magnates, rules which were explicitly said to be part of the 'usage and custom of France'.[69]

These new rules were laid down explicitly within this new lexical representation of aristocratic power, framed by the words *feoda, hominagium* and *ligium hominagium*. Their terms were unambiguously standard

[67] *The Charters of Duchess Constance of Brittany and her Family, 1171–1221*, ed. J. Everard and M. Jones (Woodbridge, 1999), A15. In July 1202, Arthur had performed liege homage to Philip for his '*feodum* of Brittany, Anjou, Maine and the Touraine', recorded in one of Philip's charters, and later transcribed in abbreviated form in Register A. *Recueil*, II, nos. 723, 829. The phrase *propter fidele servitium* does begin to appear in Philip's acts from 1203–4; it may well be that the influence here was (broadly defined) Angevin, as a slightly different version of it was standard among English royal *acta* and was used in Arthur's charters as *pro fideli servitio*.

[68] See *Layettes*, I, nos. 713, 734, 1033.

[69] For the adoption of custom-formulae in *actes*, see D. Power, *The Norman Frontier in the Twelfth and Early Thirteenth Centuries* (Cambridge, 2004), 144–61. But it was still optional. Non-royal counterparts to royal documents could remove the statement, as occurred in Stephen, bishop of Noyon's notification of 1213 which contains the famous phrase that the kings of France were not accustomed to do homage: whereas Philip's diploma (surviving in Register C: Paris, Archives Nationales, JJ7, fo. 56r) describes this as the 'usage and custom of the kingdom of France' (*Recueil*, III, no. 1309), Bishop Stephen's notification simply calls it the 'usage and custom approved until this day' (*Layettes*, I, no. 1053).

and public. On 1 May 1209, Philip, along with five named magnates and 'many other magnates of the kingdom of France', agreed a new rule about inheritance.[70] The document linked the agreement of these six individuals with the idea of a public *regnum*: six men from the *regnum Francie* agreed 'unanimously' and 'made firm' the rule with 'public assent' (*assensu public*). The rule was explicitly new: it was to take force from 1 May onwards and was concerned with 'feudal holdings'. In case anyone was unsure what this meant, the document helpfully defined it: a feudal holding was 'whatever is held from a liege lord (*de domino ligio*) or when a division has been made in whatever way'. The definition of 'feudal holding' was thus extremely broad and vague. That, presumably, was the point. It stipulated that all those who hold parts of the same fief (i.e. when a fief was divided) should hold first from the 'lord of the fief' with no intermediary. What this meant was that all should be tenants of the lord of the fief, rather than each other. In this way, the rule laid down a powerful position that required, at least in its ambition, the reshuffling of landed relationships into a single hierarchy which led back, inextricably, to the king.

It has been shown that it was extraordinarily difficult to enforce the 1209 rule, nor did it apply everywhere.[71] Yet, although enforcement and compliance are important to consider when understanding rules and the relationship between rules and the exercise of authority, it is still important to consider, first, how rules conceptualise the ruled and, second, what authority or authorities claim the right to make, endorse and disseminate those rules. Both these considerations can be illustrated through the example of the judgement over the inheritance of Theobald IV to Champagne. This has traditionally been used to underline the growth of Philip's seigneurial authority over his magnates, yet it is worth reconsidering. In July 1216, a letter patent of Philip announced the judgement of the 'peers of the kingdom' concerning the disputed inheritance of the county of Champagne.[72] The claim of young Theobald IV, under the protection of his mother, Blanche of Navarre, to the county of Champagne had been challenged by his cousin, Philippa, and her husband, Erard of Brienne. Theobald's claim was upheld not by Philip but by the peers of the kingdom and other lay and ecclesiastical magnates, who invoked a rule in order to do so. The rule is given in full in the letter patent: 'after anyone is seised of any fief by the lord of the fief, the lord of the fief ought not to receive

[70] *Recueil*, III, no. 1083.

[71] P. Petot, 'L'ordonnance du 1er mai 1209', *Recueil de Travaux offerts à M. Clovis Brunel* (2 vols., Paris, 1955), II, 371–80, particularly 376–9.

[72] *Recueil*, IV, no. 1438. For a recent discussion of the meaning of 'pares', see *The Cartulary of Countess Blanche of Champagne*, ed. T. Evergates (Toronto, 2010), 18–19.

another in homage for the same fief for as long as he who is seised of the fief by the lord of the fief wants and is prepared to do right and to make suit at the court of the lord of the fief'. That is to say, once you had a fief, it could not be given to anyone else, unless you had done something wrong. Theobald had performed homage to Philip and had made suit at his court; the court – representing the kingdom – decreed that he had followed the rules (whether Theobald was aware of it or not) and so stated that it could not even hear Erard and Philippa's claim. By making rules concerning the practices of homage, inheritance and juris-diction which were internal to fiefs (*feoda* in 1216 or *feodales tenementa* in 1209) and by invoking the twin concepts of the *dominus feodi* and the *dominus ligius*, the king's ordinances used the new diplomatic register to claim that all similar landholdings could be understood as hierarchical, personal and juridical relationships which were subject to the same rules, regardless of geographic distance, regional difference or common sense, and that these rules pointed straight to the king.

Second, the authority which disseminated this rule was not only the king; indeed, the claim to make rules about aristocratic power was not made in opposition to it, but rather made through it. The eighteen peers, bishops and barons of the realm made the 1216 judgement but they also disseminated it.[73] It is easy to concentrate on Philip's letter patent announcing the judgement but it should not be forgotten that the very same text was also issued under the names of those who made the judgement (nine lay lords and nine bishops), an action initiated and ordered by the king himself.[74] All these letters patent follow the structure and wording of Philip's letter almost precisely and so were also written in the new lexical register of the royal writing office and had the seals of the issuer affixed to them.[75] Interestingly, despite the fact that none of these acts diverge from the text and substance of Philip's letter patent, adjustments were nonetheless made to recast a royal letter patent under the authority of another effectively. The letter patent of Odo, duke of Burgundy, for example, recorded that Blanche had been cited personally by the duke (and two others), and showed Odo's higher rank over Blanche by describing her as *dilecta et fidelis nostra* (which echoed the king's act) and then inserting his own pres-ence into Blanche's corroboration of the judgement, which occurred not

---

[73] The details of this complex and longstanding case are summarised in T. Evergates, *The Aristocracy in the County of Champagne 1100–1300* (Philadelphia, 2007), 34–42, 284–92.

[74] Philip's commands are found in *Recueil*, IV, nos. 1437–8, and *Cartulary of Countess Blanche*, ed. Evergates, nos. 285–6; see also the table found at *ibid.*, 19.

[75] *Cartulary of Countess Blanche*, ed. Evergates, nos. 24, 39–47, 396–401. Only the seal of one of the originals survives as a fragment (that of Gaucher, count of Saint-Pol: Paris, Archives Nationales, J198, no. 36).

just in the king's presence and that of his barons but, in Odo's letter, 'in the lord king's presence, in our [Odo's] presence, and in that of the barons of the kingdom of France'.[76] This contrasts with the statements in the letters of counts of lesser status. For example, the act of Gaucher, count of Saint Pol, called Blanche *karissima domina nostra*, and stated that Blanche's corroboration had occurred *coram domine rege et coram baronibus regni*.[77] In this way, although all the documents themselves would have *sounded* royal, there were a few subtle alterations in each act which personalised the 1216 judgement, and the legal rule it cited, thus further authenticating its issue and dissemination under the authority of the archbishop, bishops, duke, counts and barons who made the judgement.

At least some of these acts *looked* royal as well. Only seven of the eighteen acts of those listed in 1216 survive as originals, all now kept by the Archives Nationales in Paris. Although it has been suggested that three of these acts were written by the same scribe, it is extremely difficult to be sure about this: although there are similarities in letter forms, the speed of the ductus and the pen nibs used can be quite different. What is clear, however, is that all but one of the originals were written in hands which were similar to the more cursive script registers used for new forms of French royal document which emerged during the late twelfth and early thirteenth centuries (and which were used for the developing form of the French letter patent, *mandements* and the royal registers). Indeed, we know that these documents were drawn up on royal orders and at least one copy of each was kept in the royal archives, as they have survived through their preservation in the Trésor des chartes. But these aristocratic and episcopal letters were not just for the benefit of royal authority: further copies were drawn up for Blanche and Theobald themselves and these were deemed as just as important as the royal letter patent itself by the scribes who produced the champanois archival series during the later 1210s and 1220s because they were copied first into the comital cartulary and then into the cartulary prepared for Blanche herself. All the documents were framed as public letters, normally addressing the *universi*; we cannot know whether further copies were drawn up for preservation by the issuers or how far they were circulated more widely but what can be said is the multiple authorities

---

[76] Paris, Archives Nationales, J198, no. 38 (printed *Cartulary of Countess Blanche*, ed. Evergates, no. 39). The same extra spotlight was given to the archbishop of Reims in his deed (Archives Nationales, J198, no. 34; *Cartulary of Countess Blanche*, ed. Evergates, no. 396).

[77] Paris, Archives Nationales, J198, no. 36 (printed *Cartulary of Countess Blanche*, ed. Evergates, no. 44). John, count of Beaumont's deed calls her 'domina nostra' (cartulary copy only: *Cartulary of Countess Blanche*, ed. Evergates, no. 40); William, count of Joigny, also calls her 'karissima domina nostra' (Archives Nationales J209, no. 21; *Cartulary of Countess Blanche*, ed. Evergates, no. 43).

were deemed necessary to circulate the judgement independently.[78] Cooperation – wider acceptance of and participation in these new categories – was thus present in the way in which the 1216 judgement was disseminated.

This episode raises many questions about the multiple functions of the dissemination of documents, the authority of rule-making and the nature of political cooperation in the early thirteenth-century French kingdom. First, there was a clear and direct relationship between the judgement of the 'peers of our realm' and the dissemination of the document recording judgement containing the rule: the authority of the king, aristocrats, archbishop and bishops was required to do this. Yet the document they each disseminated was not written in their own 'house style' but in what seems to be a consciously identifiable royal diplomatic register, which was then subtly adapted to reflect the status of the issuer in question and his formalised relationship with the other named parties in the document. In short, the letters patent were simultaneously royal *and* non-royal. But the royal did not trump the non-royal, nor the other way around. Blanche and her cartulary-compilers did not see only the royal letter patent as meaningful: the champanois clerks kept all the documentation, copying each letter patent into their cartularies. In this way, the production and preservation context of the 1216 judgement not only illustrates the symbolic power of kingship but also the necessary cooption and cooperation of multiple authorities in disseminating the new framework of aristocratic and royal power and the growing body of rules (enforceable to some extent) associated with it.

It is important not to understand cooperation here solely as political action, as adherence or otherwise to the king. Indeed, there were many well-defined political resistances to the ambitions of Philip Augustus. For every Blanche of Navarre who appealed to and was protected by the king there was a Renaud of Danmartin who resisted him, often with serious consequences as King John found out so very publicly. But to think that political resistance represents governmental form in its entirety may be to mistake the trees (political actors) for the wood (the structures of power in which they operated). This is a particularly important point to grasp in the case of the French kingdom because there are so many examples of political and military resistance to the rule and ambition of Philip Augustus (and well into the reign of Louis IX). By contrast, political resistance in the twelfth- and early thirteenth-century Scottish kingdom has traditionally been analysed more in dynastic terms (rival claimants or 'pretenders' to the kingship) than as ideological positions

---

[78] The originals are *ibid.*, nos. 39, 41, 43–4, 46, 396–7, all kept in the Archives Nationales; see also the brief but extremely pertinent discussion in *Cartulary of Countess Blanche*, ed. Evergates, 17.

against the centralising power of the king, although there may have been that too but there is less evidence of it and so less historical analysis of it. Resisters in the French kingdom – whether King John, Renaud of Danmartin or Fernando of Flanders – resisted concrete royal power but not the framework of royal authority itself which was being reconstructed across two generations, often with explicit aristocratic involvement or, in other words, 'consensus'. Indeed, political resistance, as much as adherence and consensus, can underscore the legitimacy of formalised power by merely acknowledging its existence as something *to be resisted*. As in Scotland, cooperation should be understood as participation in a new discursive framework of government, encompassing actions of political resistance as much as political adherence, in which aristocratic power was redefined as dependent on the king, but yet was also part of his authority and responsible for its spread.

V Conclusion

This paper has suggested a shift in the function of the internal formulae of French and Scottish royal *acta* in the late twelfth century, at least when describing and conceptualising aristocratic power. Both moved from describing individualised relationships between king and lord to a formal and public representation of legitimate lay aristocratic power, a representation based on territory, hereditability and dependence on the king, which was crucially projected explicitly across the kingdom, and could, theoretically, be applied to anywhere within the kingdom. This formal representation of aristocratic power was, in both kingdoms, subject to ever-growing legal prescription and rule-making. The legal description which we find in Louis VII's diplomas did not always reflect practical realities and was not politically and morally neutral. Yet, like the charters of David I, Louis's diplomas described individual circumstances and occasions – and stressed royal rights while doing so – but did not attempt to place the relationship between king and lord within a preexisting and standard set of formulae. His diplomas and charters described *past* actions rather than categorised a future relationship. This changed in both kingdoms under Philip Augustus and William the Lion. In the French kingdom, a few decades after formalised representations of the relationship between royal and aristocratic power started to be used in royal *acta*, rules about that category began to be disseminated. In so doing, royal acts were prescribing that the relationship between kings and aristocrats was not one between individual king and individual lord, nor even between lord and fief-holder, but between the idea of a ruler and the idea of a ruled group, the legitimacy of whose power was, in theory, dependent on those formal rules.

The comparison with the kingdom of the Scots allows for this shift in the French kingdom to be identified more clearly, precisely because similar (but certainly not identical) trends were apparent in that far-away northern kingdom. In both kingdoms, one can identify not only the emergence of the idea of a normative relationship between royal and aristocratic power within the territory claimed by the issuing authority but also the written language used in formal documents to realise that idea. This is why giving the narratives constructed on the 'periphery' of Europe their own space to breathe and inform and challenge narratives formed at the centre is particularly important. As noted above, the kingdom of the Scots has been held up as a rather extreme example of Europeanization or, in its more insular form, 'Anglicization', and there are reasons why this has occurred.[79] But the research of historians of medieval Scotland over the past twenty to thirty years has also shown the inadequacy of thinking only in those terms. The documentary form and governmental institutions of England influenced those of Scotland but did not determine them. Indeed, the adaptations made by the scribes and officials of the Scottish royal writing office to 'English' forms reveal a clear and self-conscious understanding of the different institutional, political, social and economic contexts of the two kingdoms.[80] Thinking of Scotland along the terms of the 'core' (quite apart from the issue of where one locates the 'core' in the first place) misunderstands not only the form of Scottish royal government but also mischaracterises and oversimplifies that of the English.[81] This kind of criticism of a 'core-periphery' model of European change is well known, and has been raised in the scholarship of most areas deemed to be 'peripheral'.[82] If we cast entire regions as 'core' and thus dominant in our interpretative narratives, and others as 'peripheral', and fundamentally responsive to those narratives, we lose the opportunity to

[79] For Anglicization, see R. R. Davies, *The First English Empire: Power and Identities in the British Isles, 1093–1343* (Oxford, 2001), 142–71.

[80] For the state of the field in 2013, see the extremely full analysis in Matthew Hammond, 'Introduction: The Paradox of Medieval Scotland, 1093–1286', in *New Perspectives on Medieval Scotland, 1093–1286*, ed. M. Hammond (Woodbridge, 2013), 1–52; see further J. R. Davies, 'Royal Government in Scotland and the Development of Diplomatic Forms, 1094–1249', in *Identifying Governmental Forms*, ed. Taylor; Taylor, *Shape of the State*, 446–9; M. Hammond, 'Domination and Conquest? The Scottish Experience in the Twelfth and Thirteenth Centuries', in *The English Isles: Cultural Transmission and Political Conflict in Britain and Ireland, 1100–1500*, ed. S. Duffy and S. Foran (Dublin, 2013), 68–83.

[81] Stringer, 'Law, Governance, and Jurisdiction', 104–29.

[82] To list only two: H. Pryce, 'Welsh Rulers and European Change, c. 1100–1282', in *Power and Identity in the Middle Ages: Essays in Memory of Rees Davies*, ed. H. Pryce and J. Watts (Oxford, 2007), 37–51; S. Bagge, *From Viking Stronghold to Christian Kingdom: State Formation in Norway, c. 900–1330* (Copenhagen, 2010).

think how the narratives from the 'periphery' can challenge and build much bigger narratives of change in comparative perspective.

This is what the kingdom of the Scots does for the much more dominant example of the French kingdom (consciously by-passing, so to speak, its traditional 'model', the English kingdom). It is possible to identify real similarities not in precise language but in overall direction in the royal *acta* of both kingdoms. In both, aristocratic power came to be conceptualised as territorial, often heritable and, crucially, connected with the king. What this new, standardised representation meant and why it appeared can be linked to government.[83] During the very period when these new formulae were introduced in charter diplomatic, the more traditional institutional forms of governing were also developing and royal authority was, quite literally, geographically expanding. William's government was insisting that all aristocrats should not only have courts but also royal officials present at them and that these officials should themselves hold their own courts; Philip's government was introducing systems of travelling justices and conducting mass inquests of his forest rights, fief-holders in Normandy and the extended royal domain of Artois, the Vermandois and Valois. In both kingdoms, the shift can be characterised as a move from formally undifferentiated power between rulers and lords of many varieties (royal and non-royal) to the formally differentiated power of kings and aristocrats (many of whom might still exercise the functions of ruling).

The idea that the requirements of governments transform and simplify local practices into something standardised for their own needs is, of course, not new. In *Seeing like a State*, first published now twenty years ago, James C. Scott argued that power of the modern state (and, concurrently, its fatal flaw) was its necessary ambition 'to make a society legible', contrasting imperial/central demands for information with local and diverse knowledge, and arguing that the state always discarded the latter because it was not necessary to its own needs.[84] 'Legibility', for

---

[83] The role of university-educated masters (in law) in royal administration has been identified as a catalyst for change; see J. W. Baldwin, '*Studium et regnum*: The Penetration of University Personnel into French and English Administration at the Turn of the Twelfth and Thirteenth Centuries', *Revue des études islamiques*, 44 (1976), 199–215; O. Deschamps, 'L'essor des droits savants à l'époque de Philippe Auguste', in *Autour de Philippe Auguste*, ed. Aurell and Sassier, 145–68. However, the precise intellectual inheritance of these formulae needs more consideration, and there is no space to do so here. Reynolds argues that the study of *Libri Feudorum* had little effect on growing professional government in the French kingdom, and argues that the values about the kingdom and royal authority which underpinned thirteenth-century professional government emerged from the 'ideas, values and practices...in twelfth-century and earlier sources', Reynolds, *Fiefs and Vassals*, 258–322, at 320–1.

[84] In *Seeing like a State*, James C. Scott argued that one major aspect of the modern state (and its fatal flaw) was its necessary ambition to 'make a society legible, to arrange the

Scott, was a method of domination and coercion: the state transforms divergent local practices and knowledge into abstract categories, unifying them in the aim of obtaining revenue over newly incorporated or managed areas. In a similar sense, the introduction of a standard set of formulae in royal acts in the late twelfth century made aristocratic power legible to the king. In thinking about 'legibility', however, we should not confuse standardisation at the centre with uniformity in practice at a local or even regional level.[85] The anthropologist Maxim Bolt has recently reminded us of the necessary 'unevenness of institutionalisation', by which state institutions do not reach all areas under their authority in the same way, the difference determined by the degree and diversity of the state's interactions with its citizens/subjects and vice versa (or, in this case, lords and other rulers).[86] The development of a common vocabulary of legible aristocratic power did emphatically not make all aristocrats the same, or the French (or Scottish) aristocracy a monolith; what it did so was to project the *idea* of a formal, normative basis for the legitimate exercise of that power in relation to the king.

It is revealing of the long dominance of formal administrative institutions over our understanding of government that we have missed not only how the creation of equally formal and standardised representations of legitimate aristocratic power by the centre changed the framework of elite relationships with their ruler but also how the creation of a formal and public register of aristocratic power itself was part of governmental consolidation.[87] But this process was not one way: domination does not explain everything, particularly when the object of legibility is a powerful elite. In Scotland, the aristocracy sought out this new territorial definition of their power because, in part, this very definition was an intensification of the extensive authority which they had previously exercised and the definition had also become the way to protect their inheritance. This royally defined register was the main way a lord could be powerful, could exercise his authority, and thus it increased aristocratic power at

population in ways that simplified the classic state functions of taxation, conscription and the prevention of rebellion', which necessarily involved ignoring local knowledge. Scott's work conceptualises these legible simplifications as maps, and remarks on the 'power of maps to transform as well as merely to summarize the facts that they portray': J. C. Scott, *Seeing like a State: How Certain Schemes to Improve the Human Condition Have Failed* (New Haven, 1998), quotations at 2, 87. Scott's work is not often used when thinking about the Middle Ages, but the twin ideas of 'legibility' and 'simplification' are extremely useful here: the point of a formalised idea of aristocratic power outlined here was *not* to describe its realities and varieties but to claim it as ruled power, and, in effect, transform the phenomenon.

[85] See also Broun, 'Kingdom and Identity', 73–4.

[86] Maxim Bolt, 'Fluctuating Formality: Anthropology and the Structure of Difference', The Malinowski Memorial Lecture, London School of Economics, 17 May 2018.

[87] See, with different emphases, Reynolds, *Fiefs and Vassals*, 288–95, 316–19, 320–2, 479–92.

a local level. This did not happen in the same way in France but it did happen. The formalisation of aristocratic power by the centre did not necessarily increase aristocratic power at a local level (apart from in the case of new gifts) nor did it necessarily offer new avenues for advancement within formal institutions of government themselves. It instead protected the legitimacy of the aristocrat and his or her title-holding itself and through that protection advanced the framework of hard royal authority. The gain in aristocratic power was thus not at a local level but at a central one. Although the outcomes were different, in both kingdoms, the idea of aristocratic power itself was made, not broken, by institutional government. The development of more centralised governments, and therefore changing opportunities for status and rewards, increased and cemented elite power rather than acted against it. Once this is recognised, we can better understand how and why practical cooperation between kings and aristocrats has become one of the dominant ways of understanding central and later medieval power structures and can ask instead why forms of structural cooperation differed across Europe.

What is the significance of this position for the traditional narrative of state formation outlined at the start of this paper? First, to write of aristocratic power as a uniform phenomenon, differentiated formally from royal authority prior to (roughly) the last quarter of the twelfth century in both kingdoms may be to misunderstand the practice and structures of politics and government in the twelfth century. Further research is necessary to confirm this trend elsewhere, although we should not expect the same chronological focus or indeed trends. Late eleventh- and early twelfth-century England, for example, might well offer an earlier example, while how far the twelfth-century German empire offers an alternative narrative, seeing the emergence of territorialised princely power without a similar institutionalisation of royal authority, needs to be explored in more depth as it has been argued that the territorialisation of princely power also involved an intensification of their governing authority within the empire.[88] Equally, later thirteenth-century Norway saw the rise of governance-through-documentation but not, it appears, the emergence of a uniform idea of a territorially dependent aristocracy even though, as in Scotland, landed elites acted as officials in local administration.[89] Formalising aristocratic power, therefore, need not mean an aristocratic power outside governmental

---

[88] See G. Garnett, *Conquered England: Kingship, Succession and Tenure, 1066–1166* (Oxford, 2007); Hudson, *Land, Law and Lordship.* For Germany, see Arnold, *Princes and Territories*, ch. 3; and, more generally, Bisson, *Crisis*, 295–9.

[89] Bagge, *From Viking Stronghold to Christian Kingdom.*

institutions (as in France) but *as* those governmental institutions (as in the German empire/kingdom, and, in a different way, in Scotland).

But these are questions for other occasions. What the congruence of the two very different examples of France and Scotland discussed here suggests is that state formation did not occur as part of a structural conflict between kings (or other non-royal rulers) and aristocrats with the former gaining at the expense of the latter. The kingdom of the Scots offers an example of an institutional and (relatively) bureaucratic government which was not only based on aristocratic power but which also defined and standardised it or, in the words of James Scott, made it 'legible' at the level of royal government. The early thirteenth-century French kingdom offers a different perspective: the chancery created a formal representation of 'legible' aristocratic power which was not explicitly incorporated into the institutions of royal government, as it was in Scotland, but which later on in the thirteenth century allowed for individual aristocratic rulers (particularly if they were members of the royal family) to develop their own governmental mechanisms. This was sometimes a dangerous or at least ambivalent road, as Gaël Chenard has recently shown us in his ground-breaking work on Alphonse of Poitiers, but the institutional space was there for aristocratic government to develop alongside and with royal government rather than in imitation of it.[90] It is perhaps better to abandon finally the hopeful position that the development of institutional government was somehow bad for aristocratic power and acknowledge instead that, although the nature of its authority changed, the phenomenon of aristocratic power in and of itself grew through the government of which it constituted a part – different parts in different places, of course, but parts all the same. The removal of this causal force from our narrative of state formation means that we must reconceptualise how and why institutional governments not only developed but developed in such varied ways in the central Middle Ages. The institutional forms of Scottish and French royal governments were, after all, different, as outlined at the start of this paper. If we are to understand why the manifestations of government differed so significantly, other dynamics must be explored – such as the relationship between local and central forms of power and authority and how far preexisting methods of resource extraction were coopted by central authorities – but not, or not only, those of high politics.

[90] G. Chenard, *L'administration d'Alphonse de Poitiers, 1241–1271* (Paris, 2017).

Transactions of the RHS 28 (2018), pp. 65–88 © Royal Historical Society 2018
doi:10.1017/S008044011800004X

THE WOMAN TO THE PLOW; AND THE MAN TO THE HEN-ROOST: WIVES, HUSBANDS AND BEST-SELLING BALLADS IN SEVENTEENTH-CENTURY ENGLAND*

By Christopher Marsh

READ 22 SEPTEMBER 2017

ABSTRACT. This paper investigates the representation of marital relations in some of the most successful broadside ballads published in seventeenth-century England. It explains the manner in which these have been selected as part of a funded research project, and it proceeds to question an existing historiographical emphasis on ballads in which marriages were portrayed as under threat due to a combination of wifely failings (scolding, adultery, violence) and husbandly shortcomings (sexual inadequacy, jealousy, weakness). Best-selling ballads were much more sympathetic to married women in particular than we might have expected, and the implications of this for our understanding of the ballad market and early modern culture more generally may be significant. These ballads, it is argued, were often aimed particularly at women, and they grew out of an interesting negotiation between male didacticism and female taste. Throughout the paper, an attempt is made to understand ballads as songs and visual artefacts, rather than merely as texts.

A surprisingly strong case can be made for seeking the origins of English pop music not in the 1950s, but in the 1590s (or thereabouts). As the sixteenth century drew to a close, broadside ballads – single sheet songs that sold cheaply on the streets and covered a range of themes – were becoming big business in London and beyond. *A Ditty delightfull of mother watkins ale*, for example, evidently set feet tapping up and down the country with its jaunty melody and its irresistible innuendo.[1] Like many modern pop songs, its subject was sex, and the lines delivered by its male protagonist –

*I would like to express my gratitude to the Arts and Humanities Research Council and the British Academy for generously funding the research upon which this paper is based.

[1] *A Ditty delightfull of mother watkins ale* (?Abel Jeffs, *c.* 1592). All the ballads discussed in this paper were printed in London. The tune can be found in Claude M. Simpson, *The British Broadside Ballad and its Music* (New Brunswick, 1966), 745. All ballad citations in this paper will retain the original capitalisation because it seems possible that the precise layout of the words was an important aspect of the publishers' strategy.

'For I will without faile/Mayden, give you Watkins ale' – ensured that it stimulated moral outrage, again with modern parallels. One commentator called it a 'lascivious under song', while another marvelled that any self-respecting printer could issue 'such odious…ribauldrie as Watkins Ale'. This may also have been the song that was initially licensed for printing by the Stationers' Company – as 'A ballad of a yonge man that went a wooying &c' – but which was subsequently 'Cancelled out of the book, for the undecentnes of it in Diverse verses'. The imagined substance, Watkin's ale, was not, of course, a rejuvenating beverage but instead, to use the careful expression of the ballad scholar Tessa Watt, 'a bawdy allegory for the male generative fluid'.[2] The last decade of the sixteenth century also saw Thomas Deloney, a weaver turned wordsmith, churning out hit after hit in a compositional purple patch to rival that of Lennon and McCartney in the 1960s.[3]

In Deloney's time, the format of the ballad was evolving as the business developed, and by the 1620s a standard broadside included a title, multiple verses, one or more woodcut pictures and the name of a recommended tune (musical notation was rarely included – instead, we have to find the melodies in books of instrumental pieces, dance tunes or songs). Tunes and pictures were regularly recycled, sometimes appearing on many different ballads, and most of the sheets – printed on poor-quality paper – were used and displayed until they fell apart. We would know little of the genre were it not for the activities of educated men such as John Selden and Samuel Pepys, who collected ballads and pasted them into volumes, thus preserving for posterity so many pieces of ephemera.[4] Of course, early modern balladry differed from modern pop music in many ways too. The cult of the celebrity artist and the notion of a definitive performance were absent, for example, and there were many more songs on public execution and the need for repentance than we typically see in the charts today. It can nevertheless be claimed that this was where English pop music – commercially driven, based in London and aiming at a mass audience – had its roots.

[2] Henry Chettle, *Kind-Harts Dreame* (1593), C2r; Estienne de Maisonneufve, *Gerileon of England. The second part* (1592), A4r; Hyder E. Rollins, *An Analytical Index to the Ballad-Entries in the Registers of the Company of Stationers of London* (Chapel Hill, 1924), no. 3058; Tessa Watt, *Cheap Print and Popular Piety 1550–1640* (Cambridge, 1991), 67.

[3] On Deloney's songs, see Christopher Marsh, 'Best-Selling Ballads and the Female Voices of Thomas Deloney', forthcoming in *Huntington Library Quarterly*.

[4] On balladry in general, see Natascha Würzbach, *The Rise of the English Street Ballad, 1550–1650* (Cambridge, 1990); Watt, *Cheap Print*; Christopher Marsh, *Music and Society in Early Modern England* (Cambridge, 2010), chs. 5 and 6; *Ballads and Broadsides in Britain, 1500–1800*, ed. Patricia Fumerton and Anita Guerrini (Farnham, 2010); Angela McShane, 'Ballads and Broadsides', in *Cheap Print in Britain and Ireland to 1660*, ed. Joad Raymond (Oxford, 2011), 339–62; *Broadside Ballads from the Pepys Collection*, ed. Patricia Fumerton (Tempe, Arizona, 2012).

In most modern pop songs, the romantic characters are single and sexually driven, but marriage is scarcely mentioned. Early modern ballads, in contrast, tend to assume that marriage is part of the context: tales are told of single men and women who seek marriage and, crucially for this paper, there are also many songs that feature married couples. These are topics of great interest to social historians, and early modern ballads – which are increasingly available in digital online facsimiles – have provided us with important and abundant source materials.[5] There is not space to survey this work in detail here but it seems appropriate to draw attention at the outset to what is arguably a distorting tendency in much of the existing literature. In a nutshell, ballads are most frequently deployed in order to illustrate arguments about marriages that were threatened from within primarily by female failings: adulterous lust, subversive scolding and murderous intent.[6] In some of the ballads favoured by scholars, vigorous husbands are commended for rising to the challenge, using violence against their insubordinate wives if necessary. In others, feeble men are mocked and castigated for a range of shortcomings, including sexual inadequacy, jealousy and an inability to exert authority. Admirable wives are thin on the ground. Indeed, the content of ballads about courtship and marriage is often labelled misogynistic and interpreted as evidence of profound male anxiety. Historians highlight titles about tortured males – *Cuckolds Haven: OR, The marry'd mans miserie*, for example – and Anthony Fletcher has said about balladry, 'the creation of female gender here is confined to a familiar catalogue of vices that should be avoided or that men had it in their

---

[5] See, in particular, http://ballads.bodleian.ox.ac.uk/ and http://ebba.english.ucsb.edu/. In this paper, I will refer to the EBBA website regularly so that readers can view the ballads that cannot be displayed here. The quickest way to find a song is to type the EBBA number into the search box.

[6] See, for example, Laura Gowing, *Domestic Dangers: Women, Words and Sex in Early Modern London* (Oxford, 1996), 186–7, 207–8, 223; Stuart A. Kane, 'Wives with Knives: Early Modern Murder Ballads and the Transgressive Community', *Criticism*, 38 (1996), 219–37; Kirilka Stavreva, 'Scaffolds into Prints: Executing the Insubordinate Wife in the Ballad Trade of Early Modern England', *Journal of Popular Culture*, 31 (1997), 177–88, and *Words Like Daggers: Violent Female Speech in Early Modern England* (Lincoln, NB, 2015), 46–8; Jacqueline Eales, *Women in Early Modern England 1500–1700* (1998), 31–2, 98; Barry Reay, *Popular Cultures in England 1550–1750* (1998), 24; Elizabeth A. Foyster, *Manhood in Early Modern England: Honour, Sex and Marriage* (1999), 104, 111, 193–4; Bernard Capp, *When Gossips Meet: Women, Family and Neighbourhood in Early Modern England* (Oxford, 2003), 12–14; *Women and Murder in Early Modern News Pamphlets and Broadside Ballads, 1573–1697*, ed. Martin Randall (Aldershot, 2005); Simone Chess, '"And I my vowe did keepe": Oath Making, Subjectivity and Husband Murder in "Murderous Wife" Ballads', in *Ballads and Broadsides*, ed. Fumerton and Guerrini, 131–48; Frances E. Dolan, 'Tracking the Petty Traitor across Genres', in *Ballads and Broadsides*, ed. Fumerton and Guerrini, 149–72; Sarah F. Williams, *Damnable Practices: Witches, Dangerous Women, and Music in Seventeenth-Century English Broadside Ballads* (Farnham, 2015).

power to check'.[7] Thus, wild wives and the challenge they posed to troubled husbands are considered to have been the dominant themes, and ballads about marriages in which the woman murdered the man have proved particularly appealing. There are some important exceptions – a more rounded account of ballad-marriages can, for example, be found in the work of Joy Wiltenburg, Sandra Clark and Eleanor Hubbard – but relationships endangered from within have certainly caught the imagination.[8]

There is an interpretative difficulty here. Historians pull from the existing ballad-collections texts that suit their particular purposes, but in doing so they often create the impression that they are characterising marriage-ballads *in general* (and sometimes the argument is explicit). This matters: ballads were the most widely available form of print in the period – freely accessible even to the illiterate because they were so often performed – and they therefore offer us insights into commonplace tastes and attitudes (though it is notoriously difficult to define these insights).[9] If we get ballads wrong, the consequences for our understandings of early modern culture and society more generally may be significant. Clearly, we need a methodology that is based on principles more sophisticated than lucky dip and source-mining.

For this reason, I am currently working with Angela McShane, the musicians of The Carnival Band and a number of invited singers to identify, record and display online 120 of the seventeenth century's most successful ballads. The aim is to select ballads not because they illustrate particular topics that interest us but because they were best-sellers in their own age. Sadly, there are no sales figures and the exercise is therefore challenging. We feel, however, that we have compiled as robust a list of hits as the evidence will allow, using the following indicators of popularity: the number of known editions of individual ballads and the distribution of these editions through time; the number of surviving *copies* of each song; evidence that publishers were keen to assert their copyright in specific titles (based on records kept by the Stationers' Company);

---

[7] *Cuckolds Haven* (Francis Grove, 1638), EBBA 30036; Anthony Fletcher, *Gender, Sex and Subordination in England 1500–1800* (New Haven, 1995), 117.

[8] Joy Wiltenburg, *Disorderly Women and Female Power in the Street Literature of Early Modern England and Germany* (Charlottesville, 1992); Sandra Clark, 'The Broadside Ballad and the Woman's Voice', in *Debating Gender in Early Modern England 1500–1700*, ed. Christina Malcolmson and Mihoko Suzuki (Basingstoke, 2002), 103–20; Eleanor Hubbard, *City Women. Money, Sex and the Social Order in Early Modern England* (Oxford, 2012), 14–15, 112, 126–31.

[9] Arguably, we are still bedevilled by a wish to use ballads as representational 'mirrors' of social life. It surely makes more sense to regard them as an integral and influential *feature* of quotidian existence. Ballads were embedded and involved in early modern lives, rather than being a set of black-and-white snapshots captured from above.

the survival of songs beyond the seventeenth century, both in print and in vernacular tradition; and the capacity of songs to generate new names for existing tunes, a rough and ready sign of their success.

Our methodology aims to compensate for the inevitable privileging of songs that lasted many years by including criteria that allow more explosive but shorter-lived songs to qualify for inclusion. It also aims to balance the inevitable influence of the collectors by identifying indicators that instead reflect the broader priorities of the publishers. The limitations of the evidence mean that the results of this exercise are defensible rather than definitive, but there is no doubt that all of the selected songs were extraordinarily successful. When it comes to our efforts to understand these songs as historians, our distinctive emphasis is upon the integration of texts, tunes, pictures and performances. A somewhat restrictive 'lyrics-only' approach has characterised scholarly work on printed ballads for many decades, including much of what has so far been cited. Other recent work, however, attempts to develop a more holistic approach.[10]

The following pages will discuss a selection of these songs, concentrating in particular on those that feature marriage as a prominent theme. Roughly twenty-five of the 120 ballads fall into this category, and they can be used to address the following questions: how were husbands and wives represented in hit songs of the seventeenth century, and how might this representation encourage historians to re-think balladry and, perhaps, gender relations more widely? Let us begin with the simple observation that very few of our twenty-five hit songs have featured prominently in previous scholarly discussions of marital relations as represented in early modern ballads. When historians choose their songs, these are not usually the songs they choose.[11]

---

[10] The 'lyrics only' approach informs many works, including Würzbach, *Rise of the English Street Ballad*; and Robin Ganev, *Songs of Protest, Songs of Love: Popular Ballads in Eighteenth-Century Britain* (Manchester, 2010). For more multi-media perspectives, see Christopher Marsh, 'The Sound of Print in Early Modern England: The Broadside Ballad as Song', in *The Uses of Script and Print, 1300–1700*, ed. Julia C. Crick and Alexandra Walsham (Cambridge, 2004), 171–90, and 'Best-Selling Ballads and their Pictures in Seventeenth-Century England', *Past and Present*, 233 (2016), 53–99; Theodore Barrow, 'From "Easter Wedding" to "The Frantick Lover": The Repeated Woodcut and its Shifting Roles', in *Studies in Ephemera: Text and Image in Eighteenth-Century Print*, ed. Kevin D. Murphy and Sally O'Driscoll (Lewisburg, 2013), 219–39; Alexandra Franklin, 'Making Sense of Broadside Ballad Illustrations in the Seventeenth and Eighteenth Centuries', in *Studies in Ephemera*, ed. Murphy and O'Driscoll, 169–93; Una McIlvenna, 'The Power of Music: The Significance of Contrafactum in Execution Ballads', *Past and Present*, 229 (2015), 47–89; Williams, *Damnable Practices*; Megan E. Palmer, 'Picturing Song across Species: Broadside Ballads in Image and Word', *Huntington Library Quarterly*, 79 (2016), 221–44.

[11] In the influential books by Anthony Fletcher, Elizabeth Foyster, Bernard Capp and Laura Gowing – all cited above – there are roughly 132 references to named ballads,

Most of our songs do not, therefore, sit comfortably with the historio-graphical emphasis on ballad-marriages that were endangered by a chal-lenging wife. Three might just about qualify, and the strongest candidate among them was *The lamentable fall of Queen Elenor, who for her Pride and wickedness by Gods judgements sunk into the ground at Charing-Cross and rose at Queen hive*. This describes the cruelty and sinfulness of Edward I's queen, Eleanor of Castile, who, according to its narrative, committed numerous outrages, including the vile murder of the mayor of London's honest wife, and adultery with a friar. Eleanor clearly is a dan-gerous woman, and her husband the king is well meaning but a little inef-fectual. This is not, however, a ballad that says critical things of English marriages *in general*. Quite the opposite: Eleanor's wickedness is very clearly related to the fact that she is Spanish, and 'her spight to women-kind' is carefully noted. Thus, she is the enemy of her sex rather than its representative. Furthermore, the apparently exemplary marriage of the mayor and his wife, 'the London Lady good', suggests that healthy English relationships at all levels of society are threatened not by internal stresses but by the vanity and viciousness of a foreigner (sinister Spaniards were particularly appealing to English audiences when this song was originally composed, probably soon after the Armada of 1588). Appropriately enough, Queen Eleanor eventually loses her life after being swallowed mysteriously into the ground and then regurgitated several miles away.[12]

A further eight ballads are similar in that they bear some relation to the scholarly emphasis on wicked wives and harassed husbands, but in all cases there are unexpected subtleties and complications. We have, for example, the only title in our chart that portrays a woman who murders her husband – making it also one of the few that has already been discussed by historians.[13] The ballad, composed by Thomas Deloney in the 1590s, is actually three songs in one, all set to a sombre and immensely popular tune, 'Fortune my foe', that had powerful asso-ciations both with romance and with the 'last dying speeches' of con-demned killers. The first of the three songs on this sheet is entitled *The Lamentation of Master Pages wife of Plimmouth*. It tells the tale of Eulalia

only three of which appear on our full list of 120 hit songs (and all three are mentioned very briefly). Once again, an exception is Wiltenburg, *Disorderly Women*. This discusses several of our hit ballads, though they are not generally distinguished from other titles in terms of their immense popularity.

[12] *The lamentable fall of Queen Elenor* (1586–1625; F. Coles, T. Vere and W. Gilbertson, 1658–64), EBBA 31939. The tune has not been found. Similarly troublesome women can be found in the hit songs *A Godly Warning for all Maidens* (c. 1603; W. Thackeray and T. Passinger, 1686–8), EBBA 20238, and *A good Wife, or none* (c. 1624; Francis Coules, 1624–80), EBBA 30086.

[13] *Women and Murder*, ed. Randall, xi–xii; Kane, 'Wives with Knives', 219; Stavreva, 'Scaffolds into Prints'; Foyster, *Manhood*, 105–6.

Page who, in 1590, was executed for the murder of her husband, along with her collaborating lover, George Strangwidge, and two hired killers. Singing from the heart and in her own voice – as channelled by the male author – Eulalia faces execution and describes her journey along a road to ruin. She begins,

> Unhappy she whom fortune hath forlorne,
> Despis'd of grace, that proffered grace did scorne,
> My lawlesse love that lucklesse wrought my woe,
> My discontent content did overthrow.
>
> My loathed life too late I doe lament,
> My hatefull deed with heart I doe repent:
> A wife I was that wilful went awry,
> And for that fault am here prepar'd to die.[14]

Thus far, the song fits the pattern that characterised most ballads about husband-killers. In several respects, however, it is strikingly different from others on the same theme. Eulalia is portrayed with considerable sympathy and is allowed the space to explain her conduct. She accepts the legitimacy of her punishment but explains that she was 'forced' into marriage by her greedy parents, her father in particular, and that she was already engaged to Strangwidge, her 'husband true'. The song also omits the kind of graphic detail about the murder and the execution that filled otherwise comparable ballads. And Eulalia is represented much more positively in the ballad than she was in a prose account of the same case.[15] Even her acknowledged weakness is rooted in her romantic constancy. This is no cardboard cut-out of the husband-killing 'petty traitor' but in fact a surprisingly subtle and sophisticated account of one honest and loving woman's descent into criminality under the tragically combined influence of true love and an oppressive father. It seems likely that the song's immense popularity was connected, at least in part, with its complex and uncategorical portrayal of the

---

[14] *The Lamentation of Master Pages wife of Plimmouth* (*c.* 1590; H. Gosson, *c.* 1609), EBBA 20054. For the tune, see Simpson, *British Broadside Ballad*, 227. Excerpts from most of the ballads discussed in this paper were played in the lecture, some from our new recordings and some in live performance. A film of the lecture can be accessed at https://royalhist-soc.org/category/rhs-video-archive/.

[15] For general comments on the representation of female murderers, see Frances E. Dolan, *Dangerous Familiars. Representations of Domestic Crime in England, 1550–1700* (Ithaca, 1994), 49–50; *Women and Murder*, ed. Randall, xiii; and Kane, 'Wives with Knives', 226–7. The contemporary pamphlet account of the case is in *Sundrye strange and inhumaine Murthers, lately committed* (1591), B2r–B4v. In this version, Mistress Page is much more wicked, deceitful and culpable than she is in the ballad.

murderer whom it made famous.[16] This raises interesting questions about the nature of its audience, a point to which we will return.

Other hit ballads in this sub-group of eight steer clear of murder but nevertheless follow a comparable line in representing with some sympathy wives who bring danger to their households. In *Prides fall*, a Dutch woman – married to a wealthy merchant – explains in graphic terms how her personal vanity led God to place in her womb a monstrous baby, designed as a warning to all 'fair dainty Dames' (Figure 1). The baby's strange physical characteristics reflect the mother's vanity and both the woodcut artist and the wordsmith went to considerable and unusual pains in visualising a creature that scared all witnesses.

> For it affrighted so
> all the whole company,
> That e're one said in heart,
> 'vengeance now draweth nigh'
> It had two faces strang[e],
> and two heads painted fair,
> On the brows curled locks,
> such as our wantons ware [i.e. wear].
>
> One hand held right the shape
> of a fair looking-glasse,
> In which I took delight
> how my vain beauty was;
> Right the shape of a Rod,
> scourging me for my sin:
> The other seem'd to have,
> perfectly seen therein.

The baby dies, but not before delivering a stern – and remarkably precocious – warning to the astonished townsfolk. This *is*, then, a ballad about the dangers of female sinfulness – the word 'wanton' is used repeatedly – and yet, as with Mistress Page, the wayward wife speaks for herself (as it were) and expresses her deep remorse. She turns her sin into something positive by seeking to influence other women, and the song ends with the lines, 'Maid and Wife, let my life,/be warning to you all'. The tune is also distinctly upbeat and it was strongly

---

[16] Joy Wiltenburg has noted that successful murder ballads tended to 'invite intensive imaginative participation' by presenting vividly the 'inner turmoil' of the repentant criminal. See Joy Wiltenburg, 'Ballads and the Emotional Life of Crime', in *Ballads and Broadsides*, ed. Fumerton and Guerrini, 173–88.

Figure 1 *Prides fall* (edition of 1663–74). Euing Ballads, 269. By permission of the University of Glasgow Library, Special Collections.

connected by association with another hit ballad about a heroic male apprentice, a resonance that contributes a curiously positive vibe to *Prides fall*.[17] Of course, the anonymous song is probably a man's imagining of a female persona – it is difficult to escape such ventriloquism in the seventeenth century – but it is not a straightforwardly hostile representation of the Dutch wife. At the very least, she stands in the spotlight, delivering ninety-eight lines of spoken text, only three of which mention her husband even in passing.

[17] *Prides fall: Or, A warning for all English Women* (1585–1616; F. Coles, T. Vere and J. Wright, 1663–74), EBBA 31879; *The Honour of a London Prentice* (c. 1580–1600; W. Thackeray and T. Passinger, 1686–8), EBBA 21266. The latter ballad was probably an Elizabethan composition. The melody can be found in various early modern sources, ranging from sixteenth-century instrumental collections to eighteenth-century song books (see Simpson, *British Broadside Ballad*, 14).

Other songs in this sub-group feature female adulterers but, once again, their portrayal in our hit ballads is rather different from the blunt and brutal representations of lascivious wives that have been highlighted in the scholarly literature. In *The lamentable Ditty of Little Mousgrove, and the Lady Barnet*, for example, an aristocratic wife, Lady Barnet, seduces an attractive local man, Little Mousgrove, luring him to her flower-strewn bower for an hour of passion (Figure 2). Her husband learns of the assignation and bursts in upon the couple as they lie in bed. The *denouement* is bloody: Lord Barnet slays Little Mousgrove in a sword-fight, then kills his wife, and finally takes his own life. In the closing lines, we *are* warned about the consequences of lust, and yet the song – when heard in its entirety – certainly does not feel like a fierce condemnation of a wicked wife. Even in the moralising final verse, Lady Barnet is described as a 'worthy wight', and the multiple deaths that occur are more like the climax of a tragic love story than an account of sin and its foul-smelling fruits.[18] The pictures, as so often, are recycled from other sources. On the right, for example, a commonly encountered soldier represents the angry Lord Barnet as he approaches a bed-scene that also began life elsewhere (viewers must make their own sense of the fact that the Lady and her lover appear to be sharing those precious post-coital moments with some visiting clerics).

The lamentable Ditty shares one of its pictures with our next song, *A new Ballad of the Souldier and Peggy* (Figure 3). There were several editions of this ballad in the second half of the seventeenth century, and its lovely lilting melody – described on the sheet as 'a new Northerne Tune' – subsequently became known as 'Peg and the soldier'.[19] The song tells the story of another female adulterer who places her marriage in jeopardy, but its conclusion sets it apart from many more merciless accounts of such characters. Peggy has a baby at home but she nevertheless runs off willingly to Ireland with a seductive soldier. Her 'good husband' is understandably distraught when he realises that Peggy has sailed away on a lustful impulse. After hiring a nurse to feed the baby, he expresses his anger but chooses other targets than his wife:

> He cursed the Carpenter
> that made the ship,
> And eke the Plummer,
> for plumming so deepe:

---

[18] *The lamentable Ditty of Little Mousgrove* (H. Gosson, *c.* 1630), EBBA 20172. Folksong versions of this narrative were regularly collected in twentieth-century America where it was known under various names, including 'Little Matty Grove'. The original tune is lost.

[19] *A new Ballad of the Souldier and Peggy* (F. Coules, *c.* 1640), EBBA 30250. For the tune, see Simpson, *British Broadside Ballad*, 572.

Figure 2 *The lamentable Ditty of Little Mousgrove* (edition of *c.* 1630). Pepys Ballads, 1, 364–5. By permission of the Pepys Library, Magdalene College, Cambridge.

> he banned the wind
> and the water so cleere,
> That carried her over sea
> with a souldier.

When life on the road proves a disappointment to Peggy, she returns home and begs forgiveness. Her husband, remarkably, welcomes her back immediately, asking only that she promise not to stray again.

Although Peggy is at fault – she *is* a 'wanton lewd woman' – she is also treated rather generously, both by her husband and by the narrator. We might expect a more savage act of judgement, like the one at the climax of the 'Little Mousegrove' ballad. Instead, Peggy's waywardness is presented as almost excusable – 'For youth it is wanton/ and will have a fling' – so long as the lesson is learned, 'And Peggy is at home with her husband againe'. The mood of the tune contributes to the 'all's

Figure 3 *A new Ballad of the Souldier and Peggy* (edition of *c.* 1640). Roxburghe Ballads, I, 370–1. © The British Library.

well that ends well' tone, and the recycled pictures track the narrative in a rudimentary manner. On the left, we see the soldier who, having represented Lord Barnet on the previous ballad, now stands beside an interesting illustration of a woman with a sword at her side. This image also appeared subsequently on a song – popular but not quite one of our hits – about the female soldier, Mary Ambree, who brought England glory with the great deeds she performed in the Netherlands. Clearly, she carried an association with soldiering from one ballad to the next (more mysteriously, however, Mary Ambree has apparently mislaid the sword).[20] On the song about Peggy, two woodcuts on the

[20] *The valorous Acts performed at Gaunt, By the brave bonny Lasse Mary Ambre* (William Gilbertson, 1647–65?), EBBA 36066. Successful woodblocks were often altered and copied; the difference between the two pictures is not, therefore, unusual.

right complete the tale. Here, she is no longer the bold young woman running off with a soldier but instead the conventional wife who stands beside her happy husband (everybody had seen both of these pictures dozens of times). The assumptions that underlie the ballad are, of course, conventionally patriarchal – the wife goes astray, and her deliverance consists in returning to live with a husband who forgives her as God forgives him – but this song can hardly be said to express the 'crude if jocular misogyny' that Bernard Capp and others have found to be characteristic of the cheaper forms of print in general.[21]

The fourteen ballads that complete our collection of marital megasongs carry us even further from this emphasis, suggesting that the role of balladry within early modern debates about marriage and gender relations more generally may have been misunderstood. Some of these ballads idealise marriage and present to the listener wives and husbands who live together in love and happiness. *The Happy Husbandman: OR, Country Innocence*, for example, opens with the lines,

MY young Mary do's mind the Dairy,
while I go a Howing, and Mowing each Morn;
Then hey the little Spinning Wheel
Merrily round do's Reel
while I am singing amidst the Corn:
Cream and Kisses both are my Delight
She gives me them, and the Joys of Night;
She's soft as the Air,
As Morning fair,
Is not such a Maid a most pleasing Sight?

While I whistle, she from the Thistle
does gather Down, for to make us a Bed,
And then my little Love does lie
All the Night long and dye
in the kind Arms of her nown dear Ned;
There I taste of a delicate Spring,
But I mun not tell you nor name the thing,
To put you a Wishing,
And think of Kissing,
For Kisses cause sighs, and young Men shou'd sing.

---

[21] Capp, *When Gossips Meet*, 12. The other ballads in this sub-group of eight are: *The Woful Lamentation of Mistris Jane Shore* (c. 1624; F. Coles, T. Vere and J. Wright, 1663–74), EBBA 32019; *A Lamentable Ballad of Fair Rosamond* (c. 1593; W. Thackeray and T. Passinger, 1686–8), EBBA 20235; *A New little Northren Song* (H. G., c. 1631), EBBA 20122; *An excellent Ballad of the Mercer's Son of Midhurst* (c. 1624; J. Clarke, W. Thackeray and T. Passinger, 1684–6), EBBA 20258.

The song is almost nauseating in its portrayal of an idyllic rural marriage in which the spouses perform their distinct but complementary roles with a coy smile on their faces and a sentimental song in their hearts. Their lives are full of love-making but devoid of trouble-making (wisely, they leave politics to others). This feels, of course, like a town Tory's imagining of country life, and we are told that London wives are greedy and domineering in comparison to the paragon described here. It is difficult at first to see why this song was so popular, but if we listen as well as look, then some sense of its appeal can be recaptured. The melody, described on the sheet as 'a pleasant new Court Tune', is beautiful, capable perhaps of conjuring something sublime from something ridiculous.[22]

Most of our remaining songs are different in that they *do* demonstrate an acute awareness of the dangers to marriage but, crucially, these dangers are typically the work of forces external to the relationship rather than the result of tensions between husband and wife. Frequently, marriages are threatened or complicated by the disapproval of parents or relatives, and the ballad-makers' sympathies are invariably with the couple rather than their critics. One ballad, printed repeatedly during the seventeenth century, bore the title, *A constant Wife, a kinde Wife, A loving Wife, and a fine Wife, Which gives content unto mans life*. In several editions, the repeated capital Ws in the title make the point that finding a worthy woman to wed is the song's principal focus. Written in the man's voice, the first half of the ballad describes the battle he fought to free his beloved from the evil clutches of her disapproving family ('She likely was for to be rich,/ and I a man but meanely'). He smashes his way into her uncle's house, rescues his sweetheart and marries her without the consent of her family – and he urges other men to adopt a similarly belligerent attitude to the enemies of true love. In calmer mood, he then devotes the second half of the song to praising his new wife, commending her physical beauty, her virtue, her wisdom and her obedience. The woman in this song, though set at its centre, is a passive figure, a desirable trophy over which men fight, but she is nothing like an adulterous scold.[23]

---

[22] *The Happy Husbandman* (P. Brooksby, 1685–8), EBBA 21041. The tune was composed for the ballad and can be found in Simpson, *British Broadside Ballad*, 502. For other generally positive representations of marital relationships in our group of hit ballads, see *A pleasant Song of the Valiant Deeds of Chivalry* (c. 1592; F. Coles, T. Vere, J. Wright and J. Clarke, 1674–9), EBBA 30400; *A pleasant new Ballad of the Miller of Mansfield* (c. 1588; E. Wright, 1611–56), EBBA 30162; *The Shepherd and the King* (c. 1578; A. M., 1686–93), EBBA 32009.

[23] *A constant Wife, a kinde Wife* (F. C., c. 1631), EBBA 20181. For the tune, see Simpson, *British Broadside Ballad*, 445. See also *An excellent Ballad of a Prince of Englands Courtship to the King of France's Daughter* (1585–1616; Alex. Milbourn, 1686–93), EBBA 30068.

The woman featured in *A worthy example of a vertuous wife* was a far more active presence. The song was popular in England from the 1590s right through into the eighteenth century. It tells the story of a woman from ancient Rome who, having married against her father's will, grasps the opportunity to achieve reconciliation with him after he is imprisoned and starved by the emperor. And where the man in our previous ballad uses his fists to effect a rescue, the heroine of this song must deploy more subtle and feminine means. To cut a long story short, she tricks the authorities into allowing her access to the old man, and then keeps him alive by secretly breast-feeding him through the bars of his cell every day for a year (he 'was most faire and fat to see,/yet no man knew which way'). The emperor eventually realises what has happened and, impressed by such virtuous devotion, pardons the prisoner and rewards his daughter with 'great preferments'.[24] The song acknowledges no sources but it is clearly based on ancient Roman stories recorded by Valerius Maximus and Pliny the Elder as examples of familial devotion. Valerius told two similar tales, and the one that he developed most fully actually featured an imprisoned mother rather than a father. Pliny, interestingly, recorded only this all-female version. By the sixteenth century, however, a single narrative about Cimon (the father) and Pero (the daughter) was firmly in fashion, and it subsequently became known as 'Roman charity'. It appears that early modern minds preferred the version in which a woman fed a man, perhaps because this intensified the incestuous *frisson* and reflected the topical complexities of patriarchy-in-practice.[25]

There are several interesting points to be made about this hit song. Its focus is not actually the woman's marital relationship, except indirectly, and yet the title and the final verse highlight her status as a 'vertuous' and 'loving' wife. The story is really about her conduct as a daughter, and the insistence upon her wifeliness at the song's top and tail perhaps has the effect of tying different types of female dependence and obligation together. Ballads about active women – transvestite soldiers, for example – very often conclude with verses about marriage, in which convention reclaims those who might seem to have threatened it. This is necessary here too, for the men in this song are not impressive: her father is pathetic, the emperor is autocratic and the husband hardly features. The 'vertuous

---

[24] *A worthy example of a vertuous wife, who fed her father with her own milk* (*c.* 1596; E. W., *c.* 1635), EBBA 30398.

[25] See Valerius Maximus, *Memorable Doings and Sayings*, trans. and ed. D. R. Shackleton Bailey (2 vols., Cambridge, MA, 2000), I, 501; *Pliny. Natural History*, trans. and ed. H. Rackham (10 vols., London and Cambridge, MA, 1938–62), II (1942), 587. The pivotal scene in this tale was painted during the early modern period by Rubens, Caravaggio and many others.

wife' is a feisty, resourceful and active woman who stars in her own show. She has previously defied her father, and now she defies the emperor – labelling him a 'tyrant' – and tricks his guards. She deploys traditional womanly wiles – 'wringing hands and bitter teares' – in order to do good and get her way. She also displays more clearly admirable feminine qualities such as selflessness, and the instruments through which these qualities are revealed – her own breasts – could hardly be more conventional in their symbolism. She is a complex creation, clearly set up for our admiration, and the tune – strongly associated with a heroic *male* ballad about the medieval battle at Chevy Chase – adds to the positive atmosphere.[26] We cannot know who bought this ballad, nor why it was so successful, but we might speculate that this virtuous wife worked her way, in exaggerated and exoticised guise, through the daily dilemma that faced many early modern English wives: how to find fulfilment within patriarchy through the somewhat paradoxical or counter-intuitive project of making it their own. The ballad was simultaneously a fantastical escape from 'reality' and a sturdy tool with which to work on it.

It is perhaps difficult to reconcile the popularity of the woman who fed her father with the undoubted appeal of Thomas Deloney's *Excellent Ballad of Patient Grissel*. In this version of an old story previously told by Boccaccio, Petrarch and Chaucer, a marquis marries a beautiful but poor woman called Grissel, and soon faces murmuring criticism from his noble advisers for marrying so far beneath him. He loves Grissel truly, but resolves that he must prove her moral worth to the doubters by subjecting her to a terrible series of ordeals. He removes her children, telling her (falsely) that he has had them killed, and he banishes her back to her father's miserable cottage. Grissel bears it all with patience and constancy, obeying each of her husband's outrageous commands until, finally, he reunites her with her children and explains that she has now passed all the necessary tests.[27] It is an unsettling ballad, and very different in its portrayal of the featured wife from the song we have just considered. Its appeal to men is obvious enough, but the reasons why women might have felt drawn to it, perhaps cherishing it alongside their copies of *A worthy example of a vertuous wife*, are harder to fathom. Chaucer had argued forcefully that no wife could be expected to copy Grissel, but the author of a seventeenth-century chapbook about her, taking issue

---

[26] *A memorable Song on the unhappy hunting in Chevy-Chase* (*c.* 1624; F. Coles, T. Vere and J. Wright, 1663–74), EBBA 30408. The tune was one of the most popular of the period (see Simpson, *British Broadside Ballad*, 97).

[27] *An Excellent Ballad of Patient Grissel* (*c.* 1624; F. Coles, T. Vere and W. Gilbertson, 1658–64), EBBA 31768. The tune is lost. On this and other representations of Grissel in the period, see Judith Bronfman, 'Griselda, Renaissance Woman', in *The Renaissance Englishwoman in Print. Counterbalancing the Canon*, ed. Anne M. Haselkorn and Betty S. Travitsky (Amherst, 1990), 211–23.

with those who complained about 'the absurdity of the example', urged that this is exactly what women should do.[28] Arguably, it was possible to admire Grissel not primarily for her obedience but instead for her refusal to buckle under unimaginable pressure from a cruel husband. Within this view, her extreme passivity becomes almost a species of defiant action, and – like the woman who fed her father – she survives and eventually thrives. Of course, there is a fine line between admiring obedience and admiring the capacity to suffer without complaint, but the genius of Deloney resided, arguably, in his ability to devise songs that appealed to men and women simultaneously but for different reasons. Such songs clearly stimulated debate, and the ballad 'Of Patient Grissel' was said to be a favourite choice for display on the walls of country homes.[29]

In our last ballads, marriages are endangered not by disapproving observers but by a range of other circumstances, none of which has anything to do with stresses within the core relationship. Indeed, most of the marriages are strong and loving, exemplary even, but assaulted from outside. There is one about Catherine Willoughby, duchess of Suffolk, who fled England with her husband and baby during the 1550s in order to escape persecution for her godly Protestantism. Another introduces us to a more humble bride, who dies suddenly on her wedding day after dispensing godly and practical advice to her husband and friends (she sensibly suggests that they hire a carpenter to turn her marital bed into a coffin). In both songs, the wives take centre-stage, their courageous conduct praised and promoted. They are often surrounded by men and conventional in their femininity, but they shine nonetheless.[30] The same is true of *The Constancy of SUSANNA*, which recounts the famous Biblical tale: Susanna, wife of Joachim, is forced to take a stand against two lecherous elders of Babylon who first make a pass at her, and then, angered by her resistance, accuse her falsely of committing adultery with another man.[31] The opening verses run,

[28] Geoffrey Chaucer, *The Canterbury Tales*, ed. Jill Mann (2005), 336; *The ANCIENT, True, and Admirable History of Patient Grisel* (1619), C4v.

[29] So said Sir Robert Cotton, quoted in Hyder Rollins, 'The Black-Letter Broadside Ballad', *Publications of the Modern Language Association of America*, 34 (1919), 336.

[30] *The most Rare and Excellent History, Of the Dutchess of Suffolks Callamity* (c. 1592; F. Coles, T. Vere and J. Wright, 1663–74), EBBA 31743; *The Brides Buriall* (c. 1603; H. G., c. 1635), EBBA 30586. The tunes can be found in Simpson, *British Broadside Ballad*, on 588 and 368 respectively. See also *A Lamentable ballad of the tragical end of a Gallant Lord* (c. 1570; F. Coles, T. Vere and W. Gilbertson, 1658–64?), EBBA 31955, and *A most excellent Ballad, of an old man and his wife* (E. [A.], 1620), EBBA 20028.

[31] *The Constancy of SUSANNA* (c. 1562; W. Thackeray, J. Millet and A. Milbourn, 1689–92?), EBBA 33840. Constancy was a key virtue for ballad-women and, intriguingly, our 120 hit songs were much more likely to include the word 'constant' and/or related terms than were ballads in general. 'Constance' was also a fashionable girl's name in England during the seventeenth century, fading away in the decades after 1700 (www.ancestry.co.uk/).

There was a man in Babylon,
of reputation great by fame:
He took to wife a fair woman
Susanna was she cal'd by name:
A woman fair and vertuous,
Lady, Lady,
Why should not we of her learn thus,
To live godly.

Vertuously her life she led,
she feared God, she stood in awe,
As in the story you may read,
was well brought up in Moses Law,
Her parents they were godly folk,
Lady, Lady,
Why should we not then talk
Of this Lady.

The ballad-writer, working in the late sixteenth century, begins with a man of high status – Joachim – but then quickly abandons him in favour of his much more interesting wife. The author feels the need to justify his decision – 'Why should not we of her learn thus,/To live godly'? – but it was clearly a good one, and Susanna's song sold for centuries. Two hundred years after the ballad was composed, a Welsh fiddler, Alawon John Thomas, wrote into his notebook a tune called 'Susannah' which is recognizably a version of the Elizabethan melody.[32] The original ballad has Susanna at its heart, and the refrain – 'Lady, lady' – keeps her there, even when Daniel, sent by God, arrives to save her at the end.[33] Of course, it can be argued that Susanna's appeal lay partly in her capacity to titillate men – the woodcuts used by printers in the seventeenth century came to follow the greater artworks of the age in concentrating on the moment of attempted seduction and depicting Susanna as almost nude – but this was surely not enough to carry her song up the charts.[34] However we look at her, however we *listen* to her,

[32] *A Fiddler's Tune Book from Eighteenth-Century Wales*, ed. Cass Meurig (Aberystwyth, 2004), 127. I am grateful to Judith Marsh for bringing this source to my attention. For another version of the melody, see Simpson, *British Broadside Ballad*, 412. This interesting tune was Elizabethan and originally had romantic associations as a result of its connection with Elderton's song, *The panges of love*. Arguably, the ballad about Susanna was an unusually successful attempt to redirect these associations towards something more godly.

[33] This refrain also appears in the earlier ballad by Elderton (it was clearly the 'hook' in both songs, and playwrights regularly made reference to it).

[34] Compare the various editions that are included at http://ebba.english.ucsb.edu/. Artists who depicted Susanna and the elders included Ruben, Van Dyck and

Susanna is a long, long way from the scolding and lascivious wives who have tended to dominate the literature on balladry and gender.

Our final song is a little closer to the conventional view of ballad-marriages in that it discusses a relationship that is endangered by a difference of opinion between the wife and the husband. It will help to draw strings together and matters to a close. Martin Parker's *The Woman to the PLOW; And the Man to the HEN-ROOST* was printed repeatedly after its first appearance during the 1620s (Figure 4). Its status as a hit is also suggested by the survival of closely related narratives in later folk-song and by the prominent inclusion of its title in a fascinating medley – a coloured drawing that creates the illusion of an overlapping pile of printed papers – devised by Samuel Moore in the early eighteenth century.[35] In the song, a married couple criticise one another's work and decide to swap tasks, with results that are as disastrous as they are predictable:

As he to Churn the Butter went,
One morning with a good intent,
The Cot-quean fool did surely dream,
For he had quite forgot the Cream,
He churned all day, with all his might,
And yet he could get no Butter at night…

And shortly after on a day,
As she came home with a load of Hay,
She overthrew it, nay and worse,
She broke the Cart, and killd a Horse,
The good-man the same time had ill luck,
He let in the Sow, and she kil'd a Duck.

Here, there are clear points of contact with the types of ballad that have previously been highlighted by historians. Conflict is at its heart, as husband and wife clash over their proper economic roles and spheres of influence. The sexual inadequacy of the husband is not mentioned explicitly but it is alluded to in the label 'Cot-quean' – a man who busies himself with women's matters – and emphasised more strongly in a little woodcut of the man with horns. After its appearance here, this picture became one of the stock images for ballads about cuckoldry

Rembrandt. The scene was also used regularly in domestic wall-paintings, and many representations are listed in auction catalogues of the period.

[35] *The Woman to the PLOW* (F. Grove, *c.* 1629), EBBA 32024. Several versions of the tale, under names such as 'Father Grumble' and 'Old Dorrington', can be found by searching the various databases available at www.vwml.org/vwml-home. I am grateful to Tim Somers for bringing the medley to my attention: Samuel Moore, Medley (*c.* 1700), Victoria and Albert Museum, E.128–1944.

Figure 4 *The Woman to the PLOW* (edition of *c.* 1629) Euing Ballads, 397. By permission of the University of Glasgow Library, Special Collections.

in the decades that followed.[36] On *The Woman to the PLOW*, the picture implies that the husband can expect to be cuckolded, and probably that he deserves it, even if it has not happened yet. He is argumentative, calling his wife a 'whore' at the outset, but his empty masculine bluster merely masks his foolishness, and at the end he has no choice but to back down.

In other ways, however, this ballad – like most of the songs mentioned above – distinguishes itself from those typically highlighted by historians (and let us remember that this one was a major hit in its own time). We could not, for example, call it misogynistic or even desperately anxious, nor could we characterise it as obsessed with the notorious female vices.[37] Indeed, the wife is scarcely criticised at all and, by the end, the author's sympathies clearly lie with her (the pictures chosen to represent her are, by prior association, also more solidly positive than the male woodcuts). The sub-title implies that she must 'cure' her cotquean-husband, and she

[36] See, for example, *THE Hen-peckt CUCKOLD: OR, The Cross-grain'd Wife* (J. Millet, 1685?), EBBA 21793.

[37] Anthony Fletcher detects 'a misogynist streak' in ballads on male and female work but does not mention this extremely popular song (Fletcher, *Gender, Sex and Subordination*, 230).

does so primarily by tolerating his misguided intervention until he realises his mistake. And while the husband is scorned, he does nevertheless find his way out of the thicket in which he has entangled himself. The marriage is in trouble but the problem is eventually solved; we can therefore see this as a companionate relationship in which wife and husband, working together by working apart, prove capable of managing their difficulties (of course, there is now plenty of work to suggest that the 'separate spheres' model deployed in the ballad bore only a passing resemblance to the daily experiences of most people).[38] The role models are eventually and essentially positive, as in most of the ballads surveyed above, and these super-successful songs display a notable preoccupation with the resolution of crisis through interpersonal reconciliation. The fact that the female role model in this particular ballad is the more positive of the two may tell us something about the core audience for the song. Although it begins, 'Both Men and Women listen well', there is a sense in which Parker appears to aim particularly at female consumers, allowing and encouraging them to laugh at their interfering husbands. Female and male labour are accorded equal value, and it is the wife who earns praise for quietly sorting out her foolish man. Other wives with interfering husbands are advised 'To serve them as this Woman did' (there is a nice ambiguity to the term 'serve' here). Perhaps the title of the lost tune provides another clue: 'I have for all good wives a song'.

This suggestion deserves development. We have very little concrete evidence about gendered patterns of ballad-consumption, and all propositions must therefore be tentative, but it does seem probable that many of the ballads discussed above were aimed primarily at and consumed primarily by women. There is anecdotal literary evidence to suggest that women loved ballads, perhaps even more than men did. As early as 1584, the publisher of a collection of ballads assured potential readers, 'Here may you have such pretie thinges,/ as women much desire'. Ballads, said John Earle a few decades later, were 'chanted from market to market, to a vile tune and a worse throat; whilst the poor country wench melts like her butter to hear them'.[39] Women

---

[38] See, for example, Amanda Flather, *Gender and Space in Early Modern England* (Woodbridge, 2007), 43–50, and 'Space, Place and Gender: the Sexual and Spatial Division of Labour in the Early-Modern Household', *History and Theory*, 52 (2013), 344–60; Gowing, *Domestic Dangers*, 5–6, 26, and '"The Freedom of the Streets": Women and Social Space, 1560–1640', in *Londinopolis. Essays in the Cultural and Social History of Early-Modern London*, ed. Paul Griffiths and Mark S. R. Jenner (Manchester, 2000), 134–5, 137–8.

[39] Clement Robinson, *A Handfull of pleasant delites* (1584), A1r; John Earle, *Micro-cosmographie* (1628), B61. Several suggestive sources are gathered together in Würzbach, *Rise of the English Street Ballad*, 263–4, 266, 275, 278, 279, 280–2. On female consumers of balladry, see also Sarah F. Williams, 'Witches, Lamenting Women, and Cautionary Tales: Tracing "The

were sometimes said to have a particular taste for love-ballads. We might be tempted to dismiss this as a male slur designed to imply female frivolity, but Margaret Cavendish agreed, commenting in one letter that ballads were properly the music of spinsters and housewives in company on a winter evening. Other evidence suggests the role played by women in selling ballads.[40] Furthermore, references within our twenty-five songs seem to suggest that the ballad-makers, most of whom were male, often had female consumers firmly in mind. The songs contain forty direct appeals to either women or men, and three-quarters of these favour females: ballads are aimed at 'dainty dames', 'You maidens', 'English women', 'maid and wife' and so on. Of the eighteen titles that highlight either male or female characters, fourteen choose women and only four pick men. And ballad-makers were also far more willing than we might have imagined to flatter female characters: the ten adjectives applied most frequently to women in our twenty-five hit marriage-ballads included 'fair', 'comely', 'sweet', 'bright', 'good' and 'virtuous', and only one term – 'wanton' – was clearly pejorative (and thirteen of its seventeen appearances occurred in a single song).[41] This begins to look rather like a negotiation between male didacticism and female taste, with female taste more than holding its own. It calls to mind the evidence assembled by Jacqueline Pearson to show how female theatre-goers influenced the content of male-authored plays in the later seventeenth century.[42] In the case of balladry, there emerges from the negotiation a set of songs that emphasise the female side of marriage, presenting wives whose conventional femininity is either strong, spirited and admirable or wayward but deserving of sympathy. Male authors and publishers – promoters of 'transvestite ventriloquism', to use Elizabeth Harvey's phrase – were, of course, aiming to shape female opinion, but if they wanted to make money they also needed to let female opinion shape their products.[43] We might note, in passing, a wealth of theoretical work on 'active audiences' for modern pop music

Ladies Fall" in Early Modern English Broadside Balladry and Song', in *Gender and Song in Early Modern England*, ed. Leslie C. Dunn and Katherine R. Larson (Farnham, 2014), 31–46; Clark, 'The Broadside Ballad and the Woman's Voice'; Pamela Brown, *Better a Shrew than a Sheep. Women, Drama and the Culture of Jest in Early-Modern England* (Ithaca, 2003), 90.

[40] Margaret Cavendish, *CCXI Sociable Letters* (1664), 429. See also Clark, 'The Broadside Ballad and the Woman's Voice', 103. The female ballad-singers who feature regularly in the artistic output of William Hogarth are discussed in Elizabeth Kathleen Mitchell, 'William Hogarth's Pregnant Ballad Sellers and the Engraver's Matrix', in *Ballads and Broadsides*, ed. Fumerton and Guerrini, 229–50.

[41] *The Woful Lamentation of Mistris Jane Shore.*

[42] Jacqueline Pearson, *The Prostituted Muse: Images of Women and Women Dramatists 1642–1737* (New York, 1988), 33–41.

[43] Elizabeth D. Harvey, *Ventriloquized Voices. Feminist Theory and English Renaissance Texts* (1992), 1, 16.

and other cultural forms. As consumers, we are capable of making products our own not just by purchasing them but by doing our own thing with them once they are in our hands or our heads; we can receive, re-jig or reject the messages towards which the creators may have aimed to guide us.[44]

It seems certain that these ballads were successful partly because they allowed and encouraged women to take them on, take them over and breathe new life into them. All sorts of escapes into fantasy-worlds were possible through reading and singing, and all sorts of personal re-imaginings too. The woman who inhabited one of our ballads could pass comment, discreetly, on her own marriage and the marriages of others, or she could travel as far from her own daily life as possible. These possibilities fit well with recent work emphasising the influence of female singers over the content of Thomas Campion's ayres and the importance of women's musical voices more generally.[45] Judith Bennett has used late medieval song to argue that it helped women to 'negotiate the contradictions and complexities of…patriarchy'. Katie Barclay, writing about early nineteenth-century Scotland, has shown how the ballad-repertoires of female singers differed from those of their male counterparts, partly because men and women memorised contrasting verses from the same song, resulting in versions that had distinctive and gendered emphases.[46] Throughout these centuries, women somehow found their voices through the words of men, and male composers knew that it made good sense to facilitate this process. In the estimation of Sandra Clark, ballad-writers in particular were 'as concerned to address women's concerns as men's'.[47]

Other categories of early modern ballads may have catered more to male audiences. The most clearly political of our hit ballads, for

---

[44] There is a useful overview in Keith Negus, *Popular Music in Theory* (Cambridge, 1996), ch. 1. See also David Morley, 'Active Audience Theory. Pendulums and Pitfalls', *Journal of Communication*, 43 (1993), 13–19; *The Audience Studies Reader*, ed. Will Brooker and Deborah Jermyn (2003); Jim Huimin, 'British Cultural Studies, Active Audiences and the Status of Cultural Theory', *Theory, Culture and Society*, 28 (2011), 124–44.

[45] Scott Trudell, 'Performing Women in English Books of Ayres', in *Gender and Song in Early Modern England*, ed. Dunn and Larson, 15–29; *Musical Voices of Early Modern Women. Many-Headed Melodies*, ed. Thomasin LaMay (Farnham, 2005); Lynda Phyllis Austern, 'Women's Musical Voices in Sixteenth-Century England', *Early Modern Women*, 3 (2008), 127–52.

[46] Judith M. Bennett, 'Ventriloquisms. When Maidens Speak in English Songs, *c.* 1300–1550', in *Medieval Woman's Song. Cross-Cultural Approaches*, ed. Anne L. Klinck and Ann Marie Rasmussen (Philadelphia, 2002), 201; Katie Barclay, '"And Four years space, being man and wife, they Loveingly agreed": Balladry and the Early Modern Understandings of Marriage', in *Finding the Family in Medieval and Early Modern Scotland*, ed. Elizabeth Ewan and Janay Nugent (Aldershot, 2008), 30–3.

[47] Clark, 'The Broadside Ballad and the Woman's Voice', 110.

example, seem to mention women much less frequently and much less positively than the marriage-ballads.[48] We might also need to include within the 'predominantly male' category those ballads – highlighted by historians and mentioned at the outset – in which wives are sexually driven, power-hungry scolds and husbands are under pressure to assert their authority. There *were* many such ballads but, a little strangely, they hardly feature on our list. This too may imply the economic power of the female consumer, and it suggests that the time has come for historians of balladry and marriage to think less about *Cuckolds Haven* and more about *The Constancy of SUSANNA*. Just for the record, there is one extant copy of the former but sixteen of the latter.

---

[48] There are no women, for example, in the immensely successful song, *Win at First, Lose at Last: Or, A New game at CARDS* (1660; F. Cole, T. Vere, J. Wright, J. Clark and T Passinger, *c.* 1682), EBBA 20818.

Transactions of the RHS 28 (2018), pp. 89–106 © Royal Historical Society 2018
doi:10.1017/S0080440118000051

SACRED LANDSCAPES, SPIRITUAL TRAVEL: EMBODIED HOLINESS AND LONG-DISTANCE PILGRIMAGE IN THE CATHOLIC REFORMATION

By Elizabeth Tingle

READ 21 APRIL 2017

AT THE UNIVERSITY OF CHESTER

ABSTRACT. Long regarded as a medieval tradition which declined into insignificance after Luther, pilgrimage expanded considerably from the mid-sixteenth century, until well after 1750. This paper examines long-distance journeys to shrines, rather than sacred sites themselves, to explore how landscapes travelled were perceived, experienced and used by pilgrims in the Counter-Reformation. Using theory such as phenomenology, the focus is on autobiographical accounts of pilgrimages to two case-study sites, the Mont Saint-Michel in Normandy, northern France, and Santiago de Compostela in Galicia, north-west Spain, roughly between 1580 and 1750. These were shrines with origins in the early medieval period and which attracted a clientele over long distances. These pilgrimages were also in some way affected by religious conflict in the sixteenth century, whether by direct attack by Huguenots as at the Mont, or by war-time disruptions of its routes as with Compostela, as well as the theological and polemical attacks on the practice of pilgrimage itself by Protestant authors. Pilgrimage studies have examined 'place' – the shrine – but a focus on 'landscape' allows for a consideration of wider religious and cultural contexts, relations and experiences in this period of religious change.

In 1604, the Jesuit Louis Richeome described the purpose of pilgrimage in *The Pilgrim of Loreto*:

All men have always been and remain, pilgrims and travellers on the earth...and those to whom we give the special term 'Pilgrim', travelling towards a specific destination in the world...are no more than ordinary men, unless they intentionally do more. For all mortals walk by necessity towards the grave, but if they are wise pilgrims, they direct themselves towards the heavenly kingdom.[1]

---

[1] Louis Richeome, 'Le pèlerin de Lorète', in *Les oeuvres du R. Père Richeome* (2 vols., Paris, 1628), I, 215.

In simpler terms, the *Dictionnaire universelle* of 1690 defined pilgrimage as 'a journey of devotion' while later reference works described a pilgrim as one 'who, out of piety, journeys to a place of devotion'.[2] Throughout, the emphasis was on travel. The destination could be physical – a place – but also spiritual, the attainment of grace. Pilgrimage was thus intimately bound to journey and ultimately to the landscape in which this occurred. While studies of both pilgrimage and landscape have flourished in the last two decades, their connections have attracted less attention. While there has been significant interest in place-based spiritual experiences, there has been relatively little interrogation of the relationship between sacred places, their landscape aesthetics and accounts of spiritual experience.[3] In this paper, the relationship between journeys of devotion and the physical environment will be examined, in an exploration of the impact of the Reformations on European Catholic perceptions of religious space.

For as long as we can ascertain, humanity's search for the sacred was frequently connected to physical sites, whether a temple, shrine or natural feature. In his work of 1959, *The Sacred and the Profane*, Mircea Eliade proposed that the sacred was defined by space and time.[4] From the 1960s onwards, anthropologists and historians developed this paradigm to define sacred space 'as an essential category of human experience' which, as Eric Nelson writes, 'emerges and persists as both an experienced physical location and an imagined set of cognitive associations'.[5] Historians of the Reformations have paid particular attention to the concept of sacred space, for it had an important role in the shaping, defining and contesting of religious identity. How God operated in the physical world – immanence – was one of the great questions of the Reformation, for the working of divine power in sacred places was contested. Protestants largely rejected sacred materiality and 'tended towards iconoclasm and asceticism as attempts to foreground the importance of immateriality to spirituality'.[6] Catholics, however, retained the belief that grace could work in special locations and through physical objects. The greatest expression of immanence was the real presence in the eucharist but also in saints' remains and holy places, whose

---

[2] Antoine Furetière, *Dictionnaire universelle* (3 vols., Paris, 1690), III, 85; for example, *Le dictionnaire de l'Académie Française*, 4th edn (2 vols., Paris, 1762), II, 338, which was widely copied.
[3] *Christian Pilgrimage, Landscape and Heritage: Journeying into the Sacred*, ed. V. della Dora, A. Maddrell, A. Scafi and H. Walton (2014), 1.
[4] Mircea Eliade, *The Sacred and the Profane. Nature of Religion*, trans. W. R. Trask (New York, 1959).
[5] Eric Nelson, 'The Parish in its Landscape: Pilgrimage Processions in the Archdeaconry of Blois, 1500–1700', *French History*, 24 (2010), 320.
[6] Daniel Miller, *Stuff* (Cambridge, 2010), 71.

efficacy was reaffirmed by the Council of Trent in 1563.[7] In the Counter-Reformation, therefore, shrines were rebuilt and embellished, cults restored and defended and landscapes of sacrality were revived and refined. Pilgrimage reemerged across Catholic Europe as a marker of revived religious confidence and an overt statement of orthodoxy in the face of Protestant attacks.

Long regarded as a medieval tradition which declined into insignificance after Luther, religious travel in fact expanded considerably from the mid-sixteenth century, until well after 1750. Many shrines were small, attracting a local clientele but the great pilgrimages of the Middle Ages also revived: Rome and its satellite Loreto, Einsiedeln, Altötting, Puy-en-Vélay, Montserrat, Santiago de Compostela and others. According to Joe Bergin, there reemerged a 'complex, interlocking geography of national, provincial and local sites of devotion and pilgrimage'.[8] This paper will examine long-distance journeys to shrines, rather than sacred sites themselves, to explore how these were perceived, experienced and used by pilgrims in the Counter-Reformation. Shrines themselves will not be examined. The focus will be on two case-studies, pilgrimages to the Mont Saint-Michel in Normandy, northern France, and Santiago de Compostela in Galicia, north-west Spain, roughly between 1580 and 1750. These were sites with origins in the early medieval period and which attracted a clientele over long distances. These pilgrimages were also in some way affected by religious conflict in the sixteenth century, whether by direct attack by Huguenots as at the Mont, or by war-time disruptions of its routes as with Compostela, as well as the theological and polemical attacks on the practice of pilgrimage itself by Protestant authors. Pilgrimage studies have been attentive to 'place' – the shrine – as 'a material site of meaning-making, representation and experience', but while place, particularly notions of sacred place, is significant, a focus on 'landscape' allows a consideration of wider contexts, relations and experiences in this period of religious change.[9]

Recently, the process of journeying to and from holy sites, the landscape aesthetics of pilgrims and their spiritual experiences have been examined by anthropologists studying contemporary movements, from the Hajj to the Camino in Spain.[10] The pilgrim route, destination shrine and their wider landscapes are often deeply inter-twined as part

---

[7] Session XXV of 3–4 Dec. 1563. *Decrees of the Ecumenical Councils*, ed. Norman Tanner (2 vols., London and Washington, DC, 1990), II, 796–7.

[8] Joe Bergin, *Church, Society and Religious Change in France 1580–1730* (New Haven and London, 2009), 246–8.

[9] *Christian Pilgrimage, Landscape and Heritage*, ed. della Dora, Maddrell, Scafi and Walton, 5–6.

[10] *Reframing Pilgrimage. Cultures in Motion*, ed. Simon Coleman and John Eade (2004), 5.

of the pilgrim experience.[11] Simon Coleman and John Eade argue that various forms of motion – embodied, imagined, metaphorical – are constitutive elements of many pilgrimages, for 'in certain cases…mobile performances can help to construct – however temporarily – apparently sacredly charged places'.[12] The performance of journeying and the body-centred experience of movement has been a key element of research in many social sciences, a result of the influence of theorists such as Michel Foucault for whom the body was central to the modern system of discipline and control, and of anthropology with its interest in the ritual, symbolic and classificatory roles of the body.[13] Thus, the body has been interpreted as an 'effect of deeper structural arrangements of power and knowledge' and 'a symbolic system which produces a set of metaphors by which power is conceptualised'.[14] Movement of the body is 'a performative action consciously and unconsciously effecting social and cultural transformations'.[15] Pilgrimage provides the catalyst for certain kinds of bodily experiences in a ritual framework of movement, a performance of acts linking the individual to the sacred. Scholars have sought to reappreciate the visual and material agencies in landscape in shaping subjectivities and geographical imaginations; landscapes are not blank canvases but complex textures, '"speaking back" to the beholder staring at or traversing it'.[16] However, most anthropologies of journeys and landscapes use living subjects and witnesses. Reconstructing the perception and experiences of the post-medieval Jacquelot on one of the French routeways to Compostela or the Miquelot journeying across Normandy to the Avranches coastline is more of a challenge.

A key theoretical and methodological tool for understanding the relationship between human and landscape has been that of phenomenology. As Chris Tilley writes,

> knowledge of landscapes, either past or present, is gained through perceptual experience of them from the point of view of the subject…The objective is to describe a rich or 'thick' description, allowing others to comprehend these landscapes in their nuanced diversity and complexity and to enter into these experiences through their metaphorical textual mediation.[17]

[11] *Christian Pilgrimage, Landscape and Heritage*, ed. della Dora, Maddrell, Scafi and Walton, 1.
[12] *Reframing Pilgrimage*, ed. Coleman and Eade, 1.
[13] Michel Foucault, *Discipline and Punish: The Birth of the Prison*, trans. Alan Sheridan (1977); Michel Foucault, *A History of Sexuality*, 1: *An Introduction*, trans. Robert Hurley (1979).
[14] Bryan S. Turner, 'The body in Western society: social theory and its perspectives', in *Religion and the Body*, ed. Sarah Coakley (Cambridge, 1997), 15–16.
[15] *Reframing Pilgrimage*, ed. Coleman and Eade, 16; see also John Urry, *Sociology beyond Societies: Mobilities for the Twenty-First Century* (2000).
[16] *Christian Pilgrimage, Landscape and Heritage*, ed. della Dora, Maddrell, Scafi and Walton, 7.
[17] Christopher Tilley, *Interpreting Landscapes. Geologies, Topographies, Identities*, Explorations in Landscape Phenomenology 3 (Walnut Creek, CA, 2010), 25.

Embodiment is a central term here. Experience of landscape is one 'that takes place through the medium of his or her sensing and sensed carnal body'.[18] The researcher 'enters into the landscape and allows it to have its own effect on his or her perceptive understanding. This approach means accepting that there is a dialogic relationship between person and landscape.'[19] Of course, this subjective methodology is riven with hazards when related to living humans whose opinions can be asked; for past societies, it has huge problems, not least of anachronism. However, if we look at landscape phenomenologically through the auto-biographical accounts of sixteenth- and seventeenth-century pilgrims, the primary source basis for this paper, we do learn something of their priorities and interests. We can see that 'the landscape is both iconic and a central spiritual resource in its own right' for it combines 'visual spectacle, cultural interest and embodied experience'.[20] Thus seen, 'landscape and its landforms are...not mere blank canvasses passively imprinted with meanings, but complex textures "speaking back" to the beholder staring at or traversing it'.[21] Both the landscapes themselves and their meanings to contemporaries also changed over time.

I The landscape of religious travel

Of the natural landscape itself, pilgrims make few observations and there was little change over time in this absence of description. The overwhelming sense from pilgrim writers – in contrast to some other travellers, who might admire a view, for example – is that of incon-venience, hazard, barrier and danger, that of the sublime in the ori-ginal sense of the word. The landscape throws up obstacles to overcome, to reach the holy destination. Indeed, the more a place showed itself to be wild, the more grace was bestowed on the pilgrim for the arduous journey.[22] For pilgrims to the Mont Saint-Michel, the island/promontory was 'La Merveille', an architecture marvel built on a rock in one night by angels, but its tidal access made it treacherous to approach. Jacques-August de Thou described the Mont in these terms in 1580:

one must be surprised that from a sterile desert, far from all commerce, with access so difficult that one can hardly approach it by boat even when it is bathed by the sea, that

---

[18] *Ibid.*, p. 25.
[19] *Ibid.*, p. 26.
[20] *Christian Pilgrimage, Landscape and Heritage*, ed. della Dora, Maddrell, Scafi and Walton, 1.
[21] *Ibid.*, 6–7.
[22] S. Germain de Franceschi, *D'encre et de poussière: l'écriture du pèlerinage à l'épreuve de l'intimité du manuscrit* (Paris, 2010), 293.

the faith of our ancestors made such a marvellous place, and that they overcame such obstacles and difficulties.[23]

Claude Haton remarked that pilgrims travelled from the mainland to the Mont led by a local guide, a necessity for visitors who were unfamiliar with the shifting sands and the sea.[24] The tides were treacherous. A mid-seventeenth-century Breton pilgrim, Pierre Le Gouvello, went over the sands without a guide and got caught by the incoming sea. He managed to swim to safety and thereafter recited forty Ave Marias daily in honour of St Michael.[25] An eighteenth-century English visitor, William Wraxall, saw 'in the churchyard of Genet, a grave where 5 persons were interred, who perished within these few days, and similar accidents are common'.[26]

The Compostelan pilgrim had high mountains and rivers to cross and the journey generally lasted several months rather than days or weeks. Again, sublime landscape observations prevail. The Italian priest Domenico Laffi from Bologna travelling in the 1660s described the Alpine foothills between Cesara and Montgenièvre in France as

> extremely dangerous. One goes between great crags and sheer rock faces which by the look of them are about to fall. The ravine is about two leagues long and strikes terror in everyone, because of the many who have been killed by avalanches and broken fragments that are continually falling from the mountains.[27]

The climb through the Pyrenean pass was also frightening: after St Jean Pied de Port:

> We walked all the while between precipitous mountains, which are terrifying just to look at. They seemed as if they were always about to fall on top of you. Night fell while we were still among these precipices...We kept on climbing the very high and rugged hills for a stretch of seven leagues. It was a frightening and dangerous journey. In the end, with the help of God and St James of Galicia we reached the very top of the Pyrenees...There is a small very old chapel here. We went in – there are neither doors nor windows that can be closed – and sang the Te Deum Laudamus, to give thanks to God for having brought us here safe and sound, in his infinite mercy.[28]

Laffi calls the Paradise Bridge near to Burguete in Spain the bridge of Hell, for 'it spans a big, deep river that runs between two high hills... the water, though it is clear, in fact looks black. It is so fast-flowing

[23] 'Mémoires de Jacques-Auguste de Thou depuis 1553 jusqu'en 1601', in *Choix de chroniques et mémoires sur l'histoire de France*, ed. J. A. C. Buchon (Paris, 1836), 590.

[24] *Mémoires de Claude Haton*, ed. Félix Bourquelot (Paris, 1858), 895.

[25] Hyppolite Le Gouvello, *Vie du pénitent breton Pierre Le Gouvello de Kériolet* (Paris, 1890; repr. 1996), 57.

[26] N. Wraxall, *A Tour through the Western, Southern and Interior Provinces of France in a Series of Letters* (Dublin, 1786), 37.

[27] Domenico Laffi, *A Journey to the West. The Diary of a Seventeenth-Century Pilgrim from Bologna to Santiago to Compostela*, trans. James Hall (Leiden, 1997), 45.

[28] *Ibid.*, 94.

that it fills the traveller with fear and trembling. The bridge is guarded by soldiers better described as thieves and murders' and in fact Domenico was so frightened by their manner that he ran for a league after leaving the bridge.[29] Jean Bonnecaze, travelling from Pardies in Béarn in the early eighteenth century, was forced to lay up at the abbey of Roncevalles for two nights because of snow; when he went on his way, the snow was still knee deep, until he got into the lowlands.[30] In New Castile, again the weather not the landscape was memorable: constant rain soaked Bonnecaze to the skin, every day for almost a month.[31] Good landscapes were agrarian and tamed: Laffi describes approaching Avignon, with 'a beautiful, flat, countryside where there are trees bearing every kind of fruit' while that of the Béziers region was 'truly beautiful, growing every kind of fruit and cereals'.[32] Fruitful nature, not wild landscape, was approved. The model of the Via crucis – the way of the Cross, in imitation of Christ – was everywhere else.

Some pilgrims died en route. The parish registers of the diocese of Le Mans contain numerous references to pilgrims who died on the journey to and from the shrines of Saint-Méen near to Rennes and that of the Mont Saint-Michel. In 1677, the parish register of Cuillé records the death and burial of Julien Le Ray, returning with his wife from the shrine at Saint-Méen to their home at Saint-Sulpice on the Loire.[33] On 29 August 1679, a poor pilgrim called René Trouain died of a 'virulent malady' in the barn of Jean Ferre in La Roë parish, Ferre having permitted the sick man to sleep there. In Trouain's pocket, the parish priest of La Roë found certificates from the parish priest of La Couture in the Vendée and from one of the priests of the Congregation of the Mission of Saint-Méen, who attested to Le Ray's having taken communion on 16 July. After the burial, the priest of La Roë sent the certificates to the priest of La Couture, to inform the community of the man's death.[34] In 1709, the parish priest of Colombiers-du-Plessis recorded the death and burial of Benoist Simon, aged thirteen to fourteen years old, travelling with another boy Louis Obouyer, returning from the Mont to their homes in Saint-Maurice,

---

[29] *Ibid.*, 113.
[30] N. de Caumont, G. Manier and J. Bonnecaze, *Chemins de Compostelle, Trois récits de pèlerins 1417–1726–1748*, ed. Valérie Dumeige (Paris, 2009), 175.
[31] *Ibid.*, 174.
[32] Laffi, *A Journey to the West*, 49, 67, 69
[33] Archives Départementales (AD) de la Mayenne, parish register Cuillé E dépôt 204/ E7 1677, www.archinoe.fr/cg53/visualiseur/visu_etatcivil.php?id=530002805&PHPSID= aoffbb6763ba8dfe153b5ffdfbd18ae4&w=1366&h=768.
[34] AD Mayenne, parish register La Roë, Mairie 1679, www.archinoe.fr/cg53/visualiseur/ visu_etatcivil.php?id=530006409&PHPSID=aoffbb6763ba8dfe153b5ffdfbd18ae4&w=1366& h=768.

Burgundy.[35] The landscape was perceived, often justifiably, to be a realm of hardship and danger. The shrine was the destination and the journey had to be endured to reach this goal. This was a landscape perception that persisted among pilgrims even when sightseeing travellers began to view the natural world in different terms in the eighteenth century.

The landscape recorded by pilgrims was above all a human landscape and its most frequently noted feature was the landscape of hospitality: where and how they obtained sleep, food and drink. Many of the classic guides of the Compostelan pilgrimage are little more than itineraries of roads and overnight stays. Among the most notable features of the Camino of the later Middle Ages was the network of pilgrims' hostels provided by religious houses, confraternities and wealthy donors, providing a landscape of support for the modest or pious middling-sort traveller. The same was true of other long-distance routeways as well. By the later sixteenth century, in France, this tradition had begun to decay, a result of the depredations of the religious wars and economic problems reducing the financial support of these establishments. For example, at Pons, the *hôpital neuf* was one of the main hostels between Tours and Bordeaux and like many such establishments, combined care of the poor sick with hospitality for pilgrims. It was located in the southern suburb of the town, with the hospital accommodation built immediately on the west side of the road and a chapel on the east side, linked by a vaulted arch that spanned the route to Compostela. By the early sixteenth century, its buildings were in bad repair. In 1534, the *parlement* of Bordeaux ordered that the administration of its revenues should be taken over by competent officers. Subsequently, its administration was handed over to the knights of St John of Jerusalem, as a declaration of the prior Marc Gillier in 1547 shows. The wars of religion were severe in the region of the Saintonge, however, and in 1568–9 Pons was besieged and the hospital badly damaged, losing its roof. Pilgrimage slowed in the region in these years, because of violence and insecurity on the roads.[36]

There was some restitution of French accommodation and support in the first half of the seventeenth century. In Pons in 1605, the pilgrim hospital was repaired and a new bell installed, financed by Antoinette de Pons, the local seigneur.[37] In an inventory of 1676, the hospital is

[35] AD Mayenne, parish register Colombiers-du-Plessis E dépôt 52/E13 1709, www.archinoe. fr/cg53/visualiseur/visu_etatcivil.php?id=530002213&PHPSID=a0ffbb6763ba8dfe153b 5ffdfbd18ae4&w=1366&h=768.

[36] AD Charente-Maritime H supplément 184 L'Hôpital Neuf de Pons; Pascal Even, 'L'Hôpital Neuf de Pons', in *Saint Jacques et la France*, ed. Adeline Rucquoi (Paris, 2003), 492–5.

[37] AD Charente-Maritime H supplément 184 L'Hôpital Neuf de Pons.

recorded as having fourteen beds for pilgrims in the great hall and a further three in a little side room for women and girls; upstairs, there were two beds reserved for clergy pilgrims.[38] In 1617, the duke d'Épernon founded a hospital in Cadillac, dedicated to St Marguerite in honour of his wife, with twelve beds for the sick in one section and in another, six beds for passing poor pilgrims, who would also be given bread, wine and warmth for a maximum of two nights.[39] The hospital of Saint-Jacques in Paris was receiving pilgrims until 1672, when it transferred its functions to Saint-Gervais.[40] In Bordeaux, the Jesuits took over administration of the hospital of St James in the 1570s, overseeing its function as a foundling and pilgrim hostel. They replaced the priests of the former collegiate foundation with a lay hospitaller and a porter and put the finances on a sounder footing.[41] In 1567–8, the income had been 1,500 livres and the expenditure 2,136 livres; accounts are patchy but in 1601 the income had risen to 4,634 livres of which only 360 livres was used for pilgrims, the rest for the other functions of the hospital. The hospital in Bordeaux was active into the later seventeenth century, recording an annual average of 4,021 pilgrims for the years 1666–9.[42] In 1673, there were sixteen beds, 'all cleanly kept' and the linen comprised eighty sheets and a hundred towels, 'the said linen all bleached and cleanly maintained'.[43] In the same period, the hospice of Saint-Jacques de Rodez was receiving about 2,000 pilgrims a year.[44] But in the reign of Louis XIV, the crown and city governments rationalised local hospital provision and poor relief, reducing institutional support for pilgrims as a result.[45] Also, laws of 1671 and 1687 forbade the pilgrimage to Compostela or anywhere outside of the kingdom, without permission of a secretary of state counter-signed by a bishop. This slowed pilgrimage through France.

In Spain, conversely, the dense provision of hostels and convents providing accommodation was maintained into the eighteenth century,

[38] AD Charente-Maritime H supplément 185 L'Hôpital Neuf de Pons.

[39] P. Barret and J.-N. Gurgand, *Priez pour nous à Compostelle. La vie des pèlerins sur les chemins de Saint-Jacques* (Paris, 1978), 162.

[40] Guillaume Manier, *Pèlerinage d'un paysan picard à Saint-Jacques de Compostelle au commencement du XVIIIe siècle*, ed. Baron Bonnault d'Houët (Le Mesnil sur l'Estrées, repr. 2002), xvi.

[41] AD Gironde H non classé Jésuites Saint-James, H 2315 (3) Privilèges, droits etc.; Jean Cavignac, 'Un Hôpital doublement spécialisé: l'hôpital Saint-James de Bordeaux (1564–1660)', *Actes du 97 Congrès national des sociétés savantes, Nantes, 1972, section philosophie et histoire* (Paris, 1977), 199–200.

[42] AD Gironde H non classé Jésuites Saint-James, H 2315 (3).

[43] AD Gironde H non classé Jésuites Saint-James, H 2317 Novices, Pèlerins.

[44] Barret and Gurgand, *Priez pour nous à Compostelle*, 168.

[45] Dominique Julia, 'Pour une géographie européenne du pèlerinage à l'époque moderne et contemporaine', in *Pèlerins et pèlerinages dans l'Europe moderne*, ed. Philippe Boutry and Dominique Julia (Rome, 2000), 34.

although its quality varied. We get a sense of the variety and importance of the landscape of hospitality on the Camino in the account of Guillaume Manier, an early eighteenth-century pilgrim from Picardy. Manier stayed in a few pilgrims' hostels in France, mostly in the larger cities: Paris, Pons, Bordeaux and one night sleeping in the old, ruined hostel of Ingrandes.[46] In Spain, the formal landscape of hostels was better, at least in the lowlands: Manier spent most nights here in monastery guest houses and pilgrim hospices: Santo Domingo, Burgos, Hontanas and Laôn, and on the return journey, Oviedo, Madrid, Pamplona and Roncevalles.[47] Castrojeriz had six hostels in the early modern period, each catering for a specific demographic; for example, that of San Juan took men only, for whom it had six beds, three for paupers and three for pilgrims.[48] The Hostal Real of Santiago de Compostela took fewer pilgrims and more sick and poor Galicians as the seventeenth century progressed, but even at the end of the century it was a favoured destination for many. Of the members of the confraternity of St James of Mâcon who recorded their journey in their register in 1716, one quarter stayed in the Hostal Real.[49] The quality of hostel accommodation was often poor by the eighteenth century, however. Bonnecaze stayed at Silheiro hostel, which he described as 'miserable' and in the Augustinian hostel of Laôn – where he had good care for a fever he contracted – he spent a night in a bed between three dead men, who died of an epidemic ravaging the hospital.[50] There remained in Spain a greater sense of the importance of charity to travellers, but the means with which they were supported clearly declined.

Just as important for pilgrim travellers were inns and accommodation in private houses. The Three Queens at Monarville, south of Paris, and the Saint-Jacques at Bayonne, for example, were important staging posts for pilgrims, where fellow-travellers could exchange information and form groups for part of the journey.[51] But for modest pilgrims such as Manier, private hospitality, in cottages and farms, for a few sous a night, was vital. For example, between 4 and 7 September, Manier slept in a barn near Notre-Dame de Cléry, at a farm near Chambord and at a farm, on straw, at Mantlan, outside of Blois.[52] In October, he records having slept in a stable, on bracken and on boards, in different

---

[46] Manier, *Pèlerinage d'un paysan picard*, 6, 23, 34.

[47] *Ibid.*, 59, 142–4.

[48] Julie Candy, *The Archaeology of Pilgrimage on the Camino de Santiago de Compostela. A Landscape Perspective*, BAR International Series 1948 (Oxford, 2009), 98.

[49] Georges Provost, 'Les pèlerins accueillis à l'hôpital real de Saint-Jacques', in *Pèlerins et pèlerinages dans l'Europe moderne*, ed. Boutry and Julia, 130.

[50] Caumont, Manier and Bonnecaze, *Chemins de Compostelle*, 177.

[51] Manier, *Pèlerinage d'un paysan picard*, 17, 43.

[52] *Ibid.*, 16, 19, 27.

villages in south-west France.[53] In Spain, informal hospitality was also important, despite the greater number of hostels, particularly in the mountains. Jean Bonnecaze relates how he spent a night sleeping in a muddy barrel, paying three sous for a rack to keep him out of the wet.[54] Food as charitable alms was also available in many larger communities. Laffi noted in the 1670s that most towns in southern France gave out the *passado* to pilgrims, usually in the form of bread and wine, and that this continued in Spain.[55] The eighteenth-century Neapolitan pilgrim Nicola Albali, contrasted France and Spain: he was particularly struck by the organisation of food distribution to the poor and pilgrims in the larger Spanish towns.[56] Sleeping, eating, keeping warm and dry, the basics of human existence, made the institutions of hospitality the core landscape features of pilgrimage. The main change over time, in France more than Spain, was the increasing 'privatisation' of accommodation, as the old charitable foundations decayed under economic and political pressures.

Routeway markers were a feature of both the Compostelan and Montois pilgrim landscapes. Some were for practical assistance – to indicate the correct way – and others were markers of historical events, sacred and profane. The most frequently encountered marker was a cross, frequently of stone but also of wood. Philippa Woodcock has shown that the roads pilgrims took to the Mont through the county of Mayenne were marked by crosses and wayside chapels.[57] Pilgrims of a confraternity from Caen travelling to the Mont in 1634 noted that their trumpeter sounded his horn from time to time along the route, particularly before wayside crosses.[58] Thirty-three St James's crosses are known from the old diocese of Chartres.[59] Such crosses might have important social functions for pilgrims: in 1726, four young men from the Franche-Comté arrived at the village of Carlepont in Picardy, on their way to Compostela. The entrance to the village was marked by a cross called la Croix Minard; the pilgrims were received there by two of the leading inhabitants of the community with tambour and ensigns and given

---

[53] *Ibid.*, 43–5.

[54] Caumont, Manier and Bonnecaze, *Chemins de Compostelle*, 175.

[55] Laffi, *A Journey to the West*, 48.

[56] Dominique Julia, 'Curiosité, dévotion et politica peregrinesca. Le pèlerinage de Nicola Albani, melfitain, à Saint-Jacques de Compostelle (1743–45)', in *Rendre ses vœux: les identités pèlerines dans l'Europe modern (XVIe–XVIIIe siècles)*, ed. P. Boutry, P.-A. Favre and D. Julia (Paris, 2000), 281.

[57] Philippa Woodcock, pers. comm.

[58] Michel de Saint-Martin, *Le voyage fait au Mont Saint-Michel (en 1634) par la confrèrie de St-Pierre de Caen avec 22 ecclésiastiques et plusieurs habitants des autres paroisses, dont M. Pierrre de Rasivignan, fils ainé de M. de Chamboy, gouverneur de la ville et chasteau de Caen* (Caen, 1654), 428.

[59] Georges Provost, 'Identité paysanne et "pèlerinage au long cours" dans la France des XVII – XIX siècles', in *Rendre ses vœux*, ed. Boutry, Favre and Julia, 395.

hospitality.[60] Pilgrims might also begin their journeys at such crosses. For Bonnecaze, the most notable feature of the plain of Roncevalles was again man-made: here, legend stated that Roland and his knights were killed in battle with the Vasques and a large iron cross was erected there. Bonnecaze and his companions said prayers at the cross, for the souls of the Christians killed at that site.[61] Laffi also notes in Spain the creation of way markers. At Hornillos, it was easy to lose the way on the sandy plain, but pilgrims made cairns of stones by the side of the correct routes; likewise, in woods with multiple paths, pilgrims stripped the bark from trees to indicate the right way to pass.[62]

Another key feature of the landscape of long-distance pilgrimage was the encounter with sacred nodes, that is, shrines and sacred sites along the way, recharging the holy batteries of the pilgrims, making the journey a cumulative experience. The landscape of long-distance pilgrimage was not simply a routeway or a nodal system of hospitality, but it incorporated a great number of activities and a range of places that were considered important to visit, see and participate in, sacred places in their own rights. Effectively, long-distant pilgrimages were a linear series of pilgrimages, each shrine offering indulgences and other spiritual benefits that accumulated for the pilgrim, where s/he gave thanks for the journey thus far and took a 'sacral recharge' to help him or her along the way.[63] Andrew Spicer and Will Coster call these routeways 'veins of sacred force', with the chapels, shrines and wells erected along them acquiring their own status as holy ground.[64]

In France, the sixteenth-century religious wars saw the destruction of many shrines, greater and smaller, or their decay through lack of travellers' financial support. Between Pons and Blaye in south-west France, for example, there had been 'stations' at the abbey of Notre Dame de la Tenaille, which possessed nails from the crucifixion, and at the church of the abbey of Plein-Selve. Both of these were destroyed by Protestant forces and never restored.[65] There was, however, some resurgence in passage shrines after the religious wars had ended. Woodcock has found that the parish churches of Hambers and Bais, just off one of Mayenne's western routes to the Mont, underwent rebuilding in 1588 and 1612 respectively, marked with cockleshell decorations, perhaps to

---

[60] Manier, *Pèlerinage d'un paysan picard*, 1.

[61] Caumont, Manier and Bonnecaze, *Chemins de Compostelle*, 175.

[62] Laffi, *A Journey to the West*, 142.

[63] Julia, 'Curiosité, dévotion et politica peregrinesca. Le pèlerinage de Nicola Albani', 298.

[64] 'Introduction', in *Sacred Space in Early Modern Europe*, ed. Will Coster and Andrew Spicer (Cambridge, 2005), 9.

[65] Jean Glénisson, 'De Pons à Blaye, sur le chemin de Saint-Jacques', in *Saint Jacques et la France* (Paris, 2003), 469–84.

attract pilgrims off the route to visit chapels dedicated to St Michael.[66] In Spain, sites maintained their physical structures and there were clearly 'must-visit' places. Manier recounts devotions at the cathedral of Santo Domingo, where he heard the story of the innocent hanged and acquired some votive cockerel feathers; Burgos, where he visited the famous statute of Christ in the Augustinian convent and bought paper Christs, touched against the figure; the Augustinian convent of Oviedo, where he gained indulgences for touching relics and acquired two rosaries similarly touched to the sacred objects.[67] Pilgrims treated the landscape as one of 'stations' of religious observance, with the pilgrimage being a procession through a sacred space.

Travelling priests such as Laffi were anxious to find a church in which to say mass every day, and, indeed, the churches and altars where he celebrated made the pilgrimage special. When Laffi arrived in an episcopal city, he went straight to the bishop for a dimissory letter, for permission to celebrate mass in the diocese. Highlights of his pilgrimage were his saying mass in Milan, in the cathedral of Embrun, the church of the Trinitarians in heretic-dominated Montpellier, the cathedral of Pamplona; the altar of the Crucifix at the Augustinian convent of Burgos and Santiago itself.[68] Further, Laffi and his companions gained much from participating in local rites and ceremonies, when they happened upon them. So, they attended the public showing of the shroud of Turin as they passed through the city; they were guests at a wedding in Cesana and a funeral in Pontferrada; they participated in the Corpus Christi procession in Orthez and a Holy Sacrament procession in Logroño and received indulgences in Santo Domingo de la Calzada and San Juan de Ortea.[69] Pilgrims integrated themselves into the sacred landscape of their journey through physical presence in religious rites.

A marked feature of Counter-Reformation pilgrimage was the frequency with which all pilgrims, lay and clerical, participated in the sacraments along the route to the shrine. A pilgrimage of the confraternity of Saint-Michel of Caen to the Mont in 1634, led by the son of the royal governor of the city, was conceived of as such at least by one of the chaplains who wrote up the journey for publication. The company spent its first night in Villedieu, where their priests sang mass at the church of the commandery of St John; then Avranches, where the party sang None and Vespers in the cathedral, then in the abbey church of the Mont Saint-Michel itself. The return journey went via Coutances cathedral and mass; Saint-Lô, with prayers and mass in the church; Bayeux cathedral,

[66] P. Woodcock, pers. comm.
[67] Manier, *Pèlerinage d'un paysan picard*, 54, 59, 108, 112.
[68] Laffi, *A Journey to the West*, 137.
[69] *Ibid.*, 35, 93, 126, 131.

again with mass, then returning to Caen for a final Te Deum.[70] Nicola Albani's landscape of sacrality was marked by indulgence acquisition, confession and sacraments. Albani went to confession in the south of France whenever he encountered an Italian-speaking priest; in Spain, he confessed at Monserrat, Saragossa and Madrid, where again Italian confessors could be found, and at Compostela he undertook a general confession lasting for over four hours. In Albani's case, confession and eucharist were linked to his great interest in gaining indulgences, which he notes with satisfaction in his account of his travels.[71]

So, we can see from this exposition some of the physical landscape features which were important to early modern pilgrims on these northern routes. They were not so much of the natural world as that of humans, the framework of hospitality, route markers of the road-scape and a network of shrines and sacred places. This was a nodal landscape, where food for body and soul was sought and consumed at key locations. As Candy argues, 'by thinking about the body as an artefact and as the means by which to perceive and become involved with the world it becomes easier to visualise the connection between people and the material components of the shifting landscapes that they encounter and interact with'.[72] A pilgrimage incorporated a number of activities and a range of places that were considered important to visit, see and participate in.[73] A pilgrimage journey was a metaphysical, sacred landscape, one that shifted and changed with the material and devotional opportunities available to pilgrims, over time.

II The spiritual landscape of pilgrimage

The landscape of pilgrimage was much more than a physical experience of inns and shrines, rivers and mountains, however. The way in which the pilgrim interpreted and experienced these material sites was much less about their physicality and much more about their intellectual and spiritual context, that of the mental universe of the pilgrim him or herself. Phenomenology encourages us to think carefully about the physical landscape, its relationship with power structures, gender, social group and other factors, but it has a key methodological limitation: it is effectively present-centred, for it cannot reconstruct the thoughts of past people. What makes the pilgrim's journey holy and therefore a landscape sacred, is his/her understanding of it, not ours. In this, pilgrims

---

[70] Saint-Martin, *Le voyage fait au Mont Saint-Michel (en 1634)*.

[71] Julia, 'Curiosité, dévotion et politica peregrinesca. Le pèlerinage de Nicola Albani', 299, 301.

[72] Candy, *The Archaeology of Pilgrimage*, 17.

[73] *Ibid.*, 22.

were well prepared in the early modern period, which saw the production of a wealth of guidance literature. Authors, generally members of
religious orders, produced special booklets and pamphlets for pilgrims
travelling to particular shrines, which combined history, miracles,
prayers, meditations and devotions, for the journey as well as the
shrine visit itself. Shrines themselves commissioned pamphlets which
included prayers and meditations to use on location or at home –
where they became spiritual exercises – or stimulated devotional works
which were entirely for the imaginary: Jerusalem, which became pretty
much inaccessible in this period and therefore entirely a spiritual
journey; Our Lady of Loreto in Italy, for whom 'guides' were produced
by Luis de Granada and Louis Richeome among others; Notre Dame de
Liesse, a royally favoured site near Paris; even small-scale shrines such as
Verdelais near Bordeaux and Fieulines in Picardy.[74] Confraternities also
provided for and promoted pilgrimage to their long-distant shrine by
providing literature and other meditational aids for their members.[75]
Two features of this literature affected the pilgrim's view of the landscape
of travel. First, as Wes Williams argues, narrative structure inscribed in
the pilgrim journey was modelled on the Passion narrative, of difficulties,
struggle, death, resurrection and redemption.[76] The journey, especially if
arduous, favoured intimacy with God through asceticism and penance.
Walking was a form of prayer; tiredness and the injuries along the
way, a true participation in the suffering endured by Christ on his way
to the cross. The road could be seen in eschatological terms, an image
of life as a quest for eternal life, whose trials – such as the possibility of
sickness and death – were a cause of anxiety but also an assurance of sal-
vation.[77] The pilgrim's journey was an elementary and primordial form
of penitence, a permanent prayer, more meritorious than it was
painful.[78]

Secondly, authors counselled their readers on appropriate actions and
behaviours to ensure a righteous outcome. From the end of the sixteenth
century, much of this literature was linked to interiority, the refashioning
of the Christian through meditation, prayer and participation in the
sacraments. The spiritual profit of the journey had great significance,

[74] Luis de Granada, *Istruttione de' Peregrini che vanno alla Madonna di Loreto, et ad altri luoghi Santi* (Macerata, 1575); Richeome, 'Le pèlerin de Lorète'. For discussion of other examples, see Bruno Maes, *Les livrets de pèlerinage. Imprimerie et culture dans la France moderne* (Rennes, 2016).

[75] Stefano Simiz, *Confréries urbaines et dévotion en Champagne (1450–1830)* (Villeneuve-d'Ascq, 2002), 214–29; M.-H. Froeschlé-Chopard, *Dieu pour tous et Dieu pour soi. Histoire des confréries et de leurs images à l'époque moderne* (Paris, 2006).

[76] Wes Williams, *Pilgrimage and Narrative in the French Renaissance* (Oxford, 1998), 173.

[77] Jean Mesnard, 'La quête du pèlerin de Saint-Jacques selon Alphonse Dupront', in *Saint Jacques et la France*, ed. Rucquoi, 17.

[78] Barret and Gurgand, *Priez pour nous à Compostelle*, 115.

'the very act of being on a pilgrimage encompassed a set of deeply rooted ideas about exile, sojourns in foreign lands, the metaphor of the road and the life of Christ himself' for the church 'rested upon an intellectual and spiritual genealogy that cast mankind as fated to live in perpetual exile… The righteous were those who persevered on their journey and chose the correct path through Christ.'[79] Thus, Robert Quatremaire's pamphlet, *L'histoire abrégée du Mont Saint-Michel*, instructed pilgrims in 'the motive and methods for usefully and righteously making the pilgrimage to the glorious archangel St Michael'. He wrote that pilgrims should not be too interested in the landscape because they 'must not have the motive of satisfying human curiosity when on such a holy journey'.[80] Visiting such a place was not about sight-seeing, the aim was 'to enliven the pilgrim's faith, revive his hopes, warm his charity' by witnessing places where God had made manifest aspects of his divine wisdom.[81] Pilgrims should travel 'with great fervour', 'with sobriety', 'in silence' and abstain from evil conversation, then confess and take communion when they reached the shrine. Monsieur de Quériolet, a Breton nobleman turned ascetic priest, journeyed to and from Compostela 'so deep in meditation upon Our Saviour's Law and greatness, that for fear of being distracted, he always walked at some distance from his companion and they talked only when necessary'.[82] Increased emphasis on transformations in the self we see in pilgrim tracts perhaps prompted more emphasis on the journey itself than on the destination.[83]

Finally, the landscape of pilgrimage could be entirely imagined or interior, for spiritual journeys increased in popularity as a devotional device in the Counter-Reformation. True pilgrimage was interior. Pilgrimage guides were written for the actual pilgrim but also for the virtual pilgrim, who could imagine the landscape features of the stages of the described journey, as a meditative act. Luis de Granada's influential work *Le vrai chemin* was structured as a journey to Jerusalem although unlike 'real' pilgrimage books, it was addressed overtly to young women, who rarely undertook long-distance travel, illustrating its interior, spiritual design.[84] Wes Williams argues that Jerusalem gradually ceased to exist as a primarily real place in the early modern European imagination,

[79] Candy, *The Archaeology of Pilgrimage*, 7.

[80] Robert Quatremaire, *L'Histoire abbregée du Mont Saint-Michel* (Paris, 1668).

[81] Dominique Julia, 'Le pèlerinage au Mont-Saint-Michel du XVe au XVIIIe siècle', in *Culte et pèlerinages à Saint Michel en Occident. Les trois monts dédié s à l'archange*, ed. Pierre Bouet, Giorgio Otranto and André Vauchez (Rome, 2003), 306.

[82] M. Collet, *La Vie de Monsieur de Quériolet, prestre et conseiller au parlement de Rennes, ami du Père Bernard* (Saint-Malo, 1680, 1771), 82.

[83] *Reframing Pilgrimage*, ed. Coleman and Eade, 10.

[84] Luis de Granada, *Le vrai chemin et adresse pour acquerir et parvenir à la grace de Dieu* (Paris, 1579); Williams, *Pilgrimage and Narrative*, 85.

being gradually replaced by an imagined Jerusalem, less a place than a topic, part of a narrative or devotional sequence and a means to prayer.[85] This is true of the majority of distant destinations. Richeome's pilgrim of Loreto was likewise for the spiritual as much as the physical pilgrim. Quatremaire's and Le Charpentier's booklets for pilgrims to the Mont could be used at home as well as away, being full of prayers and devotions enhanced with a woodcut illustration of the archangel Michael and the Mont. Meditative reading became 'cognitive mapping' of sacred landscape: the 'inner landscape merges the perceived experience of the place with the imagined symbolic meaning of the place to the individual'.[86]

The Catholic Reformation thus saw the promotion of new spiritual and devotional activities at all social levels, although they differed in terms of time, place and social group. Interiority to some degree was key; spiritual life turned inwards, religious persons 'adopted wholeheartedly the practice of mental prayer and the faith underwent a process of internalization and turning towards Christ'.[87] Throughout Europe, sacramental penance altered with the introduction of individual confession in the discretion of the confessional box, first introduced by Archbishop Carlo Borromeo in Milan diocese. The booth 'facilitated a private conversation between priest and penitent and encouraged the use of the sacrament for individual spiritual direction'.[88] The general confession became widespread, to evoke deeper contrition and more profound self-knowledge. More frequent reception of communion was advised. While historians have rightly questioned the degree of penetration of such practices down the social scale, it is clear from the popularity of pilgrimages and that of the acquisition of plenary indulgences from shrines – which required confession and communion to 'action' them – that these new spiritualities were being adopted by individuals of humble social backgrounds. Philip Soergel's comments on southern Germany are also true of France, that already by the seventeenth century, clerical writers such as Martin Eisengrein 'were beginning to link extra-sacramental practices such as pilgrimage to the examination of conscience and to insist that these institutions could deepen knowledge of an individual's unworthiness' are pertinent here.[89] Within the

---

[85] Williams, *Pilgrimage and Narrative*, 172.

[86] Pamela J. Stewart and Andrew Strathern, *Landscape, Memory and History. Anthropological Perspectives* (2003), p. 5.

[87] S. T. Nalle, *God in La Mancha. Religious Reform and the People of Cuenca, 1500–1650* (Baltimore, 1992), 135.

[88] Robert Bireley, 'Early Modern Catholicism as a Response to the Changing World of the Long Sixteenth Century', *Catholic Historical Review*, 95 (2009), 239.

[89] Philip M. Soergel, *Wondrous in his Saints. Counter-Reformation and Propaganda in Bavaria* (Berkeley, 1993), 119.

framework of the concept of pilgrimage, the encouragement of many ordinary people to interiorised spirituality was enacted. Spiritual imaginary and physical pilgrimage were interrelated.

III Conclusions

Recent research has stressed the role of practice and performance in the shaping and experiencing of landscape. The assemblage of the self – in this case, Christian pilgrims on long-distance journeys – through embodied encounters with the landscape have come to the fore.[90] A pilgrim journeyed through a landscape and landforms that were not merely blank canvases passively imprinted with meanings but were complex textures. Pilgrims recorded – and likely saw – primarily a landscape of human activity, roads, wayside markers, bridges, inns, houses, interspersed with special places of divine intervention, leading up to the final, great achievement of attaining the destination shrine. Natural wonders were observed; nature was wild, untamed and frequently hostile; but this was not the first interest of the pilgrim. The landscapes through which pilgrims passed were also understood allegorically, their natural features and the hardships of the road narrated in biblical terms. As Candy states, 'for pilgrims, immersed in the rhythm and "liminal space" of walking, and already susceptible to certain ideas and opinions, the sequences of encounters could set in motion more complex ideas about topography, the meaning of the pilgrimage, religious experience, mythical landscape and their role within it'.[91] Such was the spiritual value of journey and landscape that it was used as a meditative device for all Christians, whether or not they travelled physically.

The shrine, pilgrim route and the wider landscape were deeply intertwined as part of the pilgrim experience, whether physical or metaphysical: as Maddrell argues, 'landscape is the land itself and the way in which we perceive and represent it. It is both a thing and a way of seeing. Landscape is an insistently visual concept, shaped in the very act of our perceiving it, by our mindscape, but it is also an historical text.'[92] Pilgrim landscapes were for the body to achieve, but for the soul to understand. As Ignatius Loyola wrote, himself a well-travelled pilgrim in both physical and spiritual modes: 'We must remind ourselves that we are pilgrims until we arrive at out heavenly homeland, and we must not let our affections delay us in the roadside inns and lands through which we pass, otherwise we will forget our destination and lose interest in our final goal.'[93]

---

[90] *Christian Pilgrimage, Landscape and Heritage*, ed. della Dora, Maddrell, Scafi and Walton, 6.
[91] Candy, *The Archaeology of Pilgrimage*, 133.
[92] *Christian Pilgrimage, Landscape and Heritage*, ed. della Dora, Maddrell, Scafi and Walton, 6.
[93] *Monumenta ignatiana: epistolae et instructions* (12 vols., Madrid, 1903–11), Ep 6:523.

Transactions of the RHS 28 (2018), pp. 107–134 © Royal Historical Society 2018
doi:10.1017/S0080440118000063

CASTLES AND THE MILITARISATION OF URBAN SOCIETY IN IMPERIAL JAPAN*

By Oleg Benesch

READ 21 APRIL 2017

AT THE UNIVERSITY OF CHESTER

ABSTRACT. Castles are some of Japan's most iconic structures and popular tourist destinations. They are prominent symbols of local, regional and national identity recognised both at home and abroad. Castles occupy large areas of land at the centre of most Japanese cities, shaping the urban space. Many castles have their roots in the period of civil war that ended in the early seventeenth century, and now house museums, parks and reconstructions of historic buildings. The current heritage status of Japan's castles obscures their troubled modern history. During the imperial period (1868–1945), the vast majority of pre-modern castles were abandoned, dismantled or destroyed before being rediscovered and reinvented as physical links to an idealised martial past. Japan's most important castles were converted to host military garrisons that dominated city centres and caused conflict with civilian groups. Various interests competed for control and access, and castles became sites of convergence between civilian and military agendas in the 1920s and 1930s. This paper argues that castles contributed both symbolically and physically to the militarisation of Japanese society in the imperial period. The study of these unique urban spaces provides new approaches to understanding militarism, continuity and change in modern Japan.

Japanese castles are most poetic and picturesque in their expression, and they recall to us so many of the numerous gallant and heroic romances of medieval times. They are indeed so elegant that they do not look like defences for fighting, but rather the expression of a supreme art inherent to the people. Perhaps nothing could, therefore, express

*The arguments introduced here build on a forthcoming monograph, co-authored with Ran Zwigenberg, *Japan's Castles: Citadels of Modernity in War and Peace* (Cambridge, 2019). I would also like to thank David Clayton, Nathan Hopson, Jon Howlett, Helena Simmonds, the anonymous readers for the *TRHS* and the audience in Chester for their feedback and suggestions. This research was supported by the Great Britain Sasakawa Foundation and Japan Foundation Endowment Committee. Japanese names that appear in this paper and references are rendered in the standard Japanese format, with the family name first. Japanese scholars writing primarily in English are rendered with the family name second in references.

better than Japanese architecture that Japan and her people are more interested in the beautiful than the bellicose.[1]

Kishida Hideto (1899–1966), 1936

As we read Kishida Hideto's words, published in English for a foreign audience, we are struck by the date of his writing. Is Kishida sounding a subtle but prescient warning, or is he an apologist for Japanese militarism who shoehorned contemporary concerns into a discussion of medieval fortifications? We struggle to reconcile his views with our knowledge of the events of the subsequent decade, including the terrible events at Nanjing and Pearl Harbour, as well as at Hiroshima and Nagasaki. Of course, not even a prominent architectural historian like Kishida would have known what the future held in 1936. On the other hand, Japan had already experienced the Manchurian Incident (1931), withdrawn from the League of Nations (1933) and embarked on the military expansion of its informal empire in China. On the domestic front, the remaining vestiges of the liberal order were under sustained attack, especially by elements within the military, and February 1936 saw a major coup attempt by young officers who seized parts of central Tokyo and assassinated several senior politicians. The focus of this rebellion was the Imperial Castle, home to both the emperor and the First Division of the Imperial Guard, and surrounded by the important ministries of state. Tokyo, like almost all major Japanese cities, continued to be defined by the layout of the pre-modern castle town, with power and authority radiating outward from the castle area.

Castles were more than just historic sites in imperial Japan (1868–1945), and Kishida was one of many scholars who formulated cultural theories on the basis of Japan's castle architecture. The previous year, the architectural historians Ōrui Noboru (1884–1975) and Toba Masao (1899–1979) wrote of Japan's castles that they

> were of severe simplicity but of commanding force. Free from any showiness such as might have been born of feminine minds, those castles were so made as to be expressive of fearless composure of mind, invincible fortitude, unshaken faith – the qualities representing the noblest mind and the highest spirit of the samurai.

Further linking past and present, they continued, 'What may be seen in the same light is the Japanese sword of olden times, as well as the Japanese warship of modern times. Their beauty is of the samurai, viz. of the inherent spirit and soul of the Japanese people.'[2]

Writings in Japanese were even more explicit. In his monumental 1936 study of Japanese castles, the prominent castle researcher and architect Furukawa Shigeharu (1882–1963) argued that castles were vital in this

---

[1] Kishida Hideto, *Japanese Architecture*, 2nd edn (Tokyo, 1936), 108.
[2] Orui Noboru and Toba Masao, *Castles in Japan*, Tourist Library, 9 (Tokyo, 1935), 72–3.

time of 'national emergency', that threatened Japan's very existence. According to Furukawa, 'ancient castles are nothing other than the background for and an extension of the bushido spirit ("the way of the warrior") that was born from the pure "Japanese spirit"'. Furukawa lauded the recent designation of castles as national treasures, as they were symbols of the 'solid bushido ideals that flowed through all of the nation's citizens' and mandated 'benevolent self-sacrifice'. Furukawa invoked key elements of the imperial ideology, including the notion of warriors 'falling like cherry blossoms', and that 'duty is heavy as a mountain while one's [mortal] body is light as a feather', paraphrasing the 1882 Imperial Rescript to Soldiers and Sailors.[3]

The parallels drawn by castle researchers reflected the close relationship between castles and militarism, which was mediated through an idealised samurai masculinity that was held up as the model for all Japanese in the first half of the twentieth century. Kishida's English text was also a response to this sentiment, emphasising Japan's supposedly peaceful nature for a foreign readership in the face of contemporary events. A similar contradiction was evident in the Pan-Pacific Peace Exhibition, a 'mega-event' held in Nagoya in 1937. In spite of its name, the exhibition drew on castle imagery in its promotional materials, and included live-fire exercises, torpedo demonstrations and many other military events.[4] As this study argues, castles played a key symbolic and practical role in the militarisation of Japan's urban society in the decades before 1945. This dynamic echoed developments in other countries, but was ultimately unique to Japan's historical conditions.

Historians examining the Second World War in Asia have long debated the applicability of the term 'fascism' to Japan, as well as the idea of a Japanese *Sonderweg* by which modernisation led to war.[5] Scholarship during and after the war was often teleological, tracing Japanese militarism to at least the establishment of imperial rule at the beginning of the Meiji period (1868–1912).[6] The supposed Japanese focus on hierarchies, especially the emperor, was fundamental to Ruth

---

[3] Furukawa Shigeharu, *Nihon jōkaku kō* (Tokyo, 1974), 607. For a discussion of cherry blossom symbolism in imperial Japan, see Emiko Ohnuki-Tierney, *Kamikaze, Cherry Blossoms, and Nationalisms: The Militarization of Aesthetics in Japanese History* (Chicago, 2002).

[4] For an examination of this 'mega-event', see Nathan Hopson, '"A Bad Peace?" – The 1937 Pan-Pacific Peace Exhibition', *Japanese Studies* (Sept. 2018).

[5] For example Hak Jae Kim, 'The Fatal Affinity of the "Sonderweg" Revisited: The Diffusion of Emergency Powers in Germany, Japan and Korea (1871–1987)', *Journal of Historical Sociology*, 30 (2017), 110–42; Erik Grimmer-Solem, 'German Social Science, Meiji Conservatism, and the Peculiarities of Japanese History', *Journal of World History*, 16 (2005), 187–222.

[6] For a more recent example, see Iritani Toshio, *Group Psychology of the Japanese in War-Time* (1991), 160–7.

Benedict's (1887–1948) influential *The Chrysanthemum and the Sword: Patterns of Japanese Culture* (1946).[7] The narrative that a small clique of militarists exploited a traditional 'cultural weakness' to manipulate society into imperial expansion and war was useful to Americans and Japanese seeking to bury the past and forge a new alliance in the early Cold War.[8]

More recently, historians of Japan have focused on the role of everyday people in the creation of the ultra-nationalistic system in the 1930s.[9] Yoshimi Yoshiaki's conceptualisation of 'grassroots fascism' is one of the most influential contributions in this context.[10] The relationship between the people and state in imperial Japan, especially the apparent convergence of popular and official nationalisms in the 1930s, is complicated by our understanding of the Taisho period (1912–26). While the Meiji period and early Shōwa period (1926–89) are often placed into larger narratives of imperial power and military expansion, the era of 'Taisho democracy' (*Taishō demokurashī*) has been portrayed as a progressive and internationalist interlude. To proponents of the longer-term view of Japanese militarism, the Taisho period is often explained as a brief aberration of superficial liberalism.[11] To others, such as Frederick Dickinson, the significant continuities were between the anti-military feelings of Taisho and the more comprehensive pacifist reaction after 1945.[12]

This study approaches the militarisation of Japanese society by examining physical space, specifically castles. Although the designation 'Taisho democracy' is useful for certain political and cultural trends, an alternative concept of 'Taisho militarism' explains the gradual convergence of military and civilian interests from the late 1910s onward. Castles were sites of struggles between the army and civil society. Garrisons based in repurposed castles created an unparalleled urban military presence which intimidated and suppressed popular protest movements in the early twentieth century. At the same time, castles were increasingly valued as historic sites and symbols of local civic pride. Castles became subjects of serious and sustained academic study at Japanese universities in the late 1920s, while the army conducted its

---

[7] Ruth Benedict, *The Chrysanthemum and the Sword: Patterns of Japanese Culture* (New York, 1946), 21–2.

[8] John Dower, *Embracing Defeat: Japan in the Wake of World War II* (New York, 1999), 488–521.

[9] *The Culture of Japanese Fascism*, ed. Alan Tansman (Durham, NC, 2009).

[10] Yoshimi Yoshiaki, *Grassroots Fascism: The War Experience of the Japanese People*, trans. Ethan Mark (New York, 2015).

[11] For an overview of the early historical debates, see *Japan Examined: Perspectives on Modern Japanese History*, ed. Harry Wray and Hilary Conroy (Honolulu, 1983), 172–98.

[12] Frederick Dickinson, *World War I and the Triumph of a New Japan, 1919–1930* (Cambridge, 2013).

own castle research with the assistance of Toba Masao and other leading scholars from 1932 onward.[13] On the ground, civil society groups sought public access to castles that were restricted military spaces. At the heart of these tensions was an almost universal appreciation of castles throughout Japan. Popular interest in castles, combined with the identification of castles with the modern army, led to a convergence of civilian and military culture and space. This convergence in turn contributed significantly to the militarisation of urban society in the decades before 1945.

In the following, this paper begins with an overview of castles in the Meiji period, when they were dismissed as feudal relics to be demolished, sold or repurposed, often for use by the newly established military. This paper then examines the rediscovery of castles as historic sites in the early twentieth century, as well as the role they played in the suppression of dissent by the military in the 1910s and early 1920s. The final sections focus on a case-study of Osaka Castle (Figure 1) to examine popular interest in castles, and how the army used its control over castles to leverage this popular interest into support for the military as the heir and guardian of Japan's supposedly ancient and noble martial traditions in a time of national crisis.

I Castles in the modernising process

Between 1867 and 1868, a confederation of domains from south-western Japan overthrew the Tokugawa shogunate that had ruled Japan since the turn of the seventeenth century. Hoisting the banner of imperial loyalty, the victorious rebels created a new government centred around the fifteen-year-old Meiji emperor. This 'restoration' of an ancient system of imperial government simultaneously ended more than six centuries of warrior rule. The Tokugawa system had been ostensibly founded on the authority of the samurai class as the martial rulers of Japan, even if this military order oversaw more than 250 years of peace during its tenure. The best-known accoutrements of warrior power included the two swords that all samurai were exclusively obliged to carry, as mentioned by Ōrui and Toba above. In order to ensure the stability of the Tokugawa order, samurai were physically removed from their lands and made to live in the more than 200 castle towns, the main centres of population in early modern Japan. Each castle town was the administrative centre of a domain, the ruler of which pledged

---

[13] Nakai Hitoshi, 'Honpō chikujō shi hen iinkai to *Nihon jōkaku shi shiryō* ni tsuite', *Chūsei jōkaku kenkyū*, 7 (1993), 34–53. In the 1980s, the post-war generation of scholars held vigorous debates on the role castle researchers played in supporting Japan's wartime efforts. For an overview of these debates, see Yamaki Takao, 'Meiji kara haisen made no jōkaku kenkyū no nagare ni tsuite', *Chūsei jōkaku kenkyū*, 1 (1987), 184–232.

Figure 1 Osaka Castle in 2018. Photograph by the author.

loyalty to the Tokugawa but had considerable autonomy in his own lands.

One important restriction on domain lords, or *daimyō*, in the Tokugawa period was the requirement that they spend alternate years in the capital, Edo (later Tokyo), the ultimate castle town and possibly the largest city in the world by 1700, with over one million inhabitants. In addition to their lavish residences in the capital, the *daimyō* were each required to maintain a castle in their domain. In order to prevent rebellion against the shogunate, castle modifications and construction had to be approved, and each domain was ostensibly limited by the shogunate to a single castle. Castle maintenance weakened the *daimyō* financially, as most domains spent roughly 10 per cent of their annual revenue on the upkeep of walls, moats, bridges, residences and other structures.[14] There was considerable dissatisfaction with this arrangement, as castles were merely symbols of military and state power. There had been no significant military conflict in Japan since the early seventeenth century, and the design of the Japanese castle had changed little since

---

[14] Nakai Hitoshi, Katō Masafumi and Kido Masayuki, *Kamera ga toraeta furoshashin de miru Nihon no meijō* (Tokyo, 2015), 10.

the peak of its development around this time, while developments in weaponry had rendered them militarily obsolete.

For many *daimyō*, the Meiji restoration presented an opportunity to achieve their long-standing aims to relieve themselves of the burden of castle maintenance. As part of the acknowledgement of imperial rule, the more than 260 *daimyō* symbolically 'returned' their lands and castles to the emperor immediately following the restoration. Most *daimyō* now became 'governors' of their domains, and their stipends were greatly reduced, often by 90 per cent. This meant that castle maintenance might now command all of a domain's revenue, and at least thirty-nine domains applied to the government for permission to demolish their castles between 1868 and 1872.[15] Castles were also auctioned off to raise much-needed funds to help support former samurai who had lost their livelihoods in the transition.[16] The Meiji period was envisioned as a modernising age of 'civilisation and enlightenment', and applications to demolish castles typically described them as 'useless things'.[17] Castles were unpleasant reminders of the 'feudal' past.[18] Hundreds of gates, walls and buildings were sold to be carted off or demolished during the first years of Meiji, while moats and other spaces were repurposed for agriculture and more 'useful' purposes.[19]

Japanese castles occupied vast areas at the centre of major cities, having initially been built on a far larger scale than their contemporary European counterparts. As Christopher Dresser (1834–1904) wrote of the Imperial Castle in Tokyo following a trip to Japan in the late 1870s, 'The Castle enclosure is surrounded by a broad moat, on the inner side of which rise the vast walls of the fortress: and if we may judge from its appearance, no castle in Europe is more impregnable.'[20] Figure 2 shows the main entrance to the Imperial Castle in the Taisho period, with portraits of the emperor and empress.[21] One reason for the difference in scale was that Japanese cities lacked defensive walls, and all of the fortification work was centred on the castle. The castle in turn had

---

[15] Hirai Makoto, 'Meiji ki ni okeru haijō no hensen to chiiki dōkō: Ehime ken nai no jōkaku, chinya wo rei toshite', *Ehime ken rekishi bunka hakubutsukan kenkyū kiyō*, 7 (Mar. 2003), 26; Ichisaka Tarō, *Bakumatsu ishin no shiro: ken'i no shōchō ka, jissen no yōki ka* (Tokyo, 2014), 203.

[16] Hirai, 'Meiji ki ni okeru haijō no hensen to chiiki dōkō', 29.

[17] Ōrui Noboru and Toba Masao, *Nihon jōkaku shi* (Tokyo, 1936), 694.

[18] For a discussion of problems with the application of the concept of 'feudalism' to Japan, see Thomas Keirstead, 'Inventing Medieval Japan: The History and Politics of National Identity', *Medieval History Journal*, 1 (1998), 47–71.

[19] Gilbert Rozman, 'Castle Towns in Transition', *Japan in Transition: From Tokugawa to Meiji*, ed. Marius B. Jansen and Gilbert Rozman (Princeton, 1986), 343.

[20] Christopher Dresser, *Japan: Its Architecture, Art, and Art Manufactures* (1882), 13.

[21] Although English texts tended to use the term 'palace', the Japanese refers explicitly to a 'castle' in line with the official designation.

IMPERIAL PALACE OF NIJUBASHI TOKYO.   橋重二城宮   (所名京東)

Figure 2 The Imperial Castle (Kyūjō) in Tokyo. Postcard from the author's collection.

to be of a sufficient size to compensate for the absence of merchant storehouses and other potential supporting infrastructure within. Perhaps the most important factor was the different pace at which changes in the military occurred in Europe relative to Japan.[22] In Europe, medieval castles had been obsolete for centuries, and urban fortifications were repurposed, sold off, dismantled and worn down as their land and materials continued to be valuable long after they lost their military meaning. Those that survived into the modern period typically did so on a considerably smaller scale than urban castles in Japan.

In Japan, these processes which took centuries in Europe occurred at a greatly accelerated rate. The 1860s were dominated by samurai in regional militias, although there were some attempts to introduce Western weaponry and drill.[23] To consolidate its power, suppress unrest and resist foreign threats, however, the Meiji government created a modern conscripted national army. The samurai were deemed to be obsolete and a potential threat to the new order. The rapid transitions in the early 1870s meant that the planned establishment

[22] William R. Thompson and Karen Rasler, 'War, the Military Revolution(s) Controversy, and Army Expansion: A Test of Two Explanations of Historical Influences on European State Making', *Comparative Political Studies*, 32 (Feb. 1999), 3–31.

[23] Colin Jaundrill, *Samurai to Soldier: Remaking Military Service in Nineteenth-Century Japan* (Ithaca, 2016).

of the Imperial Japanese Army occurred when the fate of the newly obsolete castles had yet to be resolved, and it was decided that these should hold the new military garrisons. Following a nationwide survey undertaken by a team from the War Ministry in 1872, roughly fifty-eight castles and other fortifications were selected for military use. Another 144 castles, along with over 100 other sites, were given to the Finance Ministry for 'disposal'.[24] Many of these surplus castles were auctioned off and dismantled, converted into official or unofficial public parks, repurposed to house schools and administrative buildings, or underwent a combination of these transformations.

The castles designated for military use included the largest and most important structures, and in 1873 regional commands were set up in the castles in Sendai, Tokyo, Nagoya, Osaka, Hiroshima and Kumamoto. Fourteen infantry regiments were subsequently established, of which one was located with each of the six regional commands. The other infantry regiments were located mainly in castle sites elsewhere, in some cases with their battalions spread across multiple sites. Outside of Tokyo, for most of the period 1874–84, infantry regiments and battalions were based in and around fourteen former castles, as well as five other non-castle sites. The expansion of the military in the 1880s added ten infantry regiments, all of which took over former castle sites.[25] At all of these sites, most or all existing buildings were sold off or demolished and replaced by modern barracks and other facilities. With regard to the few infantry regiments and battalions outside of former castles in the period before 1894, these were located primarily in cities that had not been castle towns, or represented auxiliary sites in cities where the army was already using the castle space.

II Castles and the discovery of heritage

Before the turn of the twentieth century, the military took a practical approach to castles. Its priorities were recruiting and training a modern force, maintaining order through several major rebellions in the 1870s and fighting major wars with China (1894–5) and Russia (1904–5). A few important castle structures were repaired during this time, most significantly the wooden keeps at Nagoya, Himeji and Hikone, which were among the largest in Japan. These structures were unofficially protected by the Imperial Household Ministry, which donated money for the most urgent repairs in 1878 and 1879, but

[24] Moriyama Eiichi, *Meiji ishin / haijō ichiran* (Tokyo, 1989), 18–19.
[25] Data from Katō Hiroshi, Ibuchi Kōichi and Nagai Yasuo, 'Meiji ki ni okeru rikugun butai heiei chi no haichi ni tsuite', *Nihon kenchiku gakkai Tōhoku shibu kenkyū hōkoku kai* (June 2004), 203–8.

many other gates, outbuildings and walls continued to be demolished or removed at castle sites throughout Japan. These early efforts to preserve castles were limited and driven by a combination of foreigners and Japanese with considerable foreign experience. The German consul Max von Brandt (1835–1920) claimed to have convinced the army to spare the Nagoya Castle keep during a visit in 1872.[26] Another key figure was the government official Machida Hisanari (1838–97), later the first director of the Imperial Museum. Japanese visitors to Europe in the late nineteenth century were often taken to the dozens of castles that continued to have ties to European royal families, and the Iwakura Mission to the West in 1871–3 visited many such sites. For his part, Machida was impressed by the use of the Tower of London as a military museum during a stay in England in the 1860s, and in 1872 appealed to the statesman Ōkuma Shigenobu (1838–1922) to halt the destruction of the castles at Nagoya and Inuyama.[27] This appeal may well have been on Ōkuma's mind when he authorised the protection of the castles at Nagoya and Hikone six years later.[28]

These early protection efforts were few and far between, however, and did not extend to a broader appreciation of castles, which were still widely viewed as 'feudal' relics. Attitudes only began to shift from the 1890s, in line with a popular reassessment of the Japanese past. While the first two decades of the Meiji period had been dominated by movements towards modernisation and Westernisation under the banner of 'civilisation and enlightenment', a nativist backlash against foreign influences began to gather strength from the 1880s as part of a search for a 'Japanese' identity.[29] In Japan, as in other newly created nation-states, the creation of a national identity also entailed the rehabilitation of discredited symbols of the pre-modern past, including both samurai and castles. At the same time, Western practice continued to serve as a model, and the rehabilitation of the Japanese past favoured those aspects that had European equivalents. This could be seen most clearly in the rehabilitation of the samurai, which was done primarily through the formulation of the ideology of bushido, the so-called 'way of the warrior'. Although bushido was portrayed as an ancient ethic and the very 'soul of Japan', it was largely a product of the 1890s, and was heavily inspired by Victorian ideals of chivalry and gentlemanship

---

[26] Max August Scipio von Brandt, *Dreiunddreissig Jahre in Ost-asien: Erinnerungen eines deutschen Diplomaten, 2. Band* (Leipzig, 1901), 281–2.

[27] Nishimura Yukio, 'Kenzōbutsu no hozon ni itaru Meiji zenki no bunkazai hogo gyōsei no tenkai: "rekishi teki kankyō" gainen no seisei shi sono 1', *Nihon kenchiku gakkai ronbun hōkoku shū*, 340 (June 1984), 106.

[28] *Ōkuma haku hyakuwa*, ed. Emori Taikichi (Tokyo, 1909), 255–9.

[29] Donald H. Shively, 'The Japanization of the Middle Meiji', in *Tradition and Modernization in Japanese Culture*, ed. Donald Shively (New Jersey, 1971), 77–119.

that were admired in Japan at the time. Promoted as an ethic that guided all Japanese, bushido was given apparent legitimacy by its supposed relationship with the idealised former samurai, as well as by its correspondence with contemporary Western ideals.[30]

Castles experienced a similar rehabilitation in the 1890s, as the passage of time and generational shifts meant that the reality of the pre-Meiji order was becoming a distant memory. This applied to the oppressive nature of the samurai and to castles – the greatest extant symbols of the class-based former order. At the same time, the Meiji government was endeavouring to build national unity and patriotism by pardoning and even celebrating aspects of the Ancien Régime.[31] Prominent members of the Tokugawa family and their supporters were acknowledged for their contributions to the nation. The conversion of the traditional Tokugawa stronghold Nagoya Castle into an imperial detached palace in 1893 was an important step. The shogun's power and authority had been comprehensively appropriated by the conversion of Edo Castle to the Imperial Castle, but most of the original structures were destroyed in the first decade of Meiji.[32] In contrast, the protection of the Nagoya Castle keep with imperial funds in 1878, followed by the imperial family's use of the original palace buildings there as a residence, demonstrated an appreciation of the Tokugawa heritage as something other than a 'feudal' relic. The widespread invocation of feudal symbols by European royal families, including their use of castles as residences, further legitimised this appropriation of castles by the Japanese imperial house.

In 1889, the Army Ministry sought to expand its existing facilities, and to raise funds for this undertaking it declared nineteen of its castle sites to be surplus to requirements. In a further acknowledgement to the old order, the former *daimyō* families who had owned the castles before 1868 were given the first option to purchase the castles at very preferential rates.[33] Many did so, thereby reestablishing their formal links with their former domains, as the *daimyō* had been compelled to move to Tokyo with the establishment of the prefectural system in 1871. Even if very few former *daimyō* physically relocated to their ancestral homes after 1889, their symbolic return to their castle towns boosted regional and national pride. By 1905, samurai and Japan's martial heritage were being celebrated in the context of victories over China and

---

[30] Oleg Benesch, *Inventing the Way of the Samurai: Nationalism, Internationalism, and Bushido in Modern Japan* (Oxford, 2014).

[31] Carol Gluck, 'The Invention of Edo', in *Mirror of Modernity: Invented Traditions in Modern Japan*, ed. Stephen Vlastos (Berkeley, 1998), 262–84.

[32] Fujio Tadashi, 'Tenshu no fukugen to sono shūhen: Ōsaka to Tōkyō', *Jūtaku kenchiku* (May 1999), 160–5.

[33] Matsushita Takaaki, *Guntai wo yūchi seyo: rikukaigun to toshi keisei* (Tokyo, 2013), 36.

Russia. By this time, the popular image of castles had shifted from instruments of oppression to positive markers of identity in many cities, as seen
in thousands of postcards, travel guides and other records.[34] This shift
was enhanced by the fact that many former castle sites had been converted into public parks and exhibition sites, furthering popular identification with castles.[35]

The popular appreciation of castles was reflected in several developments. Civil society groups throughout Japan established local castle
preservation societies in a movement that gathered pace from the late
1910s.[36] One high-profile phenomenon was the adoption of castle
imagery by the city of Nagoya and the surrounding Aichi Prefecture.
At the Fifth National Industrial Exhibition in Osaka in 1903, the Aichi
Prefectural Pavilion was built as a mock castle keep, reflecting
Nagoya's status as the home of the largest keep in Japan.[37] This
pattern would continue through to 1945, as the regional representatives
from Nagoya and Aichi would almost invariably construct a castle-like
structure at national industrial exhibitions. Meanwhile, the real
Nagoya Castle keep remained a highly restricted bastion of authority
and could only be viewed from afar by ordinary Japanese, as shown in
Figure 3.

In 1906, Kōfu, a former castle town in the mountains west of Tokyo,
held a major regional exhibition in the spacious grounds of its ruined
former castle. The organisers used the occasion to build a temporary
keep out of wood at the highest point of the ramparts. Illuminated by
electric lights, this structure proved widely popular, with over 23,000
people paying the two Sen price of admission to climb the keep during
the six weeks of the exhibition.[38] Four years later, in the city of Gifu
north-west of Nagoya, the Gifu City Preservation Society took advantage
of a new bridge construction to build their own keep atop the ramparts of
Gifu Castle. It had never previously had a keep. Using scrap materials
from the old bridge, the Society built a two-storey structure with metal
siding atop the mountain overlooking the city, which became a tourist

---

[34] *Furu ehagaki de miru Nihon no shiro*, ed. Gotō Toyokimi and Nishigaya Yasuhiro (Tokyo, 2009), i–viii.

[35] Nonaka Katsutoshi, '"Haijō" go no jōshi ni okeru kōen ka no keiki to keika, kinsei jōkamachi no kōshin to saihen ni yoru kindai ka', *Randosukēpu kenkyū*, 79 (2016), 419–24.

[36] Nakajima Naoto, 'Shōwa shoki ni okeru Nihon hokatsu kai no katsudō ni kansuru kenkyu', *Toshi keikaku ronbun shū*, 41 (2006), 905–10.

[37] Fujio Tadashi, 'Aichi-ken baiten: mō hitotsu no Nagoya jō tenshu', *Ouroboros*, 14 (13 July 2001).

[38] Nonaka Katsutoshi, 'Jōshi ni kensetsu sareta kasetsu mogi tenshukaku no kensetsu keii to igi: senzen no chihō toshi ni okeru mogi tenshukaku no kensetsu ni kan suru kenkyū, sono 3', *Nihon kenchiku gakkai keikaku kei ronbun shū*, 78 (2013), 1553–4.

Figure 3 Tourists using telescopes to view the golden figures atop the Nagoya Castle keep from the far side of the moat. Postcard from the author's collection.

draw and a popular destination for hikers.[39] The decade after 1910 also saw the first major publications on Japanese castles, as well as articles in national newspapers, including by the art historian Ōrui Noboru, who highlighted the 'masculinity' of Japanese castles in 1912.[40] By the 1910s, castles were popular tourist destinations, and were firmly established as symbols of local, regional and national identity throughout Japan.

III Military castles and urban society in Taisho Japan

The conflicts with China and Russia were accompanied by major expansions of the Imperial Japanese Army. Relative to the period before the Sino-Japanese War, the number of regular infantry regiments doubled to forty-eight by 1902.[41] This increased further to seventy-two by 1908 in the wake of the Russo-Japanese War. Due to the rapid growth of Japanese cities in the late Meiji period, these troops could not all be garrisoned within and around existing urban castle sites, and the army had sold many of its holdings in the 1880s. Only five of the twenty-four new

[39] Nonaka Katsutoshi, 'Sengoku ki jōkaku no jōshi ni kensetsu sareta mogi tenshukaku no kensetsu keii to igi: senzen no chihō toshi ni okeru mogi tenshukaku no kensetsu ni kan suru kenkyū, sono 1', *Nihon kenchiku gakkai keikaku kei ronbun shū*, 75 (2010), 837–42.

[40] Ōrui Noboru, 'Honpō jōkaku no bikan', *Shinri kenkyū*, 1 (1912), 636.

[41] Kato, Ibuchi and Nagai, 'Meiji ki', 203–8.

infantry regiments formed in 1896–1902 were placed in castles.[42] The cost of land was an important factor in the selection of sites, and regional cities often discounted or even donated land in a fierce competition to attract lucrative military installations.[43] At the same time, the military also maximised its use of valuable urban space in and around castles, and increased and expanded its presence where this was possible. Several existing 'military cities' saw additional infantry regiments, administrative buildings and other units placed in and around the castle site.

Significantly, the army did not vacate urban castle sites for cheaper suburban ones, in spite of the logistical difficulties and expense of being located in the centres of major cities, as well as the much-needed money that could have been generated by selling castle land to eager developers. Events in Tokyo after the Russo-Japanese War demonstrated the utility of having a major armed force at central urban locations. The terms of the Treaty of Portsmouth that ended the war in September 1905 were seen as a major disappointment by the general public, which had been fed a steady diet of glorious victories and sacrifices by the government and media that did not reflect Japan's serious losses or the extent of Russia's remaining resources. Nationalistic groups portrayed the agreement as a treasonous act by the Japanese negotiators, with some even fantastically demanding that the depleted army again take to the field to obtain better terms. On the day of the treaty signing, 30,000 protestors gathered in Hibiya Park, on the south-east corner of the Imperial Castle just across the inner moat. The large police force in place to control the crowd became a target for anti-government hostility, and rioters destroyed the majority of police boxes in the area and burned down two police stations, in addition to causing other damage; 17 people were killed and more than 1,000 injured before the government mobilised the Imperial Guard from the north bailey of the Imperial Castle to restore order. Rioters welcomed the guardsmen with calls of 'Long live the emperor!' before dispersing.[44] This reflected popular respect for the emperor and military, in contrast with distrust of police and elected politicians, but it would also have been clear to the rioters that they stood no chance against the elite troops of the Imperial Guard, who ultimately held a monopoly of physical force in the urban centre.

[42] *Ibid.*

[43] Matsushita, *Guntai wo yūchi seyo*.

[44] Shumpei Okamoto, 'The Emperor and the Crowd: The Historical Significance of the Hibiya Riot', in *Conflict in Modern Japanese History: The Neglected Tradition*, ed. Tetsuo Najita *et al.* (Princeton, 1982), 260–2, 266–7.

The Hibiya Riot clearly demonstrated the potential threat of popular unrest, as well as the effectiveness of a formidable military presence in countering this threat. Some scholars have portrayed the Hibiya Riot as the starting point of a period of 'urban mass riot' that ended with the so-called Rice Riots of 1918, the largest incident of urban unrest in imperial Japan.[45] This period of urban violence should be extended to include the aftermath of the Great Kanto Earthquake of 1923, which witnessed politically motivated massacres of Koreans and leftists. Over the course of the 1910s, a major rift developed between the military and the civilian population, as the army and navy were involved in bribery scandals, corruption and high-handed tactics that brought down the government and caused a constitutional crisis. Popular anger boosted the strength of political parties, which often profiled themselves in opposition to the military.[46] In urban areas, especially, anti-military sentiment was strong, also fuelled by international socialist movements. The hostility was reciprocated by the army, which promoted the myth of the idealised rural recruit who was physically strong with a loyal character of honest simplicity, while urban conscripts were suspected of having been exposed to socialist ideas and other 'dangerous thought'.[47]

These tensions were heightened by the disruptive behaviour of soldiers in the entertainment districts and elsewhere, as they often failed to recognise the authority of civilian police.[48] In addition, the military restrictions on access to castle space led many municipalities to try and remove the army from castles and relocate them to the outskirts of the city. It was hoped that this would mitigate the problems associated with the military presence, while continuing to reap the economic benefits it brought. In cities including Himeji, Matsuyama, Kumamoto, Nagoya and Toyohashi, the Taisho period saw civilian movements to remove infantry regiments from castle sites in order to promote economic growth and provide greater public access and movement through city centres.[49]

The conflicts between the public and military in urban Japan reached a climax in August 1918. Beginning in Toyama Prefecture on the Japan Sea coast, disturbances and riots protesting against sudden increases in the price of rice spread throughout Japan, bringing more than a million people to the streets over the course of several weeks. The

[45] *Ibid.*, 268.

[46] Tetsuo Najita, *Hara Kei and the Politics of Compromise 1905–1915* (Cambridge, MA, 1967).

[47] Yoshida Yutaka, *Nihon no guntai: heishi tachi no kindai shi* (Tokyo, 2002), 160–8.

[48] Elise K. Tipton, *The Japanese Police State: Tokko in Interwar Japan* (2012), 123–7.

[49] Kobayashi Hiroharu, 'Gunto Himeji to minshū', in *Chiiki no naka no guntai*, IV: *Koto, shōto no guntai, Kinki*, ed. Harada Keiichi (Tokyo, 2015), 89–99; Matsushita, *Guntai wo yūchi seyo*, 244–8; Tsukuda Ryūichirō, 'Tōkai gunto ron: Toyohashi to, kanren shite no Nagoya, Hamamatsu', in *Chiiki no naka no guntai*, III: *Retto chūō no gunji kyoten, Chūbu*, ed. Kawanishi Hidemichi (Tokyo, 2014), 8–37.

rioters' targets included rice sellers' shops, police stations and other emblems of wealth and authority. Countless buildings were destroyed, and residents of Osaka recounted feeling 'as though a revolution had really come'.[50] The police and other civilian authorities were overwhelmed by the scale of the disturbances, and could often only stand idly by or even retreat to avoid falling victim to the violence themselves. In response, many local governments were forced to send requests to the army to suppress the riots, a measure that was especially effective in areas with urban castle garrisons that could be immediately deployed when necessary.

In Osaka, after three days of unrest the mayor's office sent a request to the army to deploy Fourth Division troops, who quickly restored order.[51] Nagoya saw a similar timeline, with up to 50,000 rioters burning down rice merchants' shops and police stations over the course of three days, until the prefectural governor requested soldiers from the Third Division in Nagoya Castle, who put down the protests in often violent clashes with protestors.[52] Newspaper reports from throughout Japan showed the extent of the disturbances and the importance of urban castle garrisons in restoring order. Nationally, army troops were mobilised on sixty occasions during the Rice Riots, using live ammunition and bayonets.[53] The total number of troops mobilised has been estimated at 92,000, with hundreds of fatalities on both sides.[54] The majority of soldiers were deployed from castles, as in Nagoya and Osaka. In Kokura, after rioters destroyed trains and ransacked shops for alcohol, soy sauce, clothing and other goods, mounted military police and soldiers from the Fourteenth Infantry Regiment moved out from the castle to pacify the city. In Himeji, troops from the Tenth Infantry Regiment and special forces patrolled the city and arrested thirty rioters. In Sendai and Shizuoka, hundreds of soldiers overpowered thousands of rioters.[55] In Aizu-Wakamatsu, the Sixty-Fifth Infantry Regiment moved out of the third bailey of the castle to suppress the riots quickly.[56] Although the rioters often coordinated their movements to outflank the police, they were no match for the soldiers and their weaponry. Riot suppression was more difficult in cities that did not have urban

[50] John Crump, *The Anarchist Movement in Japan, 1906–1996* (Sheffield, 1996).

[51] Seki Hajime, *Seki Hajime nikki* (Osaka, 1918), www.mus-his.city.osaka.jp/news/2008/komesodo.html (accessed 26 Apr. 2017).

[52] Abe Tsunehisa, 'Kome sōdō', *Chūgakkō shakaika no shiori*, 1 (2011), 40.

[53] Leonard A. Humphreys, *The Way of the Heavenly Sword: The Japanese Army in the 1920s* (Stanford, 1995), 43.

[54] Sheldon Garon, *The State and Labor in Modern Japan* (Berkeley, 1987), 41; Andrew E. Barshay, *State and Intellectual in Imperial Japan: The Public Man in Crisis* (Berkeley, 1988), 150.

[55] 'Kome sōdō no sono go', *Osaka mainichi shinbun* (18 Aug. 1918).

[56] Saitō Mitsuo, *Aizu Wakamatsu jō* (Tokyo, 1989), 182–3.

garrisons, as in Kōchi, where several police officers were injured when they attempted to confront the mob.[57] Here, the castle had already been converted into a public park when the Forty-Fourth Infantry Regiment arrived after the Sino-Japanese War, and the army set up in Asakura Village five kilometres west of the city centre.

The response to the Rice Riots demonstrated civilian authorities' dependence on the military to suppress serious unrest. In Tokyo, although the capital did not experience as much disturbance as regional cities in 1918, the army played a decisive role in 1923 in the aftermath of the Great Kanto Earthquake. This disaster is estimated to have killed more than 100,000 people, and tremors and fires destroyed much of the city. The army assisted in firefighting and relief efforts, but also used the chaos to pursue groups deemed 'undesirable' by the government. The military police murdered prominent anarchists, and contemporary accounts strongly suggest soldiers were involved in the killing of thousands of Koreans living in Tokyo.[58] Certainly, the declaration of martial law immediately after the earthquake gave the army control over the city. In spite of the atrocities, many people appreciated the superficial stability brought by military authority in the wake of the earthquake, which even led to a moderate improvement in popular views of the army.[59]

By the early 1920s, the army was established as the ultimate arbiter of physical force in major urban areas, and this caused considerable tension with civilian society. Individual soldiers, for example, often suffered abuse when they ventured out of the garrisons into public.[60] Tensions were also due to the relatively large size of garrisons, as Japan's military developed initially from the German model, maintaining a large standing army relative to Britain or the United States.[61] Furthermore, in spite of a series of retrenchments in the 1920s that ostensibly shifted the focus towards greater use of military technology such as the tanks and aircraft observed in Europe during the First World War, Japanese military thinking continued to centre around infantry tactics such as bayonet charges.[62] The infantry had an exceptionally large influence within the military from the early Meiji period, when it provided 90 per cent of total personnel.[63] Castles further raised the infantry's profile in society

---

[57] 'Kome sōdō no sono go'.
[58] Humphreys, *The Way of the Heavenly Sword*, 54–9.
[59] *Ibid.*, 52–3.
[60] *Ibid.*, 46–9.
[61] *Ibid.*, 82.
[62] *Ibid.*, 84–5.
[63] Jaundrill, *Samurai to Soldier*, 116.

by giving it a significant urban presence, especially in contrast with the navy which was massed in dedicated ports well away from major cities.

IV Castles and military soft power

The struggles over the control of urban space in imperial Japan reached a climax in Osaka in the 1920s. At the start of the Meiji period, Osaka was a prime candidate for the new capital of Japan, and the castle was slated to host the emperor, military and civilian government. Although most of these functions were ultimately moved to Tokyo, Osaka Castle became a major military base, the home of the Fourth Division and the Osaka Army Arsenal. The city itself built on the economic power of the military and Osaka's long-standing mercantile traditions to prosper throughout the imperial period, growing to surround the vast castle site. By late Meiji, Osaka Castle was known as the site of the largest arms factory in Asia, and at the time of Japan's surrender in 1945 the arsenal alone employed roughly 66,000 workers.[64] By this point, the land controlled by the military in and around the castle was more than three square kilometres, similar in size to Central Park in New York City, and considerably larger than London's Hyde Park and Kensington Gardens combined.[65]

The great Tokugawa keep of Osaka Castle had burned down in 1665, and many more buildings were destroyed after the Tokugawa surrender in 1867. The massive ramparts rising up from the broad moat retained their imposing presence, however, and Osaka Castle remained the symbol of the city. Control over the castle was key to demonstrating authority in the region, and the imperial forces conducted the surrender ceremony with the Tokugawa atop the highest ramparts.[66] Although castles were generally treated as unloved reminders of the feudal past in the early Meiji period, and Osaka Castle was highly restricted military space for most Japanese, the government and military soon observed the fascination that von Brandt and other Western visitors had for castles. English-language newspapers carried instructions for visiting the castle, provided notifications of closures and announced the publication of military postcards 'illustrating ancient methods of Japanese warfare as well as modern guns, boats, etc.'.[67] As Nogawa Yasuharu has shown, foreign

[64] Fujio, 'Tenshu no fukugen to sono shūhen: Ōsaka to Tōkyō', 161; Matsushita Takashi, 'Ōsaka hōhei kōshō to Ōsaka sangyō shūseki to no kankei sei: tekkō, aruminiumu, kikai kinzoku kakō gijutsu kara kōsatsu', *Sankaiken ronshū*, 24 (2012), 10.

[65] Miyake Kōji writes that other calculations put the number of arsenal workers at the time of surrender at more than 200,000 and the total size of the arsenal land at almost six square kilometres. Miyake Kōji, *Ōsaka hōhei kōshō no kenkyū* (Kyoto, 1993), 404, 408.

[66] *Ōsakajo no kindaishi*, ed. Ōsakajō tenshukaku (Osaka, 2004), 7.

[67] *Japan Chronicle* (10 Dec. 1902), 574.

dignitaries in Japan often requested to visit Osaka Castle, and the government was generally keen to show off its rapid military development through tours of the arsenal. Prospective foreign visitors to these sites submitted applications to the military via their embassies, and these were typically approved. The content of these applications reveals that the historic castle structures were a large draw, comparable to the arsenal, and that by the time of the Russo-Japanese War applications were almost exclusively to the historic sites with few requests to see the arsenal.[68]

As the symbol of Osaka, the castle also became an important site for domestic tourism over the course of the imperial period. By the early 1920s, the central area of the castle was open daily from 8 to 4, welcoming thousands of eager visitors.[69] This development was also driven by the castle's connection with the warlord Toyotomi Hideyoshi (1537–98), who unified much of Japan and built the ramparts of Osaka Castle. When the Meiji emperor entered Osaka in 1868, he lauded Hideyoshi as a great figure while criticising the Tokugawa house as having usurped his power.[70] Around the time of the Sino-Japanese War, Hideyoshi was widely hailed in official and popular campaigns for his invasions of Korea in the 1590s, which were portrayed as models for modern Japanese imperial expansion.[71] In 1915, on the 300th anniversary of the fall of Osaka Castle to the Tokugawa armies and the death of Hideyoshi's son, Hideyori (1593–1615), Hideyoshi was posthumously awarded the highest court rank.[72] Hideyoshi and the castle became fixed points of identification for Osakans, especially in the Taisho period as the city grew rapidly in size and population.

Having become aware of the popularity of the castle, the army sought to mobilise its symbolic value to mitigate anti-military feeling. The army regularly hosted public events in the parade grounds, and flights to Kyoto also departed from within the castle.[73] As elsewhere in Japan, military manoeuvres and regimental festivals were highlights of the social calendar and drew thousands of onlookers, including members of the imperial family. These events generated countless souvenirs that relied

[68] Nogawa Yasuharu, 'Ōsaka jō tenshukaku fukkō zenshi: rikugun shiryō ni miru Ōsaka jō no kankōchi ka to Naniwa Jingū zōei mondai (tokushū Nishi Ōsaka)', *Ōsaka no rekishi*, 73 (2009), 94–6.

[69] *Ibid.*, 100–1.

[70] Miki Seiichirō, 'Hōkokusha no zōei ni kansuru ichikōsatsu', *Nagoya Daigaku bungakubu kenkyū ronshū shigaku*, 33 (1987), 206.

[71] *Ōsakajō no kindaishi*, ed. Osakajō tenshukaku (Osaka, 2004), 41.

[72] 'Koju ichii Toyotomi Hideyoshi zōi no ken' (10 Nov. 1915) (Japan Center for Asian Historical Records: A11112488700).

[73] Endō Shunroku, 'Ōsaka-fu ka no nyūei, enshū, zaigō gunjinkai', in *Chiiki no naka no guntai*, ed. Harada, IV, 170–1.

heavily on castle and samurai imagery. Shops operated by the army in the castle and inside the Takashimaya department store sold official post-cards, maps and other souvenirs relating to the castle, army and Toyotomi Hideyoshi.[74] Newspapers regularly reported visits to the castle by Japanese and foreign dignitaries. Castles also served educational purposes, such as when more than 3,000 students were invited to Osaka Castle in 1919 for a tour of the historic ramparts and demonstrations of artillery and a new tank design. Coverage of the event included photographs of children admiring the tank as well as the commanding views across Osaka from atop the ramparts.[75] Through these events, the army sought to reduce public animosity and establish its own legitimacy as the caretaker of Hideyoshi and Osaka's heritage as embodied by Osaka Castle.

In 1923, the influential Seki Hajime (1873–1935) became mayor of Osaka, following several years in other high offices in the municipal government. Seki oversaw many ambitious plans to raise both the profile of Osaka and general quality of life in the city, even if these aims were sometimes in conflict and not always realised. The first of these goals was attained in 1925, when a redistricting plan helped Osaka's population reach two million people, temporarily surpassing Tokyo and making Osaka the sixth largest city in the world.[76] This was known as the 'Great(er) Osaka period' (*Dai Ōsaka jidai*). This rapid expansion was difficult to reconcile with one of Seki's other long-standing concerns, to grow 'the lungs of the city' by creating more green space in Osaka.[77] The bleak conditions in industrial Osaka are reflected in photographs of the skyline from 1914 (Figure 4).[78] The dearth of parks and other public spaces in Japanese cities was a major concern nationwide, and was highlighted by the historian Charles Austin Beard (1874–1948), brought in to consult on Tokyo's urban planning in 1923.[79] Seki's push for park creation was in response to the miserable living conditions, when it was 'estimated that the average worker in Osaka before the First World War occupied about the same amount of living space as a Japanese sailor aboard ship'.[80]

[74] Nogawa, 'Ōsaka jō tenshukaku fukkō zenshi', 100–1.
[75] 'Ōsaka shinai seito sōkōsha kengaku daiichinichi', *Osaka asahi shinbun* (evening, 11 Apr. 1919), 2.
[76] Kinoshita Naoyuki, 'Kindai Nihon no shiro ni tsuite', *Kindai gasetsu*, 9 (2000), 92.
[77] Kitagawa Hiroshi, 'Ōsaka jō tenshukaku: fukkō kara genzai ni itaru made', *Rekishi kagaku*, 157 (1999), 17.
[78] *Ōsaka fu shashin chō*, ed. Ōsaka fu (Osaka, 1914), 29.
[79] Charles Austin Beard, *The Administration and Politics of Tokyo: A Survey and Opinions* (New York, 1923), 177–8.
[80] Jeffrey Hanes, *The City as Subject: Seki Hajime and the Reinvention of Modern Osaka* (Berkeley, 2002), 205.

Figure 4 The skyline and smokestacks of Osaka in 1914. Image supplied by the National Diet Library.

Miserable conditions for Osaka workers resulted in considerable labour unrest, including strikes at the arsenal, and contributed strongly to the Rice Riots in Osaka.[81] The army quelled disturbances, further contributing to tensions between the military and citizenry. To Seki, Osaka Castle presented an opportunity for obtaining valuable urban space for a park, and anti-military feeling meant that he could count on popular support. Proponents of the castle park conversion also tied into another movement in the early 1920s to remove the army from the castle centre and to build shrines to Hideyoshi and the legendary emperor Nintoku in the main bailey, instead. This effort was led by a nationalistic education society that claimed to have 80,000 members and sought to boost shrine attendance.[82] Although this push was unsuccessful, it firmly established the idea of creating a castle park and opened negotiations on the subject with the army. Furthermore, by invoking

[81] *Ibid.*, 200–2.
[82] Nogawa, 'Ōsaka jō tenshukaku fukkō zenshi', 104–6.

Hideyoshi, this initiative was in clear competition with the army over claims to his legacy.

These competing agendas came together in 1925 in the Great(er) Osaka Exhibition, in which the castle played a central role. The army agreed to open the main bailey to the public for the duration of the exhibition, and to allow the organisers to construct a keep-shaped tower atop the highest ramparts, offering panoramic views of the city. This mock keep was named after Hideyoshi, and contained extensive displays relating to the castle's early history. Over 700,000 visitors toured the keep during the exhibition, and their approach took them past an impressive array of modern military hardware exhibited by the army for the occasion.[83] The army thus sought to reinforce its links with Japan's pre-modern martial heritage, including the expansionist hero Hideyoshi. At the same time, the exhibition further boosted popular interest in Hideyoshi and the castle, and whetted appetites for a permanent reconstruction of the castle keep in a new public castle park. This plan was soon taken up by Seki and local business leaders, encouraged by the visiting statesman Gotō Shinpei (1857–1929), who had served as mayor of Tokyo in a long career that included heading several government ministries.[84]

For the army, although the Great(er) Osaka Exhibition had been a useful propaganda event, there was no appetite for surrendering the centre of the castle to the public on a permanent basis. In addition to security issues, army leaders were embarrassed by the poor state of their deteriorating buildings, and were reluctant to expose these to further scrutiny by curious visitors to the castle.[85] This resulted from the military's dire financial situation following the retrenchments of the 1920s, which simultaneously presented an opportunity for proponents of the castle park. The army was willing to make concessions in exchange for economic support, in this case paying for a new administrative building. Following extensive negotiations, it was agreed that the army would allow the construction of a permanent keep inside a new castle park. In the end, the allocated public green space was only 10 per cent of that originally envisioned by the city, demonstrating the overwhelming power of the army in the negotiations.[86] Furthermore, the army insisted that the plans include the construction of a monumental new headquarters

[83] Kinoshita, 'Kindai Nihon no shiro ni tsuite', 92; Kinoshita Naoyuki, *Watashi no jōkamachi: tenshukaku kara mieru sengo no Nihon* (Tokyo, 2007), 263.

[84] Kitagawa, 'Ōsaka jō tenshukaku', 16.

[85] Nogawa, 'Ōsaka jō tenshukaku fukkō zenshi', 109.

[86] Hashitera Tomoko, 'Kaienji no Ōsaka jō kōen to Taishō ki no keikaku an ni tsuite: kindai no Ōsaka jōshi no riyō ni kan suru kenkyū', *Nihon kenchiku gakkai Kinki shibu kenkyū hōkoku shū* (2002), 1032.

building for the Fourth Division, to be located directly across from the reconstructed keep in the main bailey.

The city council approved the plans in February 1928, and 1.5 million Yen in donations and pledges were raised from the public in less than six months.[87] The new army building took up more than half the funds, and was built from concrete to resemble a medieval European castle. The design echoed that of contemporary armouries, prisons and other military buildings in Europe and the United States.[88] The focal point of the project was the reconstruction of Hideyoshi's castle keep, also built from steel-reinforced concrete at a cost of 471,000 Yen. As the first major concrete reconstruction of a castle keep, the project was beset by problems. With the field of castle research still in its infancy in Japan, the city tasked the municipal architect Furukawa Shigeharu with the project on the basis of his prior experience with shrine construction.[89] The lack of detailed historical materials complicated the project, as did the selection of Hideyoshi's early keep rather than the more extensively documented Tokugawa keep, for which the ramparts were designed.[90] The use of concrete also caused problems, as the centuries-old ramparts had to be reinforced to withstand the 11,000-ton keep.[91] The project was also delayed by personnel issues, with several key people leaving before its completion in 1931. Furukawa himself left early that year due to an unspecified personal conflict, but made his thoughts on the project known in a detailed book on the subject that ran to almost 500 pages and established him as one of the most authoritative castle researchers in Japan.[92] One of Furukawa's complaints related to the lack of 'high-level research' into the historical castle, which frustrated the attempts to recreate accurately the 'masculine shape' of Hideyoshi's original keep.[93]

The Osaka Castle keep was opened on 7 November 1931, in a major ceremony attended by hundreds of prominent persons, including Seki, the head of the Fourth Division and the city council. Celebrations were held throughout the city, with parades and extensive decorations. Newspapers focused on the contribution of the 'people of Osaka' in rebuilding the keep, which instantly became the symbol of the city

---

[87] Kitagawa, 'Ōsaka jō tenshukaku', 16.

[88] For example, see Nancy Todd, *New York's Historic Armories: An Illustrated History* (Albany, 2006).

[89] Furukawa Shigeharu, *Kinjō fukkō ki* (Osaka, 1931), Foreword 1.

[90] *Ibid.*, 2.

[91] *Ibid.*, 465–8; Amano Kōzō, Sazaki Toshiharu, Watanabe Takeru, Kitagawa Hiroshi, Ochiai Haruoki and Kawasaki Katsumi, 'Shōwa no Ōsaka jō fukkō tenshukaku no kiso kōzō ni tsuite', *Dobokushi kenkyū*, 17 (1997), 405–11.

[92] Furukawa, *Kinjō fukkō ki*, 462, 468–9.

[93] *Ibid.*, 464.

(Figure 5).[94] The connection with Osaka residents was further reinforced by restricting entry to the keep to locals for the first nine days of its opening, while the inside of the keep contained a local history museum as well as a special exhibition on Hideyoshi. The keep also had broader national significance, and its opening officially commemorated the enthronement of the Showa emperor several years before. The national appeal of the keep could be seen in events such as a November 1932 visit by the emperor, Seki and leaders of the Imperial Reservists Association.[95] In addition to these events, tens of thousands of ordinary people visited the castle, taking in the military installations and the imposing new headquarters building along the way.

The building of the Osaka Castle keep was a national event that both reflected and influenced broader trends elsewhere, especially major cities with large castles and military presences. In Sendai in the north-east, tensions between the public and the Second Division resulted in an agreement whereby the city built a new gate for the army, which opened part of the castle as a park in 1926.[96] In Kumamoto in the south-west, the civilian Kumamoto Castle Preservation Society worked to restore a seventeenth-century turret in 1927, attracting over 100,000 visitors in its first year of opening. Kumamoto Castle was controlled by the Sixth Division, and the public interest in the castle resulted in competing plans to reconstruct the lost keep by the army and preservation society. These conflicts contributed to the fact that the keep reconstruction was not realised, even though both sides invoked commemoration of the imperial enthronement, as in Osaka.[97] In Nagoya, where most of the castle was controlled by the Third Division, the castle keep was opened to the public in 1931. The keep was Japan's largest original castle structure, and after it had served as an imperial detached palace for more than three decades, the Imperial Household Ministry donated the main bailey along with the keep to the city in 1930 to avoid paying for costly maintenance and repair.[98] Within a few months, the keep and other structures were listed as national treasures and opened to the public,

[94] Kitagawa, 'Ōsaka jō tenshukaku', 16–17.

[95] 'Tenshukaku go tōrin', *Yomiuri shinbun* (17 Nov. 1932), 4.

[96] Katō Hiroshi, 'Dai ni shidan to Sendai', in *Chiiki no naka no guntai*, I: *Kita no guntai to gunto, Hokkaidō, Tōhoku*, ed. Yamamoto Kazushige (Tokyo, 2015), 35–6.

[97] Nonaka Katsutoshi, 'Kumamoto, Hagi, oyobi Wakamatsu ni okeru jōshi de no mogi tenshukaku no kensetsu kōsō to sono haikei: senzen no chihō toshi ni okeru mogi tenshukaku no kensetsu ni kan suru kenkyū, sono 4', *Nihon kenchiku gakkai keikaku kei ronbun shū*, 79 (2014), 1346–8.

[98] *Japan Times*, 24 Aug. 1930.

閣守天園公城阪大るせ建再で力の民市　（所 名 阪 大）
Osakajo Park and Castle Tower reconstructed by Citizen.
(Famous Place in Osaka)

Figure 5 'Osakajo Park and Castle Tower reconstructed by Citizen'.
Postcard from the author's collection.

Figure 6 'Headquarters of Kwanto (Kwantung) Army and Japanese Embassy, Hsin-ching (Xinjing)'. Postcard from the author's collection.

thereby bringing together military, civilian and imperial interests in a popular and publicly accessible space.[99]

By the early 1930s, vocal opposition to the military in broader society had decreased considerably, as Japanese involvement on the Asian continent expanded. The army projected its castle symbolism across the empire, as seen in the Kwantung Army Headquarters built in Shinkyō/Xinjing (now Changchun) in 1936 in the shape of a Japanese castle (Figure 6). Within Japan, castles also gained symbolic power in Japanese cities throughout the 1930s. Many towns used their castles for tourism and exhibitions, often with a militaristic and imperial theme. Himeji hosted the National Defence and Natural Resources Great Exhibition on the army parade ground in the castle in 1936, celebrating the castle, military, industry and tourism. Even in smaller towns without an army garrison, castles combined Japan's idealised samurai heritage with the modern military and technological advancement. The rural market town of Iga-Ueno rebuilt its lost keep in 1935, celebrating the occasion with an 'industrial and cultural' exhibition that included pavilions representing Japan's colonies, as well as a 'National Defence Pavilion' of the type that were ubiquitous at exhibitions at the time. The castle keep itself was celebrated as a 'command tower for industry

[99] *Hozon: Architectural and Urban Conservation in Japan*, ed. Siegfried R. C. T. Enders and Niels Gutschow (Stuttgart, 1998), 31.

Figure 7 Postcard commemorating a marine review in Osaka in the 1930s. The castle and smokestacks are shown in both the photograph and ornamental frame. From the author's collection.

and Japan's traditional bushido spirit'.[100] As the demand for new recruits grew, military and imperial exhibitions were important propaganda tools, and increased rapidly in number in the 1930s.[101] These events were often held in castle spaces or used castle themes to encourage identification with an idealised ancient Japanese martial spirit (Figure 7).

The local conflicts over the course of the Taisho period and beyond changed the functions of and meanings attached to castles while raising their profile. By boosting popular interest in and identification with castles, the conflicts over castle space ultimately contributed to the militarisation of society in the 1930s. The responses to popular unrest established beyond doubt the physical authority of the military in urban Japan. The struggles over control of castle sites between the military and civil society reaffirmed this hierarchy, while also raising the profile of castles as key symbols of local, regional and national identity. This development was reinforced by the partial conversion of castles to parks, local history museums and sites of memory, typically linked with both the military and the imperial house. In this way, the historical

[100] *Iga bunka sangyō jō rakusei ki'nen zenkoku hakurankai shi*, ed. Mie Ken Ueno Chō (Ueno, 1938), 2.
[101] Naoko Shimazu, *Japanese Society at War: Death, Memory and the Russo-Japanese War* (Cambridge, 2009), 241–8.

conditions of Japan's urban space contributed significantly to the convergence of popular and official interests that fed into the militaristic totalitarianism of late imperial Japan. To return to Kishida Hideto, the Japanese people, like people everywhere, may well have been 'more interested in the beautiful than the bellicose', but the military's appropriation and use of castles made the two most difficult to separate.

Transactions of the RHS 28 (2018), pp. 135–148 © Royal Historical Society 2018
doi:10.1017/S0080440118000075

BUILDINGS, LANDSCAPES AND REGIMES
OF MATERIALITY*

By William Whyte

READ 21 APRIL 2017

AT THE UNIVERSITY OF CHESTER

ABSTRACT. Beginning with a surprisingly exuberant response to the landscape
recorded by a distinguished scholar, this paper explores the agency of things and
places though time. It argues that the recent 'material turn' is part of a broader
re-enchantment of the world: a re-enchantment that has parallels with a similar
process at the turn of the nineteenth century. Tracing this history suggests that
within the space of a single generation the material world can be enchanted or disenchanted, with things and places imbued with – or stripped of –agency. In other
words, different periods possess what we might call different regimes of materiality.
Any approach which assumes the existence of material agency throughout history,
or which imports our assumptions into a period which did not share them, will
necessarily fail. Before we look at the material world, therefore, we need to
examine how the material world was looked at, how it was conceptualised and
how it was experienced. We need to apprehend its regime of materiality.

Landscapes, we are assured by the organisers of the Royal Historical
Society symposium, *Putting History in its Place*, 'are not merely canvasses
on which human action is played out, but constitute active social and cultural agents in producing change'. During the course of our discussions,
we witnessed just how that might work out across a range of landscapes
and a broad swathe of periods and places. Of course, as a modernist,
there is always a fear that my subject is simply not as exotic or as exciting
as those that went before – and the fact that my paper came last of all
only enhanced that fear. But let me start with a modern – a twentieth-
century – example of the power of place, nonetheless: one every bit as

*My sincere thanks to Jennifer Hillman, Tom Pickles and Katherine Wilson for the invi-
tation to speak, and to the Royal Historical Society for its support. I have explored some of
the ideas in this paper at conferences in Belfast, London and Oxford and am deeply grateful
for the opportunity to develop them over a number of years. I must also thank Dan Hicks
and Sim Koole for bibliographical suggestions, and – as always – acknowledge my debts to
Zoë Waxman for her invaluable help and advice.

odd as anything from the early modern or medieval eras, and one that raises – I believe – an important range of issues for historians of all periods.

I want to begin with a story taken from an autobiography published in 1994: the memoirs of Sir Kenneth Dover, a classicist, a rationalist and a man, as one biographer notes, almost painfully determined to expose his own experiences 'to critical scrutiny'.[1] Recalling his time in the Royal Artillery regiment as it swept through Italy in the latter part of the Second World War, Dover remarks on a somewhat surprising event which occurred in the mountains of Campagna, just a few miles south of the commune of Mignano Monte Luca. 'It was', writes Dover,

> an absolutely still day, with a blue sky from one horizon to the other, and the Matese massif was covered from end to end with snow. The scene struck directly at my penis, so I sat down on a log and masturbated; it seemed the appropriate response.

What, though, is the appropriate response of the historian to this rather unlikely reminiscence? For journalists in the mid-1990s, who headed a report of Dover's disclosure 'Oxford Don Takes Memoirs in Hand', this was simply a laughing matter. For the author himself, anxious – in his own words – to avoid the suggestion that his recollections amounted to nothing more than *Confessions of a Wanker*, and keen, presumably, to distinguish his writings from the shame-faced masturbatory memoirs of Jean-Jacques Rousseau, this physical, sexual response to a landscape could be simply and easily rationalised. 'The explanation of such events', Dover concludes, 'is scientific rather than philosophical.'[2] In other words, he saw this somehow as a natural response: natural in the sense that this was a simple, physiological reaction; and natural, too, in that it reflected some primal, essential, subconscious connection between a man and the natural world.

Clinicians are inclined to agree. Certainly, a recent encyclopaedia of human sexuality notes that it is not untypical for 'a person so inclined' to respond erotically to 'a pleasing landscape or art work'.[3] But philosophers might well beg to differ. Indeed, for the political philosopher Jane Bennett, considering what she calls 'the sex appeal of the inorganic' opens up all sorts of questions about human relationships with – and responsibility for – the environment.[4] And for historians, of course,

---

[1] Stephen Halliwell, 'Dover, Sir Kenneth James (1920–2010), Greek Scholar and College Head', *Oxford Dictionary of National Biography*, www.oxforddnb.com/view/10.1093/ref:odnb/9780198614128.001.0001/odnb-9780198614128-e-102682, accessed 13 Apr. 2018; see also D. A. Russell and F. S. Halliwell, 'Dover, Kenneth James, 1920–2010', *Biographical Memoirs of Fellows of the British Academy*, 11 (2012), 153–75.

[2] Kenneth Dover, *Marginal Comment: A Memoir* (1994), 114.

[3] *Human Sexuality: An Encyclopaedia*, ed. Vern Bullough and Bonnie Bullough (New York and London, 2013), 54.

[4] Jane Bennett, *Vibrant Matter: A Political Ecology of Things* (Durham, NC, 2010), 61. In this, she follows the terminology coined by Mario Perniola.

Dover offers a self-evidently inadequate account. Far from exposing this experience to critical scrutiny, his recourse to the rhetoric of nature and science ducks the important question of what was actually happening on that mountainside in Italy in 1944.

In the first place, as Dover, the author of a pioneering work on *Greek Homosexuality*, was well aware, sexuality and sexual practice are never just about science.[5] They have a history. And masturbation has a history every bit as rich and interesting as any other aspect of the history of sex (given its apparently perennial popularity, it can hardly not).[6] Secondly, and every bit as importantly, 'nature' is a category that cannot – or, at any rate – should not be reduced to the simply or supposedly 'scientific'. As the huge and ever-expanding field of environmental history continues to demonstrate, nature has a history too.[7] Even Dover's sense that he was witnessing a 'scene' – a landscape maybe – reveals his place within history: for both the notion of the scenic and the scene he describes have a history; they offer a glimpse of that most modern category, one defined by Edmund Burke in 1757 – the category of the sublime.[8] Caspar David Friedrich's *Wanderer Above a Sea of Fog* (1818) may have been doing nothing more alarming than gazing out into the mountains, but the sensibility depicted here is exactly that with which Dover identifies.[9] And in Friedrich's other paintings of the German alps, we see not just the same sensibility but the same aesthetic.[10] Dover's response in that way, too, was particular: shaped not just by science (whatever that means), but by history.

Yet even this conclusion does not go far enough. It is clearly important that we do not simply replace abstract 'science' with an equally abstract 'history' when trying to explain Dover's experience. Even when contextualised within the history of sexuality and the history of landscape, there

[5] Though it must be said his references to masturbation are somewhat reductive, see, e.g., Kenneth Dover, *Greek Homosexuality* (Cambridge, MA, 1989), 148.

[6] Thomas Lacqueur, *Solitary Sex: A Cultural History of Masturbation* (New York, 2003). On the silences surrounding the subject in history, see David Stevenson, 'Recording the Unspeakable: Masturbation in the Diary of William Drummond, 1657–1659', *Journal of the History of Sexuality*, 9 (2000), 223–39.

[7] For a useful introduction, see Andrew C. Isenberg, 'Introduction: A New Environmental History', in *The Oxford Handbook of Environmental History*, ed. Andrew C. Isenberg (Oxford, 2014), 1–22.

[8] Edmund Burke, *A Philosophical Enquiry into the Sublime and Beautiful* (Oxford, 2015), esp. 34, 47, 109–11. The sublimated sexuality of Burke's sublime is discussed in Richard C. Sha, *Perverse Romanticism: Aesthetics and Sexuality in Britain, 1750–1832* (Baltimore, 2009), 166–71. The extent to which a 'sexual element' is always found in the sublime is briskly summarised in Camille Paglia, *Sexual Personae: Art and Decadence from Nefertiti to Emily Dickinson* (New Haven and London, 2011), 269.

[9] Joseph Leo Koerner, *Caspar David Friedrich and the Subject of Landscape* (2009), 212–13.

[10] Werner Hofmann, *Caspar David Friedrich*, trans. Mary Whitall (2005), 22, 25.

remains a question at the heart of his account: the question with which this symposium sought to grapple; the question of agency. Dover's description is intriguing. He sketches in the scene – the 'blue sky', the snow-covered mountains – and then observes that this 'struck directly at my penis'; masturbation, he concludes, 'seemed the appropriate response'. But who is doing what in this recollection? Should we see Dover as the only active agent here? Or should we take seriously his implication – an implication he does not explore, and perhaps was not even conscious of evoking – that he was somehow responding to something the landscape was in some way doing to him?

These are crucial questions – critically important for anyone trying to put history back into its place, and vital for understanding landscapes and buildings in the past. For one of the most remarkable developments in scholarly life over the last two decades or so has been not just the renewed emphasis on objects and things which might be summed up in the 'material turn', but also – associated with, but distinct from this fashion – what appears to be a more profound re-enchantment of the world.[11] Anthropologists like Tim Ingold have reanimated animist notions of objects and landscapes.[12] Art historians like W. J. T. Mitchell have likewise returned to questions of totemism and fetishism and even asked the question 'what do pictures want?'[13] Archaeologists like Chris Gosden have widened this quest, not only enquiring 'What do objects want?', but also 'emphasizing the manner in which things create people'.[14] Philosophers like Jane Bennett have self-consciously sought to articulate what she describes as an 'enchanted materialism';[15] a 'childlike sense of the world as filled with all sorts of animate beings, some human, some not, some organic, some not'.[16]

And this re-enchantment of the world has – perhaps perforce – a special purchase on the study of the landscape: one that can be seen in the work of Ingold on perceptions of the environment,[17] or Mitchell on landscape and power.[18] Indeed, the landscape has become the site of a particular sort of enchantment: an unlikely mysticism which affects

[11] See especially Graham Harvey, *Animism: Respecting the Living World* (2017), 213–30.

[12] Tim Ingold, 'Rethinking the Animate, Reanimating Thought', *Ethnos: Journal of Anthropology*, 71 (2006) 9–20.

[13] W. J. T. Mitchell, *What Do Pictures Want? The Lives and Loves of Images* (Chicago and London, 2005).

[14] Chris Gosden, 'What Do Objects Want?', *Journal of Archaeological Method and Theory*, 12 (2005), 193–211, at 194.

[15] Jane Bennett, *The Enchantment of Modern Life: Attachments, Crossings, and Ethics* (Princeton, 2011), 92.

[16] Bennett, *Vibrant Matter*, 20.

[17] Tim Ingold, *The Perception of the Environment: Essays on Livelihood, Dwelling, and Skill* (new edn, London and New York, 2011).

[18] *Landscape and Power*, ed. W. J. T. Mitchell, 2nd edn (Chicago and London, 2002).

even those who seem to fight shy of the mystical. How else, for instance, to explain the ways in which avowedly post-humanist writers like social and political theorist Diana Coole are now nonetheless willing to approve such gnomic, quasi-mystical comments as those of Cézanne, as quoted by that other great mystic Maurice Merleau-Ponty: 'The landscape thinks itself in me and I am its consciousness'?[19]

This twenty-first-century re-enchantment of the world is almost – though perhaps not quite – as surprising as Kenneth Dover's decision to drop his trousers atop that Italian hill. After all, the disenchantment of the world was meant to be a characteristic of modernity. Indeed, for Weber, it is the definitive aspect of modernity; 'the key concept within Weber's account of the distinctiveness and significance of Western culture', as Ralph Schroder once observed.[20] Sociologists and historians, at least until recently, embraced disenchantment as an unquestioned fact: tracing the *Secularization of the European Mind in the Nineteenth Century* with the saintly Owen Chadwick,[21] or uncovering the vestigial, atrophying remains of *Religion in Secular Society* with the equally proper but infinitely more sceptical Bryan Wilson.[22]

The disenchantment of the world also meant the disenchantment of the landscape, of course, and in the distinguished form of Keith Thomas – Dover's successor as president of Corpus Christi College, Oxford, by the way – disenchantment found its prophet. *Religion and the Decline of Magic* (1971) and *Man and the Natural World* (1983) were both, in a sense, Weberian, and both traced disenchantment – even alienation – from the world. 'The seventeenth and eighteenth centuries', Thomas concludes, 'had seen a fundamental departure from the assumptions of the past.'[23] That departure – that disenchantment – was, it is clear, both product and progenitor of modernity. It is thus especially telling that in her brilliant book of 2011, *The Reformation of the Landscape*, Alexandra Walsham reaches quite the contrary conclusion. Covering a still greater period than Keith Thomas, she finds no disenchantment; rather, Walsham observes that 'the overall effect of the religious,

[19] Quoted in Diana Coole, 'The Inertia of Matter and the Generality of Flesh', in *New Materialisms: Ontology, Agency, and Politics*, ed. Diana Coole and Samantha Frost (Durham, NC, and London, 2010), 92–115, at 104. Compare this to the assertion on p. 20 of the introduction that this is a 'posthumanist' study.

[20] Ralph Shroeder, 'Disenchantment and its Discontents: Weberian Perspectives on Science and Technology', *Sociological Review*, 43 (1995), 227–50, at 228. See also Richard Jenkins, 'Disenchantment, Enchantment and Re-Enchantment: Max Weber at the Millennium', *Max Weber Studies*, 1 (2000), 11–32.

[21] Owen Chadwick, *The Secularization of the European Mind in the Nineteenth Century* (Cambridge, 1975).

[22] Bryan Wilson, *Religion in Secular Society* (Harmondsworth, 1969).

[23] Keith Thomas, *Man and the Natural World* (1983), 90.

intellectual, and cultural movements' she outlines 'was to redefine rather than remove the presence of the sacred in the material world'.[24]

What accounts for this re-enchantment? How, in the forty years between *Religion and the Decline of Magic* and *The Reformation of the Landscape* could scholars have come to differ so much? There are doubtless many explanations – generational, political, methodological. In the short space available to me, I can only gesture towards some of the key themes and most important works. An undeniably important development was what has become known as the material turn: a move or movement which, as we all know, emerged out of a deepening dissatisfaction with the linguistic turn;[25] a dissatisfaction voiced most forcefully by the Italian theorist Roberto Esposito in his ringing declaration that 'By transforming the thing into a word, language empties of it of reality';[26] and a process rather wonderfully illustrated in A. S. Byatt's novel of 2001, *The Biographer's Tale*, which opens with a postgraduate, poststructuralist student, sitting bored in an English literature class, pondering the 'fatal family likeness' of all his seminars. 'We found the same clefts and crevices, transgressions and disintegrations, lies and deceptions beneath, no matter what surface we were scrying', he observes. As his lecturer expatiates on Lacan and Freud once again, he concludes that he has had enough. 'I thought', he writes, 'I must have things.'[27] That a whole generation of scholars has agreed explains much about scholarship since then.

This search for things has been accompanied – and energised – by a renewed interest in the history of the body and in the history of emotions. Both have redirected our attention towards traditions of thought – especially phenomenology in its various different forms – that seek self-consciously to re-enchant. Heidegger is a continual reference point here; as is Husserl and Merleau-Ponty. Without their example, the work of philosophers like Edward Casey or archaeologists like Christopher Tilley would be unimaginable.[28] Without Tilley or Casey, the history of landscape, in particular, would be very different indeed.[29] Other

---

[24] Alexandra Walsham, *The Reformation of the Landscape: Religion, Identity, and Memory in Early Modern Britain and Ireland* (Oxford, 2011), 567.

[25] Dan Hicks, 'The Material Cultural Turn: Event and Effect', in *The Oxford Handbook of Material Culture Studies*, ed. Dan Hicks and Mary Beaudry (Oxford, 2010), 25–99.

[26] Roberto Esposito, *Persons and Things*, trans. Zakiya Hanafi (Cambridge, 2015), 9.

[27] A. S. Byatt, *The Biographer's Tale* (2001), 1–2.

[28] Edward S. Casey, *Getting Back into Place: Towards a Renewed Understanding of the Place-World*, 2nd edn (Bloomington and Indianapolis, 2009); Christopher Y. Tilley, *A Phenomenology of Landscape: Places, Paths and Monuments* (1994).

[29] Tilley is, for example, cited in Walsham, *Reformation of the Landscape*, 6. Casey has proved influential in the work of historians like Helen Gittos, *Liturgy, Architecture, and Sacred Places in Anglo-Saxon England* (Oxford, 2015), 277.

theorists, like the French philosopher and historian Michel Serres, have also offered a phenomenologically informed approach which seeks to re-enchant. 'We consider a landscape, as a whole and in detail', he writes in his influential tract on *The Five Senses*, 'it considers us as a landscape.'[30]

There is, of course, an ethical dimension to all this. The contemporary re-enchantment of the world owes much to anxieties about the environment – especially human-made climate change. In Jane Bennett's words, the project of imputing agency to the world is driven by the 'hunch…that the image of dead and thoroughly instrumentalised matter feeds human hubris and our earth-destroying fantasies of conquest and consumption'.[31] There is also a hope that a re-enchanted world will find space for a more progressive politics. Breaking down the boundaries between subject and object, human and non-human, it is argued, will also break down divisions between people. Recognising the entanglement of matter and meaning, humans and the world in which they live, suggests Karen Barad, in a book which draws on quantum physics to make its point, will enable the creation of an ecological, egalitarian, feminist political philosophy. 'We are of the universe', she concludes, 'there is no inside, no outside. There is only intra-acting from within and as part of the world in its becoming.'[32]

All these forces – intellectual, ethical and, doubtless, simply professional – have been given further impetus by wider historical changes. I can only sketch them in for now; but they do need to be acknowledged. The fall of the Soviet Union and the rise of fundamentalist religion has had a shattering effect on modernisation theory, with its assumption of a secular future for all.[33] The relative decline of the West has also led to questions about what was believed to be its normative path to modernity. For whilst modernisation theory – with all its disenchantments – has retained a surprising purchase in precisely those parts of the world that seem to challenge it most, the rise of the rest and slide of the West have had their effects.[34] Dipesh Chakrabarty's *Provincializing Europe* is a good example of this – and the fact it concludes with a

[30] Michel Serres, *The Five Senses: A Philosophy of Mingled Bodies*, trans. Margaret Sankey and Peter Cowley (2016), 51.

[31] Bennett, *Vibrant Matter*, ix.

[32] Karen Barad, *Meeting the Universe Halfway: Quantum Physics and the Entanglement of Matter and Meaning* (Durham, NC, and London, 2007), 396.

[33] The changing atmosphere is wonderfully summed up in the work of the sociologist Steve Bruce – from *God is Dead: Secularization in the West* (2002) to *Secularization: In Defence of an Unfashionable Theory* (Oxford, 2011).

[34] See, for instance, James Fergusson, *Expectations of Modernity: Myths and Meanings of Urban Life on the Zambian Copperbelt* (Berkeley, 1999). I explore some of these themes in William Whyte, 'Modernism, Modernisation, and Europeanisation in West African Architecture, 1944–1994', in *Europeanization in the Twentieth Century: Historical Approaches*, ed. Martin Conway and Kiran Klaus Patel (Basingstoke, 2010), 210–28.

discussion of magic is emblematic of the ways in which enchantment and re-enchantment have become important parts of a broader challenge to a monolithic notion of modernity.[35] Similar themes can be found in the work of that great founding father of actor-network theory, Bruno Latour.[36] Indeed, with his bold claim that *We Have Never Been Modern* and in his most recent book *Facing Gaia* we encounter the intriguing entanglement of material agency, political idealism, doubts about modernisation theory and a certain amount of mysticism or even enchantment.[37]

So much for the present day. My reason for spending such a long time outlining this context is not just that much writing on the material turn seems to ignore or downplay the process of re-enchantment which has become such an important part of it. It is also – indeed, it is preeminently – because our early twenty-first-century experience is so remarkably reminiscent of an earlier, early nineteenth-century, moment. The eighteenth century was, as numerous scholars have noted, a period of disenchantment. Inheritors of the Cartesian dualism against which so many of our contemporary writers now rail; disciples of the Newtonian worldview with its fixed laws and predictable causality; imbibers of the Kantian notion of matter as essentially inert and passive: the thinkers of the age of the Enlightenment are in all sorts of ways precisely those sorts of people who helped shape the modernisation thesis and who saw the disenchantment of the world as a necessary, desirable end.[38]

To be sure, we now know much more the ways in which this disenchantment proved partial, fragmentary, episodic. We understand that the eighteenth century found room for miracles and Enlightenment; for the alchemy as well as the physics of Newton; for much magical thinking.[39] It is now pretty uncontroversial to argue, as Paul Kléber Monod does in a recent book, that the period 'witnessed a remarkable revival of occult thinking'.[40]

[35] Dipesh Chakrabarty, *Provincializing Europe: Postcolonial Thought and Historical Difference* (Princeton and Oxford, 2000), 240–3.

[36] Bruno Latour, *On the Modern Cult of the Factish Gods* (Durham, NC, 2010), 61.

[37] Bruno Latour, *We Have Never Been Modern*, trans. Catherine Porter (Cambridge, MA, 1993); *idem, Facing Gaia: Eight Lectures on the New Climatic Regime*, trans. Catherine Porter (Cambridge, 2017).

[38] See especially Edward Casey, *The Fate of Place: A Philosophical History* (Berkeley, 1997). For Kant, for instance, the sublime and sexual experience detailed by Kenneth Dover would be simply the consequence of a – somewhat disordered – mental process. 'Sublimity', he observes, 'does not reside in any of the things of nature, but only in our own mind': Immanual Kant, *The Critique of Judgement*, trans. James Creed Meredith (Oxford, 1952), 114.

[39] Jane Shaw, *Miracles in Enlightenment England* (New Haven and London, 2006); Rob Iliffe, *Priest of Nature: The Religious Worlds of Isaac Newton* (Oxford, 2017).

[40] Paul Kléber Monod, *Solomon's Secret Arts: The Occult in the Age of Enlightenment* (New Haven and London, 2013), 227.

Yet even if one acknowledges that the eighteenth-century experience and understanding of the world was more complex and multi-faceted than a simple caricature of Enlightenment ideals might suggest, the truth remains that 'the modern scopic regime', as Martin Jay puts it, did apparently 'triumph' in this period.[41] With this triumph came a celebration of the enlightened individual's subjectivity: a focus on the distance between the viewer and that which was viewed; a disenchantment of a sort precisely because it emphasised the dynamic role of the observer and the passive role of the world around him (and it was almost always him). This was a development which united those who, following Locke, were fundamentally empiricist and those who, following Descartes, preferred to focus on how the mind interpreted sensation. For both occultist and rationalist, too – and for those who were both – the material world was subject to man; not a force in its own right. It was an odd consensus oddly summed up in the aesthetic theorist William Gilpin's disagreements with his neighbour William Lock in 1769. 'I have had a dispute lately', he wrote, 'on an absurd vulgar opinion, which he holds – *that we see with our eyes*; whereas I assert, that our eyes are only mere glass windows; and we see with our imagination.'[42] Either way, of course, the active agent was the viewer and the recipient of that action was the world beyond.[43]

Just as is the case today, debates about landscape give a good index of what was thought and felt. Landscape, after all, was a relatively new coinage and a relatively new concept. It was also hugely fashionable. Landscape design and landscape painting were of intense interest for a remarkable range of people, 'those', as Conal Shields once put it, 'for whom "nature" was nearly, if not quite, something to be ignored: those for whom it was to be subdued or transformed: those for whom it was to be gazed at and enjoyed'.[44] In all these cases, of course, the landscape was treated as an object of interest rather than a subject – much less an agent – in its own right. By the end of the eighteenth century, it had become controversial to maintain that landscapes had any inherent quality of their own. Instead, many cleaved to the claims of writers like Richard Payne Knight, who argued that the picturesque landscape, for instance, was nothing more than 'a way of seeing, a subjective

---

[41] Martin Jay, *Downcast Eyes: The Denigration of Vision in Twentieth-Century French Thought* (Berkeley, 1994), 105.

[42] Quoted in J. Mordaunt Crook, *The Dilemma of Style: Architectural Ideas from the Picturesque to the Post-Modern* (1987), 21.

[43] See also Jonathan Crary, 'Modernizing Vision', in *Vision and Visuality*, ed. Hal Foster (Seattle, 1988), 29–50, at 33.

[44] Conal Shields, 'Introduction', to *Landscape in Britain, c. 1750–1850*, ed. Leslie Parris (Exhibition Catalogue, London, 1973), 9–13, at 9.

aesthetic in the eye of the beholder'.[45] Armed with Burke's dictum that 'No work of art can be great, but it deceives';[46] committed to Chambers's argument that 'Nature is incapable of pleasing without the assistance of art',[47] designers like Humphry Repton, in the words of one expert, turned landscape design 'into a species of furnishing'.[48] Here was disenchantment indeed.

Attitudes towards architecture echoed this sense of the material world as passive, animated only by human action. This was increasingly true even of sacred architecture, which is conventionally understood as somehow intrinsically different: an embodiment, in the title of one influential text, of *Theology in Stone*;[49] a space capable of evoking emotion and – in the words of Mary Carruthers – a place which 'has, as it were, moving parts…an engine of prayer, not simply its edifice'.[50] Yet, as historians of eighteenth-century America have shown in particular, the construction of churches which simply followed secular fashions,[51] and which down-played any sacred function, was in many respects a distinctive feature of the period.[52] Far from being an engine of prayer, much less an active agent of any sort, the late eighteenth-century church was simply a gathering place: a box for preaching in; a vessel which only came alive when it was filled by its congregation.[53] Little wonder churches remained locked and closed for most of the week: these practical, fashionable spaces were essentially inert. Like the wider landscape of which they were a part, it was human activity and human agency which counted; the material world was always subject to that.

As I have argued elsewhere, the nineteenth century would overturn this conception of sacred space.[54] Churches were reimagined as active

[45] Stephen Daniels, *Humphry Repton: Landscape Gardening and the Geography of Georgian England* (New Haven and London, 1999), 48.

[46] Quoted in David Watkin, *The English Vision: The Picturesque in Architecture, Landscape, and Garden Design* (1982), viii.

[47] Quoted in Crook, *Dilemma of Style*, 31.

[48] *Ibid.*, 26.

[49] Richard Kieckhefer, *Theology in Stone: Church Architecture from Byzantium to Berkeley* (New York, 2004).

[50] Mary Carruthers, *The Craft of Thought: Meditation, Rhetoric, and the Making of Images, 400–1200* (Cambridge, 1999), 263.

[51] Dell Upton, *Holy Things and Profane: Anglican Parish Churches in Colonial Virginia* (New Haven and London, 1997), 228–9.

[52] Louis P. Nelson, *The Beauty of Holiness: Anglicanism and Architecture in Colonial South Carolina* (Chapel Hill, NC, 2008).

[53] John Harvey, *Image of the Invisible: The Visualization of Religion in the Welsh Nonconformist Tradition* (Cardiff, 1999).

[54] See William Whyte, *Unlocking the Church: The Lost Secrets of Victorian Sacred Space* (Oxford, 2017). For a shorter essay with a broader perspective, see William Whyte, 'Architecture', in

agents: capable of shaping belief; able to affect their congregations and even passers-by. For the influential German architect and theorist Karl Friedrich Schinkel, for instance, 'the "genuine" religious building' was, as John Toews puts it, 'a place where individuals were guided towards recognition of their inner essence through aesthetic experiences of the divine principle which animated both the universe and themselves'.[55] This new – this re-enchanted – view of architecture would shape buildings throughout the world, as the old notion of the church as an inert vessel gave way and a forest of steeples, a sea of stained-glass, a tide of encaustic tiles and marble fittings swept across cities, towns and villages. These were not merely aesthetic effects; they reflected a belief that buildings – especially religious buildings – did things to people.[56]

This transformation was not confined to churches. The belief that buildings shaped behaviour; the sense that – as one Victorian headmaster put it – *'the almighty wall is, after all, the supreme and final arbiter'*, was very influential.[57] Prisons, workhouses, schools, public buildings and private homes were all designed with this in mind.[58] The 'agency of things' that Patrick Joyce has uncovered in this period – most recently in his *State of Freedom* – was a product of this new, and newly re-enchanted view.[59] And, of course, it was not just architecture that was reimagined in light of this thinking. The townscape, the landscape, the natural world – what we might call the environment – were all, in this environmentalist view, seen as consequential, capable of shaping their human inhabitants.

Think of the housing reformer and landscape preserver Octavia Hill, for instance.[60] A woman shaped by widely shared assumptions about the impact of the environment, her life was devoted to redeeming the poor by improving their homes and granting them access to nature. So committed was she to the idea of material agency that she often neglected the capacity of humans to act, treating the recipients of her idealism as objects – 'never', in Ruth Livesey's words, 'full actors' – whilst emphasising the way in which new houses or gardens or plants could

The Oxford Handbook of Nineteenth-Century Christian Thought, ed. Joel Rasmussen, Judith Wolfe and Johannes Zachhuber (Oxford, 2017), 471–84.

[55] John Toews, *Becoming Historical: Cultural Reformation and Public Memory in Early Nineteenth-Century Berlin* (Cambridge, 2004), 129.

[56] See also G. L. Hersey, *High Victorian Gothic: A Study in Associationism* (Baltimore, 1972).

[57] Edward Thring, quoted in William Whyte, 'Building a Public School Community, 1860–1910', *History of Education*, 32 (2003), 601–26, at 619.

[58] I explore this further in William Whyte, 'Architecture', in Carolyn White, *A Cultural History of Objects in the Age of Industry* (forthcoming).

[59] Patrick Joyce, *The State of Freedom: A Social History of the British State since 1800* (Cambridge, 2013), esp. ch. 7.

[60] The following sentences draw heavily on William Whyte, 'Octavia Hill: The Practice of Sympathy and the Art of Housing', in *'Nobler Imaginings and Mightier Struggles': Octavia Hill and the Remaking of British Society*, ed. Elizabeth Baigent and Ben Cowell (2016), 47–64.

ameliorate both the lives and the souls of the indigent.[61] Hill's emotional entanglement with things even extended to the terrible 'sense of injustice' she felt when planting a Virginia creeper in one of her tenements. She could not rid herself of the guilt that it was exposed 'to so different a fate from its companions'.[62] In Octavia Hill, we find something approaching animism in the late Victorian slums of London.

This brief sketch of an epistemological revolution 200 years ago is not only intended to signal that we have been here before; though we have. It is also meant to pose a problem: a conceptual and methodological issue for those of us interested in the effect of the material world on individuals and societies in the past; the problem with which I began this paper. Even in this now re-enchanted world, scholars remain unsure about material agency. There are those who would wish to deny any distinction between human and non-human actors: those, like the archaeologist Dan Hicks, who would reject what he terms 'the false impression that the dirt on my hands is somehow ontologically different from my hands themselves'.[63] There are those, too, like the historian Chris Otter, who would deny the term agency altogether, seeing it as an unhappy and unhelpful anthropomorphism, which – as he puts it – 'ironically, disrespects a resolutely non-human, inorganic process'.[64] For most, the solution is a still greater emphasis on materiality. Indeed, it is a routine complaint by writers of wildly divergent views that previous scholars – even, perhaps especially, those writing on the material – have not taken materiality seriously enough. For Tim Ingold, for instance, only through making – through scholars weaving, flint napping, dancing, focusing intently on things in themselves and for themselves – will we come to understand how things work and how people are things.[65] For Ian Hodder, only a willingness to abandon a human-centred analysis for one focused more firmly on things will unravel the entanglements of people and the material world.[66]

There is a virtue in this. Hodder is surely right to criticise phenomenologists like Christopher Tilley for blithely assuming that 'our own

---

[61] R. Livesey, 'Women Rent Collectors and the Rewriting of Space, Class, and Gender in East London, 1870–1900', in *Women and the Making of Built Space*, ed. Elizabeth Darling and Lesley Whitworth (Aldershot, 2007), 87–106, at 94.

[62] C. Edmund Maurice, *The Life of Octavia Hill as Told in her Letters* (1913), 193. Quoted in Whyte, 'Octavia Hill'.

[63] Hicks, 'The Material Cultural Turn', 96.

[64] Chris Otter, 'The Technosphere: A New Concept for Urban Studies', *Urban History*, 44 (2017), 145–54, at 147.

[65] Tim Ingold, *Making: Anthropology, Archaeology, Art, and Architecture* (New York and London, 2013).

[66] Ian Hodder, *Entangled: An Archaeology of the Relationships between Humans and Things* (Chichester, 2012).

embodied experiences of landscapes and monuments today must reveal to us something of the experiences of the people who once inhabited those same places in the past'.[67] But his solution – to focus yet further on the material itself – is no real solution at all, at least for my purposes, because it tells us no more about how that material was understood and experienced than the phenomenologists can. It replaces conjecture with something seemingly – literally – more solid. But it remains problematic, because it assumes, with a wonderful circularity, that if we only understood the thing we will come to understand how the thing was understood. Put more simply: just as we can have no confidence that our present-day experiences are the same of those of people in the past, so we can have no confidence that our understanding of materiality itself is the same as that of our subjects.[68]

What I have sought to show is that within the space of a generation the material world can be enchanted or disenchanted; it can be seen to possess agency, or any sort of agency can be strongly denied. In other words, different periods possess what we might call different regimes of materiality. They do not just understand the world differently; they experience it differently; they interact with it differently. As Chris Gosden acknowledges towards the end of an essay which appears to say quite the reverse, 'The world changes not just in its forms but in its feelings.'[69] Any approach which assumes the existence of material agency, which imports our assumptions into a period which did not share them, will necessarily fail to capture that. Before we look at the material world, therefore, we need to examine how the material world was looked at, how it was conceptualised.

These regimes of materiality were, of course, never secure. They were fluid and changeable. They encompassed a striking variety of different approaches. After all, when the anthropologist Daniel Miller went to explore how a people in a single street used things, he found thirty different experiences in thirty virtually identical houses.[70] Regimes of materiality might also be small scale and quite specific. They might be highly individuated even. After all, Kenneth Dover's notably enthusiastic response to the landscape reflected a regime which perhaps few other people have ever shared. But, just like the different emotional regimes explored by William Reddy in his work on *The Navigation of Feeling*, these differing regimes of materiality defined what was reasonable to

[67] *Ibid.*, 29.

[68] For a rather more enthusiastic account of phenomenology – when combined with documentary research – see Nicola Whyte, 'Senses of Place, Senses of Time: Landscape History from a British Perspective', *Landscape Research*, 40 (2015), 925–38.

[69] Gosden, 'What Do Objects Want?', 209.

[70] Daniel Miller, *The Comfort of Things* (Cambridge, 2008).

believe about the world and what was possible to experience in the world.[71] It is by uncovering and re-articulating these regimes of materiality that historians can come to understand both their subjects and how their subjects experienced the world.

This claim has an obvious implication for the study of buildings and landscapes. In a typically lapidary phrase, W. J. T. Mitchell once observed that he hoped 'to change "landscape" from a noun to a verb', from 'an object to be seen or a text to be read' into a 'process by which social and subjective identities are formed'.[72] In this paper, I have tried to suggest that both these accounts – both the idea of the landscape as fixed and the idea of the landscape as active – had different purchases at different times in history, in different regimes of materiality. If landscape is a verb, it is one that has been translated and comprehended very differently in these different regimes of materiality.

---

[71] William M. Reddy, *The Navigation of Feeling: A Framework for the History of Emotions* (Cambridge, 2001).

[72] W. J. T. Mitchell, 'Introduction', to *Landscape and Power*, ed. Mitchell, 1–4, at 1.

Transactions of the RHS 28 (2018), pp. 149–174 © Royal Historical Society 2018
doi:10.1017/S0080440118000087

ORTHODOXY AND REVOLUTION: THE RESTORATION OF THE RUSSIAN PATRIARCHATE IN 1917

Prothero Lecture

By Simon Dixon

READ 7 JULY 2017

ABSTRACT. At the height of the October Revolution in Moscow – a much bloodier affair than the Bolshevik seizure of power in Petrograd – the Orthodox Church installed Tikhon (Bellavin) as Russia's first patriarch since 1700. At the most obvious level, this was a counter-revolutionary gesture aimed at securing firm leadership in a time of troubles. It was nevertheless a controversial move. Ecclesiastical liberals regarded a restored patriarchate as a neo-papal threat to the conciliarist regime they hoped to foster; and since Nicholas II had explicitly modelled himself on the Muscovite tsar Aleksei Mikhailovich, the potential for renewed conflict between church and state had become clear long before 1917. Whilst previous historians have concentrated on discussions about canonical and historical precedent, this paper emphasises the extent to which a single individual haunted the whole debate. For, until the last moment, it was widely assumed that the new patriarch would be not the little-known Tikhon, but Archbishop Antonii (Khrapovitskii), whose attempts to model himself on Patriarch Nikon – the most divisive of seventeenth-century Muscovite patriarchs – helped to make him the most controversial prelate of the age.

'Slaughter on the streets of Moscow', noted Sergei Prokof'ev in November 1917, appalled at the bombing of an apartment he had planned to occupy: 'How clever of me not to have gone at all!'[1] While Prokof'ev read Kant in Kislovodsk, the revolution had become much bloodier in Russia's old capital than in Petrograd, where the Bolsheviks seized power on 25 October. When Red Guards captured

---

Dates follow the Julian calendar, used in Russia before the Bolshevik Revolution, thirteen days behind the Gregorian calendar in the twentieth century.

[1] *Sergey Prokofiev Diaries: 1915–1923, Behind the Mask*, trans. Anthony Phillips (2008), 240, Nov. 1917.

the Kremlin on the following day, it was besieged by *iunkers* loyal to the Provisional Government, who retook the fortress on 28 October. Once the Military Revolutionary Committee abandoned the subsequent ceasefire two nights later, vicious street-fighting ensued. Most of those who took up arms were apparently keener to thwart counter-revolution than to launch a Soviet regime.[2] But among the Moscow Bolsheviks, there were extremists such as Nikolai Bukharin, who thought 5,000 casualties an acceptable price to pay. 'One could hardly expect the socialist revolution to be as painless as some popular festival', Bukharin warned the Petrograd Soviet once victory was assured: 'This is the epoch of dictatorship and we shall sweep away with an iron broom everything that deserves to be swept away.'[3]

It was against this menacing backdrop that the first Russian Church Council since 1689 resolved on the need for firm ecclesiastical leadership. When the Council opened on the feast of the Dormition (15 August), there had been no immediate prospect that the patriarchate would be restored. Indeed, so controversial was the subject that it was introduced to a plenary session only on 11 October. Under pressure from external events, subsequent progress was swift. On 28 October, the Council resolved to curtail its debates at the Moscow Diocesan House, a few streets to the north of the Kremlin, and elect a patriarch forthwith. On 31 October, as violence raged nearby, three bishops were elected to go forward to the final drawing of lots: the Council's chairman, Tikhon (Bellavin), installed as metropolitan of Moscow as recently as July, and two of his six vice-chairmen, Archbishops Arsenii (Stadnitskii) of Novgorod and Antonii (Khrapovitskii) of Khar'kov.[4] The revolutionaries' final assault on the Kremlin on 1–2 November prevented a patriarchal election in the Dormition cathedral. So, on 5 November, thousands of Muscovites struggled past the university anatomy theatre, where fellow-citizens queued to identify corpses destined for a mass grave on Red Square, to the cathedral of Christ the Saviour.[5] There, the Council's secretary wrote out the candidates' names in front of a packed congregation and placed the slips in a casket. At the end of a liturgy conducted by Kiev's Metropolitan Vladimir (Bogoiavlenskii), Tikhon's name was drawn by a venerable monk.

---

[2] Richard Pipes, *The Russian Revolution, 1899–1919* (1990), 501–3; Diane P. Koenker, *Moscow Workers and the 1917 Revolution* (Princeton, 1981), 329–46.

[3] *The Debate on Soviet Power: Minutes of the All-Russian Central Executive Committee of Soviets, Second Convocation October 1917–January 1918*, trans. and ed. John L. H. Keep (Oxford, 1979), 96, 98, 6 Nov. 1917.

[4] *Deianiia Sviashchennogo Sobora Pravoslavnoi Rossiiskoi Tserkvi 1917–1918 gg.* (hereafter *Deianiia*) (11 vols., Moscow, 1994–2000), III, 55–6, 31 Oct. 1917.

[5] *Time of Troubles: The Diary of Iurii Vladimirovich Got'e*, trans. and ed. Terence Emmons (Princeton, 1988), 76, 5 Nov. 1917.

Though churchmen shocked by the desecration of the Kremlin's holy places had failed to broker a truce earlier in the week, they successfully negotiated a return to the Dormition cathedral through the mediation of Prince Nikolai Odoevskii-Malov, the beleaguered head of the palace administration who had known Anastasii (Gribanovskii), the liturgist charged with staging Tikhon's enthronement, as bishop of Serpukhov between 1906 and 1914.[6] According to Archbishop Arsenii, the Bolshevik authorities 'did all they could to spoil the festival', making the ritual on the feast of the Presentation of the Mother of God into the Temple (21 November) 'more like a funeral than the joyful coronation of a great church father'.[7] Bishops were obliged to abandon their carriages – treasured, if much derided, status symbols – and proceed on foot to the Trinity Gate. There, council delegates were delayed by the Kremlin's new commandant, who accused them of exceeding their allocation of tickets. 'Why do we need a patriarch? Let them walk!' onlookers hooted as Metropolitan Vladimir, a prominent right-winger, slipped on the cobbles. It was a similar story after the service, when Tikhon circumnavigated the Kremlin in a cab to bless the crowd who had been refused entrance. Metropolitan Evlogii (Georgievskii) later claimed that Red Guards on cathedral square doffed their caps in reverential silence: according to the contemporary record, those outside the Kremlin sang the Marseillaise.[8] But despite all the obstacles, Tikhon was installed wearing vestments made for his Muscovite predecessors and the Russian Church could boast its first patriarch since the death of Adrian in October 1700.

I

Since this was by any standards an historic moment, it is curious that historians should have treated it so unevenly. Most have ignored the restoration,[9] implicitly dismissing it as the sort of 'grandiose "nonevent"' that

---

[6] M. I. Odintsov, 'Moskovskii Kreml', osazhdennyi revoliutsiei: Oktiabr'-noiabr' 1917 g. Svidetel'stva ochevidtsev', *Istoricheskii arkhiv* (1997), no. 3, 64–77; A. V. Sokolov, 'Gosudarstvo i pravoslavnaia tserkov' v Rossii, Fevral' 1917 – ianvar' 1918 gg.' (doctoral dissertation, Russian State Pedagogical University, St Petersburg, 2014), 532–44; Mitropolit Anastasii (Gribanovskii), 'Izbranie i postavlenie Sviateishego Patriarkha Tikhona', *Bogoslovskii sbornik*, 13 (2005), 363–5.

[7] Prot. V. Vorobe'v and I. A. Krivosheeva, 'Mitropolit Arsenii (Stadnitskii) o sobore 1917–1918 gg. i vosstanovlenii patriarshestva', in *XIX Ezhegodnaia bogoslovskaia konferentsiia PSTGU: Materialy, tom 1* (Moscow, 2009), 253.

[8] *Deianiia*, IV, 36–75 (second pagination), 21 Nov. 1917; 'Iz "dnevnika" Professora A. D. Beliaeva', *Bogoslovskii sbornik*, 6 (2000), 123–4, diary, 26 Nov. 1917; *Put' moei zhizni: Vospominaniia Mitropolita Evlogiia*, ed. T. Manukhina (Paris, 1947), 305.

[9] There is, for example, no mention of it in Pipes, *Russian Revolution*; Catherine Merridale, *Red Fortress: The Secret Heart of Russia's History* (2013); or Laura Engelstein, *Russia in Flames:*

the exceptionally well-informed Catherine Evtuhov had in mind when describing the Moscow Church Council as one of those 'powerful and directed impulses that never achieved culmination because the Revolution happened instead'.[10] Overturning stereotypes of institutional inertia, Evtuhov herself demonstrated that a wide range of believers drawn from all sectors of society were capable of articulating a variety of Orthodox worldviews to challenge emerging secular norms.[11] Nevertheless, most of the 564 delegates who came to the Moscow Church Council from all corners of the empire were followers rather than leaders. Scarcely any of the fifty-one speakers who registered for the plenary debate on the patriarchate had anything new to say because discussion of restoration had long been dominated by the forty or so bishops, priests, scholars and intellectuals whose private and public utterances form my principal sources. Paradoxically, although much of the most distinguished recent scholarship is replete with names, its tone is deliberately impersonal so that many individuals remain all but anonymous.[12] I shall take a different approach, arguing that the debate on the patriarchate was inseparable not only from questions of canonical and historical tradition, but also from questions of contemporary politics and personality. In other words, churchmen's views on matters of principle were mediated by their opinions of each other.

Hopes of restoring the patriarchate had been expressed privately in ecclesiastical circles from the time of Metropolitan Filaret (Drozdov), Russia's leading prelate between the 1820s and his death in 1867. Public discussion dated from the 1880s. But a realistic prospect of restoration came only with the campaign for church reform that erupted with unexpected force in spring 1905.[13] By then, the Synodal system

War, Revolution, Civil War (New York and Oxford, 2017). Nicholas V. Riasanovsky and Mark D. Steinberg, *A History of Russia*, 8th edn (New York, 2011), 614, say that Tikhon was elected patriarch in 1918; Nicolas Zernov, *Eastern Christendom: A Study of the Origin and Development of the Eastern Orthodox Church* (1963), 207, gives 31 July 1917. By contrast, see Geoffrey Hosking, *Russia and the Russians from Earliest Times to 2001* (2001), 438, for 'the most important event in the history of the Orthodox Church for over two hundred years'.

[10] Catherine Evtuhov, *The Cross and the Sickle: Sergei Bulgakov and the Fate of Russian Religious Philosophy, 1890–1920* (Ithaca, NY, 1997), 191.

[11] Catherine Evtuhov, 'The Church in the Russian Revolution: Arguments for and against Restoring the Patriarchate at the Church Council of 1917–1918', *Slavic Review*, 50 (1991), 497–511.

[12] Vera Shevzov, *Russian Orthodoxy on the Eve of Revolution* (New York and Oxford, 2004), 49–51; Hyacinthe Destivelle, *The Moscow Council (1917–1918): The Creation of the Conciliar Institutions of the Russian Orthodox Church* (Notre Dame, IN, 2015), 2, 77–90.

[13] James W. Cunningham, *A Vanquished Hope: The Movement for Church Renewal in Russia 1905–1906* (Crestwood, NY, 1981); Ierei Georgii Orekhanov, *Na puti k Soboru: Tserkovnye reformy i pervaia russkaia revoliutsiia* (Moscow, 2002); and especially V. M. Lavrov *et al.*, *Ierarkhiia russkoi pravoslavnoi tserkvi, patriarshestvo i gosudarstvo v revoliutsionnuiu epokhu* (Moscow, 2008), for the research of I. V. Lobanova.

established by Peter I in 1721 was so widely discredited that even the metropolitan of St Petersburg, Antonii (Vadkovskii), told the tsar that he had 'always believed' that Russian public opinion would eventually 'declare it shameful and impossible for Holy Rus to live under such an abnormal system of ecclesiastical government'.[14] However, no consensus emerged about its replacement in a series of debates at the Pre-Conciliar Commission, which opened in a blaze of publicity in March 1906;[15] the Pre-Conciliar Conference of spring 1912, whose confidential proceedings soon leaked to the press;[16] and the Pre-Conciliar Council of June–July 1917.[17] While some churchmen promoted a restored patriarchate as the ultimate symbol of ecclesiastical self-government, others feared it as the harbinger of papal despotism. At best, opponents argued, a patriarch would benefit only bishops, whose pretensions they questioned in search of the enhanced role for laymen and parish clergy that was crucial to their rival view of *sobornost'*.

In one sense, positions were entrenched as early as 1906. 'It smells of blood, hatred, enmity and party-mindedness', Arsenii (Stadnitskii) remarked as the Pre-Conciliar Commission began to discuss the patriarchate, accurately predicting that a liberal-leaning 'left' would emerge to charge the conservative 'right' with lifeless rigidity, while the 'right' retorted with allegations of Protestantism and freethinking.[18] However, as so often in Russian history, informal personal loyalties ran across the ideological divide. A full reconstruction of these networks lies beyond the scope of this lecture. But much can be revealed by exploring reactions to the single individual who haunted the whole debate. For, until the last moment, it was widely assumed that Russia's new patriarch would be neither the little-known Tikhon, who had served long spells in the USA and Lithuania, nor Arsenii (Stadnitskii), an efficient but unimaginative disciplinarian. The man long regarded as patriarch-in-waiting was Archbishop Antonii (Khrapovitskii), the most controversial prelate of the age.[19]

---

[14] Quoted in Simon Dixon, 'The Russian Orthodox Church in Imperial Russia, 1721–1917', in Michael Angold, ed., *The Cambridge History of Christianity*, VI: *Eastern Christianity* (Cambridge, 2006), 341.

[15] *Zhurnaly i protokoly zasedanii Vysochaishe uchrezhdennogo Predsobornogo Prisutstviia (1906 g.)* (hereafter *Zhurnaly*), ed. E. Bryner *et al.* (4 vols., Moscow, 2014), especially I, 222–317, 3–19 May 1906.

[16] Sergei Firsov, *Russkaia Tserkov' nakanune peremen (konets 1890-kh–1918 gg.)* (Moscow, 2002), 414–26.

[17] *Dokumenty Sviashchennogo Sobora Pravoslavnoi Rossiiskoi Tserkvi 1917–1918 godov* (hereafter *Dokumenty*), ed. A. M. Mramornov *et al.* (5 vols., Moscow, 2012–), I:1, 326–40, 4 and 11 July 1917.

[18] Quoted in Orekhanov, *Na puti k Soboru*, 168, diary, 4 May 1906,

[19] Nikon (Rklitskii), *Mitropolit Antonii (Khrapovitskii) i ego vremia* (3 vols., Nizhnii Novgorod, 2012), reprints much primary material; *Metropolitan Antonii (Khrapovitskii): Archpastor of the*

We shall come later to Antonii's volatile cocktail of social conservatism and political radicalism. Let me begin by focusing on his view of Muscovy's relatively brief patriarchal regime, for the period between 1589 and 1700 could hardly have been more turbulent in terms of the relations between church and state. In September 1916, three years after the Romanov tercentenary had festooned Russia with a riot of Muscovite imagery, Archbishop Antonii encouraged an improbable rumour that Nicholas II had once planned to abdicate in favour of Tsarevich Aleksei so that he himself could become patriarch, much as Patriarch Filaret (Romanov) had guided his own son, Tsar Mikhail (r. 1613–45).[20] In fact, Filaret's name figured less prominently in debates on the patriarchate than that of Patriarch Nikon, whose reforms had split the church in the 1650s, and whose alleged rivalry with the autocracy was pregnant with implications for a tsar who deliberately represented himself as Mikhail's successor, Aleksei Mikhailovich (r. 1645–76).[21] In the early twentieth century, Nikon's ambition was widely regarded as limitless. Dmitrii Filosofov claimed that Nikon had even compared himself with Christ.[22] The main problem arose, however, from his adoption of the title 'Great Sovereign', also conferred on Patriarch Filaret.[23] As Russia's leading religious journalist, Vasilii Rozanov, observed in 1906, no reader of Peter I's *Spiritual Regulation* could fail to recognise the spectre of Nikon in the passage warning that a 'Supreme Pastor' – the word 'patriarch' was carefully avoided – risked being seen as 'a kind of second Sovereign, equal to, or even greater than the autocrat himself'.[24] The point had been given scholarly credibility by the historian, Nikolai Kapterev. Though his *magnum opus*

Russian Diaspora, ed. Vladimir Tsurikov (Jordanville, NY, 2014), treats most of Antonii's interests except the patriarchate. In the period covered by this lecture, Antonii ranked successively as bishop and archbishop. For convenience, and to distinguish him from his name-sake, Antonii (Vadkovskii), metropolitan of St Petersburg between 1898 and 1912, I refer to him throughout as Archbishop Antonii.

[20] *Dnevnik L. A. Tikhomirova, 1915–1917*, ed. A. V. Repnikov (Moscow, 2008), 285–6, diary, 21 Sept. 1916.

[21] Nikon's name is oddly missing from the classic study by Richard S. Wortman, *Scenarios of Power: Myth and Ceremony in Russian Monarchy*, II: *From Alexander II to the Death of Nicholas II* (Princeton, 2000). Compare Robert L. Nichols, 'Metropolitan Antonii (Khrapovitskii) and Religious Nationalism in Late Imperial Russia', in *Metropolitan Antonii (Khrapovitskii)*, ed. Tsurikov, 118–19, 129.

[22] D. Philosophoff [Filosofov], 'Le Tsar-Pape', in D. Merezhkovsky *et al.*, *Le tsar et la revolution* (Paris, 1907), Sept. 1906.

[23] For a modern treatment, see Olga B. Strakhov, 'The Title "Great Sovereign" and the Case of Patriarch Nikon', *Russian History*, 35 (2008), 429–46.

[24] Wasilii Rosanoff [Rozanov], 'La chiesa', in *I russi su la Russia*, ed. E. Trubetskoj, 2nd edn (Milan, 1906), 201–2. *Polnoe Sobranie Zakonov Rossiiskoi Imperii*, first series, VI, 317, no. 3718, 25 Jan. 1721, part 1, para. 7, declared that Russia need have no fear of 'revolts and disturbances' under a collective administration.

was completed only in 1912, the year of his election to the Fourth Duma as a moderate liberal Progressist, Kapterev's most controversial claim had first been advanced twenty years earlier. This was that Nikon 'believed and taught that the spiritual power was superior to the secular power (*sviashchenstvo vyshe tsarstva*)'.[25] In the light of such a claim, the notion that a modern bishop might imitate Nikon was incendiary. 'Patriarch Nikon set the boiars against himself', cautioned the most forthright episcopal opponent of the patriarchate in 1905, 'and in the conditions of our time a patriarch could easily set everybody against himself'.[26]

It mattered, therefore, that Archbishop Antonii (Khrapovitskii) revered Nikon as the greatest man in Russian history – a genius close to the common people – and correspondingly despised Kapterev, an outspoken critic of Antonii's brand of 'learned monasticism', as one of those unbelieving 'parasites' who opposed the restoration of the patriarchate so that they could continue 'feeding off the sick body of the church'.[27] Antonii always argued that patriarchal authority was moral rather than political. Long after the Bolshevik Revolution, he continued to insist that Nikon's 'great personality' had been 'misunderstood' by those who failed to grasp 'what a right vision he had of Russia as the symphony of the Church, on the one hand, and the Tsar, representing the state, on the other'.[28] Had he not been deposed, Antonii believed, Nikon would have healed the schism with the Old Believers, a subject close to his own heart.[29] Echoing the concern for the Eastern patriarchs expressed by this 'Christian cosmopolitan', Antonii was no less keen than Nikon for Russia to play a messianic role in the creation of a universal Christian empire.[30] Indeed, he went further by projecting onto Nikon his own idealised self-image: 'Ascetic and demagogue; ruler and hermit; artist and master; democrat and friend of the court; national

[25] N. F. Kapterev, 'Suzhdenie bol'shago Moskovskago sobora 1667 goda o vlasti tsarskoi i patriarshei', *Bogoslovskii vestnik* (June 1892), no. 6, 510; *idem*, *Patriarkh Nikon i tsar' Aleksei Mikhailovich* (2 vols., Sergiev Posad, 1909–12), I, v, and II, *passim*. Kapterev's *Tsar' i tserkovnye moskovskie sobory XVI i XVII stoletii* (n.p. [Sergiev Posad], 1906), was conceived as a contribution to contemporary conciliarist debates.

[26] Paisii (Vinogradov), bishop of Turkestan, in *Otzyvy eparkhial'nykh arkhiereev po voprosu o tserkovnoi reforme* (hereafter *Otzyvy*) (2 vols., Moscow, 2004), I, 90, 27 Oct. 1905.

[27] 'Vozstanovlennaia istina: Lektsiia Vysokopreosviashchenneishego Antoniia, arkhiepiskopa Volynskago, o sviateishem Nikone, patriarkhe Vserossiiskom, zapisannaia o. P. L.', *Mirnyi trud* (1910), no. 9, 140–71; *Otzyvy*, II, 340, 7 Jan. 1906. See also M. A. Babkin, *Sviashchenstvo i Tsarstvo: Rossiia, nachalo XX veka–1918 god* (Moscow, 2011), 114–15.

[28] Christopher Birchall, *Embassy, Emigrants, and Englishmen: The Three Hundred Year History of a Russian Orthodox Church in London* (Jordanville, NY, 2014), 252–3, quoting Abbess Elizabeth (Ampenoff) whose family hosted Antonii (Khrapovitskii) in London in 1929.

[29] *Deianiia*, II, 289, 18 Oct. 1917.

[30] Mitropolit Antonii (Khrapovitskii), *Sila Pravoslaviia* (Moscow, 2012), 341–5; *Deianiia*, IV, 127–8 (first pagination), 17 Nov. 1917.

patriot and ecumenical saint; champion of enlightenment and strict preserver of ecclesiastical discipline; gentle soul and thunderous denouncer of untruth.'[31]

II

As this striking list of binaries implies, Antonii was no 'run-of-the mill bishop, investigating and signing consistory papers'.[32] Descended from Catherine II's state secretary, he belonged to the tiny minority of nobles among an episcopate recruited overwhelmingly from the clerical estate.[33] His early career was meteoric. Appointed rector of the Moscow theological academy at the age of twenty-seven, he had a diocese of his own a decade later and in 1900, the year of his appointment to Ufa, published three volumes of collected works adorned with his own photograph.[34] By December 1901, Ufa's best-known son, the artist Mikhail Nesterov, regarded Antonii as second only to Rozanov as an ecclesiastical celebrity – the 'most forceful and most fascinating' among the growing number of Russians seeking a solution to questions of religion.[35]

Antonii's elevation to the wealthier diocese of Volhynia at Easter 1902 struck rivals as indecently premature.[36] But by then he had already sponsored a fresh generation of 'learned monks', drawn like himself from social elites untarnished by the scholastic theology taught in church schools and committed to a sustained ascetic engagement with the modern world.[37] While Synodal officials initially favoured these febrile young zealots as a 'convenient administrative weapon', their impact was inherently subversive since Antonii dreamed of 'a breadth and freedom of action' that was bound to undermine the ecclesiastical bureaucracy and offend churchmen wary of his arrogant 'generals in cassocks'.[38] Although never a charismatic preacher – his tone was shrill,

---

[31] Nikon, *Mitropolit Antonii (Khrapovitskii)*, I, 206.

[32] 'Pered sozyvom tserkovnogo sobora', in V. V. Rozanov, *Priroda i istoriia: Stat'i i ocherki 1904–1905 gg.*, ed. A. N. Nikoliukin (Moscow, 2008), 664, Nov.–Dec. 1905.

[33] Jan Plamper, 'The Russian Orthodox Episcopate, 1721–1917: A Prosopography', *Journal of Social History*, 34 (2000), 22–3, Appendix 2.1, calculates that noble bishops comprised 1.8 per cent of the total under Nicholas II.

[34] Episkop Antonii, *Polnoe sobranie sochinenii* (3 vols., Kazan', 1900).

[35] M. V. Nesterov to A. A. Turygin, 13 Dec. 1901, in M. V. Nesterov, *Pis'ma izbrannoe*, ed. A. A. Rusakova, 2nd edn (Leningrad, 1988), 198.

[36] Mitropolit Arsenii (Stadnitskii), *Dnevnik*, ed. Prot. V. Vorob'ev (3 vols. Moscow, 2006–), II, 39, diary, 6 May 1902.

[37] Patrick Lally Michelson, *Beyond the Monastery Walls: The Ascetic Revolution in Russian Orthodox Thought, 1814–1914* (Madison, 2017), 176–216.

[38] S. Vvedenskii, *Nashe uchenoe monashestvo i sovremennoe tserkovnoe dvizhenie* (Moscow, 1906), 10–11; S. V. Smolenskii, *Vospominaniia*, ed. N. I. Kabanova, *Russkaia dukhovnaia muzyka v dokumentakh i materialakh*, 4 (Moscow, 2002), 286.

his delivery rapid and his approach unemotional[39] – Antonii always had a knack of drawing attention to himself. In 1901, when Joachim III was restored to the ecumenical throne in Constantinople, Antonii published a congratulatory letter which was widely interpreted as a call for restoration in Russia.[40] In 1903, Andrei Belyi heard that he was 'going in for miraculous cures' at a convent associated with St Serafim of Sarov. Crowds pursued him after he persuaded a deaf and dumb girl to say her name and another with deformed arms to cross herself. The Synod, Belyi learned, were 'afraid' of Antonii 'because he has already more than once shown a penchant for surprises and tricks, and because he is one of the few to consider himself a [real] bishop'.[41]

When the campaign for church reform began in 1905, it was hard to deny that the hierarchy as a whole had responded feebly to Bloody Sunday because they had been infantilised by the aged chief procurator, K. P. Pobedonostsev, mocked by Rozanov as a nanny who 'feeds and dresses the babies and puts on their shoes'.[42] Antonii (Khrapovitskii), by contrast, was swift to seize his opportunity. The moment had come, he rejoiced to the Russian elders on Mount Athos, to throw off the European yoke imposed on the church by Peter I: 'Let us have the councils demanded by the decrees of the Holy Apostles and the ecumenical Fathers! Let us also have a Most Holy Patriarch, as a younger brother of the Eastern Patriarchs!'[43] First, on 20 February, Antonii denounced the intelligentsia at St Isaac's cathedral in a sermon on the Last Judgement.[44] Later, he used Pobedonostsev's inquiry about church reform of July 1905 to assert the religious significance of the patriarchate, a subject deliberately omitted from the questionnaire.[45] However, sensing that the Synod remained packed against him, Antonii realised

---

[39] See, for example, *Dnevnik Velikogo Kniazia Konstantina Konstantinovicha*, ed. T. A. Lobashkova (Moscow, 2015), 291, diary, 21 May 1910.

[40] Nikon, *Mitropolit Antonii (Khrapovitskii)*, I, 314–17.

[41] A. S. Petrovskii to B. N. Bugaev [Belyi], 27 Aug. 1903, in *Perepiska 1902–1932/Andrei Belyi, Aleksei Petrovskii*, ed. Dzh. [John] Malmstad (Moscow, 2007), 72. The source was Petrovskii's sister, a nun at the Diveevskii convent.

[42] V. V. Rozanov, *Kogda nachal'stvo ushlo...1905–1906 gg.*, ed. P. P. Apryshko and A. N. Nikoliukin (Moscow, 2005), 34.

[43] Antonii to Arkhimandrit Nifont, Good Friday [15 Apr.] 1905, in *Pis'ma vydaiushchikhsia tserkovnykh i svetskikh deiatelei Rossii startsam Russkogo Sviato-Panteleimonova monastyria na Afone*, ed. Ieromonakh Makarii (Sviataia Gora Afon, 2015), 552.

[44] 'Slovo o Strashnem sude i sovremennykh sobytiiakh', *Moskovskiia vedomosti*, 2 Mar. 1905. Apparently, only Metropolitan Antonii (Vadkovskii) restrained him from repeating his onslaught: see Arsenii, *Dnevnik*, III, 51, diary, 19 Mar. 1905.

[45] *Otzyvy*, II, 339–46, 7 Jan. 1906. Though all these responses were submitted in the name of individual prelates, most resembled the bishops' annual reports to the Synod, drawing with varying degrees of explicitness on contributions by sundry diocesan bodies and scholars. Antonii (Khrapovitskii) was one of only five hierarchs to write in the first person, the others being Paisii (Vinogradov), *ibid.*, I, 87–93, Vladimir (Sokolovskii-Avtonomov), II,

that his own chances of promotion were negligible: as he confided to a protégé, it was better to remain silent and bide his time.[46] As a result, his name scarcely figured during the brief window in March 1905 when the patriarchate seemed certain to be restored.

The context was Pobedonostsev's rear-guard action to prevent the prime minister, Count Sergei Witte, from taking church reform into the hands of the Committee of Ministers.[47] Without consulting the chief procurator, Witte had invited Metropolitan Antonii (Vadkovskii) to present topics for discussion. Shortly after Pobedonostsev regained control for the Synod, it shocked him by resolving on 22 March, while he was absent through illness, to petition for an episcopal Church Council which was expected to elect a patriarch. When the news leaked that night, General Aleksandr Kireev, a fervent patriarchist who nevertheless campaigned for lay influence in the church, expected the patriarch to be placed in the first class on Peter I's table of ranks. That would put him 'on a par with a field marshal and the state chancellor, but will scarcely give him power or independence'.[48] By contrast, the idea of granting a patriarch the sort of 'exaggerated rights' that had divorced the 'uncanonical' Synod from ordinary parish life alarmed Mikhail Novoselov and his religious-philosophical circle in Moscow. It was inappropriate, these laymen argued, for the patriarchate to be restored in this way, and patriarchists later blamed them for helping Pobedonostsev to persuade Nicholas II that both council and patriarch were 'inopportune'.[49]

By the time the tsar reached that decision on 31 March, gossips, thinking restoration guaranteed, were already discussing potential runners. When a wag quipped to Aleksei Suvorin that Pobedonostsev himself intended to become patriarch, the publisher retorted by proposing Rozanov.[50] Serious attention focused on Russia's three metropolitans, all of whom seemed flawed to Archbishop Antonii. 'The cleverest' –

153–81, Germogen (Dolganov), II, 498–511, and Lavrentii (Nekrasov), II, 536–47. Ioannikii (Kazanskii), I, 377–83, also specified his own views.

[46] Evdokim (Meshcherskii) to Arsenii (Stadnitskii), 1905, in I. V. Lobanova, 'Perepiska Arkhiereev kak istochnik po istorii Russkoi Pravoslavnoi Tserkvi Sinodal'nogo perioda', *Russkii istoricheskii sbornik*, 7 (Moscow, 2014), 130.

[47] The fullest account, Orekhanov, *Na puti k Soboru*, 34–80, exaggerates Pobedonostsev's own commitment to reform.

[48] A. A. Kireev, *Dnevnik, 1905–1910*, ed. K. A. Solov'ev (Moscow, 2010), 39, diary, 22 Mar. 1905.

[49] *Russkoe delo*, 28 Mar. 1905, in I. V. Preobrazhenskii, *Tserkovnaia Reforma: Sbornik statei dukhovnoi i svetskoi periodicheskoi pechati po voprosu o reforme* (St Petersburg, 1905), 90; I. V. Lobanova, 'Moskovskoe dvizhenie protiv vosstanovleniia patriarshestva vo vremia pervoi russkoi revoliutsii', in *Tserkov' v istorii Rossii*, 8 (Moscow, 2009), 155–67.

[50] A. S. Suvorin to V. V. Rozanov, 25 Mar. 1905, in V. V. Rozanov, *Priznaki vremeni: Stat'i i ocherki 1912 g.*, ed. A. N. Nikoliukin (Moscow, 2006), 321.

his fellow-noble Flavian (Gorodetskii) of Kiev – was 'inactive and slug-gish'; Moscow's Vladimir (Bogoiavlenskii) was 'honest and fervent, but insufficiently educated'; Antonii (Vadkovskii), the sole plausible candi-date, though 'intelligent [and] self-possessed', lacked 'fervency of spirit'.[51] He was also compromised by the collapse of Witte's scheme. Unable to see the tsar at the height of the March crisis, the metropolitan confessed to feeling isolated and conscious of his 'shaky position'.[52]

That position became shakier still as Metropolitan Antonii came under attack from the radical Right. One of his few public supporters was the monarchist lawyer, N. D. Kuznetsov, a member of Novoselov's circle opposed to both the patriarchate and Archbishop Antonii.[53] As stubborn as he was courteous, the metropolitan neverthe-less persisted. His own reply to the Synodal inquiry on church reform declared that the new patriarch should be the metropolitan of St Petersburg and on 1 June 1906, the Pre-Conciliar Commission resolved, under his chairmanship and by a majority of 33:9, that Russia's leading bishop should bear both titles jointly.[54] In the circumstances, even a man who abhorred intrigue found it hard to avoid charges of careerism from right-wingers who now had a further motive to campaign for his demo-tion: 'This means he will not be patriarch!' gloated the renegade terrorist, Lev Tikhomirov, wrongly predicting the metropolitan's downfall in November 1906.[55]

III

In fact, no patriarch could be elected in the foreseeable future because the political cards were stacked firmly against restoration. Alarmed by the unexpectedly wide range of political opinions espoused by the clergy after 1905,[56] neither the tsar nor his new prime minister, Petr Stolypin, relished the prospect of a Church Council to rival the Duma.

[51] Arsenii, *Dnevnik*, III, 52, diary, 19 Mar. 1905.

[52] V. A. Teliakovskii, *Dnevnik Direktora Imperatorskikh Teatrov, 1903–1906* (St Petersburg, 2006), 450, diary, 29 Mar. 1905, quoting D. S. Merezhkovskii.

[53] N. D. Kuznetsov, *Po Voprosam Tserkovnykh Preobrazovanii* (Moscow, 1907), 83–147, reprints speeches at the Pre-Conciliar Commission implicitly directed at Antonii (Khrapovitskii) via a critique of Nikon's papal pretensions: see, for example, *Zhurnaly*, II, 643–4. See also M. A. Novoselov to A. S. Glinka, 6 Jan. 1909, in *Vzyskuiushchie grada*, ed. V. I. Keidan (Moscow, 1997), 186; and *Dnevnik L. A. Tikhomirova, 1905–1907 gg.*, ed. A. B. Repnikov and B. S. Kotov (Moscow, 2015), 301, diary, 29 Dec. 1906.

[54] *Otzyvy*, II, 238; Cunningham, *A Vanquished Hope*, 263, 265.

[55] *Dnevnik L. A. Tikhomirova, 1905–1907 gg.*, 289, diary, 26 Nov. 1906, labels Antonii (Vadkovskii) 'a careerist by nature'.

[56] Gregory L. Freeze, 'Church and Politics in Late Imperial Russia: Crisis and Radicalization of the Clergy', in *Russia under the Last Tsar: Opposition and Subversion, 1894–1917*, ed. Anna Geifman (Oxford, 1999), 269–97.

Stolypin had particularly good reason for suspicion since Aleksei Shirinskii-Shikhmatov, a monarchist dismissed as chief procurator in June 1906 to make the incoming ministry more palatable to the Duma, made no secret of his intention to exploit the *sobor* as a 'counter-balance' to Stolypin's 'destructive parliamentary aspirations'.[57] In January 1907, Shirinskii's successor, Petr Izvol'skii, warned Nicholas II that church leaders conceived of a canonical regime 'not as an internal initiative, but as a new form of power'.[58] Since a cardinal aspiration of the patriarchists – that the patriarch should negotiate directly with the tsar – ran counter to one of the most fundamental assumptions of modern Russian monarchy, Archbishop Antonii unsurprisingly concluded, after meeting the prime minister in October, that Stolypin was 'afraid of a council and especially of the patriarchate'.[59]

The spectre of clericalism soon loomed larger still. Under Pobedonostsev, independently minded bishops had been banished, like Antonii (Khrapovitskii), to backwaters such as Ufa. But this tactic backfired after 1907 when the excesses of frontier capitalism, the national aspirations of non-Russian peoples and a burgeoning local press offered a tempting range of targets for prelates determined to convert their isolated dioceses into theocracies beyond ministerial control. In the notoriously unruly province of Saratov, Germogen (Dolganov) sponsored a populist crusade by the monk Iliodor (Trufanov) that helped to destabilise Stolypin's relationship with the tsar.[60] Serafim (Chichagov), who promoted regenerated parish councils as a way of encompassing (and thereby emasculating) the entire political spectrum, provoked charges of electoral malpractice when translated from Orel to Bessarabia.[61]

Befriending Germogen and Serafim as allies in the Synod, Archbishop Antonii largely shared their contempt for Jews, Poles and St Petersburg's Westernising elites. Nevertheless, he developed his own highly confessionalised form of Russian nationalism according to which harmful Western accretions were to be stripped away to reveal the Gospel 'incarnating itself' in the life of the common people. Antonii's tactics, too, were distinctive. Whereas most diocesan bishops distrusted the suffragans foisted on them by the Holy Synod, Antonii willingly delegated frontline combat in Ukraine to the disciples whose appointment he successfully engineered. At the Pochaev Lavra, Archimandrite Vitalii

[57] Kireev, *Dnevnik*, 157, diary, 15 July 1906.

[58] Firsov, *Russkaia Tserkov' nakanune peremen*, 393.

[59] Kireev, *Dnevnik*, 147, diary, 30 May 1906; Orekhanov, *Na puti k Soboru*, 189.

[60] Simon Dixon, 'The "Mad Monk" Iliodor in Tsaritsyn', *Slavonic and East European Review*, 88 (2010), 377–415.

[61] See, for example, N. N. Dudnichenko, *'Luchshie liudi' Bessarabii: Arkhiepiskop Serafim, Gg. Krupenskie, Sinadino i dr.* (Kishinev, 1913).

(Maksimenko), whom Antonii had rescued from expulsion as a student, printed thousands of lurid pamphlets that fanned the flames of right-wing populism across the Western Provinces, underpinning Antonii's support for the Union of Russian People.[62] Antonii's own pronounce-ments were largely reserved for the national stage, where he posed as the people's champion, scourge of the intelligentsia and nemesis of liberal theologians. Already in 1895, he had proclaimed an implicit alli-ance between church, tsar and *narod* against Russia's 'falsely-educated' elites. After 1905, a series of increasingly intemperate pronouncements – in the press, in the State Council in 1906 and as chairman of the Kiev Missionary Congress in 1908 – marked him out as the sworn enemy of liberals in both religion and politics.[63]

Antonii by no means monopolised the crucial rhetorical claim that lib-eralism was incompatible with authentic churchmanship.[64] Nevertheless, a mind that found binary opposites congenial was ideally suited to exag-gerate the contrast between the two, and no group felt his wrath more severely than the academy professoriate, whom he repeatedly denounced as impious fifth-columnists.[65] Not only did these critics of learned monas-ticism suffer the indignity of having Antonii's acolytes imposed as their rectors. They were also exposed to the sorts of personal attack embodied in his report on the Kiev theological academy in 1908, nominally confi-dential to the Synod, but printed at Pochaev and leaked to the press.[66] 'It is amazing how he loves to slander and blacken everyone that for some reason he dislikes', complained the Kazan' professor, archpriest Nikolai Vinogradov, in 1909. By November 1911, Vinogradov could see nothing 'saintly' in Antonii, who seemed 'shot through with Jesuitism and polit-icking, balks at nothing to achieve his aims, and to satisfy his diabolical

[62] Sophia Senyk, 'Antonij Xrapovickij in Volyn', 1902–1914', in *Metropolitan Antonii (Khrapovitskii)*, ed. Tsurikov, 244–63; Ricarda Vulpius, *Nationalisierung der Religion: Russifizierungspolitik und ukrainische Nationsbildung 1860–1902* (Wiesbaden, 2005), 213–40; Rachel Dilworth, 'Antonii (Khrapovitskii)' (MA dissertation, UCL, 2013), 7.

[63] See, for example, I. I. Tolstoi, *Dnevnik*, ed. B. V. Anan'ich (2 vols., St Petersburg, 2010), I, 484–5, diary, 18 July 1908.

[64] Compare, for example, Professor D. I. Bogdashevskii's letters of 6 July and 30 Oct. 1908 in '"Liubliu Akademiiu i vsegda budu deistvovat' vo imia liubvi k nei ..." (Pis'ma pro-fessora Kievskoi dukhovnoi akademii D. I. Bogdashevskogo k A. A. Dmitrievskomu)', ed. N. Iu. Sukhova, *Vestnik PSTGU*, series II (2013), no. 54, 84, 91.

[65] For example, *Zhurnaly*, II, 349, 8 May 1906. Compare Prot. P. Ia. Svetlov, 'Glavneishiia oshibki v otvetnoi dokladnoi zapiske ep. volynskago i zhitomirskago Antoniia Sviateishemu Sinodu', *Tserkovnyi vestnik*, 2 Mar. 1906, 263–6.

[66] Antonii, episkop Volynskii, *Otchet po Vysochaishe naznachennoi revizii Kievskoi dukhovnoi aka-demii v marte i aprele 1908 g.* (Pochaev, 1908), prompted a vigorous refutation from the profes-soriate: *Pravda o Kievskoi Dukhovnoi Akademii: Vynuzhdennyi otvet na izdannuiu arkhiepiskopom Volynskim Antoniem broshiuru* (Kiev, 1909).

arrogance spares no-one who wounds him in any way'.[67] Sure enough, soon after Antonii's denunciation of his study of the church schools – an implicit critique of learned monasticism – the historian B. V. Titlinov was sacked as editor of a leading ecclesiastical weekly. Reporting to the Synod, Archbishop Sergii (Stragorodskii) condemned *Tserkovnyi vestnik* (*Church Herald*) in the manner of his mentor for reflecting the views of 'the most unpleasant type of kadets [constitutional-democrats], namely, ecclesiastical kadets, i.e. people who had lost their spiritual links with the church and with historic Orthodoxy'.[68]

One can see why Metropolitan Antonii wanted to keep his namesake out of the Synod as a man who sought 'to revolutionise everything'.[69] Since 1905, Archbishop Antonii and his allies had transformed an anti-Erastian struggle for *sobornost'* into a far-reaching campaign for social and political 'enchurchment' (*votserkovlenie*) that threatened to undermine the secular authorities. During the campaign for elections to the Fourth Duma in 1912, Antonii's protégé Andronik (Nikol'skii) portrayed 'the Christianisation of national life in the widest possible sense' as a moral rather than a political aspiration.[70] However, as Dmitrii Merezhkovskii perceived, the very idea of divorcing Russia from European culture in a return to pre-Petrine values was 'much more destructive of the existing order than the most extreme ideas of our revolutionaries'.[71]

It is hardly surprising that Archbishop Antonii should have been denied a metropolitan see. He had not, however, abandoned hope of the patriarchate, and by late 1911, when a second edition of his collected works appeared, the time seemed ripe for a concerted campaign.[72] Stolypin had been assassinated in September and the recently appointed chief procurator, Vladimir Sabler, had been learned monasticism's leading patron until he was dismissed as Pobedonostsev's deputy in 1905 for supporting the restoration of the patriarchate. Together, Sabler and Antonii intended to exploit the impending tercentenary of

---

[67] "'Da blagoslovit Gospod' plody trudov tvoikh na pol'zu sviatoi tserkvi i dukhovnoi nauki" (Pis'ma protoiereia Nikolaia Vinogradova k A. A. Dmitrievskomu)', ed. N. Iu. Sukhova, *Vestnik Ekaterinburgskoi dukhovnoi seminarii* (2016), no. 13, 168, 1909, and 183, 26 Nov. 1911.

[68] *Kolokol*, 20 and 21 Oct. 1911; B. V. Titlinov, *Otvet na 'Otzyv' arkhiepiskopa Antoniia Volynskago* (St Petersburg, 1911); Rossiiskii gosudarstvennyi istoricheskii arkhiv, St Petersburg, fond 796, opis' 205, delo 260, 20 Nov. 1911.

[69] Kireev, *Dnevnik*, 347, diary, 26 Dec. 1909.

[70] Andronik (Nikol'skii), *Tvoreniia* (2 vols., Tver', 2004), II, 69.

[71] D. S. Merezhkovskii, *Griadushchii kham* (St Petersburg, 1906), 143. At the Moscow Church Council, Vasilii Rubtsov, a provincial salesman with no formal education, portrayed the restoration of the patriarchate as a betrayal of Russia's attempts to catch up with Europe: see *Deianiia*, II, 268–9, 14 Oct. 1917.

[72] Antonii, *Sobranie sochinenii*, 2nd edn (3 vols., Moscow, 1911).

the Romanov dynasty when Antonii wanted the tsar to appoint a patriarch as the prelude to the convocation of a Church Council.

In January 1912, Antonii published a defence of the patriarchate that coincided not only with his chairmanship of the first national *edinoverie* congress (intended as a harbinger of reunion with the Old Believers), but also with the tercentenary of an earlier hammer of the Poles, Patriarch Germogen. That commemoration, however, was unexpectedly overshadowed by adverse publicity surrounding the exile of the late patriarch's namesake, the bishop of Saratov, following his attack on Rasputin in December 1911.[73] Bishop Germogen, Antonii told the press, had been 'the victim of a well-known party', which, 'being unashamed of intrigues', directed 'all its strength against the chief procurator and individual bishops in order to replace them with its own close collaborators'.[74] Here was a reference to the despised 'Rasputinite heroes' whose appointment did much to discredit the church and even more to thwart Antonii's ambitions. For the moment, however, he pressed on regardless, securing in spring 1912 the appointment of a seven-man Pre-Conciliar Conference, packed with allies and chaired by Sergii (Stragorodskii) since Metropolitan Antonii was too ill to serve.

Critics such as Rozanov, who feared that a patriarchate would herald the crushing of the white clergy by the monastics, were brushed aside in the autumn.[75] By then, plans were already afoot for a lengthy sojourn in Russia by the patriarch of Antioch, Gregory IV, who in April 1913 spent four days at the specially illuminated Pochaev Lavra. On a visit timed to coincide with the consecration of his former pupil Dionisii (Valedinskii) as third suffragan of Volhynia, Antonii took advantage of the opportunity to reiterate his elevated view of episcopacy.[76] But despite press drumbeating on behalf of a restored patriarchate, other projects went awry. Nicholas II unexpectedly refused to attend the controversial canonisation of Patriarch Hermogen, whose remains had inconveniently decomposed.[77] 'Exalting Patriarch Hermogen', as Richard Wortman observes, 'would have given the church even more prominence and created a

---

[73] Arkhiepiskop Antonii, 'Vozstanovlenie patriarshestva', *Golos Tserkvi* (Jan. 1912), no. 1. On Germogen's attack, see Dixon, 'The "Mad Monk" Iliodor', 406–7.

[74] *Rech'*, 16 Jan. 1912, 'K uvol'neniiu episk. Germogena'.

[75] Antonii, episkop Volynskii, 'Bedy ot lzhebratii: Razbor glavnykh vozrazhenii protiv patriarshestva', *Golos Tserkvi* (Oct. 1912), no. 10, 132–49.

[76] Nikon, *Mitropolit Antonii (Khrapovitskii)*, I, 666–82.

[77] Gregory L. Freeze, 'Subversive Piety: Religion and the Political Crisis in Late Imperial Russia', *Journal of Modern History*, 68 (1996), 330–6. John Strickland, *The Making of Holy Russia: The Orthodox Church and Russian Nationalism before the Revolution* (Jordanville, NY, 2013), 188–208, underestimates the canonisation's significance by portraying it merely as a nationalist pageant.

symbol to rival the patriarch Filaret, the progenitor of the dynasty.'[78]
Though the war gave Archbishop Antonii new grounds for portraying
Peter I's Protestant-style Synodal regime as the enemy within, it left
little hope for a patriarchate as Rasputin strengthened his hold over episcopal appointments.

IV

Not until the February Revolution was the question of the patriarchate
divorced from that of a *sobor*. On the one hand, Nicholas II's abdication
removed the biggest obstacle to the convocation of a Church Council, for
which plans forged ahead under the Provisional Government. On the
other hand, in the absence of a tsar, the notion of a patriarchal
counter-balance now seemed anachronistic to almost everyone except
those peasants who still craved a father-figure. Neither development
boded well for Antonii (Khrapovitskii), who was powerless to prevent
the new chief procurator, V. N. L'vov, from presiding over the dismissal
of several episcopal allies. At the Moscow theological academy, Feodor
(Pozdeevskii) resembled 'a trapped beast' in the face of an inquiry
begun only days after the tsar's fall; Serafim (Chichagov) was among
those subsequently unseated at the behest of diocesan assemblies.[79]
Though it was once suggested that L'vov engineered Antonii's own
removal in order to disbar him from the impending council, his
nemesis was also locally inspired.[80] Either way, he retreated to the
Valaam monastery to write a controversial study of the Atonement
and was unable to influence the Pre-Conciliar Council, where his
enemies took their revenge at a meeting in Petrograd less than a week
after the July Days.

As before, the central question concerned the nature and extent of
executive authority in a future conciliar regime. A single executive
body comprising bishops, clergy and laymen was narrowly rejected
(8:6) in favour of a bi-cameral structure capped by an episcopal
Synod. But when Sergii (Stragorodskii) proposed a lifetime appointment
for the Synod's 'leading bishop', the professoriate suspected a covert
attempt to restore the patriarchate. It was impossible to restore an impo-
tent patriarch, insisted Professor A. I. Pokrovskii. 'By its very nature', the
patriarchate was 'based on power and splendour', and if Archbishop
Antonii's dreams were to be realised, the result would be 'a sort of

[78] Wortman, *Scenarios of Power*, 450.
[79] Mikhail Bogoslovskii, *Dnevniki 1913–1919* (Moscow, 2011), 326–8, diary, 13 Mar. 1917;
P. G. Rogoznyi, *Tserkovnaia revoliutsiia: 1917 god* (St Petersburg, 2008), ch. 2.
[80] Compare James W. Cunningham, 'The Russian Patriarchate and the Attempt to
Recover *Symphonia*', *Canadian-American Slavic Studies*, 26 (1992), 273, with Rogoznyi,
Tserkovnaia revoliutsiia, 177–80.

dictator, the leader of a multi-million strong Orthodox army, ready to dash into battle with any forces hostile to it'.[81]

Since the absent Antonii evidently haunted the meeting, it is worth pausing to consider what those present thought of him. Six of them had been his pupils; at least seven more knew him in other ways. Loyal acolytes are readily identifiable. In the late 1890s, Archbishop Sergii had served with Andronik (Nikol'skii) in one of Antonii's favourite causes, the mission to Japan. Now bishop of Perm', Andronik was the only hierarch apart from his mentor to espouse openly monarchist sentiments since the abdication.[82] Another trusty student, Father Simeon Shleev, had organised the *edinoverie* congress in 1912 when the prospect of healing the schism was crucial to Antonii's case for the patriarchate. 'The worst patriarch', Shleev subsequently assured the Moscow Council, would be an improvement on 'the best Synod'.[83] Equally favourable to a lifetime appointment were two lay experts on the Eastern patriarchates who consistently supported restoration. To Feodor (Pozdeevskii)'s friend, P. B. Mansurov, who had seen five patriarchs come and go during his diplomatic career at Constantinople, continuity seemed self-recommending.[84] No less enthusiastic was I. I. Sokolov, the historian who had supplanted Titlinov as editor of *Tserkovnyi vestnik* in 1911.[85] Sokolov's glowing account of the Constantinople patriarchate, published in 1904, claimed (somewhat implausibly) that 'the Church had always followed the principle of freedom from any encroachment by the government or the laity upon its internal affairs'.[86]

Archbishop Antonii's supporters at the Pre-Conciliar Council were nevertheless outnumbered by his detractors. Much had changed since the bishop of Ufa, Andrei (Ukhtomskii), graduated together with Andronik in 1895 and taught alongside him at the missionary seminary at Ardon in northern Ossetia, a nest of budding *antonievtsy*.[87] As the scion of a princely family committed to healing the schism, Andrei initially seemed a model disciple. However, alienated by his mentor's

---

[81] *Dokumenty*, I:1, 330, 11 July 1917.

[82] Arkhimandrit Sergii, *Na dal'nem Vostoke*, 2nd edn (Arzamas, 1897); Ierom[onakh] Andronik, *Missionerskii put' v Iaponiiu* (Kazan', 1899); Rogoznyi, *Tserkovnaia revoliutsiia*, 50–2.

[83] *Dokumenty*, I:1, 329–30, 335–6, 11 July 1917; *Deianiia*, II, 343, 21 Oct. 1917.

[84] *Dokumenty*, I:1, 332–3, 11 July 1917; *Zhurnaly*, I, 277; P. B. Mansurov, *Tserkovnyi Sobor i Episkopy – ego chleny* (Moscow, 1912), 8, 11–12. Mansurov was Archbishop Antonii's principal lay ally in the affair of the heresy of the name on Mount Athos.

[85] *Otzyvy*, II, 273–85; *Zhurnaly*, I, 255–7; *Deianiia*, II, 383–91, 23 Oct. 1917. I. I. Sokolov, *Pravoslavnaia grecheskaia tserkov'* (St Petersburg, 1913), helped to publicise Patriarch Gregory IV's visit.

[86] Ivan Sokolov, *The Church of Constantinople in the Nineteenth Century*, trans. Hieromonk Nikolai Sakharov with an introduction by Kallistos Ware (Oxford and Bern, 2013), 833.

[87] I. A. Slanov, *Ardonskaia dukhovnaia seminariia* (Vladikavkaz, 1999).

scabrous vocabulary and by the insults of the radical Right, he had long since abandoned Antonii. By May 1917, when Andrei was defeated as L'vov's candidate in the election for the see of Petrograd, Andronik regarded him as a socialist.[88] Such a charge could hardly be levelled against Arsenii (Stadnitskii). Yet although he remained on civil terms with Archbishop Antonii, personal experience dating back to the 1890s had left him distrustful of the *antonievtsy* and he opposed Antonii's 'head-splitting experiments' in the church schools.[89] So did every professor at the Pre-Conciliar Council except Sokolov. Vladimir Zavitnevich, a campaigner for academic autonomy at Kiev, subsequently warned the Moscow Council against Antonii's 'poetic' representation of a patriarchal regime, knowing from experience that in practice things might be different.[90] The Moscow canonist, Il'ia Gromoglasov, had likewise been 'staggered' by Antonii's 'insulting' public report on his master's thesis. In 1910, Gromoglasov was dismissed on the pretext of earlier political journalism; Pokrovskii had been sacked the year before.[91] With Antonii's shadow hovering over them, the meeting voted 12:6 against a lifetime appointment for the Synod's leading bishop – in other words, against restoration of the patriarchate. Little else could have been expected, Antonii complained, so long as the Pre-Conciliar Council was dominated by the 'gang of renegade Holy Joes (*kuteiniki*)' whose cards he had marked as early as 1905: 'Let them be damned!'[92]

V

Patriarchists therefore came to the Moscow Church Council in August 1917 with little hope of success. Three developments transformed their prospects. First, the mood in church circles hardened after the July Days had cast doubt on the Provisional Government's ability to preserve order.[93] It was this shift in sentiment that contributed to the election of

---

[88] Rogoznyi, *Tserkovnaia revoliutsiia*, 41–2, 151–3.

[89] Arsenii, *Dnevnik*, I, 277–9, diary, 20 Jan. 1898, 355–6, 20 Sept. 1900; Arsenii (Stadnitskii) to Kirill (Smirnov), 18 Aug. 1911, 'Arkhivnye dokumenty Sviashchennomuchenika Kirilla (Smirnova), mitropolita Kazanskogo, iz fonda mitropolita Arseniia (Stadnitskogo) 1907–1918', 246.

[90] Lavrov *et al.*, *Ierarkhiia*, 120.

[91] I. M. Gromoglasov to N. N. Glubokovskii, 31 July 1909, in T. A. Bogdanova, 'Iz akademicheskikh "istorii": zameshchenie kafedry tserkovnogo prava v Moskovskoi Dukhovnoi akademii v 1910 godu', *Vestnik tserkovnoi istorii* (2007), no. 1, 41; V. A. Tarasova, *Vysshaia dukhovnaia shkola v Rossii v kontse XIX–nachale XX veka* (Moscow, 2005), 177–9.

[92] Antonii (Khrapovitskii) to Arsenii (Stadnitskii), 3 Aug. 1917 (?), in Lobanova, 'Perepiska arkhiereev', 152.

[93] J. S. Curtiss, *The Russian Church and the Soviet State, 1917–1950* (Gloucester, MA, 1965), 26–43.

Tikhon, a patron of the radical Right, as metropolitan of Moscow.[94] When the Council refused General Kornilov's appeal for support because it wanted to bless both sides – 'It was always the same with our bishops at critical moments', grumbled the conservative historian Mikhail Bogoslovskii[95] – the need for leadership became increasingly apparent. 'At the Pre-Conciliar Council, I was against the patriarchate', noted Arsenii (Stadnitskii): 'not on principle, but against the idea that it was timely in the near future.' Now he was changing his mind.[96] Secondly, the Council found itself at loggerheads with the Provisional Government, which threatened clerical impoverishment through the land transfer committees created on 21 April and which refused to reconsider its takeover of the Orthodox parish schools on 1 June. A delegation led by Archbishop Kirill (Smirnov) returned from Petrograd to tell shocked delegates on 14 October that the government planned nothing less than the secularisation of society.[97] Coincidentally, this was the second day of the plenary debate on the patriarchate. Packed with provincial teachers and officials disinclined to defer to metropolitan professors, who accounted for only 9 of the 204 laymen elected to Moscow, the chamber was in no mood to prevaricate.[98] None of the 36 peasant delegates spoke against restoring the patriarchate.

The social composition of the Council, the hostility of the Provisional Government and the deteriorating state of the country benefited not only the cause of restoration in general, but Antonii (Khrapovitskii) in particular. On 11 August, he regained the see of Khar'kov, to which he had been translated in 1913, by polling 412 votes – 396 more than his closest rival.[99] Six days later, on the anniversary of Patriarch Nikon's death, the newly restored prelate preached to members of the Council at Nikon's New Jerusalem monastery outside Moscow, claiming that it was only a matter of time before his hero followed Patriarch Hermogen to canonisation.[100] There could have been no clearer signal of the sort of regime Antonii envisaged. However, as elections for the council chairmanship

---

[94] The depth of Tikhon's political commitment remains unclear. However, like Antonii (Khrapovitskii), he patronised the Union of Russian People in his dioceses and sent greetings to national congresses of the Union of Russian Men. See *Pravye partii: Dokumenty i materialy*, ed. Iu. I. Kir'ianov (2 vols., Moscow, 1998), I, 464, 27 Sept. 1909, II, 304, 19 Feb. 1913; M. L. Razmolodin, *Chernosotennoe dvizhenie v Iaroslavle i guberniiakh Verkhnego Povolzh'ia v 1905–1915 gg.* (Iaroslavl', 2001), 77–8, 195.

[95] Bogoslovskii, *Dnevniki*, 413, diary, 31 Aug. 1917.

[96] Vorob'ev and Krivosheeva, 'Mitropolit Arsenii', 250.

[97] Cunningham, 'The Russian Patriarchate', 278–80.

[98] On the Council's social composition, see Evtuhov, *The Cross and the Sickle*, 198–9.

[99] Rogoznyi, *Tserkovnaia revoliutsiia*, 180–1.

[100] Sv[iashchennik] Evgenii Sosuntsov, 'Vserossiiskii pomestnyi sobor', in *Delo velikogo stroitel'stva tserkovnogo: Vospominaniia chlenov Sviashchennogo Sobora Pravoslavnoi Rossiiskoi Tserkvi 1917–1918 godov*, ed. Prot. Vladimir Vorob'ev (Moscow, 2009), 80.

soon proved, his brand of militant interventionism was still divisive. While Arsenii (Stadnitskii) became vice-chairman on 18 August with 404 votes in favour and 31 against, Antonii joined him on 285 votes but no fewer than 150 blackballs. Both men were chosen only after Tikhon had unexpectedly run away with the chairmanship, defeating Vladimir (Bogoiavlenskii) in the first round by 356:23 (Antonii came fourth with 19), and finally polling 407 votes with only 33 against.[101] Here was the first sign of the attractions of a dark horse, whose 'composed, almost phlegmatic' appearance set him apart from most right-wingers in the church: 'There is peace in his voice', noted Professor A. D. Beliaev, 'clarity, and moreover not the slightest sharpness'.[102]

The Council began to consider the patriarchate in its section on the supreme administration of the church to which some 266 of the 504 delegates eventually subscribed under the chairmanship of Mitrofan (Krasnopol'skii). Recently translated to Astrakhan, Mitrofan was best known as a Russian nationalist in the Western Provinces who shared both Antonii's contempt for the intelligentsia and his admiration for Patriarch Nikon, 'a simply colossal person'.[103] Laymen proved keener on restoration than clergy, whose personal experience of episcopal despots – 'little "Patriarch Nikons"', as Rozanov put it at the outset of the Pre-Conciliar Commission – made them fearful of 'a bishop squared'.[104] However, on 22 September – less than three weeks after work began and two days *before* the Moscow City Duma elections registered a sharp rise in support for the Bolsheviks – Arsenii (Stadnitskii) joined the majority of 65:38 in support of a formula proposed by Prince Evgenii Trubetskoi.[105] To the horror of Trubetskoi's fellow-liberals, this advocated a patriarch as *primus inter pares* among bishops.[106] Much activity had evidently taken place behind the scenes, where Archbishop Antonii and his supporters were at their most persuasive, coaxing rather than hectoring in the manner of their public

[101] *Deianiia*, 1, 65–70 (second pagination), 18 Aug. 1917.

[102] 'Iz "dnevnika" Professora A. D. Beliaeva', 107, diary, 4 July 1917.

[103] I. V. Lobanova, '"Nam nuzhen Patriarkh…": Dokumenty Otdela o vysshem tserkovnom upravlenii Pomestnogo sobora 1917–1918 gg.', in *Tserkov' v istorii Rossii*, 10 (Moscow, 2015), 180, 16 Sept. 1917.

[104] Prof.-Prot. Ia. Galakhov, 'Sobornaia rabota', in *Delo velikogo stroitel'stva*, 102; V. V. Rozanov, *Russkaia gosudarstvennost' i obshchestvo: Stat'i 1906–1907 gg.*, ed. A. N. Nikoliukin (Moscow, 2003), 46, 13 Mar. 1906; Lobanova, '"Nam nuzhen patriarch…"', 183, archpriest A. Ia. Iazykov, 18 Sept. 1917.

[105] Vorob'ev and Krivosheeva, 'Mitropolit Arsenii', 250; Lavrov *et al.*, *Ierarkhiia*, 129–30.

[106] Randall Poole, 'Religion, War and Revolution: E. N. Trubetskoi's Liberal Construction of Russian National Identity, 1912–20', *Kritika: Explorations in Russian and Eurasian History*, 7 (2006), 195–240, passes swiftly over Trubetskoi's ecclesiastical involvement, but it seems that he was particularly effective in reconciling peasant and elite opinion at the Council.

pronouncements. To maintain the pressure, Antonii nevertheless reminded delegates that, in the current economic crisis, a council which had already cost 400,000 roubles risked bankruptcy before a single resolution had been reached. After an initial stalemate (38:38), Mitrofan's section resolved (56:32) to take Trubetskoi's formula to a plenary session.[107] As a sign of his confidence by the first week in October, Antonii was sitting for the celebrated portrait by Nesterov, who boasted that he was painting 'the potential all-Russian patriarch'.[108]

Seizing his moment, Antonii chaired the episcopal curia for the first and only time on Sunday 8 October. Having hitherto functioned as a special interest group, hearing appeals from hierarchs dismissed earlier in the year, the curia now considered Serafim (Chichagov)'s proposal for a more interventionist approach to conciliar business. Conscious of the delicacy of their position, the bishops agreed only to select a representative to express their views on any particular issue at a plenary session. Bishop Mitrofan was mandated to present the case for the patriarchate without delay, even though his section had yet to perfect its scheme.[109] Slicing through the historical and canonical maze, Mitrofan justified restoration on grounds of leadership, a quality soon praised by others keen to install a fearless *vozhd'*: 'We need a patriarch as a prayerful representative of the Russian Church – a representative of heroic deeds and audacity – and as someone to stand up for the Russian Church. All the rest is unimportant.'[110]

Since only Archbishop Antonii fitted this bill, he was the sole bishop (effectively the sole potential candidate) selected to speak on 18 October, when the Council, alarmed by the proliferation of brief, underdeveloped interventions, voted 217:144 to restrict the debate to six orators on each side.[111] Feigning surprise at being called early, just as he had done in the State Council in 1906, Antonii launched into some characteristically personal remarks, objecting that his critics had dishonestly ascribed his support for the patriarchate to covert monarchism. Any church required leadership, he claimed, and it was not Patriarch Nikon but that 'great destroyer' Peter the Great who was responsible for 'everything bad' in Russian Orthodoxy.[112] By then, Andronik (Nikol'skii) had preached in favour of the patriarchate at Sergiev Posad, where the talk was soon of 'hysterics' on both sides.[113] In fact,

---

[107] Lavrov *et al.*, *Ierarkhiia*, 131–2.
[108] M. V. Nesterov to A. A. Turygin, 6 Oct. 1917, in Nesterov, *Pis'ma*, 272.
[109] *Dokumenty*, IV, 43–9, 8 Oct. 1917.
[110] *Deianiia*, II, 235, 11 Oct. 1917; Evtuhov, 'The Church in the Russian Revolution', 506–7.
[111] *Deianiia*, II, 276–8, 18 Oct. 1917.
[112] *Ibid.*, II, 289, 18 Oct. 1917.
[113] 'Iz "dnevnika" Professora A. D. Beliaeva', 114–16, diary, 15 and 22 Oct. 1917.

though Bishop Mitrofan, a prominent right-winger in the Third Duma, liked to tweak the liberals' tails by referring to parliamentary procedures, the atmosphere at the Council remained civil, if tense, since patriarchists were determined to secure the passage of the transition formula, presented as a compromise designed to reconcile the 'supreme power' of the Council with the restoration of a patriarch.

Personalities were now to the fore. The claim by the Moscow archpriest Nikolai Dobronravov that such a petty-minded episcopate could generate no plausible candidate for the patriarchal throne was echoed by Professor Titlinov, who insisted that the office required someone capable of 'moral charm'. 'No such person is visible on our horizon', Titlinov pointedly declared, adding that 'the important psychology in our time is not individual, but social: and to social psychology the idea of the patriarchate says precisely nothing'.[114]

Still, he could sense that the mood was against him, and so it proved. A well-known turning point in favour of restoration came on 23 October, when Archimandrite Ilarion (Troitskii) gave an emotional address claiming that the heart of Russia beat in the Dormition cathedral, whose empty patriarchal throne he compared with the wailing wall of Jerusalem.[115] Although Ilarion has sometimes been placed on the ecclesiastical 'left', by 1917 he had long since marked himself out as a critic of Western progress, and no council delegate would have missed, in his reference to a 'beating heart', an image beloved of Archbishop Antonii.[116] Equally familiar was Ilarion's insistence that there was no need to fear a papal patriarch, since his powers would be controlled by the Council. Five days later, as the Kremlin was temporarily recaptured from the revolutionaries, Bishop Mitrofan reminded liberals who complained that the patriarch's powers remained undefined that the Duma itself had been created on the basis of the ambiguous October Manifesto. Last-ditch amendments to the transition formula proposed by Petr Kudriavtsev – a Kiev professor once denounced by Antonii (Khrapovitskii) as 'an academic Voltaire' – succeeded only in adding the word 'supervisory' (*kontroliruiushchii*) to the list of the Council's powers ('judicial, administrative, legislative'). Restoration was rapidly approved and the nervous chamber settled down to hear Kirill (Smirnov) describe the violence of the previous day, when he had been

---

[114] *Deianiia*, II, 358, 21 Oct. 1917.

[115] *Ibid.*, 377–83, 23 Oct. 1917.

[116] Compare Dimitry Pospielovsky, *The Russian Church under the Soviet Regime 1917–1982* (2 vols., Crestwood, NY, 1984), I, 30, with Michelson, *Beyond the Monastery Walls*, 210–12. On Antonii's notion of the patriarch as a 'heart beating for the whole Church', see Lobanova, 'Nam nuzhen patriarkh', 173, 12 Sept. 1917 (A. V. Vasil'ev, a self-fashioned neo-Muscovite poet who had been Rozanov's superior at the Office of State Comptrol in the 1890s).

refused admission to the Kremlin because he could not say whether he represented the government or the Bolsheviks.[117] 'In the current anarchy one can understand why a patriarch might now seem desirable even to those who previously did not want it', Professor Beliaev noted on 29 October. 'In peaceful circumstances, under the full, firm and unconditional authority of the secular government, the question of the patriarchate might have been decided in the negative or passed with an insignificant majority.'[118]

That evening, a meeting of the Council steering committee (*sovet*) accepted a proposal from seventy-nine council delegates that each delegate should nominate three candidates – the first three to secure an overall majority would go forward to the drawing of lots.[119] The meeting was attended only by the Council's secretary and by Tikhon, Arsenii, Antonii and archpriest A. P. Rozhdestvenskii, a professor opposed to restoration. Since their discussion was not recorded, we cannot know whether Antonii objected to the decision. However, at the plenary session next day, one of his most loyal episcopal acolytes, Pakhomii (Kedrov), was put up to argue (in vain) that the final choice be made by the bishops alone. Another disciple, Evdokim (Meshcherskii), successfully ensured that candidates for the final draw required an absolute majority, and the Council also accepted an amendment from the thirty-eight-year-old inspector of the Lithuanian Seminary, Viacheslav Bogdanovich, that delegates should be permitted to nominate only one man.[120] That afternoon, Antonii received 101 of the 257 valid nominations (16 ballot papers were blank). His closest rival, Kirill (Smirnov), scored only 27; Tikhon came third with 23, Arsenii fifth with 14. Nine of the twenty-five nominees attracted only one supporter.[121] Only when the opportunity to cast multiple votes was restored on 31 October did Tikhon and Arsenii regain ground. In the first round of the final ballot, in which 155 votes were required for an overall majority, Antonii scored 159, Arsenii 148 and Tikhon 125. In the second round, Arsenii polled 62 more votes than Tikhon, whose name went forward to the final draw only after a third round of voting.[122]

Changes in voting patterns since August must be analysed with caution since this ballot, like the poll for the council chairmanship, was secret and the turnout had fallen owing to the chaos in Moscow and the possible

[117] *Deianiia*, III, 9–12, 28 Oct. 1917; Nikon, *Mitropolit Antonii (Khrapovitskii)*, II, 131.
[118] 'Iz "dnevnika" Professora A. D. Beliaeva', 116–17, diary, 29 Oct. 1917.
[119] *Dokumenty*, II, 128–9, 29 Oct. 1917.
[120] *Deianiia*, III, 44–5, 30 Oct. 1917.
[121] *Ibid.*, 51, 53, 30 Oct. 1917.
[122] *Ibid.*, 55–6, 31 Oct. 1917.

secession of some liberals.[123] Nevertheless, it seems clear that a significant number of delegates were now prepared to suspend their reservations about Archbishop Antonii, sensing that the qualities required in a patriarch were different from those desirable in a council chairman, especially in the transformed political circumstances. It must also be stressed that Antonii was by no means a creature of the episcopal curia. Since attendance there averaged only in the high forties and not all his fellow-bishops supported Antonii, most of his votes, both at the nomination and in the final ballot, must have come from laymen and parish clergy. It was reasonable for him to conclude that his election represented the will of the majority.[124]

Ironically, that majority was punctured only by the drawing of lots, a procedure never subsequently repeated. Its precedents, scarcely discussed until the last moment, were complex.[125] The Byzantine model – in which the emperor selected bishops from a shortlist of three – had undergone significant modification in medieval and early modern Russia. There, the role of the secular power was probably less decisive than surviving royally inspired manuscripts make it seem.[126] By November 1917, however, tsarist intervention was impossible and a casting role for the Synod (rejected in episcopal elections that spring) was inconceivable.[127] Beginning with the election of Patriarch Iosif in 1642, several Muscovite patriarchs had been chosen by lot. But in their cases, the successful candidate emerged from a shortlist longer than three.[128] For a Russian precedent for the procedure adopted in 1917, it is necessary to return to medieval Novgorod, where the resort to 'a man chosen by God' appears to have provided a means of resolving especially divisive episcopal contests.[129] Boris Uspenskii has compared the mood of Novgorod's republican popular assembly (*veche*) with that of the Moscow Church Council in 1917–18.[130] However, judging from the

---

[123] The Council's standard voting procedure, evidently designed to foster consensus, was for delegates to stand in their places, non-contents being counted first. Where no clear majority emerged, the chair could call for a division or a formal vote. See *Deianiia*, I, 49–51 (first pagination), especially paras. 174, 175, 177.

[124] Evlogii, *Put' moei zhizni*, 301.

[125] The Pre-Conciliar Commission debated lots only once, with reference to the election of laymen and clergy to a future council: see *Zhurnaly*, I, 100–2.

[126] See Paul Bushkovitch, 'The Selection and Deposition of the Metropolitan and Patriarch of the Orthodox Church in Russia, 1448–1619', in *Etre catholique – être orthodoxe – être protestant: confessions et identités culturelles en Europe médiévale et moderne*, ed. Marek Derwich and Mikhail V. Dmitriev (Wrocław, 2003), 123–50.

[127] Rogoznyi, *Tserkovnaia revoliutsiia*, 144–50, especially 149.

[128] B. A. Uspenskii, *Tsar' i patriarkh: Kharizma vlasti v Rossii (Vizantiiskaia model' i ee russkoe pereosmyslenie)* (Moscow, 1998), 303–7.

[129] *Ibid.*, 290–303; Michael C. Paul, 'Episcopal Election in Novgorod, Russia, 1156–1478', *Church History*, 72 (2003), 251–75

[130] Uspenskii, *Tsar' i patriarkh*, 307.

debate on 30 October, delegates were preoccupied rather with the example of the contemporary Eastern patriarchates. As Professor Sokolov had explained at a fringe meeting the day before, these offered a variety of options. The suggested model, as the Council subsequently heard, approximated to the practice of the patriarchate of Alexandria.[131] But no one knew better than Sokolov that Alexandrian elections had been controversial within living memory.[132] And whatever their grasp of rival electoral mechanisms, it seems probable that the central merit of the system adopted by the Moscow Church Council delegates was that it offered a clear resolution to a bitterly fought election in increasingly unpredictable times. The result was doubly ironic: it was only the resort to divine intervention that rescued ecclesiastical liberals who had harped on the majority principle since 1905 from the electoral triumph of their bête-noire – Antonii (Khrapovitskii) – who himself had spent the previous decade decrying the falsity of parliamentary democracy.

VI

Having argued that the politics of restoration make sense only if we allocate a central role to Archbishop Antonii, it is natural for me to end by speculating what might have happened had he been elected in Tikhon's place. On the day that Tikhon's name was drawn, a relieved Bogoslovskii concluded that the church had escaped the anarchy engulfing the state by selecting 'an individual around whom Orthodox Russia will unite' – 'a spiritual centre towards which the scattered, the lacerated, the jaded and the tormented must gravitate':

> When yids and scoundrels stand at the head of the state, it is comforting to have a pure and holy father at the head of the church. Under the tsar, it ought, perhaps, to have been possible to manage without the patriarchate. But now it can render priceless service for Russia.[133]

Things did not work out that way, and it is hard to imagine a better outcome for the church had the more abrasive Antonii triumphed. Over the autumn of 1917, ecclesiastical opinions had hardened in favour of a man who could get things done, much as they had in society more generally. Aside from his resilience, however, Antonii resembled Lenin only in his ability to defame his enemies and scheme

---

[131] *Deianiia*, III, 38–51, especially 42–4, 30 Oct. 1917.

[132] I. I. Sokolov, 'Izbranie Aleksandriiskikh patriarkhov v XIX veke: istoricheskii ocherk', *Khristianskoe chtenie* (Mar. 1915), no. 3, 358–78, opens with the riven Orthodox community in Cairo in the late 1860s. For a recent treatment, see *Rumyniia i Egipet v 1860–1870-e gg.: Pis'ma rossiiskogo diplomata I. M. Leksa k N. P. Ignat'evu*, ed. O. E. Petrunina (Moscow, 2016).

[133] Bogoslovskii, *Dnevniki*, 454, diary, 5 Nov. 1917.

against them. And although Lenin long remained nervous of the church's counter-revolutionary potential, it was he who held the whip hand. In January 1918, in the aftermath of the decree separating church from state, Patriarch Tikhon resorted to a favoured tactic of the ecclesiastical 'right' by anathematising the 'madmen' whose 'satanic' acts had covered Russia in blood.[134] His anathema made no difference and the church remained powerless to direct the strong current of popular religiosity that continued to flow through revolutionary Russia. Instead, the sorts of elite dissension we have considered widened over the following decade into multiple schisms, intensified when renovationist churchmen deposed Tikhon in April 1923 and annulled his anathema on the Bolsheviks. After Tikhon's death in 1925, the patriarchate fell into abeyance until 1943. And while Antonii emigrated to lead the Russian Church Abroad until his death in 1936, many of the most prominent individuals discussed in this lecture became martyrs for their faith, swept away by Bukharin's iron broom.

[134] 'Poslanie Sviateishago Tikhona, Patriarkha vseia Rossii', *Bogoslovskii vestnik* (1918), nos. 1–2, 74–6.

Transactions of the RHS 28 (2018), pp. 175–195 © Royal Historical Society 2018
doi:10.1017/S0080440118000099

'WHO THE HELL ARE ORDINARY PEOPLE?' ORDINARINESS AS A CATEGORY OF HISTORICAL ANALYSIS*

By Claire Langhamer

READ 10 FEBRUARY 2017

ABSTRACT. Ordinariness was a frequently deployed category in the political debates of 2016. According to one political leader, the vote for Brexit was 'a victory for ordinary, decent people who've taken on the establishment and won'. In making this claim, Nigel Farage sought to link a dramatic political moment with a powerful, yet conveniently nebulous, construction of the ordinary person. In this paper, I want to historicise recent use of the category by returning to another moment when ordinariness held deep political significance: the years immediately following the Second World War. I will explore the range of values, styles and specific behaviours that gave meaning to the claim to be ordinary; consider the relationship between ordinariness, everyday experience and knowledge; and map the political work ordinariness was called upon to perform. I argue that the immediate post-war period was a critical moment in the formation of ordinariness as a social category, an affective category, a moral category, a consumerist category and, above all, a political category. Crucially, ordinariness itself became a form of expertise, a finding that complicates our understanding of the 'meritocratic moment'.

I Introduction

Filmed in the winter of 1940–1, the Crown Film Unit documentary, *Ordinary People*, offered a glimpse of everyday London life in Blitz conditions.[1] Featuring factory, department store and GPO workers alongside bombed out families and air raid shelter-dwellers, the film was clearly designed to garner foreign support for a people's war. *Ordinary People*

---

*Mass-Observation material is used by permission of the Mass-Observation Trustees. I would like to thank the Institute of Historical Research Durham for the Fellowship during which some of the early research for this paper was conducted. I would also like to thank Stephen Brooke, Lucy Robinson and Penny Summerfield for their comments on earlier drafts, the audience at the 2016 Northeast Conference on British Studies for their questions about an earlier version of this paper and the Royal Historical Society audience for their own questions and comments.
[1] J. B. Holmes and Jack Lee, *Ordinary People* (1941).

was a celebration of ordinary life in the face of exceptional circumstance. Motifs of the ordinary interject throughout, notably in tea-based hospitality, the morning milk delivery and the purchase of a 'powder-blue' cardigan: that last detail is important. This powerful representation of a single wartime day ends with a harmonica-led sing along in the shelter, a reminder of the speed with which the unusual can become the norm.

Ordinariness permeated the production of this film as well as its content. The opening titles included a pointed instruction 'To the future historian' that 'THIS FILM WAS PLAYED BY ORDINARY PEOPLE OF LONDON.' The message was reinforced through Robert Menzies's spoken-to-camera introduction to the film; an introduction that celebrated ordinary people as the custodians of a set of values essential for allied victory:

> You are going to see a film called Ordinary People. It is made by the people of London about the people of London, the plain people, the true people...Great things are happening in Britain but perhaps the greatest is the display of neighbourliness, of kindness, of cheerfulness, of uncomplaining suffering that is being given by ordinary people who secure no fame and who have no place in the headlines. In this picture you will catch a glimpse of that spirit which is the surest bulwark of Britain against senseless and indiscriminate bombing by the half civilised Hun. In brief in this picture you will see why Hitler cannot win.

Ordinary People was not of course the only wartime film that sought to valorise ordinariness. An emphasis upon the day-to-day dignity and emotional authenticity of the ordinary person underpins the documentary work of Humphrey Jennings for example. And the attempt to represent the truth of wartime experience through recourse to the ordinary transcended the documentary genre. Feature films such as *Millions Like Us* (1943) and *In Which We Serve* (1942) sold the heroism of ordinary people in extraordinary circumstances back to a mass cinema audience. In so doing, as Jo Fox explains, they placed 'the image of the ordinary within the master narrative of the people's war'.[2] Film historian James Chapman notes that 'The most celebrated films of the war are undoubtedly those which give a sober realistic portrait of ordinary people.'[3]

In this wartime context, ordinariness was located within the everyday, but was not synonymous with it. The 'People's War' provided a space within which ordinariness – as a set of values, social characteristics and emotional styles, as well as specific behaviours in particular places – was asserted and celebrated. The extreme demands of wartime

---

[2] Jo Fox, 'Millions Like Us? Accented Language and the "Ordinary" in British Films of the Second World War', *Journal of British Studies*, 45 (2006), 819–45 (quotation at 820).

[3] James Chapman, 'British Cinema and the People's War', in *Millions Like Us? British Culture in the Second World War*, ed. Nick Hayes and Jeff Hill (Liverpool, 1999), 60.

seemed to colourise the ordinary and draw attention to its texture. As sociologist Victoria Robinson has recently argued, 'the extraordinary is both embedded within and in dialogue with the mundane, rather than having a separate and unmediated existence of its own'.[4] Such a dialogue is, of course, historically contingent. Over time, the extraordinary could become ordinary and vice versa; the relationship between these categories was politically and culturally freighted in temporally determined ways.

The identity of the 'ordinary person' was also framed by context. In wartime, the category was necessarily loose because its rhetorical power rested upon its inclusivity. This imprecision facilitated an easy mapping onto the new wartime identities; experiences and forms of expertise that did not always correspond to existing social structures. As the social investigative organisation Mass-Observation noted in 1942, 'today the ordinary citizen can no longer be covered in these familiar phrases "the man-in-the-street" and "the woman-in-the-kitchen", it is now the "man-in-uniform", the "woman-in-the-workshop", or vice versa'.[5] Nonetheless, roughly drawn boundaries were periodically advanced, often in order to cohere the collective identity still further. In his BBC 'Postscript' broadcast of 30 June 1940, writer, broadcaster and pipe-smoking Yorkshireman, J. B. Priestley, confided that 'Sometimes I feel that you and I – all of us ordinary people – are on one side of a high fence, and on the other side...are the official and important personages: the pundits and mandarins.'[6] For George Orwell, Englishness (if not Britishness) was itself innately ordinary; in 1941, he called for 'a conscious open revolt by ordinary people against inefficiency, class privilege and the rule of the old'.[7] As Chris Waters has argued, this was 'a period in which the nation was increasingly reimagined on the site of the ordinary and everyday'.[8]

In this paper, I focus on the immediate post-war period. What did it mean to be ordinary once the war was over, where did the boundaries of ordinariness lie and what social, cultural and political work did the category do?

---

[4] Victoria Robinson, 'Reconceptualising the Mundane and the Extraordinary: A Lens through which to Explore Transformation within Women's Everyday Footwear Practices', *Sociology*, 49 (2015), 903–18 (quotation at 904).

[5] Mass-Observation, *People in Production. An Enquiry into British War Production* (1942), 2.

[6] Quoted in John Baxendale, '"You and I – All of Us Ordinary People": Representing "Britishness" in Wartime', in *Millions Like Us?*, ed. Hayes and Hill, 318.

[7] George Orwell, *The Lion and the Unicorn* (orig. publ. 1941; 1962), 59. For more on Orwell's 'modest celebration of ordinary Englishness', see Robert Colls, *George Orwell. English Rebel* (Oxford, 2013), 168.

[8] Chris Waters, '"Dark Strangers" in Our Midst: Discourses of Race and Nation in Britain, 1947–1963', *Journal of British Studies*, 36 (1997), 207–38 (quotation at 210).

II Framing ordinariness

The parameters of the ordinary cannot be taken for granted. Raymond Williams explored the complexity of the category in the second edition of his vocabulary of culture and society, *Keywords*, noting that

> The use of ordinary in such expressions as 'ordinary people' has a curious history and implication. What ordinary people believe can, in different contexts, mean either what 'uneducated' or 'uninstructed' people know and think, in what are then clearly seen as limited ways, or what 'sensible', 'regular', 'decent' people believe, as distinct from the views of some sect or of intellectuals.[9]

Writing from a later, historiographical, standpoint, Raphael Samuel also noted 'the ambiguities attaching to the notion of "ordinary people", a coinage of the 1930s, replacing older terms such as "everyman" and "the common people"'.[10]

After 1945, 'ordinary people' were addressed and represented in intersecting ways within newspapers, popular culture, political debate, scholarly studies and historical narratives. The heroism of a loosely defined community of the ordinary underpinned retrospective accounts of Britain at war for example. Speaking to Remembrance Day crowds in 1950, the bishop of Burnley declared that it was 'the steadfastness of the ordinary people...that decided the issue of two world wars'.[11] Postwar re-construction fantasies placed ordinariness at their heart. A widespread desire to restore, or more accurately re-make, 'ordinary life' found a particularly striking expression in a focus on home and family.[12] The expanding genre of advice literature utilised ideas of ordinariness to facilitate the creation of a happy, home-focused, audience. Marriage guidance expert David Mace declared that his book *Marriage Crisis* was written: 'for ordinary folks, and I'm going to write it the way ordinary folks will understand. If some of my friends think this is undignified, I can't help it.'[13] Psychoanalyst Donald Winnicott addressed a gendered audience of the ordinary in a series of radio talks entitled 'The Ordinary Devoted Mother and Her Baby'.[14]

The turn to ordinariness informed the production of entertainment and advertising as well as advice. Interviewed by the *Lancashire Evening Post* in May 1947, for example, radio host Wilfred Pickles explained the success of his *Have a Go!* programme, 'I am talking to ordinary

---

[9] Raymond Williams, *Keywords. A Vocabulary of Culture and Society* (1983), 225–6.

[10] Raphael Samuel, *Island Stories: Unraveling Britain. Theatres of Memory*, II (1998), 225.

[11] *Burnley Express*, 15 Nov. 1950, 1.

[12] Richard Bessel and Dirk Schumann, *Life after Death. Approaches to a Cultural and Social History of Europe during the 1940s and 1950s* (Cambridge, 2003), 3.

[13] David R. Mace, *Marriage Crisis* (1948), 8.

[14] Anne Karpf, 'Constructing and Addressing the "Ordinary Devoted Mother"', *History Workshop Journal*, 78 (2014), 82–106.

people, about ordinary things, in an ordinary way.'[15] From 1946, both *Woman's Hour* and *Housewives' Choice* sought to cohere their audiences through an appeal to ordinariness.[16] Ealing comedies such as *The Titfield Thunderbolt* (1953), *Whiskey Galore* (1949) and, of course, *Passport to Pimlico* (1949) pitted the ordinary person against officialdom; whilst a 1946 film, *The Voice Within*, advertised itself baldly as 'A powerful drama of ordinary people and a dog.'[17]

Within the context of austerity and scarcity, the language of ordinariness also proved useful to those advertising consumer goods. Here, ordinariness was used to associate sensible good judgement with the act of shopping. For example, Robinsons Shopping Centre – 'for the Ordinary People of the Hartlepools' – was advertised as 'The Plain Store for Plain People.'[18] The appeal to ordinariness was also an appeal to be trusted. The Provincial Building Society boasted that it had attracted 'Thousands upon thousands of ordinary people who want to invest their savings to show a sure, steady profit.'[19] The 'other' to ordinariness – expertise, celebrity – was an implicit, and sometimes explicit, presence in these kinds of appeals. So, for example, Anadin aspirin was advertised on the grounds that 'Tens of thousands of professional people who deal daily with the problem of pain know and use "Anadin"…They know that "Anadin", the fast and *safe* pain killer is absolutely suitable for ordinary people to use at home, at work, or wherever they happen to be.'[20] Adverts for Zubes cough mixture suggested that 'Huskiness may be very glamorous in film stars, but to the ordinary person it's neither glamorous nor comfortable.'[21]

Perhaps most significantly, the ordinary also had a salience in politics, apparently personified by Prime Minister Clement Attlee who 'in his very ordinariness, represented the hopes of millions'.[22] Attlee's autobiography, *As It Happened*, was described by Tom Hopkinson in *The Observer* as 'an extraordinary book, extraordinary for its unbelievable ordinariness'.[23] That Labour now claimed the mantle of ordinariness stands in contrast to the interwar period when its association with trade unionism was characterised as 'radical' and 'unordinary' by the Conservative party

[15] *Lancashire Evening Post*, 30 May 1947, 6.
[16] Maggie Andrews, *Domesticating the Airwaves: Broadcasting, Domesticity and Femininity* (2012), 122.
[17] *Burnley Express and Burnley News*, 21 Sept. 1946, 1.
[18] *Hartlepool Northern Daily Mail*, 17 Jan. 1947, 7.
[19] *Western Daily Press and Bristol Mirror*, 16 Oct. 1950, 1.
[20] *Aberdeen Evening Express*, 5 Mar. 1953, 10.
[21] *Sunday Post*, 3 Feb. 1946, 7.
[22] David Howell, *Attlee* (2006), 2.
[23] *Observer*, 11 Apr. 1954, 11.

of Baldwin and Chamberlain.[24] But the post-war appeal of ordinariness spread beyond party politics to political and social education. In 1951, for example, the Hartlepool Co-operative Society's education department ran a series of lectures on 'The Life of Ordinary People in Six European Cities',[25] and in 1958, the *Daily Mirror* introduced its readership to 'What they are really like in Russia today' by emphasising 'the ordinariness of these very ordinary people'.[26]

This was not all one-way traffic. If ordinary people constituted a coherent, yet usefully nebulous, market for advice, entertainment, goods and politics, they were also of interest in their own right. The popular press sought to ventilate their views and increasingly their feelings too.[27] As Adrian Bingham notes, 'the traditional conduit for this information was the readers' letter'; but the introduction of opinion polling just prior to the war had promised more systematic access to ordinary people's attitudes.[28] The most effective mobilisation of the ordinary was through the pages of the *Daily Mirror*, which repeatedly appealed to the ordinariness of its readers.[29] But the local press was the real bastion of ordinariness, with its interest in the specificities of the everyday, and commitment to cohering a place-based readership. As one reader put it: 'Only in the Local Press which one usually finds has been built up by hard work and good journalism, can the ordinary person be free to express his opinions.'[30]

The visibility of the ordinary in popular culture, commerce and politics both attracted, and was encouraged by, social scientists of various stripes. A research interest in ordinariness pre-dated the Second World War but was professionalised in its aftermath. It found a particular focus in the activities of Mass-Observation, whose work straddled the mid-century moment. Following the example set by Robert and Helen Lynd's study of 'Middletown' (Muncie in Indiana), Mass-Observation placed the ordinary – both empirically and methodologically – at the heart of a 'science of ourselves'.[31] Its founders harnessed the

[24] See Ross McKibbin, *The Ideologies of Class: Social Relations in Britain, 1880–1950* (Oxford, 1990), 289.

[25] *Hartlepool Northern Daily Mail*, 12 Nov. 1951, 10.

[26] *Daily Mirror*, 11 Sept. 1957, 12.

[27] See Adrian Bingham, *Family Newspapers? Sex, Private Life and the British Popular Press 1918–1978* (Oxford, 2009), 97–9.

[28] *Ibid.*, 97. See also Laura Dumond Beers, 'Whose Opinion?': Changing Attitudes Towards Opinion Polling in British Politics, 1937–1964', *Twentieth Century British History*, 17 (2006), 177–205.

[29] The *Daily Mirror* had, according to Donald Tyerman, editor of *The Economist*, 'performed a revolution in communication by talking to ordinary folk in ordinary folk's language about things ordinary folk are interested in'. *Daily Mirror*, 11 Aug. 1959, 9.

[30] *Buckingham Advertiser and Free Press*, 27 July 1946, 4.

[31] R. S. Lynd and H. M. Lynd, *Middletown. A Study in Modern American Culture* (1929). In its early publication, *Britain*, Mass-Observation explained that 'there has been much talk about

observational talents of 'a section of people in the population who were at one and the same time ordinary, hardworking folk and also intelligent and interesting enough to want to help us' who would 'give an extraordinary picture of England – extraordinary, though the material they report is completely ordinary'.[32] In fact, Mass-Observation's volunteer writers were most likely to be of a lower-middle-class status but a shared identity of ordinariness was used to cohere a broad church of volunteers of different, and sometimes ambiguous, class backgrounds.[33]

In numerous publications and broadcasts, Mass-Observation emphasised its engagement with ordinary people; a 1938 radio broadcast saw Humphrey Jennings and 'a man in the street' discuss 'poetry and the ordinary reader today'.[34] Those who reported on Mass-Observation reiterated this characterisation. 'Ordinary people watching how they themselves behave, how other people behave – a searchlight on living' was how the *Mirror*'s 'Cassandra' described its early activities.[35] Mass-Observation accumulated the views of 'ordinary' people in different locations throughout the war; in the latter part of the conflict, it ventilated the feelings and desires of a people on the verge of peace, often explicitly contrasting these to 'expert' or official opinion. *An Enquiry into Peoples Homes*, for example, roundly contested the view amongst planners that 'ordinary people have no idea of what they want in housing'.[36] In the later 1940s and early 1950s, Mass-Observation continued to privilege the ordinary, whether in search of 'the attitudes of ordinary people towards the future of the world', in demonstrating 'the puzzledness of ordinary people about some of the main stabilities of the past', or in offering advice to government on how it might best communicate with those same 'ordinary people'.[37]

the social relations of science, the need for extending the Science of Ourselves and for studying the everyday lives and feelings of ordinary people, a well as the customs of primitive people and the feelings of neurotics'. Mass-Observation, *Britain* (1939), 9.
For a history of Mass-Observation, see James Hinton, *The Mass Observers. A History, 1937–1949* (Oxford, 2013).
[32] Mass Observation Archive (hereafter MOA), File Report A26, Charles Madge and Tom Harrisson, 'They Speak for Themselves', BBC script broadcast 1 June 1939, 3; Charles Madge and Tom Harrisson, *Mass-Observation* (1937), 31.
[33] Hinton suggests that 'many of the panel members did not think of themselves as "ordinary". They tended to see themselves as unusual people, distinguished by their desire to self-fashion their lives free from the conventions of their social milieu.' Hinton, *The Mass Observers*, 374.
[34] 'The Poet and the Public', 10 May 1938, http://genome.ch.bbc.co.uk/58271ee8952a45f19712e00d52dc3ae9.
[35] *Daily Mirror*, 25 June 1937, 12.
[36] Mass-Observation, *An Enquiry into People's Homes* (1943), 5.
[37] MOA, File Report 2397, 'Second Report from Mass-Observation on World Organization and the Future', June 1946, 1; Mass-Observation, *Puzzled People* (1947), 12; MOA, File Report 2462, 'The Language of Leadership', Mar. 1947.

Where Mass-Observation led, post-war social science followed. As Mike Savage has demonstrated, the years after the Second World War saw sociology take a determined turn towards the ordinary, describing and categorising as it went. Women researchers were at the forefront of the new academic interest in the ordinary; interviews and surveys were their preferred method of accessing it.[38] Pearl Jephcott subtitled *Rising Twenty* – her study of young women in their late teens – *Notes on Some Ordinary Girls*, explaining that

> The girls are quite ordinary people, distinguished by no one characteristic except that in March 1945 they were all over 17 and under 21. 'Typical' is a dangerous label; but to a casual observer these particular girls seem to bear a family likeness to their million and a half contemporaries in England and Wales, and seem more or less birds of a feather with the other girls of their immediate localities. They also, on occasion, display much the same emotions and behave remarkably like certain of their predecessors to whom literature has given immortality.[39]

A decade later, Elizabeth Bott's study of *Family and Social Networks* focused explicitly on 'ordinary urban families'.[40] Her criteria were expansive; for Bott, ordinariness 'had no class connotations'.[41] Margaret Stacey also championed 'a sociology of the ordinary': 'Because I really thought we needed some empirical data about how "ordinary people" lived – not these categories who were presenting social problems.'[42] She was more specific in her 1960 study of *Tradition and Change in an English Town* identifying the 'ordinary' as one of three status groups within the Banbury working class (alongside the 'rough' and the 'respectable').[43]

And yet the claim to ordinariness did not map seamlessly on to existing social distinctions: it was an affective as well as an economic position. As we have already seen, J. B. Priestley described himself as an ordinary person; so did Eton-educated Colonel Clifton Brown, speaker of the House of Commons. 'I don't pretend to have any great qualities. I am just an ordinary person; but, I hope, a very human one', he was quoted as saying in 1945.[44] But who else laid claim to the identity or had it bestowed upon them? In the words of Labour MP, Eric Heffer, 'Who the hell are ordinary people?'[45] In 1949, the apparent ordinariness of those attending a communist meeting in the Chapeltown district of

---

[38] Mike Savage, *Identities and Social Change in Britain since 1940* (Oxford, 2010), 244.

[39] Pearl Jephcott, *Rising Twenty. Notes on Some Ordinary Girls* (1948), 19.

[40] Elizabeth Bott, *Family and Social Network. Roles, Norms and External Relationships in Ordinary Urban Families* (1957) 8.

[41] *Ibid.*, 10–11.

[42] Savage, *Identities and Social Change in Britain since 1940*, 151.

[43] Margaret Stacey, *Tradition and Change. A Study of Banbury* (Oxford, 1960), 105.

[44] *Yorkshire Post and Leeds Mercury*, 2 Aug. 1945, 1.

[45] House of Commons Debates, 17 Feb. 1971, vol. 811, cc. 1852. Heffer was speaking in a debate on industrial action.

Leeds proved puzzling to a *Yorkshire Post* reporter. He reported that the gathering included 'shop assistants, housewives, typists, a chemist, a school teacher, an insurance agent, a scientist and a number of ordinary British workmen'.[46] When the *Bucks Herald* interviewed 'ordinary people' about their hopes for 1953, those included were 'local people from various walks of life', such as a scoutmaster who hoped for a new sports field, a 72-year-old villager desirous of illuminated numbers on bus-stops, a proponent of world peace and a shop-keeper with suggestions on how to improve traffic conditions.[47]

Women were more likely to say that they felt ordinary than men, and were certainly more likely to be designated ordinary by others. Housewives were nearly always 'ordinary' and women were assumed to be housewives. So, for example, Mrs Beatrice Curtis, parliamentary candidate for the seat of Clapham in the 1950 general election, was listed in the Liberal Candidates *Who's Who of 475 Liberal Candidates Fighting the 1950 General Election* as follows:

> Is Bachelor of Arts of London University and has been lecturer at King's College, London. Since 1934 an ordinary housewife. Varied war work includes National Savings, work among Belgian refugees, etc. Has been chairman of Balham and Tooting Liberal Association since 1945, was Hon. Secretary of the Balham appeal for Lord Mayor's fund for children, and has worked hard for U.N.A.[48]

The seat was won by Labour. Even the first all-woman team to climb in the Himalayas (Dr Evelyn Camrass, Monica Jackson and Elizabeth Stark) described themselves as 'ordinary women'.[49]

And yet ordinariness was not necessarily a stable identity. Rather, it was bestowed, performed or addressed within specific contexts for particular purposes. It was a notably prominent feature within post-war local council elections, used to denote authenticity, shared experience, local knowledge or determined advocacy. The Labour party in Birmingham was 'the expression of the hope and aspirations of the ordinary people: the people who perform the useful work of society', a carefully knowing formulation that did not draw explicit attention to class difference.[50] Liberals in Hampstead preferred to act as the ordinary person's conduit, declaring that it was 'vital that the voice of ordinary people is heard through representatives free to speak their minds

---

[46] *Yorkshire Post and Leeds Mercury*, 2 Sept. 1949, 1.

[47] *Bucks Herald*, 2 Jan. 1953, 7; *Buckingham Advertiser and Free Press*, 27 July 1946, 4.

[48] MOA, Topic Collection 76, General Elections, 76-6-D, Liberal Party Election Publications, *Who's Who of 475 Liberal Candidates Fighting the 1950 General Election* (1950).

[49] Monica Jackson and Elizabeth Stark, *Tents in the Clouds. The First Women's Himalayan Expedition* (1957).

[50] MOA, Topic Collection 88, Local Council Elections: 1937–51, 84-1-D, Councils: Aberdeen to Bristol, 'Birmingham City Council By-election, Labour', 22.6.50.

without rigid obedience to a Party Whip'.[51] Conservative candidates in Leeds preferred to speak *for* the ordinary person: 'The Conservative view of a free and better life with fewer restrictions, rising confidence and a happier outlook is the hope to-day of millions of ordinary folk.'[52]

And Beatrice Curtis was not the only aspirant councillor to declare their own ordinariness. Standing as a Labour candidate for the electoral division of Swallowfield, Arthur P. Hogarth used the category to assert powerful affective bonds between himself and the electorate.

> I am quite an ordinary person – just like yourself – and I believe the essence of demo-cratic government is that it should be carried out by ordinary people – just like us. I know your problems, your hopes, your fears, because they are also my problems, my hopes, and my fears. What you want done for the happiness and well-being of your families and yourselves, I also want done for mine.[53]

Ordinariness was deployed to build emotional bridges in other contexts too, although sometimes in ways that were barely credible. In August 1951, the *Sunderland Daily Echo and Shipping Gazette* claimed that when Princess Margaret 'visits the theatre she does so as an ordinary person, usually sitting in the stalls, with a small party of friends'.[54]

The identity of those excluded from the category ordinary varied according to historical moment, the purpose of categorization and the identity of those policing it. Regardless of their own, often spirited, defini-tional claims, politicians, journalists, 'intellectuals', trade unionists, busi-ness people, farmers, 'career women', campaigners, historians – or anyone perceived to have some kind of a public voice – could be deemed to sit beyond its parameters. According to the 1957 Wolfenden Report, prostitutes were excluded from the circle of 'decent' ordinari-ness. As Julia Laite explains, 'The chief proprietor of the right to public space was the person who was liberally referred to as "the ordin-ary" or the "normal, decent" citizen. This "ordinary citizen's" "sense of decency" was conceived as under threat by prostitutes who were distinct from "ordinary citizens".'[55] Migrants – particularly those of West Indian, African or South Asian origin – could also find themselves positioned outside the parameters of ordinariness. Or they were regarded as a direct threat to a 'normal' ordinariness that was implicitly designated

---

[51] MOA, Topic Collection 88, Local Council Elections: 1937–51, 84-1-E, Councils: Cheshire to Hornsey, 'Liberal, Hampstead Borough Council', 12.5.49.

[52] MOA, Topic Collection 88, Local Council Elections: 1937–51, 84-1-F, Councils: Kent to North Riding, 'Leeds City Council, Conservative', 1.11.47.

[53] MOA, Topic Collection 88, Local Council Elections: 1937–51, 84-1-D, Councils: Aberdeen to Bristol, 'Berkshire County Council, Labour', 8.3.46.

[54] *Sunderland Echo*, 20 Aug. 1951, 2.

[55] Julia Laite, *Common Prostitutes and Ordinary Citizens* (2011), 198.

as 'white'. Describing a visit to Brixton in 1955, sociologist Sheila Patterson asserted that

> As I turned off the main shopping street, I was immediately overcome with a sense of strangeness, almost of shock. The street was a fairly typical South London side-street, grubby and narrow, lined with cheap cafes, shabby pubs, and flashy clothing-shops. All this was normal enough. But what struck one so forcefully was that…almost everyone in sight had a coloured skin.[56]

Nonetheless, within the House of Commons, the identity of the ordinary person was not infrequently contested. Within the press, it was deployed inconsistently. Within popular culture, it implied particular tastes. Within individual narratives, it could be a claim to inclusion or a challenge to vested interests. As a post-war social category, it could encompass nearly everyone or it could describe no one at all.

III The meanings of ordinariness

In 1981, David Pocock at Sussex University reinvented Mass-Observation as what was to become the Mass-Observation Project. In his appeal for volunteer writers, he mirrored the language of Mass-Observation's first phase, asserting that 'the experience of "ordinary" people is of particular importance'.[57] When Sheridan, Street and Bloome subsequently interviewed Mass-Observation Project volunteers in the early 1990s about their writing practices, few failed to claim ordinariness as a subject position.[58] One woman explained that

> I don't think ordinary people get the same chance as many perhaps academics, or so-called educated people, and people in the media, to have their say…I think ordinary really, you think of yourself as someone who hasn't perhaps achieved fame, or great success; just live a sort of normal, everyday life, going to work and with your family.[59]

For individuals such as this, the ordinary person was defined as much by who they were not, as by whom they were. Anyone whose voice went unheard within public life seemed to qualify, introducing a stark public–private dimension to the category. As Sheridan and her co-authors concluded, 'there is a sense in which being defined as "ordinary" is vague, more of a place holder waiting on how each writer will define it, rather than a given definition, "Its very difficult really; I don't think anybody's really ordinary" (M1498 interview)'.[60]

---

[56] Sheila Patterson, *Dark Strangers. A Study of West Indians in London* (1963), 1.

[57] Dorothy Sheridan, Brian Street and David Bloome, *Writing Ourselves. Mass-Observation and Literacy Practices* (Creskill NJ, 2000), 48.

[58] *Ibid.*, 214.

[59] *Ibid.*, 174.

[60] *Ibid.*, 218.

Within the immediate post-war period, however, ordinariness was less a 'place holder' and more an assertion of a (flexible) set of desirable traits. A range of values, styles and specific behaviours gave meaning to the claim to ordinariness, even if the precise identity of the ordinary person was somewhat elusive. So, for example, a reader of the *Gloucester Citizen* sought to distinguish between the political and the ordinary in a contribution to the letters page in 1949:

> How can we define the 'ordinary' from the political'. Let's take the ordinary people first: they are easier, because I flatter myself that I'm one of them. All the ordinary people want, I believe, are three things – Happiness, Contentment and Security...And of the political people? Simply that God forgot to put the power into their warped brains. So they mingle about with the ordinary people making them as miserable as themselves.[61]

The values most often ascribed to the ordinary person were decency and common sense, although kindness, authenticity, trustworthiness and transparency were also frequently advanced as defining characteristics.[62] In 1948, Foreign Secretary Ernest Bevin told the miners' conference at Whitley Bay that 'It is Moonshine that foreign affairs are something above the heads of ordinary people and a job for very clever diplomats...Foreign affairs is common sense people hoping to talk to other common sense people.'[63] Reporting on the Burgess and Maclean scandal in 1955, the *Daily Mirror* launched a scathing attack on the Foreign Office, 'crammed with intellectuals, the Old School Tie brigade, long-haired experts and the people-who-know-the-best people – have taken a mighty drop in the estimation of the very ordinary men and women of Britain who are armed with just a little bit of common sense and caution'.[64] Regardless of whether it was being addressed, quantified or represented, ordinariness was always a value-laden category.

The public assertion of ordinariness had other meanings too. When Grace Jones – wife of convicted murderer Arthur – was interviewed by the press, she sought moral sanctuary in the category. 'I shall not change my name – my very ordinary name', she was quoted as saying. 'We were a very ordinary, happy family before all this horror began – as ordinary as thousands of Joneses...The only way I can rebuild our lives is to get back to ordinariness again – and I hope my ordinary

---

[61] *Gloucester Citizen*, 22 July 1948, 4.

[62] In his study of discourses of race and nation, Chris Waters argues that 'it was largely in the 1930s and 1940s that Britons were reinvented as members of an essentially unassuming nation, a quiet, private, and ordinary people, defined by their modesty, kindness to others, loyalty, truthfulness, straightforwardness, and simplicity', Waters, '"Dark Strangers" in Our Midst', 211.

[63] *Gloucestershire Echo*, 7 July 1948, 1.

[64] *Daily Mirror*, 20 Sept. 1955, 1.

name will help me.'[65] When a twenty-five-year-old 'hotel servant' appeared in court on the charge of receiving a stolen typewriter, his lawyer argued that his client 'had not from the very beginning of his life, had an ordinary person's life'.[66] Here, an absence of ordinariness served as mitigation. The accused was sentenced to one year in prison nonetheless.

The contours of the 'ordinary person's' life were increasingly homogenized in the post-war years, although perhaps not quite to the extent that one woman assumed when she attempted to sell a wedding dress, that 'will fit ordinary size person'.[67] In the 1980s, Michael Anderson drew attention to a mid-twentieth-century 'modern life cycle', 'which had a number of clearly demarcated stages through which most of the population passed within a relatively narrow band of ages'.[68] Laura King has more recently demonstrated that a post-war 'focus on the "ordinary family" in newspapers and films, and to an extent, literature, created a rhetoric of homogeneity in terms of the experiences of different social groups, even where differences between parts of society remained'.[69] For those believed not to fit this model – by dint of sexuality or 'race' for example – ordinariness was more difficult to claim. Nonetheless, in post-war Britain, being ordinary was always more freighted than simply a description of being average or representative.

A crucial element was, of course the relationship between ordinariness and social class. 'I'm an ordinary woman', declared Celia Johnson's Laura in the 1945 David Lean film *Brief Encounter*, a claim that surely reflected the film's origins as a 1936 Noel Coward play. Laura Jesson's ordinariness speaks of Virginia Woolf's attention to 'an ordinary mind on an ordinary day' or to interwar radio programmes such as 'Music and the Ordinary Listener' in which 'Twelve little-known and seldom heard Overtures by Handel will be analysed at the piano and then played on the harpsichord.'[70] It is a notion of the ordinary rooted in middle-class suburban life. But in the wake of a 'People's War', ordinariness was increasingly located in the tastes and experiences of the British working class. As Selina Todd suggests of this period, 'the working class

[65] *Daily Mirror*, 29 June 1961, 2.

[66] *Gloucestershire Echo*, 22 June 1950, 6.

[67] *Dundee Courier and Advertiser*, 2 Jan. 1948, 1.

[68] Michael Anderson, 'The Emergence of the Modern Life Cycle in Britain', *Social History*, 10 (1985), 69–87 (quotation at 69).

[69] Laura King, *Family Men. Fatherhood and Masculinity in Britain, 1914–1960* (Oxford, 2015), 196.

[70] Lorraine Sim, *Virginia Woolf: The Patterns of Ordinary Experience* (2010), 8; 'Music and the Ordinary Listener', 7 May 1929, http://genome.ch.bbc.co.uk/b1446a0769bf4a259c4395b9924b1799.

became normative in Britain: they became "ordinary"'.[71] Indeed, Mike Savage has shown that ordinariness did important class-work in the years that followed the war, providing a coded framework within which social identity could be messy, contingent and apparently self-evident.[72] In his analysis of Goldthorpe and Lockwood's Luton-based 'Affluent Worker' interviews of the early 1960s, Savage identifies the pervasiveness of the self-identity 'ordinary': 'The working class comprises normal, authentic people. By differentiating it from a public upper-class elite, respondents could see themselves as ordinary people devoid of social distinction.'[73] Yet, as we have already seen, assertions of ordinariness did gender-work as well as class-work. In further analysis of the same material, Jon Lawrence shows that the claim to ordinariness and authenticity by male interviewees – alongside a rejection of snobbery – underpinned a particular way of 'doing masculinity' which had powerful cross-class purchase within the interview situation.[74]

IV The uses of ordinariness

According to the anthropologist of modern France, Catherine Neveu, contemporary use of the socio-political category 'ordinary citizen' often signals a non-political or uninvolved individual 'seen as more independent and detached than those involved in collective spaces or debates, and their opinions as more genuine, more "authentic" and less biased, since they are not supposed to be structured by the corporate interest or opinions or organised groups or collectives'.[75] John Clarke suggests that in contemporary Britain:

> ordinary people are valorised *because they are not political*. They are seen as occupying positions that are above or below politics: below, because they are seen to be concerned with more 'everyday' issues; above, because they are not engaged in the venal, corrupt or collusive pursuit of power and self interest in the manner of politicians.[76]

[71] Selina Todd, 'Class, Experience and Britain's Twentieth Century', *Social History*, 39 (2014), 489–508 (quotation at 501).

[72] Working on a slightly later period, Sam Wetherall has shown how the terms 'ordinary' and 'working class' were used interchangeably by community artists of the 1970s who framed a dichotomy between 'posh' and 'ordinary' art and who searched for 'a set of ordinary class-based experiences around which art could be made', Sam Wetherell, 'Painting the Crisis: Community Arts and the Search for the "Ordinary" in 1970s and '80s London', *History Workshop Journal*, 76 (2013), 235–49 (quotation at 242).

[73] Mike Savage, 'Working-class Identities in the 1960s: Revisiting the Affluent Worker Study', *Sociology*, 39 (2005), 929–46, at 938.

[74] Jon Lawrence, 'Social-Science Encounters and the Negotiation of Difference in Early 1960s England', *History Workshop Journal*, 77 (2013), 215–39 (quotation at 234).

[75] Catherine Neveu, 'Of Ordinariness and Citizenship Processes', *Citizenship Studies*, 19 (2015), 141–54 (quotation at 141).

[76] John Clarke, 'Enrolling Ordinary People: Governmental Strategies and the Avoidance of Politics', *Citizenship Studies*, 16 (2010), 637–50 (quotation at 642).

Dominic Sandbrook draws on these contemporary uses in his histories of post-war Britain, regularly employing the 'ordinary person' as a counter-weight to notions of a politicised population. For Sandbrook, ordinary people in the past are nearly always conservative and almost always uninterested in effecting change. In concluding a chapter on Cold War politics, for example, he claims that 'For all the fuss about the special relationship, or banning the bomb, or Skybolt, or nuclear testing, or the madness of modern science, it ultimately tuned out that to most ordinary people there were a lot of better things to worry about.'[77] In this usage, ordinary people do work for historical interpretation simply by dint of being 'ordinary'.

And yet as Neveu also argues, ordinariness has a 'politicising poten-tial': '"working through the ordinary" can allow us to grasp less conven-tional reworkings of citizenship'.[78] Matthew Hilton has recently argued for the making-ordinary of British politics in his study of post-war Non-Governmental Organisations.[79] For Hilton, NGOs transformed the meaning of politics by targeting specific 'ordinary' – or more accur-ately everyday – issues. In this reading, 'ordinary politics' is single-issue politics mobilised by professional, technical experts engaging a predom-inantly middle-class citizenry of concerned individuals.[80] But if politics was ordinary in post-war Britain, then ordinariness was also political. As we have already seen, the subject position 'ordinary person' had sign-ificant political purchase coming out of the Second World War. In post-war Britain, intervening as an ordinary person legitimated both opinion and knowledge claims. As a social category, the ordinary performed sign-ificant political work in terms of defining, cohering and excluding; it re-calibrated the extraordinary as it went. If ordinariness was defined in opposition to learned expertise, political power and possession of a public voice, then these categories were themselves shaped by the devel-oping character of ordinariness.

Ordinariness was a powerful position from which to resist and to chal-lenge authority, to assert rights and to make demands. Crucially, it pro-vided an individual – yet implicitly collective – counterpoint to various manifestations of 'the expert'. A growth in the authority of the expert has long been seen as a characteristic of twentieth-century Britain. For Guy Ortolano, amongst others, the period 1945 – c. 1975 was a 'merito-cratic moment'; a period in which the ideal citizen was the expert

---

[77] Dominic Sandbrook, *Never Had It So Good. A History of Britain from Suez to the Beatles* (2005), 259.
[78] Neveu, 'Of Ordinariness and Citizenship Processes', 141.
[79] Matthew Hilton, 'Politics Is Ordinary: Non-governmental Organizations and Political Participation in Contemporary Britain', *Twentieth Century British History*, 22 (2011), 230–68.
[80] *Ibid.*, 235.

citizen.[81] And yet, trust in expertise was not unconditional, particularly where it was brought to bear on the everyday and came into conflict with the authority of experience. Whether in relation to childcare practices, home design or emotional intimacy, the opinion of the expert – or 'official' – was consistently challenged and sometimes actively rejected.[82] The relationship between the ordinary person and 'authority' was explicitly exploited by the Conservative party's 'Trust the People' exhibition of 1947. As Mass-Observation reported,

> The most popular exhibit is on the first floor – a desk with about a dozen telephones. Over the desk is this poster, 'Listen to the voice of Authority'. You pick up the receiver and listen-in to a conversation between Bureaucracy and the ordinary man-in-the street showing how he is hedged and hampered on all sides by officialdom and Red Tape.[83]

The public assertion of ordinariness had a power beyond resistance to state interference. The ordinary person was both non-expert and most expert: ordinariness and expertise were not necessarily oppositional. Lived experience and feeling were set against acquired knowledge and training in all manner of areas including domestic and local issues, national politics and international relations. For example, when interviewed about the *Daily Herald Post-War Homes Exhibition* in July 1945, female visitors critiqued what they saw on the basis of their experience, and feelings, as 'ordinary' women:

> I thought I'd see a whole house – but I just didn't. I didn't bother with the little models. They're not a scrap of use to the ordinary person. What do I know about scale and measurement? I like to see the house and walk round it, and then I'll tell you if I like it or don't.[84]

A frustrated traveller on the overcrowded Dundee to St Andrews train service sought to deploy his own lived expertise to solve an apparently intractable problem: 'To the ordinary person the solution seems to be to put the 4.55 train back until after five o'clock, and leave the 5.44 train for long distance passengers.'[85] Those who confided in Mass-Observation deployed their ordinariness as a defence against renewed war – 'We ordinary people must hang together more and see that what we want we get' – and as a subject position from which to critique the direction of science: 'I am only an ordinary man, but if I can see such

[81] Guy Ortolano, *The Two Cultures Controversy. Science, Literature and Cultural Politics in Postwar Britain* (Cambridge, 2009), 17–18.

[82] Claire Langhamer, 'Everyday Advice on Everyday Love: Romantic Expertise in Mid-Twentieth Century Britain', *L'Homme. European Journal of Feminist History*, 24 (2013), 35–52.

[83] *Speak for Yourself: A Mass-Observation Anthology 1937–1949*, ed. Dorothy Sheridan and Angus Calder (Oxford, 1985), 236.

[84] MOA, File Report 2270B, 'First Report on the Post-War Homes Exhibition', July 1945, 7.

[85] *Dundee Courier and Advertiser*, 9 Nov. 1945, 2.

a misdirection of scientific research, surely those who have been trained and educated to view these problems with a keener intellect than I can see it?'[86]

Increasingly being an ordinary person was deemed to be a form of expertise in its own right. The importance of finding a place for the ordinary person on government committees and investigations was not infrequently asserted in House of Commons Debates. 'Will there be any ordinary people on the committee?' asked Godfrey Nicholson in a Commons discussion of a transport users' committee for London.[87] The *Daily Mirror*, perhaps unsurprisingly, went further. In a damning critique of the *Report of the Royal Commission on Marriage and Divorce* published in 1956, it asserted that 'The only worthwhile results would come not from a Royal Commission – but from an ordinary Commission of ordinary folk reporting on married life as they see it, and live it. For the human race goes on being human – with its own common sense outlook – though Royal Commissions come and go.'[88]

The figure of the ordinary person was used across the political spectrum both to bestow everyday authority upon political interventions and to claim that specific concerns were matters of general interest. And yet the ordinary person was not always deemed capable of speaking for himself or herself. The period was replete in ventriloquists who projected their own voice through that of the ordinary person in order to speak on their behalf. So, for example, when pipe-smoking local councillor W. D. Reid proposed an end to the smoking ban in Aberdeen Art Gallery, he spoke on behalf of the ordinary person: 'I have always felt that the Art Gallery, in its general outlook, is repellent to the ordinary person', he told the local newspaper, suggesting that 'If smoking were permitted it would make the place more attractive and more useful to the community.'[89] In the midst of the post-war death penalty debate, Cicely M. Craven of the Howard League for Penal Reform wrote to *The Times* that 'The ordinary citizen hates the whole business of the death sentence, the condemned cell, the hanging and the morbid sympathy with the murderer that it arouses.'[90]

As might be expected, the popular press saw itself as particularly well placed to act as a conduit for ordinary opinion, or at least to claim that it was doing so. When Nikita Krushchev pulled out of a Summit meeting in August 1958, the *Daily Mirror* suggested that 'The ordinary people of the

---

[86] MOA, File Report 2370, 'World Organisation and the Future', Mar. 1946, 27; MOA, File Report 2474B, 'Scientists – Magicians or Monsters?', Apr. 1947, 8.

[87] House of Commons Debates, 21 Feb. 1949, vol. 462, cc. 1590.

[88] *Daily Mirror*, 22 Mar. 1956, 2.

[89] *Aberdeen Journal*, 13 Apr. 1946, 4.

[90] *Times*, 22 Nov. 1947, 5.

world are bitterly disappointed.'[91] But the *Mirror* was not alone in inter-nationalising ordinariness. An American representative on the Council of the United Nations World Federation told a church audience in Sunderland that 'Peace for the future lies in the hands of millions of ordinary people all over the world lending their full support to the United Nations Association and so influencing their national policies and directing their statesmen.'[92] According to Anthony Eden speaking in 1948, 'In every land the ordinary people yearn for a period of tranquillity', offering the possibility of an international community of peace-loving ordinary people, a model that perhaps chimed with early interpretations of the atrocities committed during the Second World War which foregrounded the culpability of leaders over the led.[93] In a small but telling way, telephone operator Sheila Brown – winner of a 1954 *Picture Post* competition – asserted that her life's ambition was 'to own a horse-drawn caravan and to amble along indefinitely throughout Europe meeting ordinary people'.[94] The internationalism of ordinariness was, ultimately, a form of 'imagined community'; the claim to ordinariness was an assertion of a collectivity that transcended national boundaries.[95] As Ben Highmore has put it, 'the ordinary brings with it one of the most optimistic but also most daunting phrases from science fiction and horror: you are not alone'.[96]

V Conclusion

The queen's 1954 Christmas Day speech was dedicated to 'the great bulk of ordinary citizens' and 'the average men and women'. She sent

> a special message of encouragement and good cheer to those of you whose lot is cast in dull and unenvied surroundings, to those whose names will never be household words, but to whose work and loyalty we owe so much. May you be proud to remember – as I am myself – how much depends on you and that even when your life seems most mon-otonous what you do is always of real value and importance to your fellow men.

[91] *Daily Mirror*, 7 Aug. 1958, 1.

[92] *Sunderland Daily Echo and Shipping Gazette*, 30 Sept. 1946, 3.

[93] *Gloucestershire Echo*, 14 Aug. 1948, 1. Within the historiography of Germany, attempts to explain the events of the 1930s and 1940s have increasingly focused upon psychological and/or ideological explanations for the violence and murders perpetrated by 'ordinary men' or 'ordinary Germans'. For an overview, see Richard Overy, '"Ordinary Men", Extraordinary Circumstances: Historian, Social Psychology and the Holocaust', *Journal of Social Issues*, 70 (2014), 515–30. Key texts include Christopher R. Browning, *Ordinary Men: Reserve Police Battalion 11 and the Final Solution in Poland* (New York, 1992); Daniel Jonah Goldhagen, *Hitler's Willing Executioners. Ordinary Germans and the Holocaust* (New York, 1996). See also Nicholas Stargardt, *The German War: A Nation under Arms, 1939–45* (2015).

[94] *Picture Post*, 1 May 1954, 47.

[95] Benedict Anderson, *Imagined Communities: Reflections on the Origin and Spread of Nationalism* (1983).

[96] Ben Highmore, *Ordinary Lives. Studies in the Everyday* (2011), 5.

In reporting the queen's words the *Daily Mail* added portentously, 'And of course we are a nation of ordinary people.'[97]

Nonetheless, the post-war valorisation of ordinariness had its critics as well as its supporters. When Noel Coward poked fun at the ordinary in a lyrical assault on the Festival of Britain – 'We're proud to say/ In every way/ We're ordinary folk' – he was not a lone voice.[98] Ann Temple, the *Daily Mail*'s agony aunt, railed against 'domestic ordinariness' – as did, for different reasons, those characterised as 'angry young men'. Bernard Buckham in the *Daily Mirror* asserted that 'This idea which is always cropping up in different directions that you want a lot of ordinary or average people on the air is, to my mind, a complete fallacy.'[99]

Certainly by the 1960s, the ordinary could be as much something to escape – imaginatively or literally – as something to embrace. Valerie Walkerdine puts it well in her retrospective account of growing up working class in post-war Derby: 'everything about it, its sense of safety, had felt for so long like a trap, the site and origin of an ordinariness both hated and desired. It was the place in which, if I were not careful and being so vigilant, I might turn into my mother.'[100] Shifting trends in advertising also map the transition. Beefeater gin was not an ordinary gin; rather it was 'A gin to be proud of.'[101] In the *Daily Mirror*, the Cassandra column warned of the political perils of ordinariness. Prime Minister Harold Wilson 'was in danger of being the victim of the cult of domestic ordinariness'.[102] Mrs Wilson was a particular target: 'Every time she speaks the bells of ordinariness begin to chime.' Some readers agreed. 'I deplore the modern practice of trying to make ordinariness a virtue' wrote R. Smith from London.[103]

Nonetheless, ordinariness retained sufficient political purchase at the end of the sixties to be deployed by Enoch Powell in his 1968 'Rivers of Blood' speech.[104] Setting a rhetorical precedent recently echoed by Nigel Farage, Powell placed the views of a 'decent, ordinary fellow Englishman' at the centre of his particular brand of racism. As Amy Whipple has demonstrated, ordinariness was a subject position

[97] *Daily Mail*, 28 Dec. 1954, 1.

[98] Quoted in Alan Sinfield, 'The Government, the People and the Festival', in *Labour's Promised Land? Culture and Society in Labour Britain 1945–51*, ed. Jim Fyrth (1995), 181.

[99] *Daily Mail*, 8 Feb. 1954, 6; *Daily Mirror*, 13 June 1945, 7.

[100] Valerie Walkerdine, 'Dreams from an Ordinary Childhood', in *Truth, Dare or Promise. Girls Growing up in the Fifties*, ed. Liz Heron (1995), 63–77 (quotation at 63).

[101] *Daily Mirror*, 11 Nov. 1968, 22.

[102] *Daily Mirror*, 20 Nov. 1964, 10.

[103] *Daily Mirror*, 26 Nov. 1964, 6.

[104] On Powell, see Camilla Schofield, *Enoch Powell and the Making of Postcolonial Britain* (Cambridge, 2013).

adopted by many of Powell's supporters.[105] But it was also harnessed in the fight of Black Britons against racial discrimination: 'We have the right to be ordinary citizens of Britain' asserted Marion Glean in 1964.[106]

In this paper, I have argued that post-war ordinariness was a powerful, yet mutable, category that was widely harnessed as a distinctive social and political standpoint. If ordinariness has more recently been defined by what it apparently is not – political, expert, influential – then in the years immediately following the Second World War it was defined by what it apparently was. Although as a category it was malleable and messy, ordinariness was nonetheless held to denote specific values, emotional styles and social behaviours. It also had clear political uses. It operated as a particularly powerful position from which to mount an individual, and collective, critique of 'the expert'. But it was also, itself, a form of expertise.

It is, perhaps, the loose malleability of the category which explains its appeal to historians today. Over recent years, there has been a noticeable turn to the ordinary in history as well as to other disciplines.[107] Sometimes, the ordinary is conceptualised as distinct from the everyday; at other times, the two are conflated, although as literary scholar Lorraine Sims advises 'Something can be ordinary without being everyday.'[108] An appetite has emerged for 'ordinary sources' – in part defined as those that facilitate access to ordinary lives, in part defined by their very nature as ordinary.[109] And 'ordinary people' – sometimes encased by inverted commas although increasingly not – populate our histories across time and place. Yet as historians, we might do well to remember that, to quote Neveu, '"ordinariness" cannot be defined per se, or *in abstracto*…no situation, site, practice or individual is "ordinary" in itself'.[110]

I want to end by suggesting that our use of the category today might be strengthened if we have a clearer sense of its use as a social descriptor in the past. Who do we mean when we refer to ordinary people and who did the people we study mean? Given its definitional contingency, can ordinariness ever be a stable subject position? In this paper, I have

[105] Amy Whipple, 'Revisiting the "Rivers of Blood" Controversy: Letters to Enoch Powell', *Journal of British Studies*, 48 (2009), 717–35.

[106] Quoted in Kennetta Hammond Perry, *London is the Place for Me. Black Britons, Citizenship, and the Politics of Race* (Oxford, 2015), 190.

[107] Two of the most interesting interventions from anthropology and cultural studies respectively are Kathleen Stewart, *Ordinary Affects* (Durham and London, 2007) and Highmore, *Ordinary Lives*.

[108] Sim, *Virginia Woolf*, 2.

[109] Jennifer Sinor, *The Extraordinary Work of Ordinary Writing: Annie Ray's Diary* (Iowa City, 2002), 5–6.

[110] Neveu, 'Of Ordinariness and Citizenship Processes', 148.

argued that what appears to be a straightforward social history category is actually a slippery, deeply politicised, often fought-over and dynamic identity; one which people moved in and out of according to context. And, most importantly, that it was, and remains, a category with real political purchase. Perhaps, then, a little more definitional precision, allied to an enhanced understanding of the historically situated meanings of ordinariness, is needed if the description 'ordinary people' is to retain its analytical power.[111]

[111] And here I am critiquing my own use of the category, as much as anyone else's.

Transactions of the RHS 28 (2018), pp. 197–217 © Royal Historical Society 2018
doi:10.1017/S0080440118000105

ANTI-SOCIALISM, LIBERALISM AND INDIVIDUALISM: RETHINKING THE REALIGNMENT OF SCOTTISH POLITICS, 1945–1970*

By Malcolm Petrie

David Berry Prize Winner

ABSTRACT. This paper presents an alternative interpretation of Scottish politics between 1945 and 1970, a period that witnessed the decline of a once-powerful Unionist tradition, the revival of Liberalism and the rise of the Scottish National party (SNP). While existing accounts have focused principally upon social and economic factors, this study foregrounds the role of ideology and rhetoric. During the 1940s and early 1950s, Scottish Unionists were, like their Conservative colleagues elsewhere in Britain, able to construct a popular, but essentially negative, anti-socialist coalition that prioritised the defence of individual liberty. This electoral alliance, defined by opposition to Labour's programme of nationalisation and expressed via an individualist idiom, was able to attract broad support; it was, however, always provisional, and proved increasingly difficult to sustain after the Conservative party returned to office in 1951. It was, this paper suggests, the fragmenting of this anti-socialist coalition in the late 1950s and early 1960s that created the opportunity for both the Liberals and the SNP to present alternative renderings of this individualist appeal, and to emerge as credible political alternatives. Crucially, by the 1960s, individual liberty was beginning to be understood in constitutional rather than economic terms.

The quarter century following the Second World War saw the transformation of Scottish politics. In the decade after 1945, election results in Scotland largely mirrored wider British trends, with Labour initially dominant, before the Unionists, as the Conservatives were labelled in Scotland until 1965, recovered in the early 1950s.[1] From the 1959 general election onwards, however, Labour enjoyed an electoral

*I would like to acknowledge the generous support offered by the award of an early career fellowship by the Leverhulme Trust (ECF–2015–391), which facilitated the research that informs this article.

[1] The name was a legacy of the 1912 merger with the Liberal Unionists. See C. Burness, *'Strange Associations': The Irish Question and the Making of Scottish Unionism, 1886–1918* (East Linton, 2003).

supremacy that would survive for more than five decades; in contrast, the Unionists, and their Conservative successors, entered an era of sustained decline. Scottish Conservatism's travails were accentuated by the resuscitation of Liberalism and the arrival of the Scottish National party (SNP) as a credible political force. By the 1970s, a distinctive four-party Scottish electoral contest was established.[2]

Assessments of this period of political realignment have emphasised the importance of several factors. Secularisation eroded the popular Protestantism that underpinned working-class Unionism, exposing the party to accusations that it represented only a remote and Anglicised landed elite, and encouraging younger voters to view the SNP with greater sympathy. Further, the growing reliance of Scots on the public sector for employment and housing, coupled with the relative weakness of the Scottish economy from the late 1950s, entrenched support for the Labour party in urban and industrial areas, while simultaneously lending weight to nationalist criticisms of the performance of successive Westminster regimes. The improved fortunes of the SNP have, perhaps more speculatively, been attributed too to a loss of faith in British identity triggered by economic stagnation and imperial retreat.[3] Equally, political scientists have suggested that the fall in Unionist support after 1959 represented the assertion of 'natural' political allegiances, as Scotland's social and economic structure began to be reflected at the polls.[4] It is, in such a reading, the anomaly of earlier Unionist success that needs explanation, with the distinctive Scottish aspects of the party's appeal being highlighted.[5]

---

[2] W. L. Miller, *The End of British Politics? Scots and English Political Behaviour in the Seventies* (Oxford, 1981); I. G. C. Hutchison, *Scottish Politics in the Twentieth Century* (Basingstoke, 2001), 98–139; E. A. Cameron, *Impaled upon a Thistle: Scotland since 1880* (Edinburgh, 2010), 263–319.

[3] J. G. Kellas, 'The Party in Scotland', in *Conservative Century: The Conservative Party since 1900*, ed. A. Seldon and S. Ball (Oxford, 1994), 671–93; R. J. Finlay, *A Partnership for Good? Scottish Politics and the Union since 1880* (Edinburgh, 1997); R. J. Finlay, 'Unionism and the Dependency Culture: Politics and State Intervention in Scotland, 1918–1997', in *Unionist Scotland, 1800–1997*, ed. C. M. M. MacDonald (Edinburgh, 1998), 100–16; R. J. Finlay, 'Patriotism, Paternalism and Pragmatism: Scottish Toryism, Union and Empire, 1912–65', in *Whatever Happened to Tory Scotland?*, ed. D. Torrance (Edinburgh, 2012), 29–42. For contrasting interpretations of the impact of empire, see T. M. Devine, 'The Break-up of Britain? Scotland and the End of Empire', *Transactions of the Royal Historical Society*, 16 (2006), 163–80; J. O. Nielsen and S. Ward, '"Cramped and Restricted at Home"? Scottish Separatism at Empire's End', *Transactions of the Royal Historical Society*, 25 (2015), 159–85.

[4] S. Kendrick and D. McCrone, 'Politics in a Cold Climate: The Conservative Decline in Scotland', *Political Studies*, 37 (1989), 589–603.

[5] J. Mitchell, *The Conservatives and the Union* (Edinburgh, 1990); D. Seawright and J. Curtice, 'The Decline of the Scottish Conservative and Unionist Party, 1950–1992: Religion, Ideology or Economics?', *Contemporary Record*, 9 (1995), 319–42; D. Seawright, 'Scottish Unionist Party: What's in a Name?', *Scottish Affairs*, 14 (1996), 90–102;

Such developments were undoubtedly significant. The intention in this study is, nonetheless, to offer a different perspective, one that both complements and complicates existing accounts by foregrounding the role of ideology in post-war Scottish politics, as disclosed chiefly through political rhetoric. Since the 1920s, Unionists had exploited concerns over the alleged threat posed by socialism to attract the support of erstwhile Liberals, often building upon the purportedly non-partisan anti-Labour pacts established at a municipal level.[6] During the 1940s, this anti-socialist appeal was amplified by wartime experiences and the election of the first majority Labour government, imbuing Unionism with an individualist idiom centred upon the defence of individual liberty, and opposed to the expansion of the authority of central government. The principal divide within Scottish political debate after 1945 was provided not by class, or by attitudes towards the constitution, but by this contest between individualism and socialism. Efforts to understand post-war Scottish politics require an examination of why the electoral alliance assembled beneath the Unionist banner, and held together by an appeal to individual freedom, began to disintegrate. We should, then, reconsider the language used by Unionist politicians and their allies, as well as the worldview they promoted. In doing so, we may relate an assessment of Scottish politics to wider British debates, and especially those that concern the fluctuating fortunes of what W. H. Greenleaf described as the 'libertarian strand' within British political thought.[7] Libertarian in this context should, of course, not be interpreted in a literal or absolute manner, but rather as denoting an inclination to view the growing power of the central state with foreboding, alongside a scepticism regarding the viability of economic planning.[8]

The primary concern here is, then, with the attempts of politicians to secure public support, to convince voters to view matters in a certain way; the focus is, by necessity, on what politicians said. As scholars of political rhetoric have recognised, ideologies are more than sets of substantive policy positions: they are, as Alan Finlayson and James Martin have stressed, also a matter of 'a "mood", an emotional register and a style of

---

D. Seawright, *An Important Matter of Principle: The Decline of the Scottish Conservative and Unionist Party* (Aldershot, 1999). See also Finlay, *Partnership for Good*, 139–40; C. Harvie, *No Gods and Precious Few Heroes*, 3rd edn (Edinburgh, 1998), 108–9; M. Cragoe, '"We Like Local Patriotism": The Conservative Party and the Discourse of Decentralisation, 1947–51', *English Historical Review*, 122 (2007), 965–85.

[6] J. J. Smyth, 'Resisting Labour: Unionists, Liberals, and Moderates in Glasgow between the Wars', *Historical Journal*, 46 (2003), 375–401; Cameron, *Impaled upon a Thistle*, 163–8.

[7] W. H. Greenleaf, *The British Political Tradition*, II: *The Ideological Heritage* (1983), 263–346.

[8] See J. Ramsden, *The Age of Churchill and Eden, 1940–1957* (1995), 166–76; E. H. H. Green, *The Ideologies of Conservatism: Conservative Political Ideas in the Twentieth Century* (Oxford, 2002), 192–239.

presentation'.[9] The analysis that follows is designed to trace the temper of post-war Scottish politics, particularly among that half of the electorate unconvinced by the claims of the Labour party. First, the nature of the Unionist appeal after 1945 is outlined; second, the rise of discontent among Unionist supporters in the late 1950s is explored alongside the upturn in the fortunes of the Liberal party; third, the Unionist response to the 1959 general election is examined; lastly, the implications of the decrease in Unionist support during the 1960s are assessed.

I

The Unionists, in common with their Conservative colleagues in England, contested the 1945 general election on a platform of defending individual freedom and lifting the economic controls imposed during wartime. The campaign culminated with Winston Churchill's infamous radio broadcast, where, echoing Friedrich Hayek's *Road to Serfdom*, published the previous year, he warned that a Labour victory, and the ensuing introduction of socialism, would presage a slide into tyranny.[10] The result was, nevertheless, a Labour landslide, with the Conservatives enduring their worst defeat since 1906. Yet the party soon regrouped: at the 1950 general election, Labour's parliamentary majority was reduced to five; the following year the Conservatives returned to power, and remained in office for over a decade.

Traditionally, the Conservative revival was attributed to the party's acceptance of the new political landscape created by the war and confirmed by Labour's victory in 1945, one in which the primary role of government was to ensure full employment, manage a mixed economy and oversee the running of the nascent welfare state.[11] It was, in this model, not until the 1970s that this governing consensus collapsed,

[9] A. Finlayson and J. Martin, '"It Ain't What You Say…"': British Political Studies and the Analysis of Speech and Rhetoric', *British Politics*, 3 (2008), 451. See also R. Barker, 'Hooks and Hands, Interests and Enemies: Political Thinking as Political Action', *Political Studies*, 48 (2000), 223–38; A. Finlayson, 'Political Science, Political Ideas and Rhetoric', *Economy and Society*, 33 (2011), 528–49; R. Toye, *Rhetoric* (Oxford, 2013).

[10] R. Toye, 'Winston Churchill's "Crazy Broadcast": Party, Nation, and the 1945 Gestapo Broadcast', *Journal of British Studies*, 49 (2010), 655–80. On Hayek's influence on the Conservative campaign, which came via the party chairman, Ralph Assheton, see R. Cockett, *Thinking the Unthinkable: Think-Tanks and the Economic Counter-Revolution, 1931–1983* (1994), 91–9; Green, *Ideologies of Conservatism*, 219–20.

[11] For key interventions, see P. Addison, *The Road to 1945: British Politics and the Second World War* (1975); J. Ramsden, '"A Party for Owners or a Party for Earners?" How far did the Conservative Party Really Change after 1945?', *Transactions of the Royal Historical Society*, 37 (1987), 49–63; R. Lowe, 'The Second World War, Consensus and the Foundation of the Welfare State', *Twentieth Century British History*, 1 (1990), 152–82; D. Kavanagh, 'The Post-War Consensus', *Twentieth Century British History*, 3 (1992), 175–90.

amid economic crisis and the Conservative party's turn to the right under
the leadership of Margaret Thatcher.[12] Since the 1990s, however, this
interpretation has been questioned, and the extent to which
Conservative opinion remained unreconciled to the post-war settlement
emphasised. Ina Zweiniger-Bargielowska highlighted the crucial role
that opposition to rationing, particularly among female voters, played
in the Conservative victory in 1951; likewise, Harriet Jones argued that
post-war Conservatism was hostile towards redistributive taxation and
universal welfare provision.[13] For Ewen Green, notions of a post-war
consensus were weakened by the continued influence within
Conservative ranks of 'liberal-market' opposition to state intervention.[14]
As Green noted drily, the party's slogan in this era was "'Set the People
Free", not the welfare state and the mixed economy are safe in our
hands.'[15]

Still, these debates have had relatively little impact on studies of
Scottish politics, where the conviction that Unionist success hinged
upon a combination of an appeal to Scottish identity and an embrace
of corporatism remains dominant.[16] Yet this assessment is at odds with
the rhetoric often deployed by the party, infused as it could be with
Hayekian warnings that the increasing powers accrued by the central
state, while perhaps necessary during wartime, had become a threat to
personal freedom, and claims that Labour's programme of nationalisation would, if allowed to continue, lead inexorably to totalitarianism.
As the party's Western Divisional Council declared in 1948, the
Labour government had overseen the erection of 'a crazy economy' characterised by 'crushing taxation, restrictive controls, subsidies and a depre-
ciated currency': the public must choose 'between the Unionist policy of a
free economy and the democratic way of life on the one hand, and
Socialist State monopoly and eventual servitude on the other'.[17]

[12] B. Harrison, 'The Rise, Fall and Rise of Political Consensus in Britain since 1940',
History, 84 (1999), 301–24.
[13] I. Zweiniger-Bargielowska, 'Rationing, Austerity and the Conservative Party Recovery
after 1945', *Historical Journal*, 37 (1994), 173–97; H. Jones, 'A Bloodless Counter-Revolution:
The Conservative Party and the Defence of Inequality, 1945–51', in *The Myth of Consensus*,
ed. H. Jones and M. Kandiah (Basingstoke, 1996), 1–16.
[14] E. H. H. Green, 'The Conservative Party, the State and the Electorate, 1945–64', in
Party, State and Society: Electoral Behaviour in Britain since 1820, ed. J. Lawrence and
M. Taylor (Aldershot, 1997), 176–200.
[15] Green, *Ideologies of Conservatism*, 220. For a considered critique of this revisionist stance,
see R. McKibbin, *Parties and People: England, 1914–1951* (Oxford, 2010), 164–76.
[16] Harvie, *No Gods*, 104, 108–9; Hutchison, *Scottish Politics*, 74; Finlay, 'Unionism and the
Dependency Culture', 107–8. Although see the suggestive comments in: Cameron, *Impaled
upon a Thistle*, 271–7.
[17] National Library of Scotland (NLS) Acc. 10424/27: Scottish Unionist Association (SUA)
Western Divisional Council (WDC), *Annual Report 1948*, 2–3. Capitalisation in original.

Individual Unionist politicians could speak in similarly apocalyptic terms. At a constituency association meeting in late 1946, William McNair Snadden, MP for Kinross and West Perthshire, advised that the 'Socialist [i.e. Labour] policy of concentrating power into the hands of a few political bosses would result in the...final destruction of the freedom of the individual': he urged all 'anti-socialists' to unite, since, if they remained divided, 'they made certain of bringing about the very thing they had fought for six years to destroy – the Totalitarian State'. A year later, following the introduction of direction of labour, Snadden warned that the 'fundamental right of the citizen to choose his own work was being taken away [and] if they did not bring down the Government then the Government would bring down the nation'.[18] Such doom-laden predictions were, no matter how hyperbolic, a common refrain, as Unionists depicted every political issue as evidence of the need to remove the Labour government from office. At a mass rally at Callender House in Falkirk, James Reid, the Unionist MP for Glasgow Hillhead who had served as lord advocate in the wartime coalition, stated that the next general election 'would be vital for the future of this country', since if Labour were re-elected, 'they would drift to the left and freedom and prosperity would be so far gone that perhaps we should never recover'.[19] A few months later, Reid's Unionist counterpart in Glasgow Central, James Hutchison, declared that nationalisation had created 'a race of sycophants – people who were always wondering if the man above was satisfied'. The public, he lamented, 'simply did not realise just how dangerous a situation was being created for them'.[20] Alan Gomme Duncan, the Unionist member for Perth, was even blunter: if Labour secured another term, he warned, it would mark the 'last general election in this country'.[21]

Of course, none of these hysterical predictions were borne out by events; nor is it clear that the politicians who made them believed what they said. These limitations are, nevertheless, comparatively unimportant: such statements were, to use Maurice Cowling's formulation, 'a form of exemplary utterance', an 'attempt to provide new landmarks for the electorate'.[22] What matters is that it was through an explicit rejection of consensus, and the promotion of a binary political contest structured

---

[18] Perth and Kinross Council Archives MS 152/2/1/3: Kinross and West Perthshire Unionist Association minutes, 30 Nov. 1946 and 29 Nov. 1947. Capitalisation in original. Direction of labour was intended to ensure that those out of work were guided towards vacancies in productive, export-led industries.

[19] *Grangemouth Advertiser*, 24 July 1948.

[20] *Falkirk Herald*, 27 Nov. 1948.

[21] *Grangemouth Advertiser*, 18 Dec. 1948.

[22] M. Cowling, *The Impact of Labour, 1920–1924* (Cambridge, 1971), 5.

around opposition to socialism, that Unionist politicians believed they could win public backing. Clearly, this approach was not total, or necessarily coherent: the party did not reject government action in every field; notably, Unionists, like their Conservative counterparts in England and Wales, considered local government to be an important source of civic identity and an essential counterweight to the expansion of the central state.[23] The dangers of socialism stemmed from centralisation, as embodied by the 'vast State monopolies' created to administer the nationalised industries.[24]

This conception of post-war politics informed the Unionist appeal to Scottish national identity, usually treated as a cynical, if nonetheless successful, effort to provoke opposition to nationalisation from the safety of opposition.[25] There was, no doubt, a degree of electoral calculation present: it was not mere chance that the Unionist promotion of Scottish autonomy coincided with the launch of the Scottish Covenant, a mass petition in support of home rule organised by John MacCormick, the former national secretary of the SNP.[26] And, as Matthew Cragoe has shown, sympathy towards Scottish and Welsh sensibilities was integral to Conservatism's broader 'discourse of decentralisation'.[27] But it would be wrong to dismiss this simply as tactics: as with the defence of local government, the promotion of Scottish distinctiveness was effective because it could be accommodated within, and even strengthen, a preexisting critique of centralised bureaucracy. It was not just that the growing dominance of Whitehall and Westminster threatened Scottish autonomy: socialism was a form of 'despotism', a political philosophy hostile to 'individuality either in men or in nations'.[28] Equally, Churchill's deployment of quasi-nationalist language when appearing in Scotland during the 1950 and 1951 general election campaigns was tempered by his assertion that it was the prospect of the 'serfdom of socialism' that threatened the union between Scotland and England.[29] Even in the case of John MacCormick's candidacy at the 1948 Paisley by-election, when MacCormick felt he had united

[23] See SUA, *Scottish Control of Scottish Affairs* (Edinburgh, 1949).

[24] National Union of Conservative Associations, *The Right Road for Britain* (1949), 7.

[25] Harvie, *No Gods*, 108; Finlay, *Partnership for Good*, 139–40; Mitchell, *Conservatives and the Union*, 48–50; Mitchell, *The Scottish Question* (Oxford, 2014), 55–7 and 79–85.

[26] On the Covenant, see J. Mitchell, *Strategies for Self-Government: The Campaigns for a Scottish Parliament* (Edinburgh, 1996), 144–53; I. Levitt, 'Britain, the Scottish Covenant Movement and Devolution, 1946–50', *Scottish Affairs*, 22 (1998), 33–57. On MacCormick, see M. R. Petrie, 'John MacCormick', in *SNP Leaders*, ed. J. Mitchell and G. Hassan (2016), 43–63.

[27] Cragoe, '"We Like Local Patriotism"'.

[28] SUA, *Scottish Control of Scottish Affairs* (Edinburgh, 1949), 1–2.

[29] C. Harvie, *Scotland and Nationalism: Scottish Society and Politics, 1707–1994*, 2nd edn (1994), 119.

Labour's opponents on a home rule platform, local Unionists backed him only on the basis that he was the 'anti-socialist candidate'.[30]

For all that Unionism was defined by hostility to socialism, it was not narrowly partisan in outlook. If anything, the urgency of the threat alleged to be posed by Labour required the construction of a broad-based anti-socialist coalition. This strategy was evident in the 1947 pact concluded with the National Liberals, which saw the parties merge their constituency apparatus in some sixty seats.[31] As the parties declared in a joint statement, there was 'one fundamental political issue', namely 'whether the principles of liberty of the individual' and 'freedom of enterprise' would survive, 'or whether the Socialist doctrine of regimentation, state-ownership and centralised control is to prevail'.[32] National Liberalism, which originated with those Liberals who remained loyal to the National Government after the abandonment of free trade in 1932, has been largely forgotten, with the 1947 agreement viewed as marking the effective end of the party's independent existence.[33] This may have been true in England, where the relative strength of Conservatism was far greater. In Scotland, though, National Liberalism enjoyed a long afterlife, exerting influence throughout the 1950s. Of the sixty joint constituency associations established by 1950, fifteen were in Scotland; in the decade that followed, the National Liberals routinely secured the support of just under one in ten Scottish voters, while the number of candidates adopting some form of the label increased.[34] National Liberalism's appeal was especially potent in the north-east, south-west and Highlands, areas of historic Conservative weakness: here, Unionism bent towards an entrenched Liberalism. Conspicuous too was the prominence of National Liberals sitting for Scottish seats both in the leadership of their party at Westminster, and, after 1951, in ministerial roles at the Scottish Office. Between 1947 and 1964, the position of National Liberal chairman was held exclusively by Scottish MPs, while John Maclay, National Liberal MP for West Renfrewshire, served as secretary of state for Scotland between 1957 and 1962; Niall MacPherson and James Henderson-Stewart, who sat as National Liberals for Galloway and East Fife

[30] NLS Acc. 10424/34: SUA WDC minutes, 4 Feb. 1948. On the Paisley by-election, see M. Dyer, '"A Nationalist in the Churchillian Sense": John MacCormick, the Paisley By-election of 18 February 1948, Home Rule and the Crisis in Scottish Liberalism', *Parliamentary History*, 22 (2003), 285–307.

[31] Ramsden, *Age of Churchill and Eden*, 197–205.

[32] NLS Acc. 11368/4: SUA Central Council (CC) minutes, 2 Sept. 1947.

[33] The only full study is D. Dutton, *Liberals in Schism: A History of the National Liberal Party* (2008).

[34] Hutchison, *Scottish Politics*, 76–9.

respectively, were both junior Scottish Office ministers in this period.[35] The National Liberals were not, as has been suggested, simply 'absorbed' by the Unionists.[36]

More even than support at the polls or personnel in cabinet, National Liberalism offered Unionism's instinctive anti-socialism, inherited from the 1920s and defined by allegations that socialism was a close relative of Bolshevism, and posed a similar threat to organised religion and family life, a more coherent intellectual framework.[37] If, in England, former Liberals were enlisted as 'subaltern anti-socialists', across rural and provincial Scotland the Unionists, through their association with National Liberalism, operated as ersatz Liberals.[38] Post-war Unionism is, then, understood best as composite in nature, as a coalition of Conservatives, Liberals and even nationalists united by a shared opposition to socialism. Such a view was given voice by Henderson-Stewart when he addressed a meeting of Unionist and National Liberal activists in South Angus in November 1949. Warning that if Labour were returned to power for a second term then liberal values would disappear 'for a generation', Henderson-Stewart urged Liberals and nationalists to support what he termed the 'coalition led by Mr Churchill', since if there were 'a straight fight in every constituency', Labour 'would be thrashed'.[39] A year later, Maclay called similarly for a 'united front' to defeat socialism, and asked Liberals to overlook their historic opposition to Toryism and prioritise instead their shared commitment to individual freedom.[40]

The arrangement with the National Liberals was intended to act as a prelude to a wider pact with the Liberal party. Although a formal alliance would prove elusive, winning over those who traditionally voted Liberal was central to Conservative electoral strategy.[41] As the party's 1950 campaign guide argued, there was 'little fundamental difference between the Conservatives and Liberals such as exists between these parties and the bureaucratic and, at times, totalitarian control of the

[35] From 1947 until 1956, the role of National Liberal chairman was performed by John Maclay; Maclay was succeeded by James Duncan, MP for South Angus, James Henderson-Stewart, MP for East Fife, and Colin Thornton-Kemsley, who represented North Angus and Mearns.

[36] C. M. M. MacDonald, *Whaur Extremes Meet: Scotland's Twentieth Century* (Edinburgh, 2009), 205.

[37] On interwar Unionism, see I. G. C. Hutchison, 'Scottish Unionism between the Two World Wars', in *Unionist Scotland*, ed. MacDonald, 82–4.

[38] Green, 'The Conservative Party, the State and the Electorate', 192.

[39] University of Dundee Archives (UDA) MS 309/2/2/3/1: South Angus Unionist and National Liberal Association, Forfar Branch, minutes, 11 Nov. 1949.

[40] J. Maclay, *Liberalism and the Present Situation* (1950).

[41] McKibbin, *Parties and People*, 167–9.

present Socialist Party'.[42] Indeed, the dramatic fall in the number of Liberal candidates at the 1951 general election was a critical factor in the Conservative victory. But Liberal retrenchment was partly a recognition of electoral reality, as opposition to Labour overrode older party loyalties, and limited the demand for more than one anti-socialist candidate in each constituency. Winston Churchill, upon his return to office in 1951, even offered the Liberal leader Clement Davies the role of minister of education in his new cabinet.[43]

Claims that there was a return to partisan politics after 1945, or that elections in the 1950s were monochrome, two-party affairs, should thus be treated with caution.[44] Such a conclusion does a disservice to the patchwork, provisional nature of Unionism; it also overlooks the motivations of activists and voters. The 'culture of coalitionism' identified by Michael Dyer as prevailing on the centre and right of Scottish politics during the 1930s, but which he suggests was fading by the late 1940s, was in truth revitalised by antagonism towards the post-war Labour government and by the context of the cold war, which encouraged anti-communist sentiment, and granted warnings of a drift towards totalitarianism a certain plausibility, however ridiculous they appear in retrospect. To select one voice as an example: in late 1949, George Ramsay, a member of the executive committee of the Central Ayrshire Unionist association, wrote to Lord Woolton, the Conservative party chairman, to encourage the pursuit of unity with the Liberals. Despite his participation in Unionist politics, Ramsay described himself openly as a lifelong Liberal; crucially, though, while known locally as a Liberal, he was, he claimed, 'better known…as an anti-socialist', active in Unionist politics as it was the only party in the area that was 'fighting Socialism'.[45]

In constituencies with more robust Liberal traditions than Central Ayrshire, informal local agreements, designed to maximise the anti-Labour vote, were reached. The clearest example was Dundee, where cooperation between Liberals and Unionists had existed since the 1920s, a result of the city being one of the few double-member constituencies to survive into the twentieth century. When this changed ahead of the 1950 general election, and Dundee was split into eastern and western divisions, the old agreement, whereby the parties each nominated one candidate, was rendered obsolete; matters were complicated further by

[42] Conservative Party, *General Election 1950: The Campaign Guide* (1950), 580.

[43] An offer Davies declined: P. Sloman, *The Liberal Party and the Economy, 1929–1964* (Oxford, 2015), 185.

[44] M. Dyer, 'The Evolution of the Centre-Right and the State of Scottish Conservatism', *Political Studies*, 49 (2001), 30–50; M. Dyer, 'A Nationalist in the Churchillian Sense'.

[45] Bodleian Library (BL) Conservative Party Archive (CPA) Conservative Central Office (CCO) 4/3/43: George Ramsay to Lord Woolton, 27 Nov. 1949. Capitalisation in original.

the Unionist pact with the National Liberals. Throughout 1948 and 1949, the Dundee Unionist association, now incorporating the National Liberals, encouraged local Liberals to agree to an alliance.[46] In practice, this meant supporting a National Liberal candidate in both seats. Initially, the Liberals refused, insisting that they would contest Dundee West, nominating the journalist John Junor and blaming the Unionists for creating a 'situation where two anti-Socialist candidates are going forward in the Western division'. Yet there was little local appetite for separate candidacies, and an Anti-Socialist association was formed just three weeks before polling to press for a pact. Similar demands were made by the Dundee Housewives' association, an organisation that campaigned for an end to rationing.[47] Within days, Junor agreed to stand down, on the condition that if the Unionist candidate were defeated then the Liberals would be given the opportunity to contest the seat at the next election. Important here is the fact that none of this was sanctioned by the Liberal leadership; indeed, the national party promoted a last-minute Liberal candidacy in Dundee West. But this was shunned by local members, who viewed anti-socialist unity as the primary aim. Such compromises could work in the opposite direction, as in Greenock, where in 1950 the Unionists stood aside in favour of the Liberals. Likewise, in Ross and Cromarty, the Unionist association offered support to Jack Macleod, first elected in 1945 as an independent Liberal, stating that as long as candidates opposed socialism, they had little interest in party labels.[48] At the 1951 election, Unionists had reached 'anti-socialist' understandings, whether with Liberals or National Liberals, in twenty of Scotland's seventy-one constituencies.[49]

These tactics were not always successful: in Dundee and Greenock, the anti-socialist candidates, whether Unionist, Liberal or some combination of both, failed to defeat the Labour incumbents. All the same, they illustrate the extent to which Unionist electoral success in the 1950s was conditional. It rested upon two claims: first, that Labour presented a threat to individual liberty and economic freedom; second, that the Unionists were best placed to check, and then reverse, the socialist advance. The question was always how long such a defensive electoral coalition could last, and whether it could survive the transition from opposition to government.

---

[46] UDA MS 270/1/1/2: Dundee Unionist Association minutes, 10 Feb. 1948.

[47] *Dundee Courier and Advertiser*, 31 Jan., 3 and 7 Feb. 1950. On the emergence of the housewives' groups, see J. Hinton, 'Militant Housewives: The British Housewives' League and the Attlee Government', *History Workshop*, 28 (1994), 128–56.

[48] *Aberdeen Press and Journal*, 20 Oct. 1951.

[49] See the list in BL CPA CCO 4/3/319: *A United Front against Socialism*, 16 Apr. 1951.

II

The Conservatives, having defeated Labour at the 1951 general election, were returned to office with an increased majority in 1955; in Scotland, the Unionists and National Liberals together secured a majority of both votes and seats. Soon, though, the anti-socialism that underlay Conservative success began to fray, and the party's vote slumped at a series of by-elections, climaxing with the Liberal victory at Torrington in March 1958. The humiliation of the Suez crisis, which ended the career of Churchill's successor Anthony Eden, was partly responsible; there were, however, other determinants. The stringency of the individualist appeal employed by the Conservatives in opposition was always likely to prove difficult to sustain in office. Nevertheless, the return of iron and steel to private ownership, and the abandonment of Labour's plans to nationalise road haulage, could, when set alongside reductions in income tax and the abolition of rationing in 1954, be presented as evidence that the government had delivered on its pledges 'to restore freedom, to reduce the burden of taxation and to give individual men and women a better chance to live a decent life'.[50] In Scotland, Unionists could point too to the appointment of an additional minister of state to the Scottish Office, and the convening of a Royal Commission on Scottish Affairs, as evidence of their commitment to the defence of Scottish autonomy from the incursions of London.[51] For the leadership, this represented the limits of the possible: further attempts at reform of the nationalised industries, or scaling back of the welfare state, risked controversy. But for party activists and voters, this caution was a source of frustration, as rising inflation eroded the position of those on fixed incomes and fostered antipathy towards the seemingly privileged position enjoyed by organised labour, especially in the public sector.[52]

In Scotland, complaints that the government was failing to live up to its pre-election rhetoric were heard soon after the Conservatives had regained power: in 1953, there were demands from Unionist supporters for 'more evidence of the intention to reduce the government's expenditure of the taxpayer's money'. After the 1955 general election, these grievances were voiced with increasing frequency. In October 1955, Patrick Blair, secretary of the Scottish Unionist association, reported a widespread 'feeling' amongst the party's supporters that there had not been a sufficient commitment to reducing public expenditure; there was, he reported, a feeling that the government was 'too much afraid of voters

---

[50] Conservative Party, *General Election 1955: The Campaign Guide* (1955), 1.
[51] Mitchell, *Scottish Question*, 79–85.
[52] Green, *Ideologies of Conservatism*, 220; Ramsden, *Age of Churchill and Eden*, 294–303.

who will not support it anyhow at any time', and was doing 'too little' to assist 'the really stabilising element of the population'. Unionist voters, he warned, were beginning 'to say that it does not matter which party is in office – they are equally bad'. Here was an early iteration of the criticism of consensus that would come to prevail on the political right in the 1970s. The following year, Blair related a desire among Unionist voters for reductions in both the level of taxation and government spending, amid 'complaints' of what was referred to as the 'slow torture of the middle classes', some of whom were threatening either to abstain at the next election, or, worse, to vote Liberal.[53] As the annual report of the party's Western Divisional Council noted, the challenges facing the 'Middle Classes' were being 'frequently and vigorously stressed'.[54] By July 1956, the party's president, William Sinclair, was protesting that he 'found himself continually defending the Government not against recognised opponents but against declared Unionist Electors, some of whom were threatening to withdraw their support from the Party'. This anger, Sinclair made clear, was driven by concerns over 'the cost of living, inflation and the lack of resistance to Trade Union demands for more and more wages not covered by corresponding increases in production'.[55]

The most notable short-term political consequence of these expressions of discontent was the emergence of the Middle-Class Alliance (MCA) and the People's League for the Defence of Freedom (PLDF), pressure groups that demanded reductions in government expenditure, further tax cuts and, in the case of the PLDF, the removal of the legal privileges granted to the trades unions. This so-called 'middle-class revolt' has been discussed from the standpoint of national politics, as part of the background to the electoral revival of the Liberal party.[56] The activities of the MCA and PLDF, and the January 1958 treasury resignations, when the chancellor, Peter Thorneycroft, and two junior treasury ministers, Enoch Powell and Nigel Birch, stepped down in protest at the refusal of the cabinet to endorse spending cuts intended to curb inflation, have been treated too as a precursor to the politicisation of inflation in the 1970s.[57] Yet the MCA and PLDF enjoyed a presence in Scotland that should encourage a reassessment of the basis of Scottish politics during the 1950s; the Unionist leadership certainly feared that

[53] BL CPA CCO 2/3/18: Scottish Intelligence Summaries, Feb. 1953, Oct. 1955 and May 1956.

[54] NLS Acc. 10424/27: SUA WDC, *Annual Report 1956*, 3. Capitalisation in original.

[55] NLS Acc. 11368/4: SUA CC minutes, 4 July 1956. Capitalisation in original.

[56] Ramsden, *Age of Churchill and Eden*, 294–303. On Liberal attempts to exploit middle-class discontent, see Sloman, *Liberal Party and the Economy*, 209–12.

[57] E. H. H. Green, 'The Treasury Resignations of 1958: A Reconsideration', *Twentieth Century British History*, 11 (2000), 409–30.

the energies of party members were being diverted by membership of these organisations.[58] Patrick Blair cautioned Unionists against being swayed by the aggressive stance adopted by the PLDF in particular: the demand that trades unions should again be made liable for losses incurred as a result of industrial action would, he warned, create a 'tremendous surge of ill-feeling' likely to be electorally damaging. Blair pleaded that the government was trying its utmost 'to arrest inflation and maintain the value of money'.[59]

Despite Blair's efforts, it was difficult to reconcile the pragmatism of the party leadership with the distrust of state intervention and organised labour prevalent among Unionist supporters; moreover, the affinity between Liberals and Unionists, rooted in a hostility towards socialism and concern for individual freedom, was weakening by the second half of the 1950s. The Unionist vote collapsed by upwards of twenty percentage points at a series of by-elections between 1957 and 1959, each time as a result of Liberal intervention in seats not contested by the party since 1950. At Edinburgh South in May 1957, the Liberal candidate polled nearly a quarter of the vote: the Unionist post-mortem attributed the increase in Liberal support to 'disgruntlement' among 'middle-class voters' and a 'feeling that [the] government was not sufficiently Tory', a reference, it seemed, to the failure of the government to pursue further economic reforms.[60] Similar conclusions were reached by Lord John Hope, a junior minister at the Scottish Office and the MP for Edinburgh Pentlands. Hope accepted that the 'cost of living' was an issue; he suggested, nonetheless, that 'something else' had caused 'discontent' to 'develop into anger'. There was, he felt, 'a widespread feeling that the only people who had been insulated against rises in the cost of living were the people who had caused it – the Trades Unionists with their endless wage demands'.[61] Such sentiments were certainly visible: in early 1958, in a letter to the Conservative chairman Lord Hailsham, Gordon Murray, secretary of Dundee Unionist and National Liberal association, recorded local support for the recently departed treasury ministers, expressing his hope that the 'prosperity of the country [would] not be jeopardised in pandering to unjust and unrealistic demands, from whatever section they may come'.[62]

[58] NLS Acc. 10424/36: SUA WDC Education and Propaganda Committee minutes, 25 Sept. 1956; Acc. 10424/50: SUA Eastern Divisional Council (EDC) minutes, 12 Dec. 1956; Acc. 11368/22: SUA EDC minutes, 11 Apr. 1958.

[59] NLS Acc. 11368/22: SUA EDC minutes, 5 Oct. 1956.

[60] NLS Acc. 11368/24: SUA EDC Executive Committee minutes, 17 June 1957.

[61] NLS Acc. 11368/22: SUA EDC minutes, 4 Oct. 1957.

[62] BL CPA CCO 1/12/552–3: Area Files, Dundee: Gordon Murray to Lord Hailsham, 17 Jan. 1958.

The stance adopted by the Liberal party during this period is instructive. Jo Grimond, the MP for Orkney and Shetland who assumed the leadership of the party in 1956, repositioned the Liberals as a progressive alternative to Labour's state socialism.[63] Yet Grimond's defence of individual freedom, criticisms of nationalisation and the welfare state, and support for further reductions in personal taxation, represented a renewal of post-war anti-socialism and individualism rather than a departure. Notably, the Conservative government was now being reproached for being too timid in its reforms, too willing to acquiesce in the settlement inherited from Labour. Grimond accused the Conservatives of 'conserving Socialism', and of failing to address the high taxes and excessive government expenditure he believed to be the 'most damaging legacy of Socialism'. To those worried that a vote for the Liberals would allow Labour to regain power, Grimond replied that 'surely there is no point in keeping a Conservative Government in power unless it is going to be something different *in kind* from a Socialist Government'.[64]

This message was clearly intended to appeal to disillusioned Unionist supporters. In May 1958, there were reports from Unionist agents across Scotland of a Liberal revival driven by a suspicion that the government was 'pandering too much to Socialism' with the result that 'too much is being spent on the Welfare State'.[65] At the June 1958 Argyllshire by-election, the Liberal candidate William McKean, who secured almost 30 per cent of the vote, told the public that, although new to the Liberal party, 'he felt he must take a stand now against the two major parties. If we did not the individual would be crushed.' He offered a programme of tax cuts and restrictions on public and private monopolies. Speaking in his support, John Bannerman, chairman of the Scottish Liberals, echoed McKean's individualism, declaring that his party would return the state to its proper role as 'servant of the people', and would always 'look to the individual's interest'.[66]

By the close of the 1950s, the division that had sustained electoral politics in Scotland since 1945 had become confused. The Conservative record in office had, unsurprisingly, failed to match the heights of the party's rhetoric in opposition. Equally, the Liberal revival after 1955, however limited and lacking in lasting parliamentary success, suggested

---

[63] Sloman, *Liberal Party and the Economy*, 204–29.

[64] J. Grimond, *The New Liberal Democracy* (1958), 17. Emphasis and capitalisation in original.

[65] BL CPA CCO 2/5/20: Scottish Intelligence Summary, May 1958. Capitalisation in original.

[66] BL CPA CCO 1/12/556/1: Area Files, Argyll: report of meeting, Victoria Hall, Campbeltown, 29 May 1958.

that the longer the Conservative party remained in office, the more exposed it would be to criticisms that drew on the very language of liberal individualism that had been so central to its earlier victories. It was, however, the party's response to the 1959 general election that would prove critical in the ensuing realignment of Scottish politics.

III

The loss by the Unionists of their preeminent position in Scotland in 1959, a result that contrasted with continued Conservative success in England, was believed by contemporaries to be a consequence of Scotland's relatively weak economic performance. Unionists in the west of Scotland were convinced that the national decision to campaign on the theme of rising prosperity had been mistaken, with the 'fear of unemployment' and hostility towards the 1957 Rent Act, which lifted controls on private lettings, strengthening support for Labour in working-class communities.[67] This supposition has been echoed by subsequent assessments, which have stressed the electoral impact of economic concerns, and the extent to which this assisted the Labour party by increasing public support for state intervention.[68]

To be sure, the Unionists lost four seats in 1959, all to Labour: Central Ayrshire, Lanark and the Craigton and Scotstoun divisions of Glasgow. There is, all the same, a sense that the party misread these results: as Richard Finlay has rightly observed, Labour's gains in Scotland stemmed from the vagaries of the electoral system.[69] The Unionists had held the four seats lost by a cumulative majority of fewer than 2,000 votes: these were constituencies secured narrowly in the early 1950s, and the party's support had only to fall slightly for them to be lost. In truth, the Unionist vote was reasonably resilient in 1959: in tandem with the National Liberals, the party still outpolled the Labour party across Scotland. Indeed, in Glasgow, Unionist support amongst the electorate as a whole even increased marginally, despite the loss of two seats, and the party regained the city's Kelvingrove division, lost at a by-election in 1958.[70] Claims that Scottish politics had moved leftwards were thus overstated, and obscured the extent to which

---

[67] NLS Acc. 11368/39: SUA WDC minutes, 6 Nov. 1959; Acc. 10424/27: SUA WDC, *Annual Report 1959*, 2–3.

[68] Harvie, *No Gods*, 110; Finlay, 'Unionism and the Dependency Culture', 111; Mitchell, *Scottish Question*, 132–3.

[69] Finlay, *Partnership for Good*, 138–9.

[70] The Unionist vote in Glasgow totalled 34.4 per cent of the electorate in 1955, and 34.5 per cent in 1959: F. W. S. Craig, *British Parliamentary Election Results, 1950–1970* (Chichester, 1971).

Labour's vote had largely remained static. Where Unionist support did fall, this was more often due to the intervention of Liberal candidates.

Yet the signs that the ties that bound the post-war anti-socialist coalition were beginning to loosen went unheeded. Unionist commentators chose to focus instead on the contest with Labour, and to continue to treat support for the Liberals uncomplicatedly as a proxy vote for Unionism. For the *Glasgow Herald*, Unionist in loyalty, the Liberals were a party 'dedicated to individual liberty'; their improved performance in 1959 could therefore be treated as signalling 'a firm "No" to policies of restriction and control', and an indication that 'for the majority, the mixed economy now in being, and its efficient management by Conservatism, marks the acceptable limit of government interference with the individual'.[71] Perhaps, but we should note that the Liberals fought the election on a manifesto that called for an end to the closed shop, reductions in inheritance tax and for council tenants to be granted the right to buy their homes.[72] Grimond, for his part, declared that nationalisation was a 'fiasco' that would in time prove 'incompatible with freedom'; he was equally critical of 'the promise of endless welfare benefits' administered by 'the grandmother state'.[73] There were, then, those for whom the Conservative conception of the relationship between the state and the individual required refinement; after almost a decade in office, for a significant section of the electorate it was no longer enough for the Unionists to claim merely to be better than Labour.

The Unionists failed to acknowledge the threat posed by this new appeal to individualism, discarding their earlier rhetoric of liberty, and emphasising instead their willingness to intervene in the economy, a response that reflected the direction taken by the Conservative party under the leadership of Harold Macmillan.[74] The government accepted the recommendations of the 1961 Toothill enquiry into the Scottish economy, directing investment towards 'growth points'; in 1962, an economic development department was added to a steadily expanding Scottish Office.[75] A year later, a development plan for central Scotland was published, which promised a 'massive programme of national reconstruction and modernisation', and conceded that 'full employment' could 'only be maintained by conscious and far-ranging acts of policy'.[76] By the

---

[71] *Glasgow Herald*, 9 Oct. 1959.

[72] *Liberalism Leads: Liberal Policy* (1959).

[73] J. Grimond, *The Liberal Future* (1959), 22.

[74] K. O. Morgan, *The People's Peace: British History, 1945–1990* (Oxford, 1992), 209–15 and 223–8; J. Ramsden, *The Winds of Change: From Macmillan to Heath* (1996), 158–64.

[75] I. Levitt, 'The Origins of the Scottish Development Department, 1943–62', *Scottish Affairs*, 14 (1996), 42–63.

[76] *Development and Growth in Central Scotland* (Cmnd 2188, 1963), 1.

1964 general election, Sir Alec Douglas-Home, who had replaced Macmillan as premier a year earlier, could tell electors that he recognised 'that in modern conditions there must be a good deal of both central and regional planning'.[77] That year's Unionist manifesto praised the benefits of planning, pledging the creation of a 'vast new economic complex' in central Scotland.[78] As Priscilla Buchan, Unionist member for Aberdeen South since 1946, acknowledged during the campaign, her party now accepted 'far more the need for gov[ernment] to take greater responsibility to promote social and economic change'.[79] Yet these attempts to rebrand Unionism as a modernising creed, one able to deliver a more efficient form of planning than Labour, failed. The party lost a further six seats, reducing the number of Unionists MPs to twenty-four, down from the thirty-six returned in 1955; the party's share of the vote fell by almost a fifth.

The abandonment by the Unionists of the individualist rhetoric of the late 1940s and early 1950s created a space within Scottish politics for the Liberal party. The three Highland constituencies lost by the Unionists in 1964 fell to the Liberals; the presence of Liberal candidates also triggered sharp falls in the Unionist vote in the north-east of Scotland as well as in Renfrewshire and Ayrshire, and led to the loss of West Renfrewshire and Glasgow Pollok to Labour.[80] As the 1960s progressed, however, it would become clear that in parts of provincial Scotland the chief beneficiary of the growing inability of the Unionists to pose credibly as a party committed to the defence of the individual was the SNP. Scottish nationalism's espousal of an intensely individualist stance during the post-war decades remains underappreciated. Yet the nationalist vision was informed by the same fear of an overmighty central state as Unionism's anti-socialism and was often expressed in similar language. The post-war SNP was equally enamoured of the virtues of local government; in 1946, the party newspaper, the *Scots Independent*, could be found employing lengthy quotations from Hayek's *Road to Serfdom* in its editorial column.[81] These inclinations were heightened by an identification with the small nations of Eastern Europe occupied by the Soviet Union after 1945, which encouraged anti-communist sentiment within nationalist circles. Self-government was, as a result, often envisaged in instrumental terms, as a bulwark against a Labour government believed to harbour

---

[77] NLS Acc. 11368/90: *Sir Alec Douglas-Home: The Unionist Candidate* (Perth, 1964).

[78] *Scotland with the Unionists* (Edinburgh, 1964).

[79] NLS Acc. 11884/21: Lady Tweedsmuir papers, notes for adoption meeting, 24 Sept. 1964.

[80] Liberal intervention also contributed to the loss of Glasgow Woodside at a by-election in November 1962.

[81] *Scots Independent*, Dec. 1946, 4.

authoritarian tendencies. As the SNP's 1947 policy statement suggested, the conflict between capitalism and socialism had been rendered meaningless by the victory of the state, in whatever guise it assumed; the task now was to defend individual liberty and the rule of law, and to resist the rise of a 'despotism ruling over an irresponsible proletariat': Scots must choose 'either the road to tyranny or the way to freedom'.[82]

This individualist version of nationalist politics survived the 1950s largely intact, finding an outlet in criticisms of the welfare state, which, from a nationalist perspective, represented little more than a bribe designed to induce loyalty to the British state.[83] The SNP's 1957 conference programme duly dismissed the post-war settlement as 'a mass of taxes designed to make the individual look to the state for his needs'; what masqueraded as compassion was just 'a vote-catching fraud'. The SNP promoted 'independence for the individual Scottish citizen as well as for the Scottish nation'.[84] Following the 1959 general election, James Halliday, the party chairman who had unsuccessfully contested the Stirling and Falkirk Burghs constituency, lamented that Scottish voters appeared content to accept 'concessions and handouts' from central government in 'a spirit of meek and docile gratitude'.[85] By the early 1960s, as the SNP's electoral fortunes began to improve following positive performances at the Glasgow Bridgeton and West Lothian by-elections, what Gordon Wilson, SNP national secretary during the 1960s and later MP for Dundee East, described as the party's tradition of 'libertarianism and desire for decentralisation' appeared newly relevant to a political contest in which both major parties advocated economic planning of one form or another.[86] In those areas where the Liberals lacked a presence, particularly in central and eastern Scotland, the SNP offered an increasingly potent, and overtly constitutional, critique of the central state that tapped a historic provincial liberal tradition.

IV

Support for nationalisation and the welfare state was, no doubt, widespread amongst Scots in the post-war era; the consistent ability of the Labour party to attract the support of near half the Scottish electorate is testament enough to that. Still, to concentrate on such positive responses neglects the existence of another constituency of roughly

---

[82] *Aims and Policy of the SNP* (Glasgow, 1947; 1962 edn), 3.

[83] *Scots Independent*, 13 Oct. 1956.

[84] NLS Acc. 10090/26: McIntyre papers, *Scottish National Party: Annual National Conference, 18–19 May 1957*, 29–30.

[85] *Stirling Observer*, 1 Dec. 1959.

[86] G. Wilson, *SNP: The Turbulent Years, 1960–1990* (Stirling, 2009), 56.

equal size, one far more sceptical of economic planning and resentful of the taxes required to pay for the welfare state. For those of the latter inclination, Scotland's sluggish economic performance in the late 1950s and early 1960s was evidence that government intervention had failed, not that there was any need for more of it. This liberal, individualist strand did not disappear from Scottish politics during the upheaval of the 1960s; rather, the ability of Unionism to pose as its dominant political expression declined, and the Liberals and the SNP were able to construct new versions of this appeal.

This would become apparent in the wake of Winnie Ewing's famous victory for the SNP at the November 1967 Hamilton by-election. An opinion survey commissioned by the Conservatives to discover why they had failed to benefit from discontent with the Labour government revealed deep-rooted opposition to what was perceived as excessive government intervention in the economy, an opinion especially visceral in relation to the level of personal taxation.[87] The policy group launched to consider proposals for devolution in the wake of Edward Heath's May 1968 'declaration of Perth', which, in reaction to Hamilton, had committed the Conservatives to supporting a Scottish assembly, uncovered a similar liberal ethos and resentment of bureaucracy.[88] The group's report stressed that the popular disenchantment central to the nationalist victory at Hamilton was not unique to Scotland, but was driven by anger towards central government, by 'a feeling that decisions are taken by people far away from the objects of these decisions' and 'a sense of impotence in the face of governmental acts and policies'.[89] It was, however, no longer axiomatic that the natural political home for such sentiments was the Conservative party.

The weakening of a once-dominant Unionist tradition, the recovery of Scottish Liberalism and the rise of the SNP had, to be sure, multiple causes. But the relinquishment by the Unionists of an appeal to liberal individualism was a crucial element within this process, undercutting as it did the coherence of the party's identity, and reducing the distinction with Labour to one of degree, not kind. There was some awareness of the dangers posed by this shift within Unionist ranks: prior to the 1964 election, Lord Dalkeith, the MP for Edinburgh North, warned that party literature was placing 'insufficient emphasis' on what he felt was the 'essential difference' between the two major parties: that the Unionists,

---

[87] BL CPA CCO 550/50/1: Surveys of Scottish, Welsh and West Country Nationalism: 'The Motivations behind Scottish Nationalism', Mar. 1968.

[88] G. Pentland, 'Edward Heath, the Declaration of Perth and the Scottish Conservative and Unionist Party, 1966–70', *Twentieth Century British History*, 26 (2015), 249–73.

[89] NLS Acc. 11368/79: *Government of Scotland Policy Group: First Report to the Constitutional Committee, August 1968*, 3.

unlike Labour, did not regard 'the individual as a cog in the great state machine planned and controlled by the all-knowing man in Whitehall'.[90] Similarly, the inroads made by the Liberals into Unionist support in Angus, Aberdeenshire and the Borders was credited to a wish for 'idealism', especially among younger voters.[91] The Unionism of the 1940s and early 1950s had, alongside its traditional role as the representative of important interests within Scottish society, fulfilled this desire for ideological principle, presenting a powerful critique of socialism, and defence of individual liberty and the free economy. But by the 1960s, softened by the experience of office, the party had mislaid this intellectual confidence; there were, moreover, now other parties able to provide the electorate with liberal political ideals. Significantly, however, individual liberty was coming to be viewed through a constitutional rather than economic lens.

[90] NLS Acc. 11368/22: SUA EDC minutes, 10 July 1964.
[91] NLS Acc. 11368/5: SUA CC minutes, 11 Nov. 1964.

Transactions of the RHS 28 (2018), pp. 219–239 © Royal Historical Society 2018
doi:10.1017/S0080440118000117

THE TROUBLES WITH A LOWER CASE t: UNDERGRADUATES AND BELFAST'S DIFFICULT HISTORY

By Sean O'Connell

READ 16 SEPTEMBER 2017

AT QUEEN'S UNIVERSITY BELFAST

ABSTRACT. This paper explores the risks and rewards involved in directing under-graduate students engaged on an oral history project in Belfast. It advocates the role of oral history as a tool through which to encourage students' engagement with research-led teaching to produce reflective assignments on the nature of historical evidence, particularly autobiographical memory. The particular challenges of conducting oral history in a city beset by ethno-sectarian divisions are discussed. This factor has ensured that the historiography of Belfast has focused extensively on conflict and violence. The city's social history is poorly understood, but employing oral history enables the exploration of issues that take undergraduate historians beyond the Troubles as a starting point. This project probed what is called the troubles with a lower case t, via an analysis of deindustrialisation and urban redevelopment in Sailortown (Belfast's dockland district). It provided evidence with which to offer a new assessment on existing historiographical discussions about working-class nostalgic memory and urban social change, one that supports those scholars that problematize attempts to categorise such memory. The testimony also differed in significant ways from previous oral history research on post-war Northern Ireland.

The RHS symposium on teaching difficult histories, held at Queen's University Belfast in September 2017 was the forum for which this paper was prepared. It is not, therefore, a conventional article that dissects a historical research question over the course of 8,000 words. Instead, it explains the problems and opportunities encountered when overseeing a group of second-year undergraduates working on an oral history project in Belfast as part of the module 'Recording History'. Amongst the historical difficulties engendered by that exercise, the most obvious centred on the danger inherent when undergraduates explore life stories in a city beset by ethno-sectarian division. There is always the likelihood that interviewees will receive simple questions about schooling, work, residence or leisure preferences warily, fearing that their answers might suggest a 'sectarian' outlook. The opportunity for cultural misunderstandings taking place in the interview encounter is heightened because most Northern Irish students have limited experience of those outside their own 'community' due to cultural, educational and residential segregation. The relatively limited historiography on the social history of post-1945 Belfast limits the extent to which this factor can be minimised by administering a lengthy reading list to students. However, utilising oral history in the tutorial room produces research-led teaching in one of its most dynamic forms. Students face the challenge of assessing the contested historical perspectives that surface in personal and collective memory. As a result, conducting oral history interviews can lead students to question their pre-existing historical assumptions as they encounter the biographical and historical experiences of individual interviewees.[1] Moreover, the testimony collected by the students often provides new evidence through which to reevaluate the historiographical literature in the research area the students focus upon. For this reason, this paper also argues that oral history can play a significant role in writing a more nuanced history of Belfast in the second half of the twentieth century.

In the case-study discussed here, undergraduate students deployed oral history to investigate the dockland district of Sailortown with a focus on deindustrialisation and urban redevelopment. These twinned traumatic processes represented Belfast's second 'troubles': one with a lower case *t*, unlike its capitalised bigger brother: the headline-hogging paramilitary conflict. Visitors to a recent photographic exhibition of Belfast during the Troubles were met by images of a war zone, not only due to the presence of armed troops but because the streets they patrolled had been blitzed.[2] However, these scarred inner-city landscapes were not the result of a bombing campaign but the product of on-going urban redevelopment that disfigured vast swathes of the inner city in the 1970s. Between the 1960s and 1990s, deindustrialisation and urban redevelopment buffeted Belfast's working-class communities. Exploring experiences of and testimony about these processes not only enriches historical understanding of the city's social history, it ultimately enables a deeper understanding of ethno-sectarian cultural politics. For the researcher, whether they are an academic or an undergraduate, oral history often forces reassessment of the assumptions held at the outset of a project. The paper discusses that process, at various levels, by examining how the testimonies collected contribute to the reassessment of a number

---

[1] For further discussion of this, see Graham Smith, *Historical Insights: Focus on Research – Oral History* (Coventry, [2010]), 4.

[2] 'Photography during the Northern Irish Troubles', Ulster Museum exhibition (June – November 2017).

of historiographical conversations. The first of these involves discussion of oral history and memory in Northern Ireland. The second involves engagement with a broader historiographical argument about nostalgia and working-class social memory. The final one concerns the neighbouring historiographical theme of memory, deindustrialisation and urban change. The paper begins by outlining briefly the historiography on Belfast's social history. It then introduces the utility of oral history as a source in Belfast, outlines the history of Sailortown and explains the preparation that the students undertook before embarking on their oral history project. The final sections of the paper reveal some of the findings uncovered during the research and concludes with a reflection on the extent to which its findings challenged conventional historical knowledge about Belfast and the student's assumptions of that history, as well as their own place in it.

I Refreshing historical narratives of Belfast

In 2011, my colleague Professor Sean Connolly made an offer that could not be refused: to write about Belfast's history from the Great War to the late 1960s for the collection *Belfast 400: People, Place and History*.[3] The task was to craft a fresh historical narrative that did not ignore sectarian conflict whilst introducing other themes central to the city's social history. The task was fascinating, but it became apparent that there were significant lacunae in the historiography on issues such as leisure, work, consumption, housing and urban redevelopment in Belfast. This realisation stirred an ambition to write a more comprehensive account of Belfast, its people and their social history and to foster the enthusiasm for a new generation of history students to contribute to that process. The historical focus on political conflict has left the social history of Belfast sketchily understood. Moreover, with the island of Ireland mid-way through the 'Decade of Centenaries', marking the period from Home Rule through to Partition and its aftermath, renewed scrutiny of Irish political history threatens to re-marginalise less visible histories. It may appear hackneyed to apply to Belfast an oft-repeated E. P. Thompson exhortation, but it is time to rescue from the enormous condescension of posterity the poor carter, the shop steward at the docks, the 'obsolete' linen doffer and even the deluded followers of the 'Save Ulster from Sodomy' campaign. A history of the families on the corporation housing waiting list in 1955 remains unwritten. What were the ambitions of the young woman who was the first of her family to study at Queen's University in the 1960s? What do historians know of the taxi driver who ferries them to and from the airport on the way to conferences to discuss Ireland's tumultuous political history: was

---

[3] Sean Connolly, *Belfast 400: People, Place and History* (Liverpool, 2012).

he once a young man, with a different future mapped out, when serving his time at the ill-fated DeLorean Motor Company manufacturing enterprise? Without answers to these questions, our historical understanding of Belfast is all the poorer.

Despite the gaps, the social history of modern Belfast is not entirely virgin terrain. Particularly noteworthy is A. C. Hepburn's scrutiny of the city's residential, occupational and sectarian demography in the first half of the twentieth century.[4] His work was innovative thematically but perhaps less so in terms of its source base. Employing oral history would have enriched his analysis, although in 1970s and 1980s Belfast inquisitive outsiders, armed with tape recorders, placed themselves in enough danger to give palpitations to any modern university ethics committee. Despite this, in the same period, sociologists Ronnie Munck and Bill Rolston did employ oral history to explore Belfast.[5] The testimony focused on the political issues of the 1930s, such as the outdoor relief protests of 1932, sectarianism and political activism. Their interests aligned with those of a number of historians who have studied aspects of the city's labour history in the early twentieth century; the most recent output being C. J. V. Loughlin's study of interwar Belfast working-class labour politics.[6] Brian Barton charted a range of social historical themes in a short discussion of the socio-economic landscape of 1930s Belfast, which appears in his study of Belfast during the Second World War.[7] A limited number of historians have tackled Belfast's social history beyond 1945. They include Marianne Elliott's major history of Ulster Catholics. Her assessment of the cultural politics of the minority is enriched by her introduction, recalling her childhood on a religiously mixed Belfast estate. Elliott deals with significant social change, such as the arrival of the welfare state and changing employment patterns: themes she returned to in a recent memoir of the White City housing estate.[8] Edited collections that include treatment of Belfast's social history offer a more tentative analysis once their chronology heads beyond 1945 and into historical periods that are relatively un-harvested.[9]

[4] A. C. Hepburn, *A Past Apart: Studies in the History of Catholic Belfast 1850–1950* (Belfast, 1996).

[5] Ronnie Munck and Bill Rolston, *Belfast in the Thirties: An Oral History* (Belfast, 1987).

[6] John Gray, *City in Revolt: James Connolly and the Belfast Dock Strike of 1907* (Belfast, 1985); John Lynch, *A Tale of Three Cities: Comparative Studies in Working-Class Life* (Basingstoke, 1998); C. J. V. Loughlin, *Labour and the Politics of Disloyalty in Belfast, 1921–39 – the Moral Economy of Loyalty* (Basingstoke, 2017).

[7] Brian Barton, *The Blitz: Belfast in the War Years* (Belfast, 1990).

[8] Marianne Elliott, *The Catholics of Ulster* (2000); Marianne Elliott, *Hearthlands: A Memoir of the White City Housing Estate in Belfast* (Belfast, 2017).

[9] Frederick W. Boal and Steven A. Royle, *Enduring City: Belfast in the Twentieth Century* (Belfast, 2006); W. A. Maguire, *Belfast: A History* (Lancaster, 2009).

For example, one of the few essays in an authoritative recent edited collection that does go beyond 1945 – R. J. Morris's survey essay on urban Ulster since 1600 – could not draw upon any recent historical research and relied on work by geographers, planners and older research by historians that is due for reassessment.[10]

Imaginative literature can also inform our historical research on important social issues in the modern city, as is demonstrated by several contributors to Michael Pierse's recent edited study of Irish working-class writing.[11] One of the writers featured therein, John Campbell, can certainly enrich our understanding of Belfast working-class history. Novels such as Campbell's *The Disinherited* and others, such as David Park's *The Big Snow*, demonstrate how historical fiction opens doors to aspects of the past that historians have neglected.[12] In novels set in the 1950s and 1960s, Park offer insights on corruption in corporation housing allocation and Campbell explores labour and community at the docks. Indeed, Campbell's work was an important preparatory source for the undergraduate students who, in 2013, set out to undertake their oral history project with members of Belfast's former dockside community.

Oral history is the method that offers the richest vein of evidence through which to open up Belfast's post-war social history and I have employed it since my arrival in Belfast in 1999. The first interviews in the city explored the theme of credit and debt in working-class communities and the experience was a steep learning curve.[13] Interviews provided much to digest, both in terms of project objectives and in the trials that lay ahead in attempting to understand the city. One early encounter was with ninety-nine-year-old Mrs Rafferty, whose testimony revealed that the origins of one of Belfast's best-known money-lending businesses lay with a compensation claim from a woman shot in the mouth by a ricocheting British army bullet in the early 1920s. Mrs Rafferty shared her belief that, despite being an Ardoyne resident for over sixty years, neighbours viewed her as an 'import': she left her original home, in the North Queen Street area, in 1941 following bombing by the Luftwaffe. The street's proximity to the docks made it a target.[14] Mrs Rafferty's testimony engendered a pause for thought. If

[10] R. J. Morris, 'Urban Ulster since 1600', in Liam Kennedy and Philip Ollerenshaw, *Ulster since 1600: Politics, Economy and Society* (Oxford, 2013), 121–39.

[11] *A History of Irish Working-Class Writing*, ed. Michael Pierse (Cambridge, 2017).

[12] David Park, *The Big Snow* (2002); John Campbell, *The Disinherited* (Belfast, 2006).

[13] See Sean O'Connell, *Credit, Class and Community: Working-Class Debt in the UK since 1880* (Oxford, 2009).

[14] Interview with Mrs Rafferty (born 1904). Conducted by Sean O'Connell, 10 Oct. 2002. Where full names are used for interviewees, this is their real name. Pseudonyms are employed for interviewees that are still living. There is one exception, John Campbell, who is happy for his identity to be revealed.

she was an 'import' after six decades, how would inhabitants of Belfast's working-class districts view an interloping oral historian? Moreover, what did her comments reveal about the complex nature of communal identify in Belfast? They certainly indicated that there were issues to consider other than the commonly understood fissures caused by ethno-sectarian identity.

A further instructive interviewee was the ex-docker Terry O'Neill, a working-class autodidact who would have performed brilliantly at university if born in the 1980s rather than the 1930s. He asked to borrow a copy of my first book, a social history of the car, and furnished me with a collection of historical short stories he had published in a local magazine.[15] Terry's advice, when returning the car monograph, was that it was interesting but that I needed to include more jokes. His own narrative was packed full of them, usually to make an important point. Thus, on his childhood neighbour, the future playwright Martin Lynch, he observed 'Martin, there was seventeen of them – two sets of twins – and their father, the only time he worked was when he took his trousers off at night.'[16] Terry's anecdotal style served as a reminder to study form and convention in the act of communication that is each oral history narration. In his darkly humorous pithy sentence, Terry drew the listener's attention to the world of dockside under-employment, overcrowded homes and working-class Catholic sexual relations in mid-twentieth-century Belfast.

II Sailortown, deindustrialisation, urban redevelopment and working-class memory

These are just two of the individuals whose testimony prompted a desire to collect further oral histories of working-class Belfast. Both their testimonies drew attention to the dockland district of the city. Studying this area, known as Sailortown, provides a vehicle through which to address Belfast's experience of deindustrialisation and urban redevelopment. These two phenomena accompanied one another in a package of turbulent social change in this neighbourhood, as they did in many inner-city districts. Exploring Sailortown facilitates the deployment of questions and themes probed in histories of urban change in other working-class communities. Social historians have examined oral histories and autobiographies to debate the impact of these traumatic experiences on working-class social memory. Raphael Samuel and Paul Thompson coined the term 'urban pastoral' to identify a motif that

---

[15] Sean O'Connell, *The Motor Car in British Society, Class, Gender and Motoring 1896–1939* (Manchester, 1998); Terry O'Neill, *Terry O'Neill's Belfast* (Belfast, 1999).
[16] Interview with Terry O'Neill (born 1930). Conducted by Sean O'Connell, 15 Apr. 2001.

they felt was a strong feature of working-class communal memory. Its hallmark was an elegiac tone that surfaced in testimony in which the 'slum' represented 'the symbolic space of the world we have lost'.[17] Joanna Bourke, Chris Waters and Ben Jones made further contributions to this discussion, in their respective analyses of various forms of working-class autobiographical memory in the decades following the 'slum clearances' of the 1950s, 1960s and 1970s. Bourke identifies the strong influence of 'retrospective reconstruction' of the traditional working-class community. Working-class oral histories and autobiographies, she maintains, employ a romantic use of the phrase working-class community in recalling social relations 'through a golden haze'. This ensures that prominence is given to 'doors that are always open', whilst 'the neighbour who was never seen is neglected in favour of the neighbour who always shared'.[18] Waters addressed the process of urban redevelopment more directly in describing the strong nostalgia for a world of mills, cobbled streets and community spirit expunged by urban redevelopment. He detected evidence of melancholic reminiscence in the popularity of L. S. Lowry's paintings of industrial Lancashire and in the working-class autobiographical writing produced by groups such as Brighton's QueenSpark publications. Waters argues that a desire emerged to remember a particular form of working-class past: one centred on place and a landscape of memory. In this respect, there was an intensification of emotion towards the form of built environment that the tower block and council housing estates replaced.[19] However, more recently Jones questioned the ubiquity of nostalgia in working-class memory, describing a variety of storytelling traditions that 'defy simple categorization'. He observes many examples of less than neighbourly relations in the autobiographical sources explored by Bourke, a factor that undermines her central premise. Jones makes parallel observations about Waters's reading of the QueenSpark material. As well as being alert to the role of nostalgia in working-class testimonies, Jones urges that historians deploying these sources pay great attention to factors such as the times and locations from which memories emerge, and to narrators' gender, age and life trajectory.[20]

---

[17] *The Myths We Live By*, ed. Raphael Samuel and Paul Thompson (1990), 9.

[18] Joanna Bourke, *Working-Class Cultures in Britain, 1890–1960: Class, Gender and Ethnicity* (1994).

[19] Chris Waters, 'Representations of Everyday Life: L. S. Lowry and the Landscape of Memory in Post-War Britain', *Representations*, 65 (1999), 121–50; C. Waters, 'Autobiography, Nostalgia and the Changing Practices of Working-Class Self-Hood', in *Singular Continuities: Tradition, Nostalgia and Identity in Modern British Culture*, ed. G. K. Behlmer *et al.* (Stanford, 2000), 178–95.

[20] Ben Jones, 'The Uses of Nostalgia: Autobiography, Community Publishing and Working-Class Neighbourhoods in Post-War England', *Cultural and Social History*, 7 (2010),

Employing similar research questions in Belfast enables the exploration of the dynamics of working-class social memory in a city with the added complication of ethno-sectarian division and produces some fascinating results. Sailortown, like other Belfast districts such as the Shankill Road, experienced 'slum clearance' in similar mode to UK cities such as Bradford where planners championed a banal urban modernism, featuring soulless urban clearways.[21] Residents of the Shankill reflected subsequently on piecemeal dismemberment, as their homes made way for the Belfast urban motorway during the 1970s and 1980s.[22] Due to redevelopment in the 1980s, the population of the Shankill fell from 76,000 to 27,000.[23] Belfast also experienced poorly regarded new housing developments, such as Divis flats on the Falls Road and the Weetabix flats on the Shankill Road. For Sailortown, however, urban redevelopment was experienced more fundamentally with almost every home in the area demolished as a new urban motorway was driven straight through the tightly packed district. This coincided with significant passages of deindustrialisation. As early as 1952, the closure of the York Street Mill struck a blow to many families. Its closure represented the loss of 15 per cent of all textile jobs in Northern Ireland. The greatest surge of deindustrialisation came between the 1970s and 1990s when Belfast lost 40,000 manufacturing jobs.[24] At the docks, the introduction of containerisation decimated employment in what had been a labour-intensive industry. By 2006, a workforce of just 16 crane and forklift truck drivers had replaced over 2,000 dockers.[25] The experience replicated that in other Sailortowns across the UK. Technology-intensive new ports developed in deepwater locations away from city centres in a process that 'proved brutally complementary to the movement for city-centre clearance'. Urban motorways disfigured districts now classified as slums and created buffer zones between cities and their waterfronts.[26]

By the time a class of Queen's history students arrived there in 2013, Sailortown was a shadow of its former self. Only four terraced houses and a handful of pubs stood as a reminder of a once vibrant community. The district developed during the nineteenth century as Belfast emerged

335–74; Ben Jones, *The Working Class in Mid-Twentieth-Century England: Community, Identity and Social Memory* (Manchester, 2012).

[21] Simon Gunn, 'The Rise and Fall of British Urban Modernism: Planning Bradford, circa 1945–1970', *Urban History*, 49 (2010), 849–69.

[22] Ron Weiner, *The Rape and Plunder of the Shankill: People and Planning* (Belfast, 1976).

[23] Colin Coulter, *Contemporary Northern Irish Society: An Introduction* (1999), 88.

[24] *Ibid.*, 70.

[25] http://news.bbc.co.uk/1/hi/northern_ireland/8024702.stm.

[26] Graeme Milne, *People, Place and Power on the Nineteenth-Century Waterfront: Sailortown* (Basingstoke, 2016).

as a thriving commercial and manufacturing hub. As the docks and maritime commerce became more economically significant, terraced housing was erected for workers who serviced the area's industries. The district developed a reputation for political radicalism. The bitterly fought Dockers and Carters strike of 1907, led by James Larkin, was one of a relatively small number of episodes in the city's history where working-class solidarity trumped ethno-sectarian divisions.[27] This strike features heavily in the social memory of Sailortown. The influence of its trade union politics also surfaced in elections in the Dock Ward via the regular return of left-leaning candidates, rather than those representing the standard unionist or nationalist politicians elected routinely elsewhere in the city.[28] It was at other times, however, the cockpit of ethno-sectarian violence. There was significant bloodshed in Sailortown during 1920–2 and 1935.[29] At the outset of the Troubles in 1969, the area's labour history traditions bore fruit, in the form of citizens' patrols designed to stop bloody incursions from one community into another in the dockside's streets.[30] The area was at high risk of descending into violence because it was a relatively 'mixed' area by Belfast standards. In 1933, for example, the Dock Ward had a Roman Catholic population of 43 per cent. The figure for the city was only 24 per cent, the greatest proportion living in segregated districts such as the Falls Road, Short Strand and the Markets. However, demographic analysis of Sailortown residential patterns reveals micro-segregation, with Roman Catholics and Protestants (of various denominations) clustering at opposite ends of the same streets.[31] Clearly, there was the potential for the Queen's students to capture intriguing testimony from ex-residents of the area about everyday life in those streets and to test some of the historiographical questions about working-class social memory.

In advance of the interviews, students examined the many forms in which Sailortown is commemorated. Among the most visible are murals that have appeared in its remaining streets, particularly on Pilot Street where the Dockers Club is located. This street art celebrates the achievements of the labour movement and its anti-sectarian principles. This theme has been pursued most recently by SHIP (Shared History Interpretive Project), founded in 2006 to research and commemorate the history of Belfast's dockers. A few hundred yards past Pilot Street, a series of haunting and evocative over-sized family photographs of former residents sit on the concrete supports holding up the elevated

---

[27] Lynch, *A Tale of Three Cities*, 35.
[28] Loughlin, *Labour and the Politics of Disloyalty*, 79.
[29] Hepburn, *A Past Apart*.
[30] Interview with Sean H (born 1942). Interviewed 25 Mar. 2013 by Ryan Mallon.
[31] Hepburn, *A Past Apart*, 48–54, 176–8.

section of the M3 motorway. The sentiment they project echoes the title of the edited collection *Once There Was a Community Here*, by the ex-docker turned poet/novelist John Campbell. Local history groups and writers' groups, such as North Belfast History Workshop or the Tin Bath Writers Co-op, have added to the extensive collection of stories about the Belfast waterfront.[32] This passage from a local history publication gives a flavour of their sentiment:

> I thought about all the many houses of Sailortown, and felt sad at the slow destruction of a neighbourhood and community. A community of good people, mostly quiet and peaceful, patiently living out their existence never asking for more than three score and ten, always making the best of what life threw at them. Households where the doors were never closed, and one was always made welcome. Welcome to share in all the little things that meant so much – the births, the deaths, the childhood days, the school years, and the times of tears and laughter, the times of departures and homecomings.[33]

The Sailortown Historical and Cultural Society and Sailortown Regeneration group campaigned to commemorate the area's past and to rebuild a community. These efforts were given added impetus, in 2002, by the Roman Catholic church's decision to close St Joseph's chapel. The church had remained open despite dispersal of its parishioners across Belfast. Suspicious that the site's value to the property developers constructing commercial premises and expensive apartments in the gentrifying dockland had motivated the Catholic hierarchy's decision, ex-residents occupied the chapel and began a campaign to save it.

This was the background faced by the thirty-four undergraduate students on the module. They worked in pairs to record seventeen oral history interviews. In preparation, students were encouraged to read work by a range of oral historians. As well as classic texts dealing with all aspects of the interview, the reading list included a number of articles on issues such as interviewing across generations, interviewing as an insider/outsider, as well as the ethics of oral history research.[34] All

---

[32] Tin Bath Writers Co-op/Sailortown Cultural and Historical Society, *Tin Baths and Mangles* (Belfast, 2006); Denis Smyth, *Sailortown: The Story of a Dockside Community* (Belfast, n.d.).

[33] *Ibid.*, 2.

[34] For those considering a similar module, reading might include Paul Thompson and Joanna Bornat, *The Voice of the Past: Oral History* (Oxford, 2017); Valerie Yow, *Recording Oral History: A Guide for the Humanities and Social Sciences* (Lanham, 2015); Lynn Abrams, *Oral History Theory* (Padstow, 2010); S. Chandler, 'Oral History across Generations: Age, Generational Identity and Oral Testimony', *Oral History*, 33 (2005) 48–56; T. E. K'Myer and A. Glenn Crothers, '"If I See Some of This in Writing I Am Going to Shoot You": Reluctant Narrators, Taboo Topics and the Ethical Dilemmas of the Oral Historian', *Oral History Review*, 34 (2007), 71–93; *The Oral History Reader*, ed. Rob Perks and Alistair Thomson (2016); Erin Jessee, 'Managing Danger in Oral History Fieldwork', *Oral History Review*, 44 (2017), 322–47.

these themes were discussed in tutorials in the weeks running up to the fieldwork taking place. Students listened to and discussed existing oral interviews, read transcripts and worked to prepare interview schedules. The agreed format for the interviews focused on the broad themes of family, work and community and the impact of social change on Sailortown. In the context of interviewing in Northern Ireland, a particularly insightful article is Anna Bryson's 'Whatever You Say, Say Nothing', which used oral history to examine memory and identity in the mid-Ulster town Maghera. The article discusses Bryson's experience, as a young Catholic female whose family are from the town, of employing oral history to probe the history of leisure in Maghera between 1945 and 1969. Bryson reached a number of conclusions. The first of these was that memories of Catholic/Protestant social relations prior to 1969 were, inevitably, filtered through the prism of the Troubles and she identified 'two distinct communal narratives, each carefully reinforced with reference to both the distant and recent past'. Most striking in terms of interviews with Protestants was their depiction of the period between 1945 and 1969 as a 'golden age' of community relations, ended only by the onset of the Troubles. In contrast, many Maghera Catholics made clear statements about the discrimination their community experienced. They identified the Second World War as the only phase in which there was a recognisable reduction of communal tension.[35]

How did these findings compare with the Sailortown interviews? An initial point to make is that of the seventeen Sailortown interviewees, only two were with Protestant narrators. A number of factors explain this. It became apparent that despite the area's reputation as a mixed community, the long passage of communal strife in the decades since the dispersal of Sailortown residents had diminished cross-community friendships and associations. Asked to recommend potential Protestant research participants, Catholic interviewees either provided no suggestion or identified John Campbell, who had already agreed to take part. It is also likely that the high-profile campaign by the Sailortown Cultural and Historical Society to save St Joseph's chapel gave a 'green' tinge to the social memory of Sailortown. In hindsight, approaches to Protestant community groups and churches using a different term for the area may have been more productive. Protestant residents of Sailortown tended to cluster close to the main arterial road, York Street, while Catholics lived at the dockside end of the area's streets. Using York Street in the call for participants may have been more productive with the former group. The twelve-week module

[35] Anna Bryson, '"Whatever You Say, Say Nothing": Researching Memory and Identity in Mid-Ulster, 1945–1969', *Oral History*, 45 (2007), 51.

timetable and looming assessment deadlines meant it was not possible to rectify this issue during the project.

As might have been anticipated, based on Bryson's work, the two Protestant interviewees did not make any unprompted references to sectarianism or discrimination. What was more surprising, however, was that the Catholic interviewees offered testimony that included strong elements of a 'golden age' discourse. A common theme was of cross-community socialising in the dockside bars. John Clancy described the reaction from a group of Catholic drinkers when one of their co-religionists passed sectarian comment on a Protestant who entered a Sailortown pub:

> But one thing I do remember I happened to be down Liam McMahon's one night and I think it was Stanley…[a] Protestant guy. And some guy happened to say something of a sectarian nature to him. And three of the dockers got your man and literally – and I mean literally head first – threw him into Garmoyle Street to the middle of the road. Told him if he ever came back again they would kick him up and down, and that is a fact. Now that is the way I could describe Sailortown, in the small instance that happened in that bar. We had no time for that sort of craic.

Clancy also deployed a well-honed joke to illustrate his belief that the common experience of economic hardship could trump ethno-sectarian division: 'we had a lot in common; it was called poverty, y'know? We were that poor we used to get parcels from the third world and after a while you get fed up of eating bananas.'[36] Female narrators also tendered positive testimony on facets of community relations. Mary H recollected the delight that Catholic children shared with Protestant neighbours when an Orange Lodge's band ceremonially collected the Lodge Master, a Sailortown resident, on the way to a parade. The ritual included benefits for the local children:

> And that was a great day because there was – there was – everybody got buns and everybody got cakes and there was lemonade and there was – I'm sure there was more Catholic children outside the door than there was Protestant ones, ya know what I mean? That sorta thing.[37]

In analysing the testimony, it is necessary to remain alert to the particular circumstances of the interviews. There was a significant generational gap between interviewers and narrators. The former were often still in their teens and the latter mostly beyond retirement age. Unconscious divergence in understanding and interpretation within intergenerational interviews can shape the content of interviews and their subsequent interpretation.[38] In some cases, interviewers and

---

[36] Interview with John Clancy (born 1943). Interviewed by Tiarnán Ó Muilleoir, 12 Mar. 2013.

[37] Interview with Mary H (born 1941). Interviewed by Francesca Owens, 25 Mar. 2013.

[38] Chandler, 'Oral History across Generations'.

narrators came from different religious backgrounds. Did this mean that some narrators held back from venting about sectarianism? If they did, was this a conscious or unconscious process? To this mixture of conjecture and analysis, we must add the requirement to explore the elements of collective and individual memory that engendered each testimony. Oral historians have debated the extent to which memory is the product of the individual and personal recollection or whether it is processed through 'cultural scripts'.[39] Others have urged the consideration of 'transactive memory', in particular the pooling of memory by individuals remembering within a group context.[40] This is pertinent to this research because two students arrived to find themselves faced with more than one interviewee. Moreover, many interviewees were members of community groups whose rationale was to commemorate Sailortown. A further significant factor, in a number of ways, was gender. For example, Kathleen M could recall no crime taking place in Sailortown. This may have been a result of her gendered experience, whereby exclusion from the docks or dockside pubs left her ignorant of theft from cargo ships or of prostitution. Alternatively, she may have been adhering to a working-class female discourse of respectability, as discussed by historian Judy Giles among others.[41] Dockside prostitution is a topic exposed brutally in John Campbell's two Sailortown novels, *Corner Kingdom* and *The Disinherited*, but he also avoided discussion of the subject when asked about it in interview. The fictionalised docks created in his novels allowed him greater freedom to break from the conventions of respectability, but the fact that his interviewer was a young female also shaped the boundaries of his testimony.[42]

Campbell also writes poems and when another interviewee John Clancy recited one of them, it was a revealing moment. The recording captured a pregnant silence after he appeared ready to commence, the significance of which emerges only when comparing John's recitation with the printed poem. He had chosen Campbell's poem 'Sailortown' to illustrate a vision of a solidly communal district. The pause came as he silently scanned and decided to omit the first two stanzas:

[39] Anna Green, 'Individual Memory and "Collective Memory": Theoretical Presuppositions and Contemporary Debates', *Oral History*, 32 (2004), 35–44.

[40] Graham Smith, 'Beyond Individual/Collective Memory: Women's Transactive Memories of Food, Family and Conflict', *Oral History*, 35 (2007), 75–90.

[41] Interview with Kathy M (born 1933). Interviewed by Anne Donnelly, 26 Mar. 2013; Judy Giles, '"Playing Hard to Get": Working-Class Women, Sexuality and Respectability in Britain, 1918–1940', *Women's History Review*, 1 (1992), 239–55.

[42] Interview with John Campbell (born 1936). Interviewed by Rachel Sloan, 18 Mar. 2013; John Campbell, *Corner Kingdom* (Belfast, 1999); Campbell, *The Disinherited*.

In Sailorstown was some good men
and many a punch-up we had then,
but we'd all finish friends again,
in Sailorstown.

In Sailorstown the drink was good
and many men used it for food.
It put them in the fighting mood,
in Sailorstown.[43]

While this example might be interpreted as evidence supporting Bourke's or Waters's position on the power of working-class nostalgic memory and retrospective reconstruction, it is also a reminder to read and listen closely to the language of each narrator. Doing so demonstrates the complex and potentially contradictory memory that surfaces in the majority of narratives. In terms of the earlier observation about the 'golden age' tinge to the accounts by Sailortown's Catholics, most of these interviews contained a 'but', at which point more divisive memories seeped into the testimony. The most commonly remembered annual event in this regard was the 'Twelfth', the highpoint of the Orange Order's marching season and a celebration of Protestant ascendency. Mary H recalled a feeling of isolation during the 'mad month' of July, in which 'even your [Protestant] friends, even ones you'da said was your friends, they didn't really wanna know'.[44] Close attention to the language deployed in the testimony provided insight into the limits of the inclusivity and shared identity that were a hallmark of the more positive elements of testimony. Mary H described the Catholic side of Sailortown as 'our way, at our end'. It is also significant that this detail came in what was her second interview, one where the student arrived to find that Mary, and three other women, had joined the intended interviewee. In the same interview, the group described a Protestant matriarch from their youth; 'Big' Maisy Morton or 'Ulster Mouth', they recollected, 'knew what direction you were [from]'. This offered an indication of an ethno-sectarian undercurrent in post-war Sailortown that was not evident initially in the testimonies.[45]

Shifting our focus from the erasure of community to the experience of deindustrialisation again engenders complex testimony. In part, this is because of the nature of the port economy. In Sailortown, the experience

---

[43] John Campbell, 'Sailortown', in *The Rose and the Blade: New and Selected Poems* (Belfast, 1997). Note Sailorstown/Sailortown are both used with some claiming that Protestants are more likely to use the former.

[44] Interview with Mary H.

[45] Interview with Mary H, Emily H, Marie S, Briege H, and Annie G. Interviewed by Lindsay Johnston, 27 Mar. 2013.

of male work, particularly that of the docker, has been commemorated in murals and via the organisation SHIP. The significant female experience of work, and deindustrialisation, in the local textile and tobacco factories went largely unremarked upon in interviews. Historical analysis of water-front masculinity in interwar Liverpool describes how the dockers' inability to achieve breadwinner status, due to the casual labour system that pitted working-class men in direct competition for work with neighbours and relatives, created a particular form of workplace culture. This culture strove to retrieve masculine self-esteem in a number of ways. It embraced anti-authoritarianism, which included pilfering, and an emphasis on physicality and the demanding nature of the work. A cele-bration of rugged masculinity spilled over into the male sociability and camaraderie that was a feature of dockland pubs.[46] The oral history interviews from Sailortown, plus local history accounts and the novels of John Campbell, all reveal that this form of culture had a strong hold in the Belfast docklands. The degrading and dehumanising aspects of work were offset by notions of masculinity that highlighted the dangerous and challenging labour process. There were also post-work leisure practices that served to build masculine self-esteem. Retired docker Tommy M remembered the casual system:

> The first horn was at five to eight and dockers used to rush to get into the Dockers Corner before five to eight and…it was bedlam. And then, on the final horn, eight o'clock horn, the union representatives and the employers would have been there and would have said, 'Go ahead' and 'Pick up dockers.' And it was bedlam. Especially if there was no work; if there were two or three jobs, they'd be pushing and shoving to get to the front, and it was degrading. It was degrading. And humiliating if you didn't get a job.[47]

As in Liverpool, one element of compensation arose in the numerous pubs of Sailortown that were home to the 'very heavy drinking people' depicted in the novels of John Campbell. Tommy M recognised how masculine identity and communal self-respect was chiselled out of some unlikely sources within the workplace also:

> The camaraderie amongst the dockers was second to none…the camaraderie at the dock was visible. Yes they'd have fought, yes they'd have argued, yes they'd have been nasty, with a capital N, but there was a hyper-dependence upon recognising people who were struggling, and the comedy, and the quick wit comment was so illumin-ating, it was unbelievable…I can remember some of the comments and the nicknames, and whatever, and you needed to have a skin as thick as a cow, ten cows (laughs) to survive.[48]

---

[46] Pat Ayers, 'The Making of Men: Masculinities in Interwar Liverpool', in *Working out Gender: Perspectives from Labour History*, ed. Margaret Walsh (Aldershot, 1999), 66–83.
[47] Interview with Tommy M. Interviewed by Hannah McDade, 22 Mar. 2013.
[48] *Ibid.*

What Tommy's interview did not reveal is that such workplace camarad-erie was possible due to a process of ethno-sectarian containment. Whilst some Catholic and Protestant males rubbed shoulders in the shared space of the dockland bars, they did not enter into potentially explosive competition with each other in the dockers' schooling pens. In 1912, a split in the workforce spawned two unions on the Belfast waterfront. Protestants joined the London-based National Union of Dock Labourers (NUDL), Catholics favoured the the Irish Transport and General Workers Union (ITWGU). This was also a division between those who identified as British or Irish and, as such, it was appropriate that the NUDL-affiliated dockers were responsible for cargo heading from and to Britain via the cross-channel docks. Meanwhile, the ITGWU dockers dealt with shipping from further afield, in the deep-sea docks.[49] Similar divisions in Belfast trade unions were commonplace but the casualised nature of work at the docks and the demographic profile of Sailortown made such an arrangement all the more import-ant.[50] This pragmatic management of ethno-sectarian differences pre-vented outbreaks of violence in the waterfront workplace and helps explains the prevalence of a 'golden age' discourse that featured in parts of the testimony. In this manner, the dockside unions created an element of stability in Belfast's most mixed working-class streets in the decades before the Troubles.

III Conclusion

How do these findings contribute to our initial questions about the nature of working-class nostalgia, oral history and memory in Northern Ireland and the potential of oral history to both reinvigorate the social history of post-war Belfast and challenge students to become active learners? In respect of nostalgic memory, the testimony collected from ex-Sailortown residents exhibited an element of what scholars of deindustrialisation dub 'double erasure'. This is a twin process in which communities lose the workplace around which the local economy revolves as well as the homes in which familial identities are embedded.[51] Moreover, regeneration in Sailortown rubbed salt into the psychological wounds of its former residents. This process included the creation of new commercial premises and waterfront apartments, but an additional factor was the construction of Titanic Belfast. The

---

[49] Lynch, *A Tale of Three Cities*, 35. For a discussion of the issue of ethno-sectarian relations in the Belfast labour movement, see Loughlin, *Labour and the Politics of Disloyalty*.

[50] Loughlin, *Labour and the Politics of Disloyalty*, 122

[51] *The Deindustrialized World: Confronting Ruination in Postindustrial Places*, ed. Steven High, Lachlan MacKinnon and Andrew Perchard (Vancouver, 2017), 6.

impressive hulk of this award-winning visitor centre looms over Sailortown from the opposite side of the River Lagan. Many ex-Sailortown residents feel excluded from the heritage celebrated in Titanic Belfast. Tommy M memorably captured this point in his interview when describing a Belfast wall mural he had scrutinised:

> it was of the Titanic going out of Belfast, fantastic colours, dynamic grasp of the moment. But there's something in the mural that everybody had ignored in talking about Titanic and remembering it. It shows a truck. A truck of two metal wheels, long shafts, like a barrow, and the heave would have been twelve bags on the ship. [It] shows you on the mural the dockers landing the bags…and that's what's been missing. The Titanic has ignored docks. The Titanic festival, the Titanic money, the Titanic image, the movement called 'The Titanic' has not recognised the docks.[52]

We could dismiss this and testimony collected about Sailortown as the product of a loosely defined nostalgic impulse that has limited historical merit. To do so, would be a blunder on two counts. First, it would underplay the complex dynamics behind the deployment of nostalgic narrative. Second, it would fail to account for other forms of sentiment that appeared in these testimonies. The exploration of nostalgic memory enables historians to comprehend how individuals endow past experience with meaning and use historical memory as a starting point for social commentary. It can be 'understood as a critique of dominant stigmatising representations' of working-class neighbourhoods or communities.[53] In the case of Tommy H's comment on Titanic Belfast, his autobiographical memory offered a powerful critique of the industrial heritage/gentrification agendas. The troubles with a lower case t were experienced by Catholics and Protestants alike in the Belfast docklands. John Campbell's testimony on the loss of dockland community and work is strikingly similar to that of Tommy H. As such, the conflicted aspect of the Sailortown memories were not between essentialised communal groups divided by irreconcilable and ethno-sectarian cultural scripts. As a reading of Ben Jones's work on working-class memory suggests, internal conflict was intrinsic to the memory and lives of the individuals encountered by the students. Nostalgia did feature as a trope but it sat alongside other forms of narrative motif making it impossible to apply simple categorisation to the dominant form of memory featuring in transcripts. The interviewees were forced to reflect on the impact of deindustrialisation, the destruction of their former homes and ethno-sectarian divisions. Amidst this complex history and buffeted by the emotions it stirred, John Clancy could both edit a poem to remove the stanzas that disrupted the nostalgic tone he chose to offer at the outset of his interview and, half an hour later, say this:

[52] Interview with Tommy M.
[53] Jones, 'The Uses of Nostalgia', 358.

They were a very heavy drinking people, you know, seamen and dockers...Some very sad cases there. It wasn't the first time that – even as a boy – now, it didn't happen in my home – but sometimes you were allowed to observe – especially with some of the dockers maybe when they got paid on a Thursday or Friday night and went...into a bar. You seen the kids coming up to get money from their daddies, so as they could buy maybe a couple of fish suppers and things like that. There were some sad times like that, y'know?

This is not to be dismissed as the confused and contradictory recall of an elderly man. The testimony that Clancy offered represented his own inter-action with larger historical narratives, including the causes of the Troubles, the erasure of workplace and community, as well as the legacies of these traumatic events. In the process, elements of nostalgia rubbed shoulders with comic anecdotes and frank commentary on some of the grimmer real-ities of post-war life in a working-class community. Jones was correct to urge the consideration of time and place, age, gender and life trajectory in each act of narration. In this case-study, the issue of ethno-sectarian iden-tity was a further variable. In terms of time and place, Sailortown provided testimony that differed in key ways from that collected by Bryson in mid-Ulster. Although the Troubles ravaged Belfast and inflamed sectarian-ism, common experiences of labour history and the shared trauma of the double erasure of community and workplace ensured that inter-views with Sailortown produce elements of a golden age discourse from Catholic, as well as Protestant, ex-residents.

In taking on this complex and difficult history, the students engaged on the module produced testimony that contributes importantly to two his-torical debates. They created the research material through which to add a case-study to historiographical discussions around nostalgia and working-class memory, one that very much supports Jones's arguments about the complexity of that memory. Moreover, the research also pro-vides a new perspective on Belfast's post-war history, one that demon-strates the value of examining the troubles with a lower case t as well as those with a capital T. One question remains, however, and that is what did the students learn from the experience of undertaking oral history interviews? One answer is that it fired historical enthusiasm among many students: four of the thirty-four are now undertaking Ph.D.s, with two working on oral histories of Belfast. One group of students worked subsequently with BBC Radio Ulster to produce a radio docu-mentary that was inspired by the oral history testimony: pitching docu-mentary ideas to the BBC represents the group-work presentation element of the module.[54] More fundamentally, the module produced impressive assignments by causing the students to reflect more deeply on

[54] This documentary was broadcast on BBC Radio Ulster and BBC Radio 5 Live. It can be accessed on IPlayer: www.bbc.co.uk/programmes/b05qgo6b#play.

their work than is the case with a regular history module; a factor recognised by the external examiner who oversaw this version of the module and those in subsequent years.

This paper will terminate with an illustration of the sophisticated reflection that is encouraged by the nature of the oral history interaction. The example deployed here focuses on a final variable in the interviewing process, one discussed above: the identity of the student carrying out each interview. The students worked in pairs, with one asking the questions and the other taking responsibility for the technical elements of the recording. The pair then shared the task of transcribing their interview before submitting individual critical commentaries on the experience. Extracts from the work of two students reveal a number of further issues around teaching difficult history in this way. The extracts are from Anthony (from a Catholic/Nationalist background) and Duncan (from a Protestant/Unionist background) and their reflections on their interview with Pat (a retired docker in his seventies). Duncan wrote:

> Anthony went on to the next topic, something which he personally has a great interest in, that of sporting tradition. There was an instant bond between the two; this became noticeable throughout the rest of the interview. The two were able to exchange knowledge of Gaelic Football. I noticed a change of atmosphere not only from Pat, but also from Anthony. At one stage, Pat got that excited he jumped from his seat to get a book about his Gaelic team forgetting he was wired to a microphone, though with quick movement we were able to carry the connections with him and save the recording. This strong bond, the two had struck, was a factor throughout the rest of the interview. Although this had positive aspects, such as an in depth analysis of something which obviously meant so much to Pat, it did have negative aspects also in my opinion. This section of the interview seemed to go on for an extremely long time, with the emphasis moving away from Sailortown...As someone who was there to listen in, I could not intervene to recover what I thought was a failing interview, due to it moving fast from its original purpose, the story of Sailortown. Though on hindsight, and from transcriptions, it is clear that the interviewer did move on, and it was perhaps my initial lack of knowledge on the subject, and urge to hear about Sailortown that made it feel so long. This is without doubt a negative aspect of carrying out the interview process in pairs...When the interview was complete and we were engaged in casual small talk with Pat, he showed us a picture of himself and others and stated 'This was taken when we had burned Long Kesh.' When I asked him to repeat, his reply was that he had served a ten-year jail term for blowing up a shop in the Troubles. Personally, I found this very hard to take in as my family's personal experiences during the Troubles came flooding back. The Troubles were obviously something which Pat could relate to in a major way having served time for a terrorist offence. The ten-year jail term also led us to question the dates he had given us for his time in the docks. This was a significant chapter of Pat's life which the interview had not picked up on. Though I do feel he would have been reluctant to tell us about it.[55]

Anthony wrote:

> The momentum of the conversation itself also proved a factor in shaping the course of the interview.

[55] Critical commentary by Duncan (pseudonym), Mar. 2013.

As it was centred very much on Pat's own personal experiences, the discussion inevitably turned to his love for GAA [Gaelic Athletic Association] and, in particular, his lifelong team Patrick Pearse's. This common sporting ground between interviewer and interviewee was important in the indulgence of 'football talk' that perhaps bogged down the mid-point of the conversation but nonetheless offered a valuable insight into Pat's personal interests and the importance of sport in local life...The relaxed, anecdotal style of narrative employed by Pat, while discussing the main themes, offered an incisive yet somewhat piecemeal understanding of his own life and that of the broader community. Of course, while there is some form of chronological sequencing explained throughout the interview, Pat relied heavily on anecdotes, often deliberately ('there's another cracking story'), which greatly fluctuated any viable time-frame that could have been attached to these ad-hoc tales. However, this style of narrative is not necessarily a limitation: rather, as Ashplant points out, 'transpositions in time and place...are all now seen as potentially revealing'.[56] The shifts and discrepancies in Pat's memory are of worth to understanding the particular motivation behind what he has said, and most potently, what he has not. This is of particular relevance when we examine the end of Pat's tenure in Sailortown. While the 71 year-old's memory in many instances is amazingly sharp (particularly in his rather moving account of the death of his younger brother Gerard, when Pat was only a toddler), other later aspects of his life remain hazy or, to the outsider at least, difficult to clarify. When asked about the opposition to the road works that ultimately saw the demise of Sailortown, Pat is hesitant and rather ill-informed of the various movements established at the time to prevent such construction. The details of when he left Sailortown to live in the New Lodge also failed to be expanded upon...The reason for these discrepancies were answered soon after the tape had stopped running; when displaying a china plate adorned with an image of himself, his elder brother Hugh and a priest, he remarked, entirely at ease, that the photo was taken while they were in Long Kesh, for 'shoplifting' as he coyly described it. While expressed so freely off the record, any mention of the Troubles during the interview itself was confined to light-hearted tales of mischief, a clear indicator that Pat was possibly concerned with the direction any kind of straight, chronological questioning may have led. Perhaps the anecdotal style Pat so masterfully employed was most useful in preventing the narrative escaping from his grasp.[57]

The two extracts indicate the extent to which students embarked on the research with strongly engrained cultural experiences that had the potential to influence the intersubjective interaction within the interview as well as its subsequent interpretation. They reveal the students' different responses to a relatively run-of-the mill aspect of the interviewee's testimony and a revelatory post-interview comment. It would be inaccurate to conclude that their experience of pursuing difficult historical research changed their worldview fundamentally, but both students worked through the challenges thrown up in a contemplative fashion that demonstrates that employing oral history in the curriculum forces students to reflect innovatively about historical evidence. Moreover, this

[56] T. G. Ashplant, 'Anecdote as Narrative Resource in Working-Class Life Stories', in *Narrative and Genre: Contexts and Types of Communication*, ed. M. Chamberlain and P. Thompson (1998), 99.
[57] Critical commentary by Anthony (pseudonym), Mar. 2013.

example also reiterates the significance of the issues discussed earlier around memory and narrative style. In this case, in the moments after the interview concluded the two young students were made aware of the significant editing of the narrator's life story that had taken place and why that was the case. One student remarks intelligently on the use of anecdote as a means through which Pat subtly imposed his control on the testimony that emerged. In doing so, he built a firewall against the possibility of questions that might yield on the record revelations about his imprisonment during the conflict. Ironically, while Pat removed his role in the Troubles from his recorded testimony, his post-interview postscript provides one last learning outcome from this undergraduate exercise: this time for the lecturer. The example indicates the extent to which any project on Belfast history that attempts to focus solely on the troubles with a lower case t will inevitably face the reality of having to factor in, in one way or another, the Troubles.

Transactions of the RHS 28 (2018), pp. 241–264 © Royal Historical Society 2018
doi:10.1017/S0080440118000129

THE RISE AND FALL(?) OF AMERICA'S NEOLIBERAL ORDER*

By Gary Gerstle

READ 5 MAY 2017

ABSTRACT. This paper argues that the last eighty years of American politics can be understood in terms of the rise and fall of two political orders. The first political order grew out of the New Deal, dominating political life from the 1930s to the 1970s. The history of this order (the New Deal Order) is now well known. The other order, best understood as 'neoliberal' in its politics, emerged from the economic and political crises of the 1970s. This paper is one of the first to elucidate the political relationships, ideological character and moral perspective that were central to this neoliberal order's rise and triumph. The paper's narrative unfolds in three acts: the first chronicles the 1980s rise of Ronald Reagan and the laissez-faire Republican party he forced into being; the second shows how the collapse of communism in the late 1980s and early 1990s accelerated the globalization of capitalism and elevated neoliberalism's prestige; and the third reveals how a Democratic president, Bill Clinton, facilitated his party's capitulation to neoliberal imperatives. Political orders encourage such capitulation, the paper argues, by universalizing their own ideological principles and making alternative ideologies seem marginal and unworkable. A coda shows how the Great Recession of 2008 fractured America's neoliberal order, diminishing its authority and creating a space in which different kinds of politics, including the right-wing populism of Donald Trump and the left-wing populism of Bernie Sanders, could flourish.

Some years ago, I published with Steve Fraser a coedited book, *The Rise and Fall of the New Deal Order, 1930–1980.* The title aptly conveyed the book's contents: namely, that a political order originating in the Great Depression and the New Deal dominated American politics from the 1930s through the late 1960s and early 1970s, when decay and decline

*I wish to thank the Royal Historical Society, and its past and current presidents, Peter Mandler and Margot Finn, for persuading me to go public with my thoughts on American neoliberalism. I also wish to thank Sven Beckert, Steve Fraser, Art Goldhammer, Joel Isaac, Alex Jacobs, Ira Katznelson, Russ Kazal, Michael Kazin, Desmond King, Nelson Lichtenstein, Liz Lunbeck, Lisa McGirr, Jim Sparrow and an anonymous reader for the *TRHS* for their invaluable feedback on earlier drafts of this paper. Thanks, finally, to Jonathan Goodwin for his research assistance, to Andrew Spicer for expertly guiding this work from lecture to published paper and to Linda Randall for her copyediting.

set in. 'The New Deal Order', we wrote, possessed an 'ideological character, a moral perspective, and a set of political relationships among policy elites, interest groups, and electoral constituencies that decidedly shaped American political life for forty years.'[1]

In this paper, I use the framework that Fraser and I developed then to analyse the political order that arose out of that old order's debris. This new order I am calling America's neoliberal order. My goal is to elucidate the political relationships, ideological character and moral perspective that facilitated the neoliberal order's rise and triumph in the 1980s and 1990s, and to offer some speculations on how far it has fallen. To frame this dissection properly, I first offer a brief review of the New Deal Order itself.

I

The New Deal Order arose in the 1930s and 1940s, during the years of the Great Depression and the Second World War. At its heart stood a powerful Democratic party, dominant in its ability to win elections consistently. Southern and eastern European immigrants and their American-born children formed a key constituency in the North; white Protestant voters constituted an equally important constituency in the South. A large and mobilized labour movement provided many of the Democratic party's shock troops. They were matched in influence by sectors of the business class persuaded that their industries would benefit from the full employment, mass consumption system of regulated capitalism that the New Deal promised to create.

The New Deal Order gained its power not just from dependable electoral and business constituencies but from its ability to implant its core ideological principles on American politics. One such principle was that unfettered capitalism had become a destructive force, generating economic instability and inequalities too great for American society to tolerate. Only a strong federal government could ease this destructive chaos and manage capitalism's growth in the public interest. Keynesianism expressed this commitment to a regulated capitalism; New Dealers adopted a vernacular form of it in 1935 and 1936 and formally embraced it in the 1940s.

The New Deal's commitment to arranging a class compromise between the warring forces of capital and labour similarly expressed the imperative of curtailing capitalism's destructive chaos. Strikes abounded in the 1930s. Employers often responded with violence. To remedy this situation, the New Deal put in place a system for managing labour relations that curbed employer power and gave workers more

---

[1] *The Rise and Fall of the New Deal Order, 1930–1980*, ed. Steve Fraser and Gary Gerstle (Princeton, 1989), xi.

workplace rights than they had previously enjoyed. The New Deal thereby facilitated the growth in the labour movement from less than three million members to more than fifteen million, from less than 10 per cent of the work force to more than 35 per cent. Thus strengthened, workers were able to compel employers to share a higher percentage of their revenue and profits with their employees.

New Dealers also forced into existence fiscal and social policies that benefited the poor. A large welfare state emerged for the first time, much of it funded by the New Deal's commitment to progressive taxation. In 1935, the taxation rate on the wealthiest Americans rose to 75 per cent. In the Second World War, it rose further, to an astounding 91 per cent, the level at which it remained until the 1960s. Economic inequality, as a consequence, fell in the 1940s to its lowest point in the twentieth century, and it stayed there as long the New Deal Order prevailed.[2]

Perhaps nothing indicates the power of a political order more than its ability to shape the thinking of its opponents. Thus, Dwight D. Eisenhower, when he became, in 1953, the first Republican to enter the White House in twenty years, accepted the high rates of taxation that the New Deal Democrats had put in place. He did so with regard to the rest of the New Deal Order's ideological and policy package as well: that labour should be strong, that capitalism ought to be managed in the public interest and that a generous welfare state was a necessity. As Eisenhower wrote to his brother in the early 1950s, 'Should any political party attempt to abolish social security, unemployment insurance, and eliminate labour laws…, you would not hear of that party again in our political history.'[3] His then vice-president, Richard Nixon, shared this perspective, commenting himself after he became president in 1969: 'We are all Keynesians now.'[4] Today, uttering such statements would get an individual banished from the Republican party.

If the New Deal Order rested on durable electoral constituencies and a hegemonic ideological character, it also brought into politics a distinct moral perspective: namely, that personal fulfilment mattered, and that the government ought to amplify opportunities for individuals to achieve it. New Dealers defined fulfilment in marketplace terms, and often measured happiness by the quantity and variety of consumer

[2] Gary Gerstle, *Liberty and Coercion: The Paradox of American Government from the Founding to the Present* (Princeton, 2015), chs. 7 and 8; Thomas Piketty, *Capital in the Twenty-First Century* (Cambridge, MA, 2014).

[3] Eisenhower to Edgar Newton Eisenhower, 8 Nov. 1954, *The Papers of Dwight D. Eisenhower*, XV, *The Presidency: The Middle Way* (Baltimore, 1970–2001), 1386.

[4] Daniel Stedman Jones, *Masters of the Universe: Hayek, Friedman, and the Birth of a Neoliberal Politics* (Princeton, 2014), 221.

goods that citizens were able to purchase. But this marketplace orienta-
tion entailed more than materialism. For one, it carried a strong egalitarian message: participation in the marketplace was to be made available to
all Americans regardless of class, race, gender, religion or nationality.
New Dealers viewed consumption in qualitative terms too, believing
that a precocious and alluring marketplace would enhance the possibilities for individual expressiveness. Such expressiveness would compensate
for the growing impersonality of public life, now dominated by large
institutions – corporations, centralized labour unions and big government. New Dealers believed that the personal could be managed as skil-
fully as the economic. They had great confidence in secular expertise – in
the hard sciences, to be sure, but also in soft science: sociology, anthropology, psychiatry and social work – and in the ability of government to
spread the benefits of such expertise through the citizenry. Happiness
and expressiveness through consumption; the capacity of the marketplace
to deliver on America's egalitarian promise; and a faith in the ability of
expertise to nurture individuality: these were the components of the
New Deal Order's moral perspective.

It is worth stating what this moral perspective declined to engage: religion. Neither Roosevelt nor Eisenhower was a deeply religious man.
Eisenhower did say that it was important that Americans believe in a
god, though he also said he did not much care which deity they wor-
shipped. Keeping faith at a distance was in part strategic: suspicions
between Catholics and Protestants still ran deep, and Democrats
needed the support of both groups for their political order to flourish.
The best way to satisfy both constituencies was to keep religion out of
politics. But the absence of religion from the New Deal Order's moral
perspective reflected something deeper: a belief that a secular government was superior to one built on faith, and that religion was best left
to the private realm and individual choice.[5]

II

In *The Rise and Fall of the New Deal Order*, Fraser and I downplayed the
importance of two-, four- and six- year electoral cycles, and of particular
political actors – presidents, senators and others. Some presidents such as

---

[5] My interpretation of Eisenhower dissents from the argument offered in Kevin Kruse's
recent book, which places Eisenhower at the centre of America's post-war religious revival.
Eisenhower did bring new forms of religious observance into government but did not
partake of the fervour – or singlemindedness – that characterized the evangelical move-
ment. See Kevin M. Kruse, *One Nation under God: How Corporate America Invented Christian
America* (New York, 2015). My own view of religion and the public sphere in 1950s
America is closer to that of Kevin Schultz, *Tri-Faith America: How Postwar Catholics and
Jews Held America to its Protestant Promise* (New York, 2011).

Roosevelt were, of course, critical, as were certain elections. But not all elections and presidents mattered to the same degree. Also, our conception of the political extended well beyond the electoral process itself to encompass economic structures and interests on the one hand and configurations of moral life on the other. Fundamental changes in political life we saw as issuing from profound crises in the nation's economy, social structure and political culture. And those crises did not happen often. Between those crises, it made sense to focus less on individual politicians and more on the economic and political structures, the ideologies and moralities, on which American politics rested.

This argument for stasis and stability did not mean that we expunged conflict or change from our history of the fifty-year period extending from the Great Depression to the election of Ronald Reagan. To the contrary, our history was full of conflict. The New Deal Order itself did not emerge fully blown – plucked, as it were, from a Sears Roebuck catalogue – but in fits and starts. Certain issues such as race it could highlight but not resolve. The emphasis on individual expressiveness that it endorsed accelerated a series of changes in cultural life that it could not contain. It proved vulnerable to a war gone horribly wrong in Vietnam and then to major reorientations in the world economy that undermined the international American hegemony on which the New Deal Order had come to rest. But the order that the New Deal had birthed in the 1930s was still recognizable in the 1970s. And, then, by the 1980s and the 1990s, it was gone.

That which now draws my attention back to questions of a political order – how one forms, how it exercises political power and how it breaks up – is that another one may be in the process of passing away before our very eyes. This political order is a neoliberal one – not a perfect name for this order but the best one we have. We do not yet know whether this order will actually fall, or find ways to repair itself. But regardless of whether or not its time is up, I believe it would be useful to take the measure of its life, using the framework that Fraser and I developed to understand the New Deal Order: what have been its core constituencies? What have been its key ideological principles, and when, exactly, did they achieve hegemony over American politics? What has been this order's moral perspective? And what have been its vulnerabilities, inconsistencies and contradictions?

I start with a naming exercise, a more difficult enterprise than what confronted Fraser and me when naming the New Deal Order. Franklin Roosevelt made the phrase the 'New Deal' his calling card, and it worked. No slogan of equivalent influence has emerged to describe the order that arose out of the New Deal Order's fall. Not even the great architect of this order and its chief phrasemaker, Ronald Reagan, came up with one.

The most logical move might be to label this order with the word preferred by its creators: 'conservative'. But the word 'conservative' is not a good descriptor of the commitment to laissez-faire capitalism that lies at the heart of this order's political economy. Laissez-faire capitalism connotes dynamism, creative destruction, irreverence towards institutions and to the complex web of relations that imbed individuals in those institutions. Laissez-faire capitalism, in other words, is the enemy of what conservatives in the classical sense value: order, hierarchy, tradition, imbeddedness, continuity. Indeed, in America, the supporters of laissez-faire capitalism only took the name conservative because Roosevelt and the New Dealers stole the name 'liberalism' from them. How New Deal liberals pulled off that heist is a story for another time and place.

The word 'neoliberal' itself is not a perfect term to describe this order either.[6] On the left, it too often becomes an epithet hurled at America when the nation is thought to have exercised its power illegitimately. By these terms, an American strike on North Korea might be described as an exercise in neoliberalism. This is a form of silliness that ought to be resisted. But we should not thereby refrain from using the word 'neoliberalism', for it focuses our attention on modern efforts to infuse political economy with the principles of classical liberalism. Classical liberalism discerned in markets extraordinary dynamism and possibilities for generating trade, wealth and a rising standard of living. It sought to liberate the market from encumbrances: monarchy, mercantilism, bureaucracy, artificial borders and tariffs. It sought, in other words, to release the economy from the heavy hand of the state, in its various guises. It wanted to allow people to move around in pursuit of self-interest and fortune; to truck, barter and trade as they saw fit. Classical liberalism wanted to let individual talent rise (or fall) to its natural level. It carried within it emancipatory, even utopian, hopes of people freed and a world transformed.

All these elements of liberalism, including the emancipatory yearnings, are present in the great liberal manifesto of the late eighteenth century, *The Wealth of Nations*, by Adam Smith.[7] In nineteenth-century Europe, liberals relinquished much of this emancipatory spirit, which increasingly

---

[6] See Daniel Rodgers, 'The Uses and Abuses of "Neoliberalism"', *Dissent* (Winter 2018), www.dissentmagazine.org/article/uses-and-abuses-neoliberalism-debate; and the very interesting forum that appeared in response to Rodgers's essay: 'Debating the Uses and Abuses of "Neoliberalism": A Forum', with comments by Julia Ott, Nathan Connolly, Mike Konczal and Timothy Shenk, and a reply by Daniel Rodgers, *Dissent*, 22 Jan. 2018. www.dissentmagazine.org/online_articles/debating-uses-abuses-neoliberalism-forum, both accessed on 31 May 2018.

[7] Adam Smith, *An Inquiry into the Nature and Causes of The Wealth of Nations* (1776; New York, 1965).

became the property of the left. In the middle decades of that century, European liberals were expending as much energy guarding their ideas against the revolutionaries of 1848 and the Communards of 1870 as they were attacking monarchical states. They had come to fear the left, the alleged carrier of anarchy, as much as the right. They wanted to distinguish themselves from the left by delineating orderly and constitutional paths of political development.[8] Something of this liberal reorientation appeared in America at this time. One can discern in the late nineteenth-century writing of Theodore Roosevelt and Woodrow Wilson, for example, a concern for the destructive effects of the left and an insistence that liberalism would succeed only if it prized order, constitutional and social.[9] Nevertheless, liberalism in America retained its hopeful, even emancipatory, cast. It had, after all, been born in revolution and in such utopian declarations that 'all men are created equal'. Woodrow Wilson was nothing if not a liberal utopianist, especially in regard to world affairs, where he expressed a desire to fight a 'war to end all wars', to achieve a 'peace without a victory', and to establish an international parliament (a 'League of Nations') that would govern the world according to liberal principles.[10]

The emancipatory spirit is very much present in the thinking of those in America whom I am labelling neoliberals. In fact, the presence of this spirit helps to explain the power of the neoliberal appeal, not just on the right but in some portions of an erstwhile left, especially an erstwhile New Left. The freedom of movement, the freedom to don different identities, the ability to live as a cosmopolitan, the ability to think outside the box, as the hippie capitalist Steve Jobs did so brilliantly: these spring from a certain kind of liberal imagination. Which is why the term 'conservative' is really a poor description of this disposition.[11]

Much good work has been done by scholars in reconstructing the history of neoliberal thought, beginning with Friedrich von Hayek and Ludwig von Mises in 1930s Austria, and continuing with the emergence of new centres of neoliberal thought in America and Britain during the

[8] See, for example, Stephen W. Sawyer, 'An American Model for French Liberalism: The State of Exception in Edouard Laboulaye's Constitutional Thought', *Journal of Modern History*, 4 (2013), 739–71; Stephen W. Sawyer, *Demos Assembled: Democracy and the International Origins of the Modern State, 1840–1880* (Chicago, 2018), ch. 4.

[9] See Gary Gerstle, *American Crucible: Race and Nation in the Twentieth Century* (Princeton, expanded edn, 2017), chs. 1 and 2; Gary Gerstle, 'Race and Nation in the Thought and Politics of Woodrow Wilson', in *Reconsidering Woodrow Wilson: Progressivism, Internationalism, War, and Peace*, ed. John Milton Cooper, Jr (Washington, DC, and Baltimore, 2008), 93–124.

[10] Thomas Knock, *To End All Wars: Woodrow Wilson and the Quest for a New World Order* (Princeton, 1995); Erez Manela, *The Wilsonian Moment: Self-Determination and the International Origins of Anticolonial Nationalism* (New York, 2007).

[11] On Jobs, see Walter Isaacson, *Steve Jobs* (New York, 2013).

post-war.[12] I have learned a lot from this work, and it informs what I am doing here. But I am not primarily interested in tracking the genealogies of neoliberal thought itself. I am interested instead in when this thought became dominant in America, when it developed the capacity to sustain a political order. This story unfolds in three acts: the first is the rise in the 1970s and 1980s of Ronald Reagan and the laissez-faire Republican party he forced into being; the second is the fall of the Soviet Union and, more broadly, of communism in the late 1980s and early 1990s; and the third is the emergence in the mid-1990s of Bill Clinton as the Democratic Eisenhower, the man who arranged his party's acquiescence to neoliberalism.

III

By far the most important figure in the rise of the neoliberal order was Ronald Reagan, president from 1981 to 1989. He had once been a New Dealer himself, the only chief executive in American history who had apprenticed for that high office as president of a labour union, in this case the Screen Actors Guild in the 1940s. In the course of his union presidency, Reagan encountered communists up close and personal. They were then a powerful force in Hollywood. He developed a profound distaste for them personally, for their tactics, which he considered underhanded, and, most of all for their political principles, which he saw as collectivizing and socializing all property in the hands of a totalitarian state. I doubt Reagan was reading Hayek in the 1940s but, by the end of that decade, he shared Hayek's belief that communism was threatening the world with a new form of serfdom. If communism were to succeed, it would surely crush the West's, and America's, greatest gift to the world: freedom, and personal liberty.[13]

By the 1950s, Reagan had come to share Hayek's belief that the comprehensive regulatory apparatus established by the New Deal had opened the door to Soviet-style collectivism in America. Thus, to protect liberty, the New Deal had to be taken down. Reagan believed that America was 'the last best hope of man' in a world threatened

---

[12] See, for example, Angus Burgin, *The Great Persuasion: Reinventing Free Markets since the Depression* (Cambridge, MA, 2015); Stedman Jones, *Masters of the Universe: The Road from Mont Pelerin: The Making of the Neoliberal Thought Collective*, ed. Philip Morowski and Dieter Plehwe (Cambridge, MA, 2009); William Davies, 'The New Neoliberalism', *New Left Review*, 101 (2016), https://libsta28.lib.cam.ac.uk:2742/II/101/william-davies-the-new-neoliberalism, accessed 1 June 2018; Quinn Slobodian, *The Globalists: The End of Empire and the Birth of Neoliberalism* (Cambridge, MA, 2018); and Wendy Brown, *Undoing the Demos: Neoliberalism's Stealth Revolution* (New York, 2015).

[13] On Reagan's early years in politics, see Lou Cannon, *Reagan* (New York, 1982); and Iwan Morgan, *Reagan: American Icon* (2016).

everywhere by communist tyranny. But it would only be able to deliver on its promise if it first put its own house in order, which meant dismantling the New Deal. If Americans failed in this essential task, Reagan averred, they would be sentencing future generations to what he called 'a thousand years of darkness'.[14]

Few people took Reagan or Hayek seriously in the 1950s or 1960s. The New Deal Order was riding high. But by the 1970s, things had changed. Indeed, the economic decline of the 1970s forms the critical backdrop to neoliberalism's rise. The steady economic growth on which the New Deal Order had depended for its support stalled during these years. The combination of rising inflation and rising unemployment confounded Keynesian policymakers. The war in Vietnam, concluding with America's defeat in 1975, had unsettled US society at home and diminished the nation's prestige abroad. Suddenly, the international stage was populated with rivals to and antagonists of America beyond the communists themselves. The cartelisation of oil producers in the Middle East profoundly changed the terms of the international petroleum economy, to the disadvantage of the United States and other industrialised nations. The resurgence of manufacturing in Germany and Japan also challenged American international dominance. President Richard Nixon's decision in 1971 to abandon the Bretton Woods agreement that had underpinned America's reconstruction of world markets, trade and finance since 1945 deepened doubts about the future of America's global preeminence.[15]

Racial turmoil further unsettled the New Deal Order's politics. In response to the civil rights protests of the 1960s, the federal government had embarked on a vast programme of racial remediation to put blacks and whites on the same plane. The reach of the federal state expanded dramatically, as it sought to dismantle not just apartheid regimes in the ex-Confederate states but also informal practices of racial inequality that had long shaped corporate hiring, real estate practices and university admissions everywhere in the country. This vast expansion of the federal state did little, in the short term, to improve either the performance of the economy or to reconcile the black and white races. Enlarging government authority without a corresponding improvement in social conditions was an explosive mix, especially in a society traditionally

[14] Ronald Reagan, 'A Time for Choosing' (speech at 1964 Republican Convention, 27 Oct. 1964), in Ronald Reagan, *A Time for Choosing: The Speeches of Ronald Reagan, 1961–1982* (Chicago, 1983), 43, 57.

[15] Judith Stein, *How the United States Traded Factories for Finance in the 1970s* (New Haven, 2010); Jefferson R. Cowie, *Stayin' Alive: The 1970s and the Last Days of the Working Class* (New York, 2010); Meg Jacobs, *Panic at the Pump: The Economic Crisis and the Transformation of American Politics in the 1970s* (New York, 2016); *Rightward Bound: Making America Conservative in the 1970s*, ed. Bruce J. Schulman and Julian E. Zelizer (Cambridge, MA, 2008).

hostile to the exercise of power by the national state. These were the circumstances under which key Democratic party constituencies, including white southerners and northern white ethnics (most of them descendants of early twentieth-century immigrants from eastern and southern Europe), began to look to the Republican party for solutions to America's vexing problems.[16]

Reagan entered politics in the 1960s as an early tribune of disaffected white Americans. His surprise election to the governorship of California in 1966 – and reelection in 1970 – were early signs of a populist force rising in the Republican party. Reagan took a strong stand both against the black insurrections that were convulsing America's cities and the student rebellions that were upending the country's most prestigious universities. America would descend into anarchy, he warned, if law and order were not restored. He condemned the expanding welfare state for offering handouts to the 'undeserving poor'. He wanted to force government to abandon all efforts at 'social engineering', a goal that could be most effectively accomplished by denying the state its flow of tax revenue. He wanted to release America's capitalist energies from the straitjacket that the New Deal Order had imposed on them. He presented himself as the implacable foe of those whom he had identified as America's enemies: black nationalists and criminals; pampered university students deluded by dreams of liberation; pot-smoking hippies; tax-and-spend liberals; and, the masterminds, in the Soviet Union and elsewhere, of international communist revolution.[17]

Despite his success in California, the national news media and party organizations did not take Reagan's rise seriously. Thus, his election to the presidency in 1980 came as a shock, almost as great as that generated by the election of Donald Trump thirty-six years later. Millions in America believed that Reagan's temperament and background as an actor (and a B-list actor at that) rendered him unfit for office. He was widely disparaged as an intellectual lightweight. He had trouble identifying a book he had read. He appeared to compensate for his ignorance with an extraordinary capacity to make things up: seeing the world as he imagined it should be rather than as it was. He encouraged what looked like reckless, nuclear brinkmanship with the Soviets. He could not stop himself from name-calling, even when those names insulted powerful nations. People ran for their fall-out shelters whenever Reagan hurled the epithet 'evil empire' at the Soviet Union or talked about arming NATO forces in Germany with tactical nuclear weapons. Did Reagan have any idea what he was doing? Or was he just playing out the narrative of *Star Wars* – Luke Skywalker vs Darth Vader – in real life? When he

---

[16] Gerstle, *Liberty and Coercion*, ch. 10.
[17] Morgan, *Reagan*, ch. 5.

was not stirring up trouble in world affairs, he indulged his love for old world ceremony, much of it directed toward restyling the White House to resemble the court of Marie Antoinette. And where did he get his idea of what the court of Marie Antoinette ought to look like? From the movie, *Singing in the Rain*, of course. Reagan, not Trump, was the first fabulist to sit in the White House.[18]

But Reagan was a more serious man than Trump is. Reagan really did want to bring the Soviet Union down, and believed he could. He really did believe that the New Deal was a form of collectivist tyranny, and thought he could bring that order down too. He imposed his will on the Republican party, rendering it a far more radical organization – in its commitment to laissez-faire capitalism – than it had been. He brought into government advisers and cabinet members well connected to the intellectual circles where neoliberalism had been percolating in the 1970s. The University of Chicago had been a crucial site of neoliberalism's incubation. Hayek and Mises had both spent substantial time there in the 1950s. Milton Friedman worked in Hyde Park his entire career, becoming the foremost advocate of neoliberal thinking in the 1970s. James M. Buchanan had trained at Chicago in the 1950s, before taking his brand of neoliberalism to Virginia (first the University of Virginia and then George Mason University) where he had become famous for founding a second school associated with neoliberal economics and public policy.[19]

These intellectual circles intersected with groups of Republican party financial backers whose encounter with collectivism was less intellectual than visceral. These wealthy Americans had come to loathe the labour unions with whom they were forced to deal, as well as government agencies that were compelling them to transform HR practices radically in the pursuit of racial equity. Believing that they were engaged in a political war, these wealthy Americans allocated a significant portion of their fortunes to support foundations, think tanks and media outlets where the right kind of ideas could be developed and then deployed. The list of conservative think tanks founded in the 1970s is impressive, among them the Cato Institute, supported by the Midwest industrial titan, Charles Koch; the Heritage Foundation, funded by beer magnate, Joseph Coors and Mellon heir, Richard Mellon Scaife; and the Manhattan Foundation. Older think tanks, such as the American

---

[18] Garry Wills, *Reagan's America: Innocents at Home* (New York, 2000); Debora Silverman, *Selling Culture: Bloomingdale's, Diana Vreeland, and the New Aristocracy of Taste in Reagan's America* (New York, 1989); Michael Rogin, *Ronald Reagan, The Movie, and Other Episodes in Political Demonology* (Los Angeles, 1988).

[19] On James Buchanan, see Nancy MacLean, *Democracy in Chains: The Deep History of the Radical Right's Stealth Plan for America* (New York, 2017).

Enterprise Institute, took on new life. William Simon, secretary of the treasury under Nixon and an Ayn Rand devotee, formed an Executive Advisory Committee of prominent businessmen who were convinced that Reagan was their man. Simon had published *A Time of Truth* in 1978 calling for "'a massive and unprecedented mobilization of the moral, intellectual and financial resources" of business to "aid the intellectuals and writers" who were fighting on the side of capitalism'. This pro-capitalist Counter-Establishment was in place by 1980. And its leaders were ready to serve as consiglieres to the Reagan administration.[20]

Reagan quickly pushed through Congress neoliberal policies that had been gestating in this Counter-Establishment's think tanks. One core policy was what Reagan and others called deregulation: removing government from the business of overseeing private industry. Reagan's predecessor as president, Jimmy Carter, had already taken the first steps in this direction, rolling back the government's regulation of telecommunications, the airlines and trucking. Reagan advanced this policy by deregulating the savings and loan thrift associations, which handled home mortgages, traditionally the most regulated sector of the financial industry. He also moved quickly on two other policy fronts, closely related to deregulation; first, crushing the power of organized labour, an ambition that became clear when, soon after assuming office, he fired 10,000 unionized air traffic controllers; and second, eliminating the progressive tax regime that the New Deal had put in place, slashing the tax rates on America's highest income earners by a remarkable 60 per cent. Reagan believed that unions and a government bent on using tax revenues for purposes of redistribution harmed the operation of a free market, the productive use of capital and thus the generation of growth and wealth. The American economy would flourish only when unions and a tax-rich government were brought to heel and, if possible, eliminated. A more direct assault on the principles of the New Deal Order could scarcely be imagined.[21]

Whether Reagan would succeed to the point not only of damaging the New Deal Order but also of establishing a neoliberal one – a political

[20] As quoted in Kim Phillips-Fein, *Invisible Hands: The Making of the Conservative Movement from the New Deal to Reagan* (New York, 2008), 245. For another neoliberal manifesto from the era, see George Gilder, *Wealth and Poverty* (New York, 1981). See also Jane Mayer, *Dark Money: The Hidden History of the billionaires behind the Rise of the Radical Right* (New York, 2016); MacLean, *Democracy in Chains*; and Sidney Blumenthal, *The Rise of the Counter-Establishment: The Conservative Ascent to Power* (New York, 1986).

[21] Joseph A. McCartin, *Collision Course: Ronald Reagan, Air Traffic Controllers, and the Strike that Changed America* (New York, 2011); Nelson Lichtenstein, *State of the Union: A Century of American Labor* (Princeton, 2013); Gerstle, *Liberty and Coercion*, ch. 10; Sean Wilentz, *The Age of Reagan: A History, 1974–2008* (New York, 2008).

formation able not only to win elections but to compel the opposition to accede to its worldview – was unclear for much of the 1980s. Democrats held power in at least one of the houses of Congress across the 1980s. Many in their ranks were drawn to aspects of deregulation, but they fought tooth and nail the diminution of organized labour and Reagan's efforts to roll back the welfare state and racial remediation.[22] Meanwhile, Republican ranks were themselves divided, between traditional Republicans (including Reagan's vice-president, George H. W. Bush) who preached fiscal discipline, and 'supply-siders' such as Congressman Jack Kemp, whose major concern was to release the animal spirits of the capitalist economy without worrying too about balanced budgets or other aspects of the bottom line. For much of the 1980s, it was not clear who would win these battles.[23] But then an event of world historical importance fundamentally altered both international and domestic politics: that was the fall between 1989 and 1991 of the Soviet Union. More broadly what fell, of course, was communism, and, more consequentially, the communist century.[24]

Arguably, there was no more important event of the twentieth century than the Russian Revolution, in terms of its influence on world affairs. In the fifty years after their rise to power in Russia, communists walled off large parts of the world – the vast Soviet Union itself, then half of Europe and then China – from capitalist economics. For the first third of the Cold War era, communism was a serious threat in Western Europe; for the first two-thirds of the Cold War, it posed a similar threat across innumerable nations emerging in Africa and Asia, and across Latin America. Fascism, and Nazism, can be understood as radical right responses to communism's rise. Meanwhile, in the United States, from the 1920s forward, communism was regarded as a mortal threat to the American way of life. The Great Depression and the Second World War moderated America's anti-communism, but only temporarily. No other force had a comparable influence on world or American politics across the twentieth century.[25]

---

[22] On the persistence of Democratic party power and politics, see the essays in Julian E. Zelizer, *The Revival of Political History* (Princeton, 2012).

[23] Wilentz, *The Age of Reagan*.

[24] I have not been able to identify the first time I came across the phrase 'communist century', though I believe that the writer and historian Theodore Draper introduced me to it. For Draper's views on communism, see his *The Roots of American Communism* (New York, 1957), and *American Communism and Soviet Russia: The Formative Period* (1960; New York, 1986). Draper was a Trotskyist turned anti-communist.

[25] Eric Hobsbawm, *The Age of Extremes: A History of the World, 1914–1991* (New York, 1994); Odd Arne Westad, *The Cold War: A World History* (New York, 2017); Odd Arne Westad, *The Global Cold War* (Cambridge, 2007). On communism in America, see Harvey Klehr, *The Heyday of American Communism: The Depression Decade* (New York, 1985); Bert Cochran, *Labor*

And then this force was gone. There is not enough space here to dwell on the reasons for and timing of its decline, except to say this: communism had produced a new and pernicious form of tyranny that undermined its claims to emancipation and enlightenment. Meanwhile, the centralized command structure of communist economies proved increasingly dysfunctional, especially once the information technology revolution took hold in the 1980s. By the late 1980s, communism had lost legitimacy as a political and economic system. The consequences of communism's fall were huge. One consequence is obvious: it opened a large part of the world – Russia, Eastern Europe, China – to capitalist penetration.[26] Capitalism thus became global in the 1990s in a way it had not been since prior to the First World War. The globalized world that dominated international affairs in the 1990s and 2000s is unimaginable apart from communism's collapse.

Another consequence of communism's fall may be less obvious, but is of equal importance: it removed what had been an imperative in America (and in Europe and elsewhere) for class compromise. I have already suggested that class compromise between capital and labour was foundational to the New Deal Order. Labour had gained through this compromise progressive taxation, social security, unemployment insurance, the right to organize and limits on the inequality between rich and poor. Capital had gained assurances that government would act to smooth out the business cycle, maintain a fiscal and monetary environment that would assure reasonable profits and contain labour's power.

One could argue, and I will, that without the threat of communism, this compromise might never have emerged. The fear of communism was great in 1930s America. The Soviet state was then perceived as a success, both in its ability to extract itself from capitalist social relations and its apparent achievement of rates of economic growth in the 1930s that surpassed those that capitalist countries of the West were then mustering. The Soviet state's supporters were powerful throughout the West: in Germany, of course, prior to Hitler's seizure of power, but also in France, Italy, Spain and Greece.[27] They were a force in America, too,

---

and Communism: The Conflict that Shaped American Unions (Princeton, 1978); Ellen Schrecker, *Many Are the Crimes: McCarthyism in America* (Boston, MA, 1998).

[26] China had already opened itself to the West, a product of the rise of Deng Xiaoping in the 1970s, his repudiation of Maoism and his tentative rapprochement with the US in the 1980s. But the history of China's opening might have taken a different path in the 1990s were it not for the fall of the Soviet Union and, with it, of communist ideology, in 1991. On China's opening to the West and its economic rise, see Thomas J. Christensen, *The China Challenge: Shaping the Choices of a Rising Power* (New York, 2015).

[27] On communism's strength in Europe, see Hobsbawm, *Age of Extremes*; Tony Judt, *Postwar: A History of Europe since 1945* (New York, 2005).

and integral to the American labour movement, then the country's most important insurgent political force. No communist had a chance of winning an election in America in 1936, but a left-leaning populist such as Huey Long did. In 1935 and 1936, Roosevelt felt the threat from the left acutely, which is why he and the Democratic party agreed to the class compromise that lay at the heart of the New Deal Order.[28] If we deploy this frame of analysis to the rest of the West, we begin to notice a parallel story: namely, that the years in which social democratic regimes flourished in Europe the most were those in which the threat of a communist alternative was greatest. In my 2015 book, *Liberty and Coercion*, I argued that, absent the Cold War, the New Deal might well have been rolled back during the late 1940s. There would have been no New Deal Order and no story of a Republican president acquiescing to Democratic party ideology to write about.[29]

What were the consequences for international and domestic politics of nations once the possibility of a communist alternative was extinguished? Surprisingly, the literature on the rise of neoliberalism, which is now substantial, seems rather indifferent to this question.[30] In looking for illumination, I have found myself driven to an unexpected treatise, one much belittled in the academy, or at least in the stretches of it that I inhabit: Francis Fukuyama's *The End of History and the Last Man*. Fukuyama is wrong about the end of history, of course; but he is right about how stunning, unexpected and consequential the fall of communism was. And that with its fall, the last universal alternative to liberal democracy as a way of organizing economic and political life passed from the world.[31]

In the United States, the collapse of communism emboldened capitalists and their neoliberal supporters. Internationally, the world had been cleared of capitalism's most ardent opponent. Vast new territories and peoples could now be brought into a single capitalist marketplace. The possibilities for growth and profits seemed boundless. The United States would benefit from this growth, of course. And perhaps the class compromise that had formed the basis of the New Deal Order could now be jettisoned. There was no longer a hard left to fear.

The most discerning members of the neoliberal movement saw something else in what remained of the left: that communism had poisoned the dream of socialist emancipation long before it fell. That socialism,

---

[28] Alan Brinkley, *Voices of Protest: Huey Long, Father Coughlin, and the Great Depression* (New York, 1982); Gerstle, *Liberty and Coercion*, ch. 7.

[29] Gerstle, *Liberty and Coercion*, ch. 8.

[30] For important exceptions, see David Harvey, *A Brief History of Neoliberalism* (New York, 2005); and Wolfgang Streeck, *How Will Capitalism End? Essays on a Failing System* (2016).

[31] Francis Fukuyama, *The End of History and the Last Man* (1992; New York, 2006).

in any form, was no longer an ideal capable of moving masses, of inspiring them with a dream of secular emancipation. In a post-communist world, those in America who insisted on calling themselves leftists turned more and more to identity politics. The resulting battles over race, gender and sexuality generated considerable conflict, but they did not threaten regimes of capital accumulation as communism had done. Multi-culturalism and cosmopolitanism could thrive under conditions of neoliberalism, and they did. The pressure on capitalist elites and their supporters to compromise with the working class had vanished. This is the moment when neoliberalism, in the United States, went from being a political movement to a political order.[32]

This transition from movement to order can best be grasped via a glance at the presidency of Bill Clinton. The true test of a political order, I have been suggesting, is when the opposition acquiesces to the order's ideological and policy imperatives. Clinton facilitated that acquiescence. He was the Democratic Eisenhower.

The extent to which Clinton's administration implemented neoliberal principles is rather stunning. In 1993, Clinton signed the North American Free Trade Act (NAFTA), legislation that turned all of North America into a single common market. In 1994, he established the World Trade Organization to implement neoliberal principles internationally, a plan that became known as the 'Washington Consensus'. In 1996, Clinton deregulated the exploding telecommunication industry, now including not just phones and television but the cable and satellite sub-industries that had become so important to the new information economy. Soon after, he did the same with the electrical generation industry that fuelled (literally) the new economy. And then, in 1999, he repealed the Glass Steagall Act, the New Deal law that had done more than any other to end speculation, corruption and the boom–bust cycle in the financial industry.[33]

Across his two terms, Clinton may have done more to advance deregulation than Reagan himself had done. The Department of the Treasury, headed by Robert Rubin, formerly head of Goldman Sachs, one of Wall Street's leaving investment banks, masterminded this liberalization of the economy. One of his lieutenants, Lawrence Summers, who would later reemerge as a key player in the early Obama administration, had this to say about the journey of ostensibly Democratic party economists: 'Not so long ago, we were all Keynesians…Equally, any honest Democrat will admit that we are now all Friedmanites.'[34]

---

[32] Thomas Frank, *The Conquest of Cool: Business Culture, Counterculture, and the Rise of Hip Consumerism* (Chicago, 1998).

[33] See Wilentz, *The Age of Reagan*; and Joseph E. Stiglitz, *The Roaring Nineties: A New History of the World's Most Prosperous Decade* (New York, 2003).

[34] Lawrence H. Summers, 'The Great Liberator', *New York Times*, 19 Nov. 2006.

Exactly how this reorientation among Democratic party economists occurred is a story that has not been fully told. Part of it dated back to the 1960s, when Great Society and New Deal activists alike had tilted against the statism of the New Deal Order. The Community Action Program's attack on big city machines and the New Left's antipathy to bureaucracy had both encouraged Democratic party interest in market-based social policies.[35] Another part of the reorientation of the Democrats emerged slowly out of a series of painful political calculations, as the conviction grew among Democrats that they would not win the presidency again unless they embraced Republican party market fundamentalism.[36] A third part emerged not from pain but from the giddiness that accompanied the information technology revolution. By the early 1990s, market evangelists were sermonizing that governments may once have been needed to manage the business cycle and to minimize risk (or to turn unmeasurable uncertainty into manageable risk). But they no longer were. New information technology made it possible to shrink and even to eliminate risk, and to smooth out the highs and lows of the business cycle. The fullness and instantaneity of information that computers had made possible had put market perfection within human grasp. Much existing state regulation was therefore superfluous – or worse, an actual impediment to economic growth and development. Hence, it would be best, market evangelists argued, if governments would just get out of the way. Clinton himself had drunk from this pitcher of kool-aid, as he contemplated how best to build what he liked to call his bridge to tomorrow. After one such sip in 1996, he happily declared that, 'The era of big government is over.'[37]

Joseph Stiglitz, the Nobel Prize winning economist and prolific author, has written revealingly about how he and other likeminded progressives themselves drank too much from the same jug of high tech kool-aid. As a member and then chair of the Council of Economic Advisers, he played an important role in the Clinton administration. Democrats like him, he

[35] For the attack on big city machines by the Great Society's Community Action Program, see Allen J. Matusow, *The Unraveling of America: A History of Liberalism in the 1960s*, 1st edn (New York, 1984). On the New Left's contribution to neoliberalism's emergence, see Reuel Schiller, 'Regulation and the Collapse of the New Deal Order or How I Learned to Stop Worrying and Love the Market', and Paul Sabin, 'Environmental Law and the End of the New Deal Order', both in *Beyond the New Deal Order*, ed. Gary Gerstle, Nelson Lichtenstein and Alice O'Connor (Philadelphia, forthcoming).

[36] Lily Geismer, *Don't Blame Us: Suburban Liberals and the Transformation of the Democratic Party* (Princeton, 2015).

[37] Wilentz, *The Age of Reagan*, 323–407; George Gilder, whose 1981 book, *Wealth and Poverty*, had become a neoliberal bible, himself in the 1990s became ever more enamoured of the information technology revolution and the frontiers of market innovation it had put within human grasp. See, for example, Gary Rivlin, 'The Madness of King George', *Wired*, 1 July 2002, www.wired.com/2002/07/gilder-6/, accessed 1 June 2018.

would observe, 'had always provided a check on the mindless pursuit of deregulation. Now, we joined the fray – sometimes pushing things even further than the Reagan Administration..."We are all Berliners" was the sentiment of President Kennedy's declaration' when he visited Berlin in 1961. 'Thirty years later', Stiglitz declared, 'we were all deregulators...By adopting deregulation language [ourselves], we had in fact conceded the battle.'[38] This concession, this participation on the part of Democrats in the market intoxication of the 1990s, is yet another sign that neoliberalism had become hegemonic, its advocates compelling all political players to work within its ideological matrix.

IV

Did this order also carry with it a moral perspective, as the New Order had? Yes, I think it did, although one that was far more contested (and conflicted) than its economic ideology. This moral perspective can be usefully called 'neo-Victorian'. Its principles were laid out by a group of Reagan supporters who labelled themselves, just to confuse terminology some more, 'neoconservatives'. Prominent in their ranks were figures such as the historian Gertrude Himmelfarb, and her journalist husband, Irving Kristol; the sociologist Charles Murray and Reagan's secretary of education, William Bennett; editor of *Commentary* magazine, Norman Podhoretz, and senator from New York, Daniel Patrick Moynihan; the writer and pundit, George Gilder, whose book *Wealth and Poverty* became a manifesto of the Reagan administration. Social scientists Daniel Bell and Nathan Glazer hovered around its fringes, as did the historian and social critic Christopher Lasch. So did Fukuyama and his mentor, Allan Bloom.[39]

This neoconservative group believed that a complete embrace of the market could be corrosive, meaning that an individual's encounter with it had to be regulated in some way. If the state was not going to provide that regulation, then who would? To which the neoconservatives increasingly responded: the individual must regulate himself. They had in mind not Margaret Thatcher's individual, allegedly alone in society, but one appropriately nestled in congeries of institutions – family and church, of course, but also in the vast archipelago of voluntary organizations that Tocqueville had identified as America's most hopeful characteristic. Thus

[38] Stiglitz, *The Roaring Nineties*, 91.

[39] Peter Steinfels, *The Neoconservatives: The Origins of a Movement: From Dissent to Political Power* (1979; New York, 2013); Murray Friedman, *The Neoconservative Revolution: Jewish Intellectuals and the Shaping of Public Policy* (Cambridge, 2005); *The Neoconservative Imagination: Essays in Honor of Irving Kristol*, ed. Christopher Demuth and William Kristol (Washington, DC, 1995); Alexander Jacobs, 'Pessimism and Progress: Left Conservatism in Modern American Political Thought' (Ph.D. dissertation, Vanderbilt University, 2016).

nestled, an individual would acquire the character necessary to engage profitably and responsibly with the market. He (and I am using the male pronoun deliberately) would acquire self-discipline and self-control, and thus self-respect, 'a pre-condition for the respect and approbation of others', Himmelfarb wrote.[40] Such an individual would not consume mindlessly, or beyond his means; nor indulge in an excess of alcohol, drugs or sex. He would live by the golden rule; he would infuse his own life and the world beyond with 'moral and civic virtue'.[41] This is what the British Victorians had done so successfully, according to Himmelfarb. And it is what Americans of the late twentieth century needed to do themselves, if their society was going to flourish.[42]

Himmelfarb and her band of 'neo-Victorians' were small in number; they were secular, East Coast urban and disproportionately Jewish. And yet they articulated a set of beliefs that resonated with millions of Americans from other regions and religions. These mostly Protestant and Catholic Americans shared with neoconservatives a sentiment that the liberation movements of the sixties and seventies – civil rights, feminism and gay rights – had turned their country, and its moral codes, upside down. Husbands and fathers had lost authority in their families. Excessively generous welfare schemes were rewarding idleness and indulgence. Criminals were being coddled, relieved of responsibility for their actions. Permissiveness had permeated all corners of civil society, rendering every lifestyle, including those of single parent families, or raising children out-of-wedlock, or living openly as homosexuals, the equal of every other. Americans had to fight to get their traditional culture back. Indeed, 'culture wars' erupted everywhere in 1990s America.[43]

To contain this slide into what they regarded as the worst form of moral relativism, the neoconservatives and the evangelical movement to which it was linked counterposed a moral traditionalism. They wanted to restore the authority of the father and husband (in her social circles, Gertrude Himmelfarb preferred to be known not as Gertrude Himmelfarb but as Mrs Irving Kristol); end welfare; punish

---

[40] Gertrude Himmelfarb, *The De-Moralization of Society: From Victorian Virtues to Modern Values* (New York, 1994), 256.

[41] *Ibid.*, 257.

[42] Among US historians, the term 'Victorianism' is often used as a shorthand for the kind of moral traditionalism that Himmelfarb was espousing. The term is deployed much less in this way by British historians, who now view British society during the long reign of Queen Victoria as composed of cultural and moral tendencies too diverse to be compressed into a morally conservative frame.

[43] Andrew Hartman, *A War for the Soul of America: A History of the Culture Wars* (Chicago, 2015); Robert Hughes, *The Culture of Complaint: The Fraying of America* (New York, 1993). On the evangelical movement itself, see Frances Fitzgerald, *The Evangelicals: The Struggle to Shape America* (New York, 2017).

criminals; suppress homosexuality; rehabilitate families, and restore their capacity to nurture self-reliant, disciplined and virtuous individuals. Could all Americans benefit from this programme? Sometimes the conservative cultural warriors said yes: they were, by and large, religious men and women who had accepted the Bible's teaching that all human beings were God's children. But lurking in their perspective was the suspicion that some races and genders were better equipped to handle the rigours of independent selfhood than others. Nineteenth-century Victorianism had rested on a set of hierarchies, gender and racial; so did its late twentieth-century neo-Victorian counterpart. Opening up America to all races, religions and cultures, and putting them on the same footing, could spell disaster.[44]

This neo-Victorian moral perspective was both fundamental to the neoliberal order, and a source of perpetual conflict and contradiction. It provided assurance that America could handle the rigours of a free market economy. It bound together the white poor with white Republican party elites, articulating an ideal of strenuous self-improvement that flowed powerfully across class lines.[45] And its influence extended far into the Democratic party. Consider, again, the case of Bill Clinton. In many respects, he was the poster child of 1960s liberation. In the 1960s, he had grown his hair long, dodged the draft and smoked weed. He had married a fiery feminist, allowed her to keep her last name and nurture career ambitions as grand as his. When Bill and Hillary entered the White House in 1993 they had every intention of making it a co-presidency, full partners in power as they believed they had been in all aspects of their previous life. Bill had embraced fully the cause of racial equality, so much that Toni Morrison once exclaimed that he was the first black president. A version of the 1960s ideal of sexual liberation – that which declared (in Stephen Stills's immortal words) 'love the one you're with' – still burned brightly in him. Conservatives saw this side of him and loathed him for it; indeed they bent every muscle toward removing this man from office and, in 1998 and 1999, almost

---

[44] The suspicion of 'lesser races' mostly ran underground (the Civil Rights Revolution of the 1960s and 1970s rendered the frank expression of such prejudice more problematic than it had previously been) but occasionally it surfaced. See, for example, Richard J. Herrnstein and Charles Murray, *The Bell Curve: Intelligence and Class Structure in American Life* (New York, 1994); and Niall Ferguson, *Empire: How Britain Made the Modern World* (2003).

[45] This shared moral perspective may help solve the mystery of what bewildered Thomas Frank about Kansas, i.e., why the poor of his state seemed so willing to subordinate their class interests to those of the rich. Thomas Frank, *What's the Matter with Kansas? How Conservatives Won the Heart of America* (New York, 2004). See also Melinda Cooper, *Family Values: Between Neoliberalism and the New Social Conservatism* (New York, 2017); and Bethany Moreton, *To Serve God and Wal-Mart: The Making of Christian Free Enterprise* (Cambridge, MA, 2009).

succeeded. And yet, this sixties veteran set out as president to burnish his moral traditionalist credentials. He sought 'to end welfare as we know it'; to lock away as many criminals as necessary to restore law and order to America's cities; to discipline black nationalists whom he perceived as contravening moral norms. In his mind, as in the mind of many Americans, this kind of discipline was necessary if America were to flourish.[46]

This sort of neo-Victorian moralism clashed at points with the spirit of freedom promised by the neoliberal order. The market did not care about morality or lifestyle. It simply wanted participants, and lots of them. And it wanted each participant to curtail saving and thrift in favour of spending, debt and excess. Market experts, moreover, had become wizards at market segmentation – developing products for particular social groups defined by age, class, gender, sexual preference and national origin. The market, as a consequence, encouraged rather than suppressed a pluralism of identities and lifestyles, underwriting precisely the sort of cultural relativism that the neo-Victorians ardently sought to suppress.[47] Thus, the consensus that the neoliberal order had established around economics did not extend to culture. The neo-Victorianism that was so powerful a force in politics coexisted uneasily with market fundamentalism, so much so that its advocates felt perpetually under siege. Yet, the power of this neo-Victorianism, and its significance in politics, were undeniable, endowing the neoliberal order not just with a constellation of stable constituencies and interest groups and a set of hegemonic ideological principles, but with a moral perspective, and perhaps with moral authority.

V

The promise of neoliberalism was that it could make markets work to their full potential and thereby rekindle the kind of economic growth that managed capitalism had failed to deliver in the long 1970s. For a time, policies emanating from the neoliberal order did just that, both domestically and internationally. The United States enjoyed a marked increase both in the rate of the growth and in job creation in the 1990s. At the same time, free trade was laying a foundation for rapid growth in what had been Third World economies: China, South Korea, India and Brazil, to take only the most obvious examples.

[46] On Clinton, see William H. Chafe, *Bill and Hillary: The Politics of the Personal* (New York, 2012); David Maraniss, *First in his Class: A Biography of Bill Clinton* (New York, 1995); and Charlotte Jeffries, 'The Politics of Teenage Female Sexuality in the United States, 1981–2008' (Ph.D. dissertation, University of Cambridge, 2017).

[47] Lizabeth Cohen, *A Consumers Republic: The Politics of Mass Consumption in Postwar America* (New York, 2003); Frank, *The Conquest of Cool*.

But there were problems. Market deregulation had magnified economic instability. A stock market bust hit the US in 2001 and 2002. Recovery did seem to come in subsequent years but the price was high, in the form of creating a bubble in the housing industry. The neo-liberal economy was suffering from a fundamental problem: insufficiency of demand. Consumers, in the aggregate, did not have enough income to support what a globalized capitalist economy could now produce.

Expanding home ownership beyond its real limits was a way to close this gap between supply and demand. All kinds of borrowers who, in the past, would have been denied mortgages were now given generous loans to buy homes. The banking industry frankly acknowledged the risk involved in such lending, labelling these loans as 'sub-prime'. But bankers had convinced themselves that they could manage such lending by bundling together large numbers of sub-prime mortgages and then selling small slices of each bundle to a very large base of investors. The risk would thus be spread so wide and in such miniscule tranches that it would effectively disappear. The bankers, meanwhile, would make money from fees charged for each round of transactions, and by building into the mortgages high, though frequently hidden, interest rates.

The millions of Americans who were given the opportunity for the first time to own a home rushed to do so, causing housing prices to shoot up. Flush with equity, homeowners began to use their homes as if they were ATM machines, a constant source of cash for all sorts of big purchases: cars, HD televisions, home remodelling, college tuition for their children and expensive vacations to exotic locales. The economy hummed, Hummers clogged the roads and the stock market soared. This optimism spread to many other parts of the world. But much of it depended on a belief in unending growth in the value of real estate, a belief that justified individuals taking on huge amounts of debt. The fever broke in 2008. Banks failed, except for those too big to fail, in which case they had to be bailed out at enormous expense by governments. These bank failures plunged the US and much of the rest of the world into the worst economic crisis since the Great Depression.[48]

We know the rest: years of economic distress; an uneven and painfully slow recovery, which sharpened both the reality and experience of economic inequality, both within and between nations. Democratic governments, by and large, showed themselves to be ineffective in response. President Barack Obama led an administration that did better than most. He implemented a modest Keynesian stimulus. He undertook a serious effort to re-regulate Wall Street. His Affordable Care Act was

---

[48] For a sampling of writings on the crash of 2008, and the factors causing it, see *Panic! The Story of Modern Financial Insanity*, ed. Michael Lewis (New York, 2009).

a reassertion of the government's responsibility to manage the market-place in the public's interest, even as the legislation did as much to affirm as to repudiate the principles of neoliberalism.[49]

Still, even Obama's relative success was not enough to quell growing anger at market fundamentalism and its perceived handmaidens: free trade, free movements of people, globalization, deregulation, cosmopol-itanism. As the hegemony of neoliberalism cracked, its opponents acquired a visibility and prominence they had long been denied. This development became clear in the 2016 elections, when Donald Trump roared to victory with rhetoric that struck at the heart of neoliberal and Republican orthodoxy: free trade was a chimera that had done nothing for the American working-man; America's borders had to be reestablished, walls built, globalization reversed. Then, and only then, would domestic manufacturing be revived, good jobs generated and America's greatness restored. Trump did not think for a moment that markets were perfect; his own experience as a real estate trickster had taught him how easy it was for clever operators, both private and public, to manipulate them.

The same arguments were made by the surprise Democratic candi-date of the left, Bernie Sanders, who made socialism a credible position in American politics for the first time in seventy years. Caught in the middle was that pillar of neoliberal orthodoxy, Hillary Clinton, her hus-band's loyal mate, never quite comprehending across a long campaign why her 1990s package of policies was so out of step with the post-2008 mood. Why all the fuss about accepting $300,000 fees for giving speeches to Goldman Sachs?

The election of Donald Trump is a symptom of the crisis in the neo-liberal order, not its cause. Eighteen months into his presidency we still do not know what sort of stamp he is going to put on American political economy. During his first six months in office, Trump listened to right-wing populists such as Steve Bannon, who really did want to end neo-liberalism as we know it. The second six months was marked by the ascendancy of financial advisers such as Gary Cohn, formerly of Goldman Sachs, who were confident that the world of neoliberalism could be restored. Cohn masterminded the 2017 tax reform package, which featured a massive cut in the corporate tax rate, a measure long sought by neoliberals as a way of removing the government from the business of redistributing corporate profits. At the same time, vice-president Mike Pence engineered a rapprochement between Trump and the neoliberal (and multi-billionaire) Koch brothers, who began lending Trump political support in exchange for Trump's willingness

---

[49] For an early effort by historians to reckon with the Obama presidency, see *The Obama Presidency: A First Historical Assessment*, ed. Julian E. Zelizer (Princeton, 2017).

to hollow out government agencies charged with regulating industry and the environment.[50]

In early 2018, however, Trump reversed field again, inaugurating a regime of tariffs on goods from countries deemed by the US to be engaged in unfair trading practices. This turn toward protectionism, which made good on one of Trump's key campaign pledges, struck at the heart of neoliberal orthodoxy. So did Trump's decision to step up his attacks on central American migrants and to militarise America's southern border by deploying thousands of National Guard troops to protect it. Gary Cohn quit the White House in March 2018, as did other top advisers who had come from the Goldman Sachs bastion of neoliberalism.

Yet, we still do not know what lies ahead. There is no doubt that the political order that made neoliberalism the dominant ideology in America for thirty years cracked in the decade following the financial crash of 2008. The next ten years (2018–28) will be decisive in revealing whether that order can be repaired, or whether it will fall. Neoliberalism's future will be determined not just by elites, of course, but by social movements of the right and left that are seeking to influence the body politic. A political order restored or an America – and a world – transformed? By the late 2020s, we shall have an answer.

[50] On the Koch connection, see Mayer, *Dark Money*; and Jane Mayer, 'The Danger of President Pence', *New Yorker*, 23 Oct. 2017, www.newyorker.com/magazine/2017/10/23/the-danger-of-president-pence, accessed 1 June 2018.

Transactions of the RHS 28 (2018), pp. 265–288 © Royal Historical Society 2018
doi:10.1017/S0080440118000130

150 YEARS OF ROYAL HISTORICAL SOCIETY PUBLISHING

By Ian W. Archer

RHS Literary Director 2004–14

ABSTRACT. The 150th anniversary of the Royal Historical Society offers an opportunity for an investigation into its publications over the *longue durée*. Its slow transformation from an association of literary dilettanti to a body of professional historians in the period 1890–1910 was accompanied by changes to its publication programme: the appointment of a literary director, an improvement in the quality of papers read, the merger with the Camden Society and the commitment to a programme of historical bibliographies established the basis of the Society's publishing programme for much of the twentieth century. The interwar years saw new initiatives including the launch of *Guides and Handbooks*, but the Society was already losing momentum, and an ill-fated foray into the publication of diplomatic records stymied its reputation. The 1950s and 1960s were a period of ongoing stasis, from which the Society was rescued in the early 1970s by G. R. Elton and his allies, who promoted a monograph series and the *Annual Bibliographies*. The momentum of change was sustained by the early commitment to an electronic version of its bibliographies, and still more recently by a commitment to open access monographs. The changing profile of the Society's publications by gender of author, period and area is charted, raising questions about future directions.

I The ambiguities of 'professionalization'

Between December 1890 and March 1891, the Royal Historical Society was rocked by some of the most contentious meetings in its history. On 18 December, Council considered a paper proposing the appointment of a literary director with an honorarium of £50 per annum, who would take over the supervision of the Society's publications, tasks which were currently performed by the honorary secretary. The proposal was highly contentious, presumably because of the threat to the current secretary, Patrick Edward Dove, a barrister with historical interests whose friends rallied in his support. Discussion of the paper was deferred on two occasions in January 1891; it was eventually carried by one vote (4:3) when discussed on 19 February, but the motion that the Society proceed immediately to fill the position of literary director was then lost by one vote. The reformers had to wait until the next meeting to confirm their victory, but the motion for the appointment of Hubert Hall*[1] to the post was carried only on the casting vote of the Society's new president, Sir Mountstuart Elphinstone Grant Duff*.[2] Hall was currently a junior clerk at the Public Record Office (he was promoted to the position of senior clerk in the following year), and had an established reputation as an editor of medieval texts; he had published in *Transactions* for the first time in 1886, and been a member of Council since 1887. Appointed for initially two years, Hall would not relinquish the post until 1938 when he was in his eighties.[3]

The Society's origins had been pretty disreputable, and it had soon become the tool of Charles Rogers*, the journalist, antiquarian and Scottish Presbyterian cleric with a penchant for founding societies, on whose resources he heartily gouged. Even after the coup which removed him from the secretaryship in 1881, *Transactions* remained pretty idiosyncratic, and the Society was predominantly frequented by 'clergymen and physicians, army officers and civil servants, barristers and solicitors, bank managers, journalists, engineers, [and] teachers'.[4] John Burrow has wittily dissected the characteristics of its leading early contributors, such as George Harris, 'the eccentric polymath...a briefless barrister and a man of grandiose though thwarted ambition', Cornelius Walford, a writer on insurance matters and a statistician, Albert Wratislaw, a Slavonic scholar, and Gustvus Zerfi, 'a Romantic exile' and would-be intellectual historian.[5] Phillipa Levine has commented that in the mid-1880s the Society 'was caught uncomfortably between the amateur tradition and a desire to emulate the rigour of the new professionals'.[6] Reform was perhaps more incremental rather than revolutionary. A trickle of historians from the universities were recruited to Council; there was talk of a merger with the fledgling *English Historical Review* in 1887; the Society played a leading role in the Domesday commemoration, from which emerged two volumes of *Domesday Studies* (1888, 1891), edited by Dove; in 1889, Council announced that it was sponsoring an edition of tracts on medieval husbandry edited by Rev.

---

[1] *The Oxford Dictionary of National Biography* has proved helpful on the backgrounds, careers and values of key individuals. Rather than citing articles individually, I have adopted the expedient of identifying subjects in the *Dictionary* by means of an asterisk.

[2] RHS, Council, 18 Dec. 1890, 15 Jan. 1891, 29 Jan. 1891, 19 Feb. 1891, 19 Mar. 1891. See also R. A. Humphreys, *The Royal Historical Society 1868–1968* (1969), 23–4; T. F. Tout, 'Presidential Address', *TRHS*, fourth series, 9 (1926), is also revealing on the Society's early years.

[3] C[harles] J[ohnson], 'Hubert Hall, 1857–1944', *TRHS*, fourth series, 28 (1946), 1–5.

[4] Humphreys, *Royal Historical Society*, 1–20, quotation at 11–12.

[5] J. Burrow, 'Victorian Historians and the Royal Historical Society', *TRHS*, fifth series, 39 (1989), 125–40.

[6] P. Levine, *The Amateur and the Professional. Antiquarians, Historians, and Archaeologists in Victorian England, 1838–1886* (Cambridge, 1986), 173.

William Cunningham* and his assistant Miss E. M. Leonard, and suggested that it was contemplating the publication of 'certain collections of state papers, especially of the French Revolution and Napoleonic periods'.[7]

The driving force behind the changes of 1890–1 was Oscar Browning*, in many ways an unlikely sponsor of reform: as Burrow has suggested, his role in the Society may have been a form of rehab. His tenure as housemaster at Eton had ended with more than a whiff of sexual impropriety in 1876, but he had reinvented himself as one of the new breed of History dons at Cambridge. He was one of the first university historians to join the Council in 1884, of which he became chairman in the following year, and he proved energetic in recruiting others, particularly from Cambridge where a branch of the Society was established in 1886. But his scholarship was 'superficial, inaccurate and diffuse'; he was a terrific snob and hated by many of his fellow-dons; in the toxic politics of the Cambridge History syllabus, he stood against the research ideal promoted by the future presidents of the Society, Adolphus Ward* and George Prothero*, and stood behind Sir John Seeley's* emphasis on a schooling for statesmanship.[8] As others have remarked, there were different species of professionalism, and it is notable that two of the leading early reformers, H. V. Malden and Hall himself were archivists rather than university teachers: Philippa Levine suggests that the record office men were 'the nascent professionals in the historical field'.[9] Moreover, Browning's allies on Council, the men who carried the critical votes, are themselves revealing of its still eclectic character. Firm in their support were T. W. Rhys Davids*, the orientalist scholar and professor of Pali at the University of London, and Benjamin Franklin Stevens, a member of Council since 1888, involved in the book export business and for thirty years the London dispatch agent for the United States, but also a noted bibliographer committed to identifying sources in European archives for the history of the American Revolution. Frustratingly absent from the key meetings of 1890–1 were Lord Acton* and Seeley who were vice presidents, and Cunningham who sat on Council. At the height of the controversy, S. R. Gardiner*

---

[7] P. E. Dove, 'Preface', *TRHS*, old series, 4 (1889), n.p.; Humphreys, *Royal Historical Society*, 20–2.

[8] Burrow, 'Victorian Historians', 135–8; R. N. Sofer, *Discipline and Power. The University, History, and the Making of an English Elite, 1870–1930* (Stanford, 1994), 54–6, 90–6.

[9] Levine, *The Amateur and the Professional*, 133. For the debate over professionalization and the ambiguities of the process, see D. Goldstein, 'The Organizational Development of the British Historical Profession, 1884–1921', *Bulletin of the Institute of Historical Research*, 55 (1982), 180–93; R. Jann, *The Art and Science of Victorian History* (Columbus, OH, 1983); P. R. H. Slee, *Learning and a Liberal Education. The Study of Modern History in the Universities of Oxford, Cambridge and Manchester, 1800–1914* (Manchester, 1986); Sofer, *Discipline and Power*.

turned down the Society's presidency, and Council had to settle for the more middle-of-the road Grant Duff.

But there is no doubting that the appointment of Hall as literary director marked a key step in the development of a more serious programme of publications. The Publications Committee was put on a firm footing; *Transactions* henceforth was to appear annually; new features included the publication of editions of documents (I. S. Leadam's highly respected editions of sections of the 1517 enclosure survey eventually morphed into a book published under the Society's auspices), and an annual *tour d'horizon* of historical writing (including continental and North American scholarship) penned by Hall under the portentous title, 'The Progress of Historical Research'; still more significantly, Council announced in February 1893 its commitment to 'a continuous and uniform series of publications' with *Transactions* to be supplemented every two years by a book. Volumes in the pipeline included papers relating to English diplomacy in Russia in 1802–4 and the secret service under George III to be edited by Oscar Browning and B. F. Stevens respectively.[10] Hall's own position was consolidated in the wake of the reorganisation following Dove's bankruptcy and suicide in 1894, as he took over the secretary's duties, and his honorarium raised to £126 per annum.[11]

It has to be said that some of the aspirations of the 'reformers' proved difficult to achieve. The survey of historical literature was dropped after two years. Neither Browning's nor Stevens's much touted editions appeared for some time and under different editors.[12] Leadam's volume on enclosures proved much more expensive than envisaged because of the discovery of an additional manuscript at the eleventh hour. In terms of fulfilling the programme of a regular cycle of publications, the Society's merger with the Camden Society in 1897 was therefore crucial. The Camden Society, founded in 1838 by a group of antiquarians 'for the publication of early historical and literary remains', had by the 1880s established its scholarly credentials, with the leading historian of the Stuart period, S. R. Gardiner and key Public Record Office men, James Joel Cartwright and James Gairdner* at the helm. Its editorial standards had risen, with notable editions by Gardiner himself, and his pupil Charles Firth*. But, faced with competition from the proliferating publishing societies of the high Victorian era, its membership had fallen, and it was struggling to

---

[10] RHS, Council, 12 May 1892, 16 Feb. 1893.

[11] Humphreys, *Royal Historical Society*, 24–6.

[12] RHS, Council, 19 Mar. 1903; *Select Despatches from the British Foreign Office Archives relating to the Formation of the Third Coalition against France, 1804–1805*, ed. J. Holland Rose (Camden Society, third series, 7, 1904); *Parliamentary Papers of John Robinson, 1774–1784*, ed. W. T. Laprade (Camden Society, third series, 33, 1922).

make ends meet.[13] Cartwright wrote in desperate terms to Gairdner in June 1894: 'nothing can save us but £200 ready money...and a permanent addition of at least 100 to our number of members'; whether they could bring out T. G. Law's volumes on the Archpriest controversy on which much had been spent already would depend on the willingness of the publishers to extend credit. As Gairdner noted wrily, 'I am afraid brandy will not save us.'[14] The prospect of imminent dissolution made the Camden Society amenable to the idea of a merger, and discussions began in January 1896. The Camden Society consulted its membership in April with pre-printed postcards: there were sixty-seven ayes, three noes and three not opposed.

The Royal Historical Society benefited from the boost in membership, including new subscribing libraries, and acquired a prestigious series; its Council was afforced by three recruits from the Camden Society. The appearance of printed instructions to editors and publishers in 1898, revised in 1915 and 1925, was a sign of the centrality of publishing to the Society's *raison d'etre*, and its seriousness of scholarly purpose. The composition of the Publications Committee in 1901 testifies to the change in the Society's intellectual profile. Hall, it is true, was perhaps not the sharpest pencil in the box (Maitland noted his 'curious fluffy mind', and his edition of the *Red Book of the Exchequer* was savaged by J. H. Round among others), but there was no doubting his dedication to hard work ('the most unselfish man I have ever known' continued Maitland);[15] in any event, the historians were the prime movers. S. R. Gardiner sat alongside his protégé, Charles Firth; others included the Anglo-Saxon scholar W. H. Stevenson, and two whose reputations have fared less well at the hands of later generations: Charles Raymond Beazley, research fellow at Merton College, Oxford, and later professor at Birmingham, and a fellow-traveller of the right, and (in ecumenical spirit) the Benedictine monk, Francis Aiden Gasquet*. Among the archive professionals were Gairdner and Malden. The presence of men as varied as I. S. Leadam, a barrister with a strong

[13] F. J. Levy, 'The Founding of the Camden Society', *Victorian Studies*, 7 (1964), 295–305; C. Johnson, 'The Camden Society, 1838–1938', *TRHS*, fourth series, 22 (1940), 23–38; Humphreys, *Royal Historical Society*, 52–67.
[14] RHS, Camden Society, secretary's correspondence file, C3/2.
[15] *The Letters of Frederic William Maitland*, ed. C. H. S. Fifoot (Cambridge, 1965), 181. I am grateful to George Garnett for drawing Maitland's letters to my attention. For more on Hall, see Humphreys, *Royal Historical Society*, 40. See also T. F. Tout, 'Review of *The Red Book of the Exchequer*. Edited by Hubert Hall', *English Historical Review*, 13 (1898), 145–50, and more damning, R. L. Poole, 'Review of *Studies on the Red Book of the Exchequer*. By J. H. Round and *The Red Book of the Exchequer: A Reply to Mr J. H. Round*. By Hubert Hall', *English Historical Review*, 14 (1899), 148–50. The Round–Hall affair has been subject to comprehensive analysis by M. Procter, 'The *Red Book of the Exchequer*: A Curious Affair Revisited', *Historical Research*, 87 (2014), 510–32.

publications record, including the edition of *The Domesday of Enclosures*; Frederic Harrison*, the polymathic positivist and friend of progressive causes; and the treasurer Robert Hovenden, who combined his perfume wholesaling business with antiquarian and genealogical pursuits, shows a continued eclecticism in recruitment to Council though all had serious scholarly credentials. Browning remained, a survivor from the 1880s, perhaps less at ease among men of this acumen. He certainly ought to have been.

The merger with the Camden Society ensured that the Society could fulfil its commitment to a regular programme of publishing. Volumes appeared regularly albeit not at the rate previously achieved by the Camden Society. Costs had to be carefully monitored. Whereas in the four years up to 1897, expenditure on printing and stationery had been £297 per annum, in the period 1897–1902, it was £394 per annum, an increase which was only to some extent offset by swelling subscription income. There were periodic attempts to limit expenditure on publications; in March 1904, a cap of £350 inclusive of editorial expenses was set, any increase requiring the approval of Council; in 1921, a more sensible policy of seeking to set a target of £750 per annum averaged over three years was adopted, the difference in costs being an indication of the inflationary pressures.[16] Honoraria to editors, requests for assistance with transcription and the cost of authors' corrections tended to push costs upwards.[17] There were periodic spats with the publishers. Although the high quality of Spottiswode's product satisfied the Society, 'their system of rendering accounts and disregard of official directives is utterly opposed to economy and efficiency' Council declared indignantly in 1907.[18] One suspects that the publisher's narrative, confronted by uncertain page extents and endless corrections, would have been somewhat different.

There was a steady expansion in the circulation of the Society's publications, as its membership and the number of subscribing libraries swelled (Table 1). Moreover, there was a real effort to diversify the range of history covered. Prothero expressed a desire that *Transactions* should not be 'too exclusively insular and medieval', and Council announced that it would give preference to papers dealing with the modern period and general historical subjects.[19] A similar policy was adopted with regards to Camdens. Whereas the Camden Society had

[16] RHS, Council, 17 Dec. 1903, 17 Mar. 1904, 21 Apr. 1904, 15 Dec. 1904, 8 Dec. 1921, 12 June 1924.
[17] RHS, Council, 15 Dec. 1904, 20 Dec. 1906, 18 June 1908, 17 Dec. 1908, 16 Mar. 1909.
[18] RHS, Council, 12 Jan. 1907.
[19] G. Prothero, 'Presidential Address', *TRHS*, new series, 19 (1905), 15–17; Report of Council, 1904–5.

Table 1 *Circulation of Royal Historical Society publications,*
1902–94

Year	Membership (all categories)	Subscribing libraries
1902	526	133
1913	517	208
1928	787	258
1938	952	287
1948	836	332
1958	882	429
1968	1,013	649
1978	1,692	766
1988	1,961	691
1994	2,120	648

Source: Annual Reports of Council.

concentrated on medieval and early modern texts, there was a shift in emphasis with volumes more evenly spread, 30 per cent of the volumes published under Hall's stewardship covering the period 1700–1900 (Table 2).[20] As early as 1893, Council took

> regard of the fact that the publication of medieval records and memorials has been for many years past undertaken both by the Treasury and by private publication societies whilst the modern state papers especially such as illustrate the foreign policy and statesmanship of this country in the great crisis of its history during the revolutionary and Napoleonic wars have been almost entirely neglected by the authorities.

Worse still,

> these state papers have for many years past been known and highly appreciated by foreign historians who have made considerable use of them though necessarily in a desultory manner so that we are actually in danger of having some of the greatest episodes in our own history interpreted on the authority of our own archives by foreigners instead of by native historians.

Publication of these records 'will prove of the highest utility to students of history and will also be the honour and advantage to the Society'.[21] These patriotic sentiments notwithstanding, the country faced a greater challenge in the Great War of 1914–18, during which many of those associated with the Society took on work in the Foreign Office intelligence service, an experience which seemed to confirm the need

---

[20] Hubert Hall's 'Memorandum on the Serial Distribution of the Royal Historical Society's Publications', prepared for RHS, Publications Committee, 21 Sept. 1933, documents the shifting balance of publications.

[21] RHS, Council, 16 Feb. 1893.

Table 2 *Periods covered by Camden volumes, 1838–2017*

Date	Volumes per annum	Medieval	Early modern	1700–1900	Post-1900
1838–97	2.7	46.3 (29%)	106.5 (68%)	4.2 (3%)	0 (0%)
1898–1938	1.5	21.8 (34%)	23 (36%)	19.2 (30%)	0 (0%)
1939–68	1.26	17.5 (46%)	8 (21%)	12.5 (33%)	0 (0%)
1969–88	1.8	12 (33%)	14 (39%)	10 (28%)	0 (0%)
1989–2017	2.4	18.3 (26%)	25.2 (35%)	17.5 (25%)	10 (14%)

Note: Fractions are explained by estimating miscellany items as proportions of volumes.

for a proper understanding of international relations.[22] In 1920, the eighteenth-century political historian Basil Williams* suggested that the Society publish a series of diplomatic instructions on the model of the *Recueil des Instructions données aux Ambassadeurs et Ministres de France (1648–1789)*, and the proposal was enthusiastically endorsed, and all pretence of historical objectivity discarded, 'with a view to making known the real intentions of our foreign policy and incidentally vindicating its general straightforwardness and continuity'. Failing government support, the Society could imagine that 'no nobler field could be offered to private generosity. The publication would be no less a service to the country than to history.' The hope that these volumes could be supplementary to the target of two Camdens per annum was not fulfilled, and private funding did not materialise, but the series went ahead. It was not a scholarly success, however. Harold Temperley*, doyen of the historians of international diplomacy and member of Council, wrote a searing review of the first volume relating to Anglo-Swedish diplomacy pointing out that the English diplomatic instructions were not comparable to, and of less intrinsic interest than, the *Receuils* and that the attempt to remedy the defects by a selection of other despatches compounded the problem because the principles of selection were unclear. The *Diplomatic Instructions* series threatened 'the reputation of British historical scholarship'. It was one of several critical reviews of the series.[23]

II The origins and early years of the bibliographies

It was in the 1920s, however, that the first fruits of another of the Society's projects, its bibliographies of British history, appeared. To understand their gestation, we need to go back a bit to the turn-of-the-century concerns about the standing of British history in the international community. Britain was behind Europe and North America in developing systematic bibliographies as research aids. The Germans in particular had laid down the gauntlet with the *Jahresberichte der Geschichtswissenschaft* and its antecedents published from 1878.[24] It was perhaps significant that the pioneer of bibliographies of British history was an assistant professor at Harvard, Charles Gross (1857–1909), who

---

[22] C. Parker, *The English Historical Tradition since 1850* (Edinburgh, 1990), 109–17.

[23] H. Temperley, 'Review of *British Diplomatic Instructions, 1689–1789. Vol. i, Sweden, 1689–1727*', *English Historical Review*, 38 (1923), 281–3; idem, 'Review of *British Diplomatic Instructions, 1689–1789. Vol. ii, France, 1689–1721*', *English Historical Review*, 41 (1926), 603–4; R. Lodge, 'Review of *British Diplomatic Instructions, 1689–1789. Vol. iv, France, 1721–1727*', *English Historical Review*, 43 (1928), 433–8.

[24] Historische Gesellschaft zu Berlin, *Jahresberichte der Geschichtswissenschaft im Auftrage der Historischen Gesellschaft zu Berlin* (Berlin, 1878–1913).

had studied at Leipzig, Berlin and Paris, and took his Ph.D. from Göttingen in 1883. He was responsible for a *Bibliography of British Municipal History* (1897), and the influential *Sources and Literature of English History from the Earliest Times to about 1485* (1900). The product of a course of lectures on British history, his bibliography of medieval history provided 'a systematic survey of the printed materials relating to the political, constitutional, legal, social, and economic history of England, Wales and Ireland to 1485'.[25]

Gross's initiative focused the concerns of those who appreciated the need for critical bibliographies in other periods. Three men were particularly influential. Henry Richard Tedder* was the librarian of the Athenaeum, who in a lecture of 1885 to the Library Association at Plymouth had taken the subject of 'Proposals for a bibliography of national history'. He became a fellow of the Society in 1902, and served as treasurer from 1904 until 1924. But the discussion within the Society was opened by Frederic Harrison in a paper of 1896, which took its cue from the possibilities of the merger with the Camden Society for the type of collaboration currently being modelled by the *Dictionary of National Biography*, to produce a bibliography of English (*sic*) history.[26] The first mention of a bibliography in the Council's minutes comes in 1900 but discussion was adjourned.[27] It was Sir George Prothero, former professor of history at Edinburgh, and since 1899 editor of the *London Quarterly Review*, president of the Society from 1901 until 1905, who really made the project central to the Society's aspirations. Prothero had studied in Germany, admired Ranke and stood for a more scientific approach to the discipline. He dedicated the bulk of his presidential address of 19 February 1903 to a call for a systematic bibliography of the history of the British Isles. Drawing unfavourable comparisons with the Germans, he suggested that the Englishman was characterised by a 'muddle through' philosophy, but 'of the higher practicality, which consists in forethought, preparation, system, the qualities which make for national efficiency, he has, I fear, but a very small share'. He noted that 'in this matter of bibliographies we are, as a nation, amazingly badly off', and it was a matter of reproach that the largest listing of works on British history was contained in the Bibliothèque Nationale in Paris, while the pioneer Charles Gross was an American, an 'ornament of Harvard'.[28]

[25] *Sources and Literature of English History from the Earliest Times to about 1485* (1900), ii.
[26] F. Harrison, 'A Proposal for a New Historical Bibliography', *TRHS*, new series, 11 (1897), 11–30.
[27] RHS, Council, 15 Mar. 1900.
[28] George Prothero, 'Presidential Address', *TRHS*, new series, 17 (1903), ix–xxxiv. For Prothero, see also C. W. Crawley, 'Sir Gorge Prothero and his Circle', *TRHS*, fifth

Prothero mobilised other luminaries of the Society like Firth, but it was really the American Historical Association that drove it forward. At its meeting at Richmond, Virginia, on 30 December 1908, the Association heard proposals for a general bibliography of modern British history, and a committee under the chairmanship of the Tudor historian E. P. Cheyney was appointed. The Society followed suit in 1909, appointing a committee chaired by Prothero, and including Firth and Tedder, to build up an Anglo-American cooperation. It was decided that there should be one volume of general bibliography, and that the period-specific works on British history since 1485 should be covered in two volumes with a break date at 1714, designed to complement Gross's existing work. Some progress was made before the First World War; Prothero was appointed general editor, funds were raised by subscription and a publisher was found. But the war diverted energies and although Prothero was still working on the project shortly before his death in 1922, there was little concrete yet to show. In 1923, the scheme was scaled back; the general volume was abandoned, and the plans for the eighteenth- and nineteenth-century volumes shelved; and it was agreed that the American and British teams should take on separate responsibility for volumes respectively in the Tudor and Stuart periods.[29]

In the determination to show something for all the investment of time and money, the Stuart volume under the editorship of Godfrey Davies, a former pupil of Firth, was rushed out, probably too soon, appearing in 1928. The reception was pretty critical. Reviewers pounced on the omissions and criticised the organisation of entries under the subheadings by date of publication which had the effect of separating material on related subjects. Some lessons were learned by Conyers Read, whose Tudor volume received a warmer reception.[30] Prothero's bequest in 1934 of the bulk of his estate (valued at £22,400) and the enthusiasm of F. M. Powicke*, another reforming president (1933–7), enabled the Society (with the cooperation of the Institute of Historical Research (IHR) to embark in 1935 on a new project, the annual listing of publications on British history, modelled on American, French and German exemplars. The first volume, covering the *Writings on British History* of 1934, appeared three years later. This and the next two volumes were compiled by Alexander ('Jock') Taylor Milne, then junior librarian of

---

series, 20 (1970), 101–28; M. Bentley, 'The Age of Prothero: British History in the Long *Fin de Siècle*, 1870–1920', *TRHS*, sixth series, 20 (2010), 171–93.

[29] See the illuminating correspondence folders on Bibliography projects, 1911–74, at RHS for negotiations with publishers and fund raising initiatives.

[30] *Bibliography of British History, Stuart Period, 1603–1714*, ed. Godfrey Davies (Oxford, 1928); *Bibliography of British History, Tudor Period, 1485–1603*, ed. Conyers Read (Oxford, 1933).

the Society, and later secretary and librarian of the IHR, but progress was interrupted by his wartime service.[31]

The bibliographies represented an attempt to diversify the Society's offering by providing key research tools. It was already appreciated that a regular diet of Camdens (and a somewhat force-fed one at that, bundled as they were into subscriptions) did not meet all the needs of historians. In 1933, the Publications Committee proposed a new series supplementary to Camdens which it hoped would be of interest to students of modern history. Proposals included lists of diplomatic agents and civil servants, lists of statistical material relating to eighteenth-century commerce to be pursued in conjunction with the Economic History Society, 'a volume of chronological data', 'a volume of the historical equations of coinage and exchange' and 'materials in private muniments of business houses'.[32] It was essentially a blueprint for what became the *Guides and Handbooks* series, though progress had already been made with the lists of eighteenth-century diplomatic agents in a Camden volume edited by D. B. Horn published in 1932. In 1938, the Society was able to contemplate the publication of one additional volume per annum, but the war and the ensuing austerity put paid to that, and in any event editors made slow progress: only six handbooks had been published by 1951; the volume on British diplomatic representatives 1509–1688 (on which work had commenced in 1937)[33] did not appear until 1990. But there were impressive fruits like Powicke's *Handbook of British Chronology* (1939) and Christopher Cheney's *Handbook of Dates* (1945), a long term bestseller.

III The place of women

We have passed the half-way point of this account, and so far the only woman mentioned has been one of Archdeacon Cunningham's research assistants, Ellen Marianne Leonard of the LSE.[34] It has been very much a case of the study of *The History Men*.[35] But one of the most surprising aspects of *Transactions* is the space given to female historians in the early twentieth century (Table 3). The proportion rose steadily from

---

[31] Humphreys, *Royal Historical Society*, 35; RHS, Council, 14 Mar. 1935, 12 May 1945, 15 Dec. 1945, 15 Mar. 1947; Royal Historical Society, *Writings on British History: 1934–* (1937–86).

[32] RHS, Council, 12 Oct. 1933, with report of Publications Committee, 21 Sept. 1933.

[33] RHS, Council, 11 Mar. 1937. The series on diplomatic agents was first mooted in 1927 and was strongly supported by both Temperley and Sir Richard Lodge: Council, 8 Dec. 1927.

[34] 'Ellen Marianne Leonard – President of the Students' Union, 1907', http://blogs.lse.ac.uk/lsehistory/2016/03/24/ellen-marianne-leonard/.

[35] The swipe at J. P. Kenyon, *The History Men: The Historical Profession in England since the Renaissance*, 2nd edn (1993), is intentional.

Table 3 *Papers by women in* Transactions, *1890–2009*

Decade	Total number of articles	Number of articles by women	Number of women councillors at decade mid-point
1890–9	76	5 (7%)	0
1900–9	81	17 (21%)	0
1910–19	80	11 (14%)	0
1920–9	72	29 (40%)	2
1930–9	63	13 (21%)	3
1940–9	67	13 (19%)	6
1950–9	80	9 (11%)	2
1960–9	77	5 (7%)	0
1970–9	101	7 (7%)	2
1980–9	92	8 (9%)	3
1990–9	131	32 (24%)	11
2000–9	134	35 (26%)	10

Source: *Transactions*, tables of contents; Reports of Council.

the 1890s and peaked in the 1920s with 40 per cent of published papers by women, a proportion which has never been equalled, and from which there was steady falling off until as late as the 1990s. Women were particularly successful in the Alexander Prize essay competition, accounting for eight of the twelve winners between 1898 and 1917. The first, Frances Hermia Durham*, went on to a distinguished career in the civil service, but others, like Rose Graham* (1903), Rachel Reid (1906) and Isobel Thornley (1917), enjoyed further academic distinction. Graham, a noted medieval church historian, and tutor at Somerville College, was to become the first female member of Council in 1920 and holds the record for articles published in *Transactions* (presidents apart) with five contributions up to 1930. Other returnees included Caroline Skeel*, leading light at the women's college of Westfield in London (three articles), Maud Violet Clarke, tutor at Somerville (two), and the remarkable Inna Lubimenko (four). Lubimenko (1878–1959) had received her initial historical training in St Petersburg, but pursued a doctorate at the Sorbonne under the supervision of Charles Bémont on Jean de Bretagne, developing an interest in Anglo-Russian relations in the early modern period during her visits to London. She was the only woman to address the International Historical Congress at London in 1913, in which the Society played a leading role; in the following year, she addressed the Society on the subject of Elizabeth I's correspondence with the tsars. Further papers were published in 1918, 1924 and 1928. Her

last visit to the West was in 1928, but although she continued to correspond with her émigré sister in Paris, she was unscathed in the Stalin
years, and continued to publish in Russian.[36] Although in 1921 the
Society elected its probably most reactionary president, Sir Charles
Oman*, no friend of the cause of women in the universities, a trickle
of female councillors followed Rose Graham through the interwar
years: Caroline Skeel (1926–9), Eleanor Lodge* (1923–36), Irene
Churchill (1926–38), Hilda Johnstone (1927–30, 1931–5), Helen Cam*
(1936–40, her first term), Evelyn Jamison (1938–41) and Eileen Power*
(1939–40). But two to three women councillors at any one time was
just about as good as it was going to get before the 1990s (Table 3). At
a time when (1920), just 11 per cent of the Society's fellows were
women, and of those three-quarters unmarried, the profile of women
in the Society's publications is striking. But there were also some less
visible women, who played key roles in publications. M. Beryl Curran,
a product of Girton, published in *Transactions* and edited a volume of
diplomatic correspondence for Camden in 1903, but she had a bigger
role as the Society's secretary and librarian from 1901 to 1943: letters
to her from Hubert Hall at the end of his tenure as literary director
show that she was no mere factotum in the publishing regime, but an
active participant.[37] She was the first of the key women behind the
scenes who tolerated all the foibles of the academics and got things
done. Aileen Armstrong (secretary and librarian, 1946–70), Jean
Chapman (executive secretary, 1977–87) and Joy McCarthy (executive
secretary, 1987–2005, 2006) were cut of the same cloth;[38] Janet
Godden and Christine Linehan likewise were to be crucial to the
success of *Studies in History*. These are contributions which the distortions
of archival survival can all too easily efface.

The growing prominence of women in the Society's publications in
the early twentieth century followed by a retreat is perhaps typical of patterns in the profession more widely. The proportion of female historians
in British universities remained fairly static between the 1920s and 1970s.
Although the phenomenon is worthy of further research, it seems that at
the turn of the century there were more opportunities on the fringes of a
profession still in the process of defining itself, with very porous boundaries between professional and non-professional. Many women

---

[36] I am grateful for help with the Alexander Prize and women in *Transactions* to Katy
Cubitt and Simon Baker respectively. For Lubimenko, my research student Mikhail
Belan has provided invaluable assistance. The archivists of Somerville College and Lady
Margaret Hall in Oxford and Girton College in Cambridge have been helpful on the
careers of women scholars.

[37] RHS, box 3, folder 143/2, Hall was writing to Miss Curran at least twice a week.

[38] Joy McCarthy, 'Jean Chapman, 1934–2015', *Newsletter*, Oct. 2015; Peter Mandler,
presidential letter, *Newsletter*, Dec. 2016.

historians found work as teaching assistants and as researchers on projects like the *Victoria County History*. Durham, for example, had trained in palaeography after completing her Cambridge education, and had been employed in cataloguing family archives. The Royal Historical Society may have been publicly silent on the question of women's role in the profession, but in the wider academy some of its leading lights were supportive, and Oman was something of an outlier in his views. Archdeacon Cunningham (president, 1909–13) had been an early supporter of women's education at Cambridge; T. F. Tout* (president, 1925–9) campaigned for the same opportunities for women as for men at Manchester University, 'a medievalist in his studies but most modern in his views'. No fewer than seventeen women, six of them on the same day,[39] became fellows in 1915 during Firth's presidency (1913–17); they included Helen Cam, Irene Churchill, Hilda Johnstone, Eleanor Lodge and Eileen Power. Several of the women we have been discussing had come under the wing of Hubert Hall, perhaps unfairly dismissed as a 'dry, dull archivist of legal and diplomatic records'. He was a close friend of the Webbs and a leading light in the establishment of the London School for Economics, for which he provided palaeography classes from 1896 to 1919 as well as teaching in economic history. Other women historians had family ties to leading male historians. Eleanor Lodge, principal of Westfield College, was the sister of Sir Richard Lodge (president, 1929–33), and Hilda Johnstone, one of the first female professors in London, was Tout's sister-in-law.[40]

IV Stasis

The falling away of female contributors – between 1951 and 1970 there were eleven years in which there were no women contributors to *Transactions* – was just one manifestation of the loss of momentum in the third quarter of the twentieth century. Publication conditions post-war were indeed challenging. Costs in 1950 were said to be 100 per cent higher than in 1938, while subscription income had grown by just 50 per cent.[41] The aspiration articulated in 1938 to publish four volumes per annum could not be realised. In May 1946, it

---

[39] RHS, Council, 18 Feb. 1915.

[40] J. V. Beckett, 'Women Historians and the VCH', paper at 'London Women Historians: A Celebration and a Conversation', 2017, podcast online at www.history.ac. uk/exhibitions/womenhistorians/index.html; Carol Dyhouse, *No Distinction of Sex?: Women in British Universities, 1870–1939* (2016), 135–8, 145–6; M. Berg, *A Woman in History: Eileen Power, 1889–1940* (Cambridge, 1996), 71, 156–7; B. G. Smith, *The Gender of History. Men, Women and Historical Practice* (1998), ch. 7. I have also benefited from the insights of Caroline Barron and Jane Garnett on these questions.

[41] RHS, Bellot papers, memorandum of 20 June 1950.

was agreed that only one Camden and a volume of *Transactions* could be published each year, with a *Guide* or *Handbook* every other year, a position which was reiterated in December 1956.[42] The rate of output of Camdens slowed to the lowest rate in the series' history. Only six handbooks were published between 1945 and 1970. The format of *Transactions* barely changed. The costs of the bibliographic projects with seemingly little returns made some councillors doubt their utility. Volumes of *Writings* appeared only fitfully after the war, although the Society was spending £350–400 per annum (12 per cent of its income in 1946) on the salary of the researcher at the IHR, and by 1960 the backlog of unlisted publications dated back to 1945.[43] Likewise, there had been some loss of direction in the production of the critical select bibliographies initiated in 1909, with key councillors in the post-war years acknowledging that they had lost track of the business.[44] Attempts to pick up the threads resulted in some tetchy correspondence and fraught meetings with the Americans. Relations were at a low point in 1952. Conyers Read emerged from meetings with T. F. Plucknett (president, 1948–52) and Hugh Hale Bellot, currently the Society's secretary, with a sense that it was more interested in *Writings* than in the compendium volumes to which the Americans remained committed, ending a letter to W. K. Jordan, 'More than once…I sighed for the more capacious days of Sir George Prothero.'[45] But Bellot, shortly succeeding as president (1952–6), did his best to set things on an even keel by securing money from the Ford Foundation in 1956 to compile a retrospective listing of the *Writings* of 1901–33, which finally appeared in five volumes in 1968–70, and also to resume work on the select bibliographies, for which new volumes were commissioned from 1956 onwards.

By and large, those serving as literary director in the post-war years were historians of distinction. The post was first split on Hall's retirement in 1938 between the admittedly intellectually lightweight Valentine Judges and the much more substantial C. R. Cheney*, and although Philip Grierson (1945–55)*, Denys Hay (1955–8) and Pierre Chaplais (1958–64) served alone, thereafter the split became permanent, increasingly with a modernist serving alongside an early modernist or medievalist. But literary directors tended to be recruited from among those who thought that the existing publishing programme was a good thing, and the Society fell prey to institutional inertia. There were hardly any

---

[42] See the helpful summary of Council resolutions in letter from R. H. C. Davis to Ian Christie, 8 Sept. 1968, Bodleian Library, K. V. Thomas papers, box 21. I am grateful to Sir Keith Thomas for permission to consult his papers.

[43] RHS, Bellot papers, C. Clay to Bellot, 4 June 1946.

[44] RHS, Bellot papers, T. F. Plucknett to Bellot, undated, ?1949.

[45] RHS, folder on bibliographies of British history, Read to Jordan, 18 July 1952.

new initiatives. 60 per cent of the papers published in *Transactions* in the 1960s were on political history, sometimes rather narrowly conceived; there was little sense of the world beyond Europe apart from some excursions into US diplomacy and the admittedly scintillating paper by John Elliott on Hernan Cortes (still among the most frequently downloaded articles); the impression is of the dominance of the golden triangle in selecting speakers, and historians of the left of the calibre of E. P. Thompson or Eric Hobsbawm were conspicuously absent.

There were murmurings of discontent about the Society's purpose. As early as 1950, Dom David Knowles* asked Bellot whether the Society 'exists to be predominantly a publishing society with its meetings little more than a recording of matter for its *Transactions*, or does it envisage becoming a rendezvous for all activities of learned societies?', though his own presidency (1956–60) saw little change. Writing to Geoffrey Elton* early in his presidency, Brian Harrison quoted with approval what he had been told by E. P. Hennock at the beginning of his career that the Society was 'largely irrelevant, a sort of dignified do nothing body for people within easy striking distance of London'.[46] There were some stirrings of reform: it was under Richard Southern* (president, 1968–72) that the Society began its programme of regional conferences which began to diversify the fare in *Transactions*: the themes of the first three, history and the new techniques, history and the arts, and urban civilization (1970–2), suggest a willingness to push at the interdisciplinary and methodological frontiers.

V The Eltonian revolution in publications

But this was nothing in comparison to what was to follow. On assuming the presidency in 1972, Elton descended on the culture of complacency (at least that is how he saw it) with ferocity. Writing to Harrison in June 1973, he claimed that 'the Victorian hangover is powerful, manifest and stifling'. Writing to the treasurer in 1974, he described the Society as 'a dim and distant maw devouring one's subscriptions and turning out… volumes of not much interest in compensation'.[47] Needless to say, he was not deterred by opposition: 'It's solid conservatives like Ian [Christie] who make me think that maybe I really am the radical of my dreams.'[48] Elton questioned in particular the value of the Camden series, suggesting that there were other ways of making primary

---

[46] RHS, Bellot papers, Knowles to Bellot, 15 Nov. 1950; cf. same to same 3 Nov. 1949; Elton papers, presidential correspondence, Harrison to Elton, 12 Sept. 1973.

[47] RHS, Elton papers, presidential correspondence, Elton to Harrison, 29 June 1973; Elton to G. Davis, 9 Feb. 1974.

[48] RHS, Elton papers, presidential correspondence, Elton to K. V. Thomas, 31 Oct. 1973.

sources available, for example through microfilm reproduction. He was keen on research guides and especially on monographs.

The literary directors Keith Thomas (1970–4) and Valerie Pearl (1974–7, the first woman in that role), supported Elton's critical approach. The Society determined on a consultation of its membership about its publications strategy, the first time I think that such a survey had been attempted. The returns survive, and provide a fascinating snapshot of the fellowship's feeling about its publications. There were 136 responses, mainly (75 per cent) from historians working in England and Wales (there were just four from Scotland and two from Ireland), but with 13 per cent from North American institutions (and only one from mainland Europe). Twenty-three women (17 per cent) replied. A full spectrum of views was expressed. Just over a third (forty-nine) were pretty hostile to Camdens, but the series attracted support from seventy-eight (58 per cent), and of these, nineteen expressed themselves in pretty strong terms. G. L. Harriss declared the series 'vital', William Kellaway opined that 'nothing wears as well as a well edited text', Lawrence Stone condemned it as 'hopelessly outdated' and breaking rank with many of his fellow-medievalists Rees Davies declared that it had 'outlived its purpose'. *Miscellany* volumes were declared by another respondent to be 'a bleak inglorious graveyard at best'. Others called for a 'reformed Camden' with longer introductions and better editorial apparatus combined with a more proactive commissioning policy. Other moderates expressed themselves content with reducing the number produced to one a year to make space for other types of publication. The suggestion that microfilm publication of records should be sponsored by the Society as a substitute for editions drew withering fire ('ask a microfilm to supply the skill of a Chaplais', quipped M. R. Powicke), while some expressed scepticism about the need for more monographs, claiming that more were being published than the paper assumed. Nor did the supposedly sacrosanct *Transactions* escape censure: J. P. Cooper attacked the quality of papers at the Society's conferences, others criticised the allegedly large number of typographical errors.[49]

There was clearly no mandate for the abandonment of Camdens, but Council did agree in February 1974 that once the backlog of already commissioned volumes was cleared, just one volume should be published each year, to be supplemented by an annual publication of an 'Aid to Research', and an occasional series of short monographs of 25,000 to 30,000 words. This was a somewhat pyrrhic victory, particularly as implementation would be delayed, nor was there much consensus

---

[49] RHS, file of returns to survey on publications, 1973. See also Elton papers, presidential correspondence, P. Chaplais to Elton, 2 Feb. 1974, J. C. Holt to Elton, 17 Dec. 1973, for the notion of the 'reformed Camden'.

about a monograph series on those terms (none appeared), while practical proposals for research aids were thin on the ground and often delayed.[50] Elton was not to be deterred. In September 1975, Council returned to the question of monographs and declared that it was a matter of 'great urgency'. It was decided to publish the books commercially with a modest subsidy from the Society for editorial work, and sell them at a discount to fellows. A circular to fellows went out in the autumn of 1975, an editorial board had been constituted by May 1976 and by September of that year £10,000 had been raised sufficient to support the series for three years. The first volumes were published in 1977 by Swifts (Boydell and Brewer took over in 1985). *Studies in History* had arrived.[51]

Elton also cut the Gordian knot on the bibliographies. Recognising the key problem with *Writings* that they were not current, and the scale of the unindexed backlog, Elton sought to get the Society to sponsor the production of annual listings of publications on British history to appear within nine months of the year in which they were published, and this was implemented with the *Annual Bibliographies*. Again, he moved with astonishing speed. He carried forward the negotiations with Harvester Press, supervised a pilot project for the first quarter of 1974, recruited the specialist section editors and produced the text on his own typewriter.[52] The *Annuals* were at first designed to trade something of the *Writings'* comprehensiveness for greater topicality, but they grew in volume, reflecting the increase in historical output as well as the compilers' more liberal approach to the interdisciplinary margins; the numbers of items indexed rose from 2,033 in 1975 to 3,677 in 1989, 6,764 in 1997 and 11,237 in 2002, the last year of hard copy publication.

Whatever one thinks of his politics, or indeed his history, there is no doubt that Elton was one of the Society's great reforming presidents. The monograph series in particular was aimed at what we now call early career researchers. Elton's intense personal involvement in the early years of the series is evident in the bulging correspondence files relating to the series held in the Society's offices. The *Annuals* were foundational to the Society's later bibliographic endeavours. It is unfortunate that none of this was recognised in the published proceedings of the symposium, 'The Eltonian legacy', held to discuss his work after his death. As Patrick Collinson has remarked in the *Oxford Dictionary of National Biography* entry on Elton, 'as an act of dismemberment, it was reminiscent of the last scene of Marlowe's Doctor Faustus, or of the Orpheus legend'.

[50] RHS, Council, 8 Feb. 1974.
[51] RHS, Council, 20 Sept. 1975, 21 Nov. 1975, 5 Mar. 1976, 18 Sept. 1976.
[52] RHS, Council, 8 Mar. 1974, 21 Sept. 1974, 18 Sept. 1976.

VI The digital turn: challenges and opportunities

In December 1992, at the beginning of Rees Davies's presidency (1992–6), the Society embarked on a review of all its activities through a series of working parties, among them its publications. The current programme was upheld, albeit with a reduced priority for monographs, but a key change was the switch of publishers for *Transactions* and Camdens in 1995 from Boydell and Brewer to Cambridge University Press and the introduction of an opt-out on Camdens with a variable subscription rate.[53] The contract was renewed in 2000 on the basis of a profit-share scheme which has served the Society well in sometimes testing market conditions. The more commercial approach has released more funds to enable it to do more things, notably research support. Whereas publication costs accounted for about two-thirds of normal expenditure at the beginning of the twentieth century, and still around 50–60 per cent in the mid-1990s, by the 2010s, it was one third; the other big change is the inflow of royalty income (in 2012–13, £93,460 in grants and royalties, admittedly boosted by one-off payments from the Cambridge digital archive, against expenditure of £95,364).[54] The Royal Historical Society is now much less a purely 'publishing society' than at earlier periods in its history.

The 1992–3 review had been asked to consider other modes of publication, including electronic, but at that stage no concrete proposals were forthcoming. The digitisation of the Society's publications had to wait until 2007–10, when the combination of student demand, falling costs and enhanced revenue opportunities made the proposals attractive to publishers: the back list of *Transactions* went live on JSTOR in 2007; in 2010, Camdens were made available through the Cambridge University Press Digital Archive, a substantial addition to the resources available for the study of British history. In the period 2011–15, downloads from *Transactions* across the CJO and JSTOR platforms averaged 430 per day, while downloads from Camden fifth series were at a more disappointing 4.6 per day: is that a measure of utility or discoverability?

In the meantime, the Society had made great progress with the digitisation of its bibliographies.[55] In 1989, taking advantage of the changing technologies, it took the decision to create a searchable database,

---

[53] RHS, Council, 12 Dec. 1992, 28 May 1993, 21 Jan. 1994. Boydell and Brewer continued to publish *Studies in History*.

[54] Reports of Council.

[55] The paragraphs which follow draw on the author's personal recollections, but the story can be followed through the successive reports of Council in *TRHS*, as well as the reports to AHRB/AHRC as archived in the Publications Committee papers. There is a considerable amount of information on the BBIH project website. See also www.history.ac.uk/making-history/resources/articles/RHSB.html.

bringing together the various sources of bibliographic information, and over the next few years secured funding from the Leverhulme Trust and the British Academy. The contents of the underlying bibliographies were scanned, gaps in coverage (notably in imperial and commonwealth history, women's history and Roman history) identified and plugged and the resulting bulky print-outs sent out to an army of scholars (including many North Americans) who checked the information, and added index- ing terms, including the period covered. John Morrill, the project's mastermind and general editor, described it as 'an extraordinary modern example of what the early modern period would have called the putting out system'. Their collective labours bore fruit in the eventual publication of a CD-ROM by Oxford University Press in 1998, allowing the complex searching of around 250,000 records on British history from 1900 until 1992.

The static character of the CD-ROM, the greater flexibility of the web and the prospect of new funding opportunities shaped the next phase. The cusp of the new century was a good time for public funding of elec- tronic projects; following initial support from the Andrew W. Mellon Foundation and the Esmée Fairbairn Trust, the Arts and Humanities Research Board and its successor the Arts and Humanities Research Council provided three consecutive Resource Enhancement grants (2001–9) to enable the bibliography to be available on the internet free at the point of use, and to develop interoperability with other resources.

Under Ian Archer, its general editor from 1999 to 2012, the project now firmly based in the IHR developed successful collaborations with *London's Past Online* and *Irish History Online*. The bibliography pioneered cross-searchability with other resources like the *Oxford Dictionary of National Biography*, linkage to library catalogues and online text through OpenURL technology. Since going live in July 2002 and at the time of writing, the database has doubled in size from around 300,000 to 600,000 records. But the irony was that at the precise point at which pressures for open access were building up in the higher education sector, the Society was forced to redevelop the resource on a subscription model. The core problem is that its usefulness depends on its being current (an average of 14,230 records per annum were added in the years 2012–16), and the editing of the records brings significant costs. The Society's president, Colin Jones, and the director of the IHR, Miles Taylor, worked with Archer and Jane Winters, then head of publications at the IHR, to secure a three-way deal with the Belgian pub- lisher Brepols, which allows the salary costs to be covered, and keeps the subscription levels at the more modest end of the spectrum. In 2010, the rebranded Bibliography of British and Irish History (BBIH) was launched with significantly improved searching capabilities.

The *Studies in History* series had undoubtedly delivered in terms of providing publishing opportunities for early career historians, but there were signs by the 2010s that it was losing momentum. Reduced print runs (500 to 550 in 1993, 400 in 2000, 200 in 2015) were a problem shared with other publishers, reflecting pressure on library budgets, but more worrying was the fall in new proposals; the series seemed a less attractive proposition for early career historians, perhaps because less focused than most of its competitors.[56] This coincided with the growing pressure for open access in which the Society, having already worked under the leadership of Peter Mandler to modify government proposals for open access journals to take account of the specific circumstances of the humanities, wished to play a leading role. The challenges were considerable as university presses charged £5,000, and even dedicated open access publishers £3,500, for an open access monograph. But in 2016, the Society announced its *New Historical Perspectives* series of books which would be authored, edited or co-edited by early career historians and available both in print and digitally as open access, with all production costs being borne jointly by the Society and the IHR. In place of the mentoring previously provided by the *Studies in History* series, authors are to be invited to workshops at which their work will be subjected to critical and constructive scrutiny by a panel of experts. The first volumes are imminent at the time of writing.[57]

Diversification, innovation, wider dissemination. It is difficult in a piece of this nature to avoid a teleological narrative of progress to our current 'happy state'. It ought to be sobering to remind ourselves that the terms of the debate within the Society on publications show considerable continuity. Anxieties about a narrow focus were being expressed in the 'age of Prothero'; some of the answers given then were not necessarily the right ones as the ill-fated foray into diplomatic history showed. The Society has found it difficult to shed its reputation for catering primarily to historians of the British Isles; that dominance is built into its bibliographic project (somewhat half-hearted efforts to produce a union bibliography in the late noughties for the various European resources foundered on the issues of cost and coordination, and Brexit will be another nail in that particular coffin);[58] Camdens (which are branded 'British') have proved remarkably resilient even in the face of the Eltonian onslaught; British history has likewise remained pretty dominant in the *Studies in History* series (Table 4), though *Transactions* has been

---

[56] Paper by Andrew Pettegree, 'The Studies in History Monograph Series', RHS, Publications Committee, Apr. 2014. The proposals were initially quite contentious.

[57] S. Newman and P. Summerfield, 'New Historical Perspectives', *Newsletter*, May 2016.

[58] See the author's paper 'Towards a Closer Union: European Historical Bibliographies', RHS, Publications Committee, 23 Nov. 2007.

Table 4 *Coverage by period and area of* Studies in History *volumes, 1977–2016*

Date	Number of volumes	Volumes per annum	Medieval	Early modern	1700–1900	Post-1900	Conference proceedings	British	European	Wider world
1977–86	49	4.9	5 (10%)	16 (33%)	16 (33%)	8 (16%)	4 (8%)	31 (63%)	8 (16%)	10 (20%)
1987–96	24	2.4	2 (8%)	10 (42%)	9 (38%)	3 (12%)	0 (0%)	19 (79%)	3 (13%)	2 (8%)
1997–2006	54	5.4	9 (17%)	10 (19%)	24 (44%)	11 (20%)	0 (0%)	40 (74%)	13 (24%)	1 (2%)
2007–16	39	3.9	5 (13%)	11 (28%)	18 (46%)	5 (13%)	0 (0%)	31 (79%)	6 (15%)	2 (5%)

Table 5 *Coverage by period and area of articles in* Transactions, *1970–9 and 2008–17 compared*

Date	Number of articles	Medieval	Early modern	1700–1900	Post-1900	Other	British	European	Wider world
1970–9	101	32 (32%)	29 (29%)	23 (23%)	12 (12%)	5 (4%)	60 (59%)	30 (30%)	7 (7%)
2008–17	89	19 (21%)	15 (17%)	30 (34%)	25 (28%)	0 (0%)	43 (48%)	28 (31%)	18 (20%)

Note: Four methodological articles for 1970–9 have not been allocated by area.

more successful in diversifying in coverage, not only temporal, but geo-graphical and thematic (Table 5). One of the challenges facing the *New Historical Perspectives* series will be that it manages to diversify. And there have been real limits to the Society's willingness to innovate. It remains committed to the monograph and to conventional edited texts, both of which have their critics; some might think that its *Transactions* (essentially invited papers) sits uneasily in a world of peer review; BBIH just might be overtaken by ever more sophisticated library catalogues and is perhaps just 'too smart' for the average user. That is not to say that these modes should be abandoned – they have their staunch supporters too – but the speed with which both the publishing landscape and the nature of the profession are changing means that the Society will need to be more flexible than ever.